Herman Westeri

Controversy and Challenge

Herman Westerink

Controversy and Challenge

The Reception of Sigmund Freud's Psychoanalysis
in German and Dutch-speaking
Theology and Religious Studies

LIT

Gedruckt mit Unterstützung des Bundesministeriums
für Wissenschaft und Forschung in Wien

Bibliographic information published by the Deutsche Nationalbibliothek
The Deutsche Nationalbibliothek lists this publication in the Deutsche
Nationalbibliografie; detailed bibliographic data are available in the Internet at
http://dnb.d-nb.de.

ISBN 978-3-643-50029-8

A catalogue record for this book is available from the British Library

©LIT VERLAG GmbH & Co. KG Wien 2009
Krotenthallergasse 10/8
A-1080 Wien
Tel. +43 (0) 1-409 56 61
Fax +43 (0) 1-409 56 97
e-Mail: wien@lit-verlag.at
http://www.lit-verlag.at

LIT VERLAG Dr. W. Hopf
Berlin 2009
Fresnostr. 2
D-48159 Münster
Tel. +49 (0) 2 51-620 32 22
Fax +49 (0) 2 51-922 60 99
e-Mail: lit@lit-verlag.de
http://www.lit-verlag.de

Distribution:

In Germany: LIT Verlag Fresnostr. 2, D-48159 Münster
Tel. +49 (0) 2 51-620 32 22, Fax +49 (0) 2 51-922 60 99, e-Mail: vertrieb@lit-verlag.de

In Austria: Medienlogistik Pichler-ÖBZ GmbH & Co KG
IZ-NÖ, Süd, Straße 1, Objekt 34, A-2355 Wiener Neudorf
Tel. +43 (0) 22 36-63 53 52 90, Fax +43 (0) 22 36-63 53 52 43, e-Mail: mlo@medien-logistik.at

In Switzerland: B + M Buch- und Medienvertriebs AG
Hochstr. 357, CH-8200 Schaffhausen
Tel. +41 (0) 52-643 54 85, Fax +41 (0) 52-643 54 35, e-Mail: order@buch-medien.ch

Distributed in the UK by: Global Book Marketing, 99B Wallis Rd, London, E9 5LN
Phone: +44 (0) 20 8533 5800 – Fax: +44 (0) 1600 775 663
http://www.centralbooks.co.uk/html

Distributed in North America by:

Transaction Publishers
New Brunswick (U.S.A.) and London (U.K.)

Transaction Publishers
Rutgers University
35 Berrue Circle
Piscataway, NJ 08854

Phone: +1 (732) 445 - 2280
Fax: + 1 (732) 445 - 3138
for orders (U. S. only):
toll free (888) 999 - 6778
e-mail: orders@transactionpub.com

Contents

Introduction

It is still stunning that the man who wrote *Moses and Monotheism* as a reflection on Jewish identity and on the sense of guilt in culture and religion began his career in a Viennese laboratory studying the spinal cord of the *Ammocoetes Petromyzon*. In the 1880s Sigmund Freud was interested in physiology, nervous systems, the (mal-)functioning of the human brain. The laboratory seemed placed at distance from questions concerning sense of guilt, morality or religion. Yet, this is only appearance. Freud's teacher Theodor Meynert for example easily linked ideas on the functioning of the human brain with issues such as conscience formation and the evolution of morality and religion. And Jean-Martin Charcot, Freud's mentor in Paris, discovered the importance of the "moral treatment" of neurotic patients. He also had a profound interest in religious manifestations that are comparable to neurotic symptoms.

In Freud's earliest intellectual environment and work we already find elements of thought that will prove to be recurring issues in his later psychoanalytic theories: the relation between body (brain) and consciousness; the tensions between human drives on the one hand and cultural morality on the other hand; the relation between morality and religion; and, like his teachers, an interest in philosophy and arts that proves to be inspiring in science. When Freud discovers the importance of psychic mechanisms such as repression and resistance in the mental life of his neurotic patients, these issues gained momentum. Seen from this perspective it is less surprising that the physiologist studying the spinal cord of a fish was eventually to write studies on culture, religion and arts.

Concerning religion a certain coincidence seems to play a role. Freud's first article on religion (1907) was written at the request of a minister, Gustav Vorbrodt, the editor of the newly founded *Zeitschrift für Religionspsychologie*. Yet here becomes visible what might also be judged inevitable when we consider the emergence of psychoanalysis: the confrontation of psychoanalytic theories with religion. In a period of emergence of the human sciences (psychology, sociology, anthropology) during which they all tried to define and demarcate their own domain for academic scientific research, psychoanalysis' premise was that every cultural phenomenon could be understood as having originated from the human psychic life.[1] Psychoanalysis could thus study virtually everything. It was therefore difficult to integrate into university curricula that demanded clear defined scientific domains. At the same time it meant that many scientific disciplines were confronted with the claims made by psychoanalysis. The emergence of applied psychoanalysis in the period after Freud had published *The Interpretation of Dreams* (1900) is thus also the period in which

---

[1] O. Rank, H. Sachs, "Entwicklung und Ansprüche der Psychoanalyse", in *Imago* 1 (1912), pp.1-16.

a series of engagements with psychoanalysis starts: in philosophy, in pedagogy, in psychology, in sociology, in cultural-anthropology, and also in theology.

This book on the reception of Freud's psychoanalytic theories and methods in German and Dutch-speaking theology and religious studies elaborates on my monograph *A Dark Trace: Sigmund Freud on the Sense of Guilt*.[2] That study was an exegesis of Freud's writings concerning his theories on the sense of guilt reconstructed from his own premises. It had no implicit theological aim or objective – the aim was to contribute to our understanding of Freudian psychoanalysis and to study the meaning of the issue of the sense of guilt in contextualized Freudian thought. It was a new reading of Freud focusing on a specific, relatively unelaborated and yet seemingly central issue in his writings.

This study of the reception of Freud in theology and religious studies starts with a chapter on Freud's anthropology and views on religion. This chapter is by and large an excerption of my reconstruction of Freud's thought as presented in *A Dark Trace*. This opening chapter is necessary, firstly, in order to make clear what my reading of Freud is. I will point out that the key issue in Freud's writings on religion is the sense of guilt, i.e. religion is primarily regarded as staging and processing the sense of guilt that originates from the collisions between drive and morality. However, other important perspectives on religion are also presented by Freud, especially and to some extent paradoxically in *the* text on religion, *The Future of an Illusion*. Secondly, I present my reading of Freud as the basis for a critical analysis of the engagement with Freud in theology. I will describe how theologians dealt with Freud's anthropology and critique of religion, what aspects of Freudian thought were elaborated and what issues were neglected. The aim here is to point out the current relevance of Freudian thought for theology.

As I am relatively detached from any specific psychoanalytic school and was fortunate to work at departments at two faculties in two countries (The Netherlands and Austria) in which various psychoanalytic perspectives were elaborated upon and discussed[3], my reading of Freud is relatively undogmatic –

---

[2] H. Westerink, *A Dark Trace: Sigmund Freud on the Sense of Guilt*, Leuven University Press (*Het schuldgevoel bij Freud. Een duister spoor*, Uitgeverij Boom, Amsterdam, 2005). The following monograph also serves as resource for our discussion of Freud's psychoanalysis: P. Vandermeersch, H. Westerink, *Godsdienstpsychologie in cultuurhistorisch perspectief*, Uitgeverij Boom, Amsterdam, 2007, pp.142-182.

[3] In the field of psychology of religion in Groningen Freud was studied and evaluated from the perspective of Lacanian psychoanalysis as well as from the perspective of object relations theory (Klein, Winnicott, Bion) and self psychology (Erikson, Kohut). The Lacanian perspective was presented by Patrick Vandermeersch, a student of Antoine Vergote in Leuven who wrote major contributions in the psychology of religion in which Lacanian psychoanalysis presents a dominant theory. Object relations theory and self psychology were represented by Nel Jongsma-Tieleman, Hetty Zock and Sytze Ypma. Major publications in the department are P. Vandermeersch, *Unresolved Ques-*

as a non-psychoanalyst I am not affiliated to a specific psychoanalytic school or association. I consider the latter fact an advantage when one wants to read Freud with an open-mind.[4]

The chapters 2-6 are concerned with the reception of Freud's psychoanalysis in theology and religious studies in the German and Dutch-speaking world, i.e. the engagement with Freud in theology in Germany, Switzerland, Austria, the Netherlands and Belgium (Flanders), with a special emphasis on the reception of Freud's theories on the sense of guilt. The latter aspect is a logical effect of my own reading of Freud.

It is not the intention to analyse or even mention the writings of every scholar who occasionally dealt with Freud, and indeed, in this study no attempt is made to be complete. The choice of material is determined by a combination of criteria. The starting point is not so much the work of individual scholars, but the reception of Freud's psychoanalysis in fields of attention and areas of discussion in theology and religious studies. The scholars elaborated upon in my study are thus first of all considered to be important in initiating a field of attention or involving themselves in areas of discussion. We will thus be able to depict a landscape, a forest with a few mighty trees. The fields of attention and ar-

---

tions in the Freud/Jung Debate. On Psychosis, Sexual Identity and Religion, Leuven University Press, Leuven, 1991; N. Jongsma-Tieleman, *Godsdienst als speelruimte van verbeelding. Een godsdienstpsychologische studie*, Uitgeverij Kok, Kampen, 1996; S. Ypma, *Tussen God en gekte. Een studie over zekerheid en symbolisering in psychose en geloven*, Uitgeverij Boekencentrum, Zoetermeer, 2001; T.H. Zock, *A Psychology of Ultimate Concern. Erik H. Erikson's Contribution to the Psychology of Religion*, Rodopi, Atlanta/Amsterdam, 1990 (2004).

In the field of psychology of religion in Vienna various perspectives are combined as both object relations theory and the writings of Vergote are elaborated upon. Also, concerning the issues of guilt and sense of guilt there is excellent know-how. Major publications in the department are H. Santer, *Persönlichkeit und Gottesbild. Religionspsychologische Impulse für eine Praktische Theologie*, Vandenhoeck & Ruprecht, Göttingen 2003; S. Heine, *Grundlagen der Religionspsychologie. Modelle und Methoden*, Vandenhoeck & Ruprecht, Göttingen, 2005; M. Pratl, *Von der Schuld zum Neubeginn. Die Beichte als Übergangsritual*, LIT Verlag, Vienna/Munster, 2008.

[4] The fact that Freud never formulated a definitive psychoanalytic theory, but again and again discussed and reformulated earlier ideas, is certainly one reason for the multitude of Freud interpretations and psychoanalytic schools that have emerged over time. This seems to be a structural characteristic of psychoanalysis, rooted not only in the interminable character of psychoanalysis (both as therapy and theory) but also in the structures of the psychoanalytic movement. It is a long history of debates and quarrels between strong headed personalities with outspoken ideas. In this context there was and is a danger of becoming "dogmatic" and indeed among psychoanalysts one finds for example ego psychologist, "Lacanians" or "Kleinians" who defend some form of "true" psychoanalysis. The advantage of being a psychologist of religion unbound to a specific psychoanalytic school is the avoidance of psychoanalytic dogmatism.

eas of discussion are situated on an academic level (second criterium), that is to
say, our concern is the reception of psychoanalysis in theology and religious
studies as scientific theoretical disciplines. We are not concerned with the reception of psychoanalysis in church practices or individual/group religious life.
This means that the main authors considered can be regarded as academic
scholars. An exception is made for the Swiss minister Oskar Pfister, not only
because he is a prominent follower of Freud in search of an integration of psychoanalysis and theology, but also because of his influence on later developments. An exception is also made for Karl Beth, a professor in systematic theology (Vienna). His reading of Freud has hardly been noticed, mainly because of
his forced emigration to the United States in 1938. Yet, in our study his work is
considered in order to put Pfister's reading in perspective and in order to show
some mutual lines of development in the early engagement with Freud in German and Dutch speaking theology and religious studies, notably in the context
of phenomenology of religion. Another criterium for our choice of material is
that the authors considered either made several substantial contributions (books,
articles) to the reception of Freud, voiced an important or significant standpoint
in an area of attention or can be regarded as seminal because of the influence
they had on other authors or lines of development in a specific field. Finally, the
scholars and texts considered can be situated in either German or Dutch-
speaking theology and religious studies. This may seem an obvious criterium,
yet here also difficulties may arise. Paul Tillich's work is considered in our
study though he worked for a large part of his career in the United States pub-
lishing in English. Yet, his early writings are in German, his intellectual roots
are situated in Germany and, decisively, his influence on others both in German
and Dutch theology has been significant. He is generally considered a "German-
American" theologian. Antoine Vergote is a bilingual Belgian who worked at
the universities of Leuven (Flanders) and Louvain la Neuve (Walone). His publications are mainly written in either French or Dutch. For a full picture of his
work it is vital to consider all his key publications whether written in French or
Dutch. Vergote had a profound influence on the reception of Freud in (Dutch)
psychology of religion.

        This touches upon a more general consideration. German and Dutch-
speaking theology and religious studies cannot be isolated. Science is after all
interdisciplinary and international. We will see in our study that occasionally,
often at crucial moments in this history, influences from "abroad" are of great
importance. This mainly concerns influences either from American or French
scholars. When necessary, we will elaborate on this in our study.

        We deal with the reception of Freud within German and Dutch-
speaking theology and religious studies. The choice for this landscape is related
to my knowledge of the language and the fact that this scientific study took
place in Groningen and Vienna. Yet, there are more important motives for this
choice. Firstly, these two "worlds" reflect their own traditions as to the en-

gagement with psychoanalysis, as we will see, but also mutual interactions and cross-border influences. This allows us to distinguish and compare Freud's reception in different intellectual environments. Secondly, both theological landscapes show Catholic and Protestant scholars being involved in the engagement with psychoanalysis and the participation in fields of attention and discussions. Hence, the choice for Dutch and German-speaking theology enables us to compare Catholic and Protestant scholars in our search for recurring patterns in the history of this engagement.

This study of the reception of Freud's psychoanalysis with a special emphasis on the reception of his theories on the sense of guilt, is first of all a descriptive analysis of fields of attention in theology/religious studies and the work of those scholars who discussed psychoanalysis and either integrated or rejected (aspects of) Freud's theories in these fields. Here, the leading question is which aspects of Freud's theories were discussed, integrated and/or rejected, and which aspects of his thought were thus not elaborated upon. My reading of Freud as presented in the first part of the study will be point of reference here. Both the leading questions in the second part and my reading of Freud as point of reference already indicate that the study of the reception of Freud's psychoanalysis is more than just descriptive analytical. My own reading of Freud serves as a reference for a critical assessment the way scholars have interpreted Freud.

It is not my intention to defend a "true" reading of Freud against other readings of Freud. Such an aim would first of all contradict my own reading of Freudian thought: Freud never developed a definitive theory on the human mind; Freud's writings show constant further development and reformulation of theories, shifts of attentions and further elaborations in specific areas in the context of debates with colleagues and followers, personal fascinations, intellectual influences and the interaction with patients. There is another reason not to confront the reception of Freud with a "true" *intentio auctoris*. We will see that Freud's theories are situated in an intellectual discourse and a scientific environment that are no longer in conformity with the present state of affairs. Also, there are specific elements in Freudian thought that have been rightfully criticized such as inclination to formulate myths (or dogmas) when dealing with the ultimate origin of psychic or cultural phenomena (primal parricide, primal scene, death drive). Because psychoanalysis was in constant shift and further development, some trains of thought are unfinished, and some concepts have remained sketchy and vague. The critical confrontation of the reception of Freud with my reading of Freud thus implies being critical in two directions.

Firstly, I will critically examine the engagement with Freud, i.e. the explicit or implicit theological ideas, convictions and aims that determine the discussion of psychoanalysis in theology, and the integration and/or rejection of (aspects of) psychoanalytic thought. Seldom is such an engagement purely based on a reading of Freud's work. Mostly the reading is filtered by specific

interpretations related to psychoanalytic schools. When necessary I will illuminate these backgrounds. As my own reading of Freud serves as point of reference I will specifically (but not exclusively) focus on the reception or non-
reception of Freud's ideas on sense of guilt in theology. The key questions are:
How did scholars in theology and religious studies read Freud? How did theological views and interests interact with Freud's disturbing ideas on human nature and religion? Why was the sense of guilt in Freud's writings for a long period overlooked? And what is the potential of Freud's psychoanalytic theories
and ideas on religion for current and future theology and religious studies?

Secondly, the analysis of the reception of Freud in theology and religious studies will imply a critical review of Freud's theories in line with my
reading of Freud in the first part of this project and in line with the ideas of others suggesting reconfigurations of Freudian psychoanalysis in order to construc-
tively further theorize on specific concepts or fields of attention that are important in theology and religious studies.

The aim of this double critical review is to work through Freudian
thought and the history of its reception in order to establish what the theoretical
potential of Freud's psychoanalysis might be for current and future theology
and religious studies. Digging up the past "forgotten" issues is a way to accomplish this. In this sense, the second part of the study is a Freudian "archaeology"
in order to make conscious in what way psychoanalysis can still be made fruitful.

I want to express my gratitude to those who contributed in some vital way to the
content of the book and to the intellectual and social milieu in which this book
was written. First of all, I want to thank Susanne Heine for her subtle reading
and generous support. I thank my colleagues, Marianne Pratl and Katharina Al-
der, for their helpfull suggestions, and the other members of the Department for
Practical Theology and Psychology of Religion, Stefan Schumann and Nicole
Nungesser, for contributing to a great atmosphere to work in. I am grateful to
Patrick Vandermeersch for the past inspiring cooperations. I thank Frank Bro-
gan for his thorough proofreading of the manuscript, and Lisette Henstra for
making the layout.

1   Reading Freud on religion

1.1 Introduction

Many attempts have been made to reconstruct Freud's ideas on religion. Not only biographers[1] and scholars in psychoanalysis but also theologians have provided studies on this matter. Although there are of course exceptions, in general it seems that these reconstructions aim at providing one systematic view on religion. Often such a synthesis of Freud's theories is based on an analysis of his texts on religion focusing on a seemingly logical development from one text to another, on thematic similarities and corresponding psychoanalytic perspectives and methods. Such a view seems possible when one starts from the premise that Freud's texts on religion are the result of applied psychoanalysis, that is to say, it is suggested that after Freud established a firm psychoanalytic theory, method and practice he applied psychoanalysis on cultural phenomena in order to explain the phenomenon of religion.

The problem with this starting point is that Freud never provided a systematic psychoanalytic theory. "Psychoanalysis has never claimed to provide a complete theory of human mentality in general."[2] He indeed never concerned himself with developing an all-embracing system or synthesis, but rather moved from the analysis of patients to areas of special attention: repression, dreams, the unconscious, sexuality, resistance, transference, sense of guilt, anxiety, aggression, pleasure, etc. There is also a shift of attention concerning pathologies – from hysteria to obsessional neurosis and from thereon to further differentiation of pathologies (paranoia, melancholia, masochism) – that provides new insights and new perspectives on cultural and religious phenomena. Hence, when one overlooks his writings one recognizes a process of emergence, further development and constant reformulation of psychoanalytic theories and methods basically founded on clinical experience, on distinguishing pathologies according to their mechanisms and on introducing and applying "abstract ideas" and "basic concepts". These "must at first necessarily possess some degree of indefiniteness" in order to reformulate with more precision and thus to "advance in knowledge".[3] In this advancement Freud shows himself a true genius as he able to again and again question his own findings that at a certain moment seemed to provide a convincing and stable theoretical framework. Thus he is able to move in unexplored directions whereas often his followers hesitate to follow their master in a new line of thought. However, at this point we should

---

[1] The most important biographies on Freud are E. Jones, *The Life and Work of Sigmund Freud, Volumes 1-3*, Basic Books, New York, 1959; P. Gay, *Freud: A Life for Our Time*, Norton & Company, New York/London, 1988.
[2] S. Freud, *On the History of the Psychoanalytic Movement, SE XIV*, p.50.
[3] S. Freud, *Instincts and Their Vicissitudes, SE XIV*, p.117.

not overestimate Freud's adventurous flexibility. On the contrary, often also his followers moved in new directions causing Freud to engage in debates and stubbornly defend gained insights by focussing on the key concepts of psycho-analysis. In either case, the constancy in Freud's writings is not provided by one core theory or clearly defined basic concepts, but by the areas of attention Freud again and again returns to and by formulating his ideas in opposition to others.

We thus start off from the premise that Freud's psychoanalytic theories are not "complete" and always in further development and we regard his work not as a growing organic unity with a steady core, but we consider his work an exploration of fields of attention from various perspectives and within reformu-lated theoretical frameworks.

This starting point has important implications for our reading of Freud on religion. Firstly, it means that Freud's texts on religion have to be situated in the context of the further developments and reconfigurations of psychoanalytic theories and methods as well as in the context of mutual debates with followers. Also, Freud's theories are to be considered against the background of historical, cultural developments. As Joachim Scharfenberg already suggested reading Freud on religion implies reading the "whole Freud", i.e. reading Freud's world of thought as a constant process of development and further clarification.[4] In this study I will always consider Freud's texts on religion as part of the further developments and reconfigurations of psychoanalytic theories and methods. In my opinion, making a sharp distinction between psychoanalytic writings on the one hand and writings in applied psychoanalysis, which would enable to study Freud's texts on religion as isolated texts, on the other hand, should be rejected. I regard Freud's texts on religion as comparable to his case studies, i.e. as de-scriptive analyses of phenomena as well as interpretative analyses including fur-ther theoretical meta-psychological considerations. To give an example: *Totem and Taboo* can be seen as the application of the structures of obsessional neuro-sis on religion, yet in this text Freud also reconfigures his theory on obsessional neurosis arguing that the neurotic's excessive morality (as for example wit-nessed in the case of the Rat Man) is not only related to repressed feelings and ideas, but is based upon some piece of reality as well. In the case of the Wolf Man this piece of reality will be the primal scene in which the copulating par-ents are witnessed. The statement in *Totem and Taboo* that the Oedipus com-plex is the nuclear complex of the neurosis is the guiding principle in the latter case, whereas in the case of the Rat Man the Oedipus complex is not men-tioned.[5]

---

[4] J. Scharfenberg, *Sigmund Freud und seine Religionskritik als Herausforderung für den christlichen Glauben*, Vandenhoeck & Ruprecht, Göttingen, 1971, p.38.
[5] S. Freud, *Notes upon a Case of Obsessional Neurosis, SE X*, 153-249; S. Freud, *Totem and Taboo. Some points of Agreement between the Mental Lives of Savages and Neurot-ics, SE XIII*, pp.160-161; S. Freud, *From the History of an Infantile Neurosis, SE XVII*, chapter IV.

Secondly, we will and can not reconstruct a single theory on religion. Like Freud's oeuvre is an exploration of fields of attention from various perspectives and reformulated theoretical frameworks, so are his writings on religion. In the case of these writings the debates with followers play an eminent role also. Therefore I prefer to refer to Freud's *theories* and *ideas* on religion instead of suggesting unity or presenting a synthesis.

1.2 Hysteria and hypnosis

The emergence of psychoanalysis in the 1890s is rooted in two entangled phenomena that in the late nineteenth century proved to be fascinating – hysteria and hypnosis. For a neurophysiologist and brain anatomist such as Freud hysteria was a riddle. The disease was sometimes associated with a brain tumor.[6] In general hereditary factors were regarded to be decisive in the aetiology of hysteria. Yet, these factors could not explain the symptoms, i.e. the paralyses that could rapidly move from one part of the body to another, and the hysterical poses. In the autumn of 1885 Freud left Vienna for Paris to work at the famed Salpêtrière hospital where Jean-Martin Charcot, the expert on hysteria, taught.[7] Freud soon gained interest in Charcot's methods and findings, for though Charcot was a physician and "anatomist"[8] regarding hereditary factors as decisive in the aetiology of hysteria, he also considered the family circumstances in which the illness manifested itself. Isolation of the patient from their family was the moral or mental side of treatment. He also found that hysterical symptoms could arise from unconscious mental processes.[9] Psychological and social (moral) factors thus played a role in hysteria and its treatment.

Charcot also discovered that the spectacular *grande hystérie* showed many resemblances with what was known as hypnotic trance. Freud also showed an interest in hypnosis. In 1889 he even made a trip to Nancy where Hypolite Bernheim was experimenting with hypnosis and discovered that it was

---

[6] P. Gay, *Freud*, p.49.

[7] The admiration of Freud for Charcot is expressed in the fact that Freud translated Charcot's *Leçons sur les maladies du système nerveux faites à la Salpêtrière* in German, *Neue Vorlesungen über die Krankheiten des Nervensystems insbesondere über Hysterie*. On Charcot and Freud see for example O. Andersson, *Studies in the Prehistory of Psychoanalysis. The Aetiology of psychoneuroses and some related themes in Sigmund Freud's scientific writings and letters 1886-1896*, Svenska Bokförlaget, Stockholm, 1962, pp.47ff; F.J. Sulloway, *Freud, Biologist of the Mind. Beyond the Psychoanalytic Legend*, Burnett Books, London, 1979, pp.28-42; C.G. Goetz, M. Bonduelle, T. Gelfand, *Charcot. Constructing Neurology*, Oxford University Press, New York/Oxford, 1995.

[8] S. Freud, *An Autobiographical Study, SE XX*, p.14.

[9] J.M. Charcot, *Leçons sur les maladies du système nerveux faites à la Salpêtrière. Tome III*, Progrès Médical, Paris, 1877, p.337.

a matter of suggestion to which everybody is susceptible, i.e. every person could enter this sleep-like state in which thoughts and acts could be suggested that were later not remembered.[10] The issue of suggestion opened new perspectives. According to Bernheim it showed that both in hypnosis and in the aetiology of hysteria psychological factors were decisive. It also meant that the relation between patient and doctor needed consideration.

Charcot not only showed great interest in the similarities between hysteria and hypnosis, he was also fascinated by religious phenomena that seemed analogous to hysteria and studied these resemblances in the late 1880s. In Rubens' painting of Ignatius of Loyola exorcizing the possessed Charcot recognizes similarities between hysteria and religious possession. And in a text on faith-healing he states that miracles, such as related to prayer or charismatic movements, can appear when one considers the analogy with hysteria – sometimes the mind can have an influence on the body.[11] As the title of the text already expresses there is faith that heals (La foi qui guérit).

From the early 1890s Freud starts to write psychological reflections on his treatments of female patients. The first important text is Psychical (or Mental) Treatment.[12] It deals with psychological states associated with strong affects and a powerful will influencing the body. As an example of the latter he pointed to pilgrim's miraculous cures.[13] Events such as these show however that the individual will is not enough to explain cure. Circumstances, such as the number of people present in religious events are of importance also. From this idea he then mentions that the physician's personality can call forth certain expectations. In this regard he spoke about hypnosis as a means of dominating a person's will: the patient became obedient and faithful.[14] In other words, modern psychic treatment stands in a religious tradition in which the power of faith and suggestion was already acknowledged and expressed.

Hypnosis disappeared both as method – Freud was not a successful hypnotizer – and hence as issue for theoretical reflection. Already in the late 1890s Freud shifts his attention from hysteria to obsessional neurosis and in fact for almost two decades hysteria will hardly play a role in Freud's writings. Yet, in Group Psychology and the Analysis of the Ego (1921) the issues of sugges-

---

[10] H. Bernheim, Hypnosis and Suggestion in Psychotherapy, University Books, New York, 1964, chapter 9. Freud translated Bernheim's De la suggestion et ses applications à la thérapeutique (1886) and Hypnotisme, suggestion, psychothérapie: études nouvelles (1892) into German: Hypnotismus und Suggestion (1888) and Hypnotismus, Suggestion und Psychotherapie (1892).

[11] P. Vandermeersch, H. Westerink, Godsdienstpsychologie, p.55. The two texts by Charcot that we are referring to are Les démoniaques dans l'art (1887) and La foi qui guérit (1892).

[12] S. Freud, Psychical (or Mental) Treatment, SE VII, pp.283-302.

[13] Idem, p.289.

[14] Idem, p.291, p.296.

tion, hypnosis and hysteria are suddenly again elaborated.[15] In this major cultural study Freud focuses on two artificial highly organized groups, the army and the Church, i.e. on groups that are not formed naturally, but that are formed under pressure from outside through leaders. The Church is interesting for Freud, because here two types of identification can be distinguished: mutual identification with the faithful and identification with, or better idealization of the leader (Christ). In the context of his discussions of the horizontal identification between group members Freud returns to the issue of hysterical symptoms. Study of hysteria revealed that such identification could be contagious; girl-friends can adopt each other's hysterical symptoms.[16] A person unconsciously recognizes in the hysterical symptoms the underlying oedipal desires of the other and also of oneself. That recognition awakens the sense of guilt regarding the desires causing similar symptoms.

Hypnosis is discussed in a chapter on idealization and being in love.[17] Like identification and the sense of guilt, idealization is related to oedipal desires. Idealization is an overestimation of the love object. It can be seen in being in love with the sexual object, but also in the tendency to accept the other's authority. Such an idealization can thus be recognized in the relation between the faithful obedient patient and the hypnotizer/analyst. This relationship now represents the model for the relationship with the leader of a group. The leader is idealized, yet not as the object of being in love, but as the authority figure that "suggests" he also loves the group members.

1.3 On the stage

Psychoanalysis emerges from hysteria and hypnosis, yet also Freud's personal intuitions seem of importance. Already before he studies with Charcot in Paris, "psychoanalytic" observations can already be found in Freud's biography. In 1883 he attends the opera *Carmen* and describes this evening in a letter to his fiancée Martha Bernays. Performed on the stage Freud witnessed the tragedy unfolding in which José has to chose between passion and refinement, drive and morality, his love for Carmen and duty. He writes about different "psychologies", about those people that are able to live spontaneously and with enjoyment, and those that deprive themselves controlling enjoyment and repressing drives. This latter habit gives the quality of refinement which is more concerned with avoiding suffering, than creating enjoyment or happiness.[18]

This analysis reflects what will be the pillar of psychoanalysis – there is repression of drives; there is an inner conflict between drive and morality. This

---

[15] S. Freud, *Group Psychology and the Analysis of the Ego, SE XVIII*, p.89, p.107.

[16] Idem, p.107.

[17] Idem, chapter VIII.

[18] S. Freud, *Letters of Sigmund Freud*, E.L. Freud (ed.), Basic Books, New York, 1960, pp.50-51.

is an assessment Freud puts forward in his early studies on hysteria. The hysterics that are hypnotized or simple urged to talk about their memories of the circumstances that lead to their symptoms do not simply recollect their memories or know these circumstances. Freud discovers that there is even active resistance against this recollection. It seems that there is some kind of inner moral agent, a "moral character" with a content determined by cultural moral consensus[19], a "counter-will" that is "not-wanting-to-know" the circumstances.[20] From this Freud develops his first theory on hysteria: it is the effect of the repression of certain affect-laden representations or ideas; the symptom replaces (by conversion) the repressed. Therapy then means linking the affect to the original representation, abreacting the affect in a conscious thought process.

From Carmen to hysteria is not as big a step as it seems. The *grande hystérie* was a theatre itself. With its dramatics and its poses it was the physical staging of inner conflict. Charcot's lectures and experiments themselves with a large public attending witnessing the hysteric's behaviour were theatrical happenings. Yet, in Freud's writings the association of the stage with hysterical conflicts is only the beginning of a returning pattern: drama and tragedy as *Leitmotiv* in Freud's oeuvre.

In *Psychopathic Characters on the Stage* (1905 or 1906) Freud reflects on what attracts people in tragedies performed on stage. He argues that people can identify with the drama, that is to say, they can identify with the conflict staged. He mentions the opera – *Carmen* – as a conflict between "love and duty".[21] This short posthumous published text has often remained unnoticed and in studies on Freud's writings on religion it is never referred to. And yet, the text is of some importance. The conflict between love and duty is not only staged in drama (operas and plays) or in psychological drama (neurotic as well as "normal" mental life). It is also staged in religious drama. In other words religion is the staging of conflict. Freud suggests this when he writes that the drama originates from religious sacrificial practices. Here the central conflict is between the brutal father God representing order and law and the promethean son-hero striving for satisfaction of his drives.[22] This conflict is seen as the ground model for later secularized drama.

Here we find a train of thought that is reformulated in *Totem and Taboo* (1912-1913) when Freud writes about the Christian Eucharist resembling the Greek tragedy in which the hero suffers by taking up the "tragic guilt" thus be-

---

[19] On this issue see especially Ph. Rieff, *Freud: The Mind of the Moralist*, Doubleday, New York, 1961, pp.11-12, p.40.
[20] S. Freud, *A Case of Successful Treatment by Hypnotism, SE I*, pp.121-123; J. Breuer, S. Freud, *Studies on Hysteria, SE II*, pp.92-93; S. Freud, *The Neuro-Psychoses of Defence, SE III*, p.46.
[21] S. Freud, *Psychopathic Characters on the Stage, SE VII*, p.308.
[22] Idem, p.306.

coming the redeemer.[23] In this case Freud is referring to the Orpheus myth as a tragedy in which the son tries to take the father's place. This tragedy takes us in the heart of Freud's reconstruction of primal history and his thesis that culture including religion originates from the identification and the sense of guilt that resulted from the primal parricide committed by the sons. The totem meal and Eucharist can be compared to tragedy as both deal with the same primal oedipal conflict that is at the root of every later conflict between love and duty. It is true that Freud regards every religion is an attempt to resolve the guilt problem that lies at its root, but this can only be done by repetition, by again and again working through history and staging the primal crime as motive for redemption and atonement. This return of the repressed in religious drama will never lead to a definitive redemption or atonement. In every commemoration the ancient crime is also reissued and re-experienced. Hence, religion stages conflict over and over again.

The association of tragedy with religion remains an important aspect of Freud's view on religion. The promethean hero is already mentioned in 1905 (1906) even before Freud's followers Karl Abraham and Carl Gustav Jung elaborate on this mythical figure.[24] Eventually, Freud will write a paper on Prometheus in the period he starts working on his final major study on Moses.[25] Elsewhere I have shown that Freud describes Moses as a promethean figure descending to his people in order to bring them the fiery new religion of the Egyptian pharaoh Akhenaton, monotheism.[26] Moses is killed by his people – the primal murder is repeated – and the Jews develop a strong sense of guilt, a "tragic guilt" that accompanies their advancement in intellectuality.

Hence, in *Psychopathic Characters on the Stage* we find elements that relate Freud's earliest intuitions on drama (*Carmen*) with his latest writings on myth (Prometheus) and religion (Moses). The text becomes a knot of trains of thought when we consider the fact that also Hamlet is discussed. Freud showed a particular interest in this tragic play in the late 1890s when he working on *The Interpretation of Dreams*. Hamlet, says Freud, shows perfectly the inner conflict of the neurotic patient. "His conscience is his unconscious sense of guilt."[27] Ac-

---

[23] S. Freud, *Totem and Taboo*, p.156.

[24] K. Abraham, 'Traum und Mythus. Eine Studie zur Völkerpsychologie', in *Psycho-analytische Studien zur Charakterbildung und andere Schriften*, J. Cremerius (ed.), Fischer, Frankfurt, 1969, p.261-323; C.G. Jung, *Psychology of the Unconscious. A Study of the Transformations and Symbolisms of the Libido. A Contribution to the History of Evolution of Thought*, Princeton University Press, Princeton, 1991, part II, chapter 3.

[25] S. Freud, *The Acquisition and Control of Fire, SE XXII*, pp.183-193.

[26] H. Westerink, "Zum Verhältnis von Psychoanalyse und Mythologie. Die Einfluß Heymann Steinthals Völkerpsychologie auf die angewandte Psychoanalyse", in *Psyche. Zeitschrift für Psychoanalyse und ihre Anwendungen*, 62 (2008), 3, pp.290-311.

[27] S. Freud, *The Complete Letters of Sigmund Freud to Wilhelm Fliess 1887-1904*, J.M. Masson (ed.), Harvard University Press, Cambridge (Mass.)/London, 1985, p.273.

cording to Freud, Hamlet unconsciously identifies with his uncle who killed his father out of love for his mother. It is the oedipal triangle that Freud now for the first time uses to describe the inner conflicts of man. The difference between the Oedipus myth Sophocles' *Oedipus Rex*) and the Hamlet tragedy is that the latter continued to repress – the desire for the mother and the wish to kill the father – what Oedipus consciously, albeit unwittingly, realized (killing the father and possessing the mother).[28]

With Hamlet and Oedipus as examples the neurotic conflict becomes a general human conflict that can basically be regarded a moral conflict – amoral desires (sexual and aggressive) clash with the moral character of man. The basic model is now provided by the Oedipus complex. How did Freud come to this model? The first formulation of the Oedipus complex in *The Interpretation of Dreams* provides the answer. The Oedipus myth is about the quest for the origins of a hidden guilt that caused the city of Thebe to suffer the plague. It is the quest for guilt that leads Oedipus to discover the source of his guilt, i.e. the murder of his father and the marriage with his mother. At this point the myth not only describes basic human wishes, but becomes a model for psychoanalytical practice as well. Psychoanalysis is the analysis of the sense of guilt in order to gain inside in the fundamental psychic conflict. It is thus the analysis of the sense of guilt that leads Freud to discover the importance of the Oedipus complex.

Opera, religious drama, ancient myth, Shakespearean tragedy all stage the psychological conflict that every person can recognize in himself when witnessing the tragedy that unfolds before his eyes. This is also apparent in Freud's many references to his most beloved author Goethe whom he considered a "father" and "teacher".[29] When Freud applies the structures of inner psychical conflict on culture in *Civilization and Its Discontents* it is Goethe's *Faust* with its tragic struggle between life and death drive, the "heavenly powers"[30] determining civilization's fate, that functions as inspiration and that offers the model for presenting man's relation with culture (and vice versa) as struggle. Seen in this light *Civilization and Its Discontents* is neither a pessimistic nor an optimistic book. Whether in conflict or in alliance, man's unhappiness and discontent, but also the limited opportunities for happiness and the strange forms this takes are determined by the "heavenly powers" and by the attempts of individuals or groups to control them. Tragedy is struggle. It does not necessarily evoke resignation or repression, hence unhappiness, nor is it the celebration of Eros and temporary happiness. It is both in an endless variety of cultural forms. *Faust* ties

---

[28] S. Freud, *The Interpretation of Dreams, SE IV*, pp.241-276.

[29] S. Freud, *The Goethe Prize, SE XXI*, pp.208-212. In 1917 Freud published an article on Goethe, *A Childhood Recollection in "Dichtung und Wahrheit", SE XVII*, pp.145-156. On Freud and Goethe see K. Brath, "Goethe und Freud – eine besondere Seelenverwandtschaft", in *Psychologie Heute* 26 (1999), pp.38-43.

[30] S. Freud, *Civilization and Its Discontents*, p.133.

in perfectly: Mephistopheles declares he is the aggressive destructive principle fighting the good, i.e. the life principle of reproduction, the Eros, but not the divine.[31]

Here we touch upon a key aspect of tragedy, namely that there is no outside divine force that can interfere in conflicts forcing a decision to the good. On the contrary, Freud can only regard any influence from outside as cultural, moral or religious enforcement. This is the reason for sharply criticizing the Christian commandment to love one's fellow man or enemy. It is a commandment that, in the name of the divine, forces people to love the one's they don't love, or even hate. According to Freud, to neglect the difference between love for loved ones and love for "neighbours" or "enemies" can only mean an inflation of Eros.[32] In other words, only in conflict Eros will show its true brilliance.

The Faustian tragic struggle as *Leitmotiv* for civilization…it was not new in Freud's work – *Totem and Taboo* ends with the famous quote from *Faust* 'in the beginning was the Deed'.[33] Only Goethe could be the genius, the poet-philosopher that was able to formulate the ambivalent act from which the sense of guilt, culture and religion originated.

1.4 The obsessional neurotic's sense of guilt

The hysterics repress certain affect-laden representations or ideas; the physical symptom replaces the repressed. Freud soon discovered that these affect-laden ideas were mostly of a sexual nature. There was some kind of dissociation due to a moral conflict, a part of consciousness that was split, repressed into what Freud could now describe as the unconscious. The "talking cure" showed that the origins of hysteria should be sought in early childhood. Because Freud, as many in his time, was first convinced that the child had an unspoiled nature, he formulated his so-called seduction theory.[34] Hysteria was the result of a sexual shock that was experienced passively in early childhood and then repressed. Later, when the adolescent or young adult became aware of her/his sexual feelings, the early experiences could be (re)interpreted resulting in the self-reproaches from which the hysterical mechanism emanated. At this point, he argued, hysteria can be distinguished from obsessional neurosis: the primal sexual

---

[31] Idem, pp.120-121.

[32] Idem, p.111.

[33] S. Freud, *Totem and Taboo*, p.161.

[34] The seduction theory is formulated in three texts from 1896: S. Freud, *Heredity and the Aetiology of the Neuroses,* pp.143-156; S. Freud, *Further Remarks on the Neuro-Psychoses of Defence, SE III*, pp.162-185; S. Freud, *The Aetiology of Hysteria, SE III*, pp.191-221. See also T. Geyskens, "Freuds Letters to Fliess. From Seduction to Sexual Biology, from Psychopathology to a Clinical Anthropology", in *International Journal for Psychoanalysis* 82 (2001), pp.861-876; T. Geyskens, *Never Remembered. Freud's Construction of Infantile Sexuality*, Nijmegen, 2002.

shock is here actively experienced with (aggressive) sexual pleasure; later this will not lead to hysteric symptom formation, but to excessive sense of guilt, a strong conscience and compulsional thoughts and acts. Since Freud began to doubt the seduction stories of his female patients, he began to shift his attention towards obsessional neurosis focusing on the question how sexual pleasure could later trigger unpleasure and sense of guilt, and, related to this, on the analysis of the exaggerated inner moral conflict (in comparison to normal psychical conflict) and its origins.

It was especially through the analysis of (obsessional) neuroses that Freud discovered that the child was not "innocent" but already equipped with sexual and aggressive drives that aim at pleasure and avoiding unpleasure. Morality that opposed these impulses could not be solely regarded as the cultural morality a child had identified with – perversion showed that if the drives were strong enough such morality could easily be disregarded. Instead he now stated that morality drew its strength from the drives, or more precisely, the active sexual aggressive enjoyment in early childhood triggered a sense of guilt and it was this sense of guilt that would later give conscience its force.[35]

We cannot reconstruct Freud's technical exposés on obsessional neurosis in detail here. Important is that at the heart of the moral conflict is the sense of guilt, a feeling that links the neurotic's excessive morality with the earliest instinctual forces in the child. It is this sense of guilt that leads Freud to formulate the Oedipus complex in *The interpretation of Dreams*.

The shift from hysteria to obsessional neurosis is crucial for understanding further developments in Freud's psychoanalytical theories notably also concerning his writings on religion. There are two entangled reasons for this. Firstly, Freud's conflict with Carl Gustav Jung, which ended with a schism in the psychoanalytic movement (1913), originated by and large from the fact that Freud's main model for the analysis of individual cases and cultural phenomena was obsessional neurosis, whereas Jung as psychiatrist was more experienced with psychotic patient and hence took psychosis (schizophrenia) as starting point for analyses. Freud's *Totem and Taboo* can be interpreted as an answer to Jung's first major study on the origin and further development of culture and religion, *Transformations and Symbolisms of the Libido* (1911-1912).[36] Secondly, Freud applied his ideas on obsessional neurosis to analyse *via analogia* religious phenomena. He could do so because he basically saw religion as morality – both aim at repression of the human drives.

In *Obsessive Actions and Religious Practices* (1907) the analogy of the neurotic's compulsive actions and religious rites is central. Though there are differences between the two – the obsessional act is private; the rite is communal – Freud focuses on similarities, notably concerning the consciousness with

---

[35] S. Freud, *Draft K. The Neuroses of Defence, SE I*, pp.220-232.
[36] P. Vandermeersch, *Unresolved Questions in the Freud/Jung Debate*.

which the seemingly meaningless act or unmotivated rite is carried out.[37] This character of the act/rite can be interpreted with help of the theory of obsessional neurosis: in both cases an unconscious sense of guilt gives consciousness its strength.[38] The origin of this sense of guilt lies in the repression of an instinctual impulse. At this point Freud again acknowledges differences between compulsive acts and religious rites. In neurosis we are dealing with excessive repression of sexual drives that should be reviewed negatively, as Freud will also indicate in *'Civilized' Sexual Morality and Modern Nervous Illness* (1908).[39] In religion the aggressive egoistic drives are repressed and this is assessed more positively by Freud.[40] Although religion is associated with oppressive morality, the repression of antisocial drives is useful to society. Moreover, religion provides the opportunity to fantasize about aggressiveness, for example revenge, without actually committing an antisocial act: religious rites "always reproduce something of the pleasure which they are designed to prevent".[41]

The conflict with Jung forced Freud to formulate his views on psychoanalysis in general and on religion in particular. But not only Jung, also Freud's other followers who were working in the field of applied psychoanalysis studying arts and mythology had raised some fundamental questions concerning the nature of psychoanalytic theories and concepts, such as the Oedipus complex, sublimation and projection (see further). Freud had to react and the result was *Totem and Taboo*.

Jung had studied mythology and religion from the perspective of psychosis focusing on the vast amount of religious ideas and symbols that were differentiations emanating from a single principle, the primal libido – an emanation reflecting the transformation of the primal libido in, for example, religious thought. This process could be characterized as organic growth and evolution according to an innate voluntaristic principle ultimately aiming at the unity of

---

[37] S. Freud, *Obsessive Actions and Religious Practices*, SE IX, pp.117-127.

[38] Idem, p.123.

[39] S. Freud, *'Civilized' Sexual Morality and Modern Nervous Illness, SE IX*, 179-204.

[40] S. Heine, 'Erkennen und Scham. Sigmund Freuds biblisches Menschenbild', in *Verbum et Ecclesia* 27 (2006/3), pp.869-885.

[41] S. Freud, *Obsessive Actions and Religious Practices*, p.125. Freud's relatively mild assessment of religion can also be noticed in other texts written in this period. In a letter to his friend Oskar Pfister, a reformed Swiss minister, Freud stated that religion could provide the framework for sublimation of the drives. The problem however was that the existing religious traditions all seemed to support repressive cultural morality. However, he also reasoned that in a secularized word in which religion offered no prospects on future enjoyments, cultural morality could become even more oppressive. S. Freud, O. Pfister, *Psychoanalysis und Faith. The Letters of Sigmund Freud and Oskar Pfister*, H. Meng, E. Freud (eds.), Basic Books, New York, 1963, p.16; S. Freud, *The Future Prospects of Psycho-Analytic Therapy, SE XI,* p.146.

differentiated aspects.[42] Freud studied religion from the perspective of obsessional neurosis focusing on the sense of guilt as the motive underlying religious morality. The Oedipus complex – hardly mentioned by Freud after its first formulation – was now again explicitly put forward. Whereas Freud had focussed on the death wish of the son against the father in *The Interpretation of Dreams* and then also in his case study of the Rat Man, he now also elaborated on the desire for the mother. In fact the first part of *Totem and Taboo* on exogamy deals with this issue.

The obsessional neurosis model – predominantly a "male" model; hysterics were mainly women – serves as matrix in the final part of the book in which Freud formulates his widely criticized reconstruction of the primal events from which culture and religion originated.[43] In Freud's own words it was a "hypothesis which may seem fantastic".[44] At some point in primal history a son-horde of (ape) men kill their father and ate him. This primal father possessed the females, ruled tyrannically and was thus both feared and hated as a rival as well as admired and loved for his strength – just as neurotics hate and love their father.[45] By eating him the sons identify with this strength. So far the death of the father is satisfying, yet because of the love and admiration the killing and eating also triggers remorse which is continued in a sense of guilt. From this identification and sense of guilt the first primitive cultural and religious ideas and institutions emanate: the prohibition to posses the mother (exogamy) and the obedience to the totem god, the elevated father. This primal Deed could, according to Freud, easily be recognized in what William Robertson-Smith had described as the totem meal, the "repetition and a commemoration of this memorable and criminal deed, which was the beginning of so many things – social organization, moral restrictions and of religion".[46] In the totem meal the group hunted and slaughtered the totem animal, mourned its death and ate its flesh. It was interpreted by Freud as the annual repetition of the primal murder, a ritual that aimed at re-experiencing the ambivalent feelings associated with the murder, repeating identification and resolving the sense of guilt. The sense of guilt was thus regarded as the key issue that related natural instinctual (ape) man to later civi-

---

[42] C.G. Jung, *Transformations and Symbolisms of the Libido*, part II, chapter 2.

[43] Freud's analyses of exogamy, totemism and taboos, but also his reconstruction of primal events was not simply an application of psychoanalytic theory. The larger part of the book consists of discussions of literature on these issues and in fact Freud formulated his ideas based on this literature. The main authors he refers to are James Frazer, Wilhelm Wundt, Charles Darwin and William Robertson-Smith.

[44] S. Freud, *Totem and Taboo*, p.141. An overview of critique of this "hypothesis" can be found in E.R. Wallace, *Freud and Anthropology. A History and Reappraisal*, International Universities Press, New York, 1983, pp.113-169.

[45] S. Freud, *Totem and Taboo*, p.143.

[46] Idem, p.142.

lized enlightened man. The motor behind cultural and religious morality was this feeling originating from the ambivalent attitude towards the father.

Freud's account of primal events can be regarded as a relapse towards the seduction theory, i.e. the theory stating that a real act/event must have occurred triggering the mechanisms that eventually cause neurosis. Freud had abandoned this theory after he found that his hysterics fantasize about seduction. Yet now he had motives not to suggest that the sons had fantasized murder. Firstly, the Deed is formulated against Jung's starting point that religion emanates from innate ideas through fantasy. Secondly, the Deed does not originate from a single primal drive or life "will", but from an ambivalent attitude towards the father, an amalgam of feelings of love and hate. This is why the sense of guilt is so important in religion. These two aspects of Freud's hypothesis are often neglected in the critique, yet they concern the fundamental problems that were at stake in the Freud-Jung debate.

Related to this problem is Freud's critique of Wilhelm Wundt's theories of the origin of the taboo.[47] According to Freud, the taboo orginates from unconscious ambivalent motives, not from conscious ideas and intuitive thoughts as Wundt had suggested. Religion is not the product of conscious "intellectuality". Again, there is not a single principle from which religious phenomena originate.

Another fundamental issue was at stake in *Totem and Taboo*: how can psychoanalysis study cultural phenomena? Freud's early followers had stressed the Oedipus complex as a universal complex and hence had applied psychoanalytic theory and concepts in a range of studies on person's (artists, etc.), cultural products (operas, etc.) and cultural phenomena (mythology, etc.). Yet, like in the comparison of Hamlet and Oedipus in *The Interpretation of Dreams*, Freud did not focus on the universality of the Oedipus complex, but on the variety of cultural forms in which (aspects of) the Oedipal structures could be recognized. *Totem and Taboo* was not about proving that culture originated from *the* Oedipus complex. Instead he focused on the analysis of the sense of guilt and morality in its varieties.[48] Typical here is Freud's elaboration of Christianity.[49] For Jung this religion constituted progress and liberation from the neurotic compulsions of Jewish law. For Freud, focusing on the element of original sin, Christian doctrine was not a victory over neurotic religion. It was one more doctrine that expressed the sense of guilt in the relationship between God and humanity. It expressed something primal in the nth variation on a theme.

Within the framework of variations on how the sense of guilt is worked through, Freud could state that in the Oedipus complex "the beginnings of relig-

---

[47] Idem, pp.26ff.
[48] Compare S. Freud, K. Abraham, *A Psychoanalytic Dialogue. The Letters of Sigmund Freud and Karl Abraham*, H. Abraham, E.L. Freud (eds.), Basic Books, New York, 1965, p.120.
[49] S. Freud, *Totem and Taboo*, pp.153-155.

ion, morals, society and art converge".[50] The Oedipus complex is included within the exposition on the vicissitudes of the sense of guilt and morality. The complex is therefore not a general universal complex, but a structure that can be recognized when analyzing the cultural varieties of the sense of guilt and morality. The text is thus about the process of analysis, the archaeological deconstruction of cultural phenomena, instead of applying one psychoanalytic scheme in order to explain "everything".

Hence, compared to his followers Freud's *Totem and Taboo* shows many nuances, that later interpreters of the text all to easily overlooked. Nevertheless, the text does bare witness of two fundamental problems in Freud's view on religion that are repeated in his other writings on religion. Firstly, there is Freud's positivist approach and reductionism. The one Deed does serve as the final explanation for culture and religion. In other words, he does not limit himself to understanding cultural phenomena by analyzing oedipal structures, the sense of guilt and morality in various formations, but he also tries to explain these by reconstructing a primal cause. In this urge to explain Freud loses sight of the complexity of religion as he for example neglects the fact that "religious" ideas are already present in the primal murder scene – the sons eating the father because they *believe* they can thus participate in his strength – or when he ignores the function and characteristics of religious language. Secondly, there is the problem of the pathological view on religion. When the model for religion is obsessional neurosis it does not mean that culture or religion *is* a neurosis, but the idea that culture or religion *is like* a neurosis is reason enough to state that it is hard to see how healthy religion would look like or how an individual can be socialized in culture without developing at least some minor symptoms of neurosis. When culture and religion stem from the neurotic repression of the parricide and the sense of guilt and when neurotic repression originates from a moral conflict in which the content of morality is provided by culture and religion, Freud's argument is a vicious circle due to his use of the analogy.[51] This problem becomes visible in the case of the Wolf Man whose obsessional neurosis starts at the moment the religion he meets only for the shortest moment seems to provide the opportunity for sublimation. The repressive character of religion however immediately smothers this spark of hope and the Wolf Man is trapped in pathology again.[52] In short, when pathology is the model for culture and religion, normality becomes an anomaly.

Contrary to *The Future of an Illusion* which Freud regarded as his "worst book"[53], the much criticized *Totem and Taboo* remained a book he was proud of. It would be an important reference throughout his writings.

---

[50] Idem, p.156.

[51] Compare S. Heine, *Grundlagen der Religionspsychologie*, p.177.

[52] S. Freud, *From the History of an Infantile Neurosis*, pp.61ff.

[53] P. Gay, *Freud*, pp.524-525.

One example of this links this paragraph on the obsessional neurotic sense of guilt directly to the previous paragraph on "the stage". In *The Interpretation of Dreams*, a book that was the result of the self-analysis that started after Freud's father had died[54], Hamlet and Oedipus are discussed in a chapter on typical dreams, more precisely dreams about the dead father. In the period he was working on this text he read Robert Kleinpaul's *Die Lebendigen und die Toten in Volksglauben, Religion und Sage* [The Living and the Dead in Folk Belief, Religion and Legend] (1898), a book that dealt with religious representations on death and on the dead returning as ghost or devil to haunt the living. The material Kleinpaul drew upon was by and large the same as Freud was fascinated by: ancient myth, Shakespeare's plays, Goethe's *Faust*. Indeed, in *The Interpretation of Dreams* the Oedipus complex is solely about the death wish of sons towards fathers and its after-effects. In *Totem and Taboo* Kleinpaul's book is discussed in the context of Freud's elaborations on taboos concerning the dead.[55] It is a crucial passage for here he provides an interpretation of the taboo – fear of the dead is the reaction against a latent hostility towards the diseased loved-one – that later strongly supports his hypothesis on the origins of culture and religion. The issue of the dead returning as ghosts or demons, i.e. the return of the father in the land of the living sons, is later again discussed in *The Uncanny* (1919). Central in this text is Freud's discussion of the figure of the sand man in Offenbach's opera *Hoffmanns Erzählungen*, a figure he interprets as a personification of the feared and loved father. The most uncanny phenomena are related to death, corpses and the return of the dead. According to Freud, this indicates that under the thin surface of civilization the world view of primitive man is still the heart beat of man's attitude towards death and the dead.[56] From this primitive mentality the Christian belief in an after-life draws its strength.

The ghost of Hamlet's father, Mephistopheles revealing himself to Faust, the sand man: they are all personifications of what Freud in *Moses and Monotheism* calls "the return of the repressed" – it should thus be no surprise that in the paragraph of that book and under that heading E.T.A. Hoffmann is explicitly referred to. In *Moses and Monotheism* many lines of thought and motives from Freud's writings join, amongst them religion as tragic drama, the analogy between obsessional neurosis and religion, the return of the dead father, the sense of guilt as driving force in moral development i.e. the "advancement in intellectuality".

[54] Freud wrote in the foreword to the second edition of *The Interpretation of Dreams* (1908) that he realized that the book was the product of his reaction to the death of his father. S. Freud, *The Interpretation of Dreams, SE IV*, p.xxvi. See on this issue also D. Anzieu, *Freud's Self-Analysis*, Hogarth Press, London, 1986.
[55] S. Freud, *Totem and Taboo*, pp.58-59.
[56] S. Freud, *The Uncanny, SE XVII*, pp.218-252.

Moses and Monotheism is first of all the application of Freud's reconstruction of the origin and history of religion as depicted in *Totem and Taboo* on Jewish religion, and at the same time the Moses book is a reinterpretation of *Totem and Taboo*.[57] Freud explicitly mentions the relation between these two texts and the model of obsessional neurosis: from the time he wrote *Totem and Taboo* he had "never doubted that religious phenomena are only to be understood on the pattern of the individual neurotic symptoms familiar to us – as the return of long since forgotten, important events in the primaeval history of the human family – and that they have to thank precisely this origin for their compulsive character and that, accordingly, they are effective on human beings by force of the historical truth of their content".[58]

The similarities between Freud's primal murder scene in *Totem and Taboo* and his reconstruction of the origins of Jewish monotheism cannot be overlooked.[59] According to Freud, Moses was an Egyptian prince at the court of the reform-pharaoh Amenhotep IV (ca. 1350 B.C.) who called himself Akhenaton during his rule in which he introduced a kind of monotheism in Egyptian society. After his death the old priest class tried to restore the more primitive polytheistic religion and hence the revolutionary court had to leave. It is in this situation that Moses decides to descend[60] to the people of his choice in order to bring them Akhenaton's religion. However, the Semitic tribes, his chosen people, are not ready for his revolutionary ideas. Freud then turns to a book written by the biblical scholar Ernst Sellin in which is argued that Moses was murdered by his own people.[61] This theory is taken up by Freud – the tribes slew Moses. Then they moved on towards the land Midian where they joined with order Semitic tribes under the leadership of a second "Moses", a Midianite priest, and where they learned to worship the primitive volcano god Yahweh. Freud describes this fusion of tribes, ideas and customs as a neurotic compromise that provided not only the structures to repress the traumatic murder, but also was the fertile soil for a return of the repressed. After all, what followed after the

---

[57] On the complex genesis and the amalgam of versions of *Moses and Monotheism* see I. Grubrich-Simitis, *Freuds Moses-Studie als Tagtraum. Ein biographischer Essay*, Verlag Internationale Psychoanalyse, Weinheim, 1991, pp.79-103; A.F.M. Mampuys, *De ik-splijting van de man Mozes en de inscheuring van zijn ik. Een commentaar bij Freuds Mozeswerk, zijn ik-splijtingstekst en de Wolfmanscasus*, Groningen, 1997.

[58] S. Freud, *Moses and Monotheism: Three Essays, SE XXIII*, p.58.

[59] Idem, part II; S. Freud, L. Andreas-Salomé, *Sigmund Freud. Lou Andreas-Salomé. Briefwechsel*, E. Pfeiffer (ed.), Fischer, Frankfurt, 1966, pp.222-224.

[60] The descent of the prince Moses to the Semitic slaves is crucial in Freud's argument against Otto Rank's view on the mythical hero. *Moses and Monotheism* starts with a critique on Rank in order to argue that Moses is not a mythical hero ascending from poor circumstances to great heights, but a historical figure. S. Freud, *Moses and Monotheism*, pp.10-13.

[61] E. Sellin, *Mose und seine Bedeutung für die israelitisch-jüdische Religionsgeschichte*, Deichertsche Verlag, Leipzig, 1922

compromise was a centuries-long development in which the character of Yahweh gradually changes into Moses' Adonai. This was the most important development in Judaism: "the central fact of the development of the Jewish religion was that in the course of time the God Yahweh lost his own characteristics and grew more and more to resemble the old god of Moses, the Aton".[62] The repressed Egyptian monotheism of Akhenaton and Moses thus returns in history as "historic truth", the "real" core and origin of religion.[63] Like in *Totem and Taboo* the driving force in this development was the sense of guilt triggered by the murder of Moses, a murder that could make such a traumatic impression because it was the repetition of the ancient primal murder. Man's latent sense of guilt was thus strengthened among Jewish people due to the repetition. The impact of this sense of guilt was not limited to the realm of the belief in one God. "The Mosaic ideals" – an absolute monotheism, the rejection of magical ceremonies and a clearly emphasized strict morality[64] – became to characterize the Jewish people as these ideals imprinted certain "traits" that could be grouped under the heading "advancement in intellectuality", character traits such as "decisiveness of thought", "strength of will", "energy of action", "autonomy and independence". The Jewish people developed an own identity over a period of time through an ongoing identification with Moses.[65] The advancement in intellectuality "consists in deciding against direct sense-perception in favour of what are known as the higher intellectual processes".[66]

The murder of Moses repeated the murder of the primal father. But does it? When applying the "developments of a neurosis" on religion, Freud presents the following formula: "Early trauma – defence – latency – outbreak of neurotic illness – partial return of the repressed".[67] The key concept in the reinterpretation of *Totem and Taboo* is "latency". This concept, introduced by Freud in *Three Essays* (1905) indicating the relatively undisturbed period between early childhood sexual experiences and later adolescent sexuality, was lacking in Freud's first reconstruction of primal events. Primal parricide resulted an immediate sense of guilt which directly lead to the first creation of commandments and prohibitions. In *Moses and Monotheism* Freud now argued that a period of latency was also present in primal history.[68] This latency period in history could be called "tradition". The repressed memories of early traumatic experiences

---

[62] S. Freud, *Moses and Monotheism*, p.63.

[63] Idem, p.32, pp.127-130.

[64] Idem, p.64.

[65] Idem, pp.106-115, Ph. Rieff, *The Mind of the Moralist*, p.311.

[66] S. Freud, *Moses and Monotheism*, p.117.

[67] Idem, p.80.

[68] Idem, p.81.

were never lost but 'persisted in traditions which survived among the people' and eventually 'would end in a written record'.[69]

The Deed was thus nuanced – the sense of guilt was not the relatively short remorse from which the sons developed their first cultural and religious convictions and institutions. Latent in the latency period was the sense of guilt which thus became the motor drive in tradition. Religious tradition was about "fixations to the ancient history of the family history and survivals of it" on the one hand and "revivals of the past and returns, after long intervals, of what has been forgotten" on the other hand[70], a development that could only be explained as the effect of "a growing sense of guilt".[71] Eventually, the growing sense of guilt lead to a return of the repressed in consciousness: "the dark traces of the past" lurked in the mind "ready to break through into its more conscious regions".[72] Unfortunately, such enlightenment was only momentary in dark ages. Christianity soon regressed taking up primitive religious elements – it could not continue the high moral standards of Judaism. Anti-Semitic traits soon became one of Christianity's characteristics. Judaism could not free itself from the sense of guilt and thus unconsciously accepted anti-Semitism as punishment.[73] These later developments are new variants to the old theme: religion as the aftermath of the culpabilization of human culture.

1.5 The apparatus "man"

The sense of guilt is key issue in Freud's writings: describing the conflict between drive and morality, later reformulated as the tension between id and superego in both individual life and in culture. It was an issue that Freud already dealt with in his earliest psychoanalytic writings on the neuroses and that was

---

[69] Idem, p.69. The issue of tradition and the transmission of memory-traces has been heavily debated in the past decades. After Yosef Yerushalmi had criticized Freud's Lamarckism, i.e. the theory of the inheritance of pychic dispositions such as the sense of guilt, Jacques Derrida, Richard Bernstein and Jan Assmann have defended Freud arguing that these psychic dispositions are not active but reactive – they "react in a particular manner to certain excitations, impressions and stimuli" (idem, p.98). They have developed theories on the transmission of unconscious memory-traces in what Derrida describes as a cultural 'archive', Bernstein refers to as 'tradition' and Assmann has called "cultural memory". Y.H. Yerushalmi, *Freud's Moses. Judaism Terminable and Interminable*, Yale University Press, New Haven/London, 1991; J. Derrida, *Archive Fever. A Freudian Impression*, University of Chicago Press, Chicago/London, 1996; J. Assmann, *Moses the Egyptian. The Memory of Egypt in Western Monotheism*, Harvard University Press, Cambridge (Mass.)/London, 1997; R.J. Bernstein, *Freud and the Legacy of Moses*, Cambridge University Press, Cambridge, 1998.

[70] S. Freud, *Moses and Monotheism*, p.84.

[71] Idem, p.86.

[72] Idem, p.87.

[73] Idem, p.87, p.136.

also the key issue in his early and late major writings on culture and religion. The moral conflict was clearly related to the repression of conscious material into the unconscious. This unconscious was not a discovery of Freud – in the 19th century philosophers such as Eduard von Hartmann had already introduced the concept to indicate a basic monistic principle that was both source and goal of the world process.[74] Jung with his concept of the primal libido and its evolutions stands in this romantic tradition. Freud however was not a philosopher but a neurophysiologist who, acquainted with the classic model in which man is a composition of body and soul (consciousness), was confronted with the task to develop a model of the mind in which the psychic processes he had discovered (repression, conversion, unconscious representations, etc.) could be integrated. This starting point is clearly expressed in his first attempt to formulate a theory on the mental life: "The intention is to furnish a psychology that shall be a natural science: that is, to represent psychical processes as quantitatively determinate states of specifiable material particles".[75]

The unconscious is the "missing link"[76] between body and consciousness.[77] It is influenced by the physical on the one hand and consciousness on the other hand. The concept of "psychical apparatus" indicates this perfectly well. In *Project for a Scientific Psychology* this psychical apparatus consists of neuron-systems (φ, ψ en ω) that relate the nervous system to psychic processes. To view this text as a work of transition from neurophysiology to psychoanalysis would be a mistake. The neuron-systems as such will move to the background, but the idea that the psychical apparatus is related to physical processes can be found throughout Freud's writings as is indicated in concepts such as "tension", "energy" or "discharge". (It can thus be described as if it were an electric machine.) Even in one of his latest writings Freud holds that the psychical apparatus is the *terra incognito* between the body and the consciousness.[78]

The psychical apparatus can be described as topic, as being "extended in space and of being made up of several portions" with mechanisms.[79] In *The Interpretation of Dreams* the first topic model is introduced: the psychical appa-

---

[74] E. von Hartmann, *Philosophie des Unbewußten. Versuch einer Weltanschauung*, Carl Duncker's Verlag, Berlin, 1869, pp.1-4. On the unconscious in the romantic era see G. Gödde, *Traditionslinien des "Unbewußten". Schopenhauer – Nietzsche – Freud*, Edition Discord, Tübingen, 1999.

[75] S. Freud, *Project for a Scientific Psychology, SE I*, p.295.

[76] S. Freud, G. Groddeck, *Georg Groddeck. Sigmund Freud. Briefwechsel*, Limes Verlag, Wiesbaden/Munich, 1985, p.22.

[77] On the Freudian unconscious see J. Corveleyn, "Het onbewuste", in A. Vergote, P. Moyaert et al. (eds.), *Psychoanalyse. De mens en zijn lotgevallen*, DNB/Uitgeverij Pelckmans, Kapellen, 1996, pp.125-170 ; A. de Block, *Vragen aan Freud. Psychoanalyse en de menselijke natuur*, Uitgeverij Boom, Amsterdam, 2003, pp.23-37.

[78] S. Freud, *An Outline of Psychoanalysis, SE XXIII*, pp.144ff; S. Freud, *Some Elementary Lessons in Psychoanalysis, SE XXIII*, pp.281-286.

[79] S. Freud, *An Outline of Psychoanalysis*, p.145.

ratus consists of three spatial systems, the unconscious, the preconscious (the censoring "screen" between the other two topics) and consciousness. This apparatus is the subject of psychoanalysis, a subject neglected by physiologists who only studied the body and by philosophers (psychologists) who focused on consciousness.[80] Hence, "psychoanalysis acts as an intermediary between biology and psychology' as it is concerned with the study of phenomena situated 'on the frontier between the spheres of psychology and biology".[81]

Two key concepts or mechanisms are crucial in Freud's understanding of the psychical apparatus. The first concept is that of the drive defined as the "psychical representative of an endosomatic source of stimulation"[82], "a concept on the frontier between the mental and the somatic, as the psychical representative of the stimuli originating from within the organism and reaching the mind" thus connecting consciousness and body.[83] The drive represents the physical in the realm of the psychical – the bodily stimuli become psychic needs.[84] (Vice versa, the hysteric bodily symptom represents psychic need.) In *Three Essays* Freud distinguishes two main drives: the sexual drives (which serve the survival of the species) and the ego drives (which serve the preservation of the individual), yet throughout his writings there are a number of drives that are specifications or amalgams of the main drives – the epistemophilic drive, the play drive, the herd drive, etcetera.

A second key concept is that of the pleasure principle. This principle builds upon Gustav Fechner's constancy principle indicating that the psychical apparatus naturally and automatically aims at the lowest possible "constant" tension. In *Project for a Scientific Psychology* and in *The Interpretation of Dreams* it is introduced to indicate the most important regulative mechanism in the unconscious. Drives can be described as quantities of tension that are experienced as unpleasure. Repressed representations also cause unpleasure that needs "discharge". In the psychical apparatus, Freud argues, a wish or need is nothing else as an attempt to discharge tension and to turn unpleasure into pleasure (satisfaction). Pleasure is thus a tensionless state. In *Beyond the Pleasure Principle* (1920) Freud renames the mechanism as "Nirvana principle".[85] There he also introduces the concepts of life and death drives (Eros and Thanatos) indicating a progressive life-affirming drive (containing both sexual and egoistic aspects) and a destructive anti-progressive drive that aims at a return to an inorganic primal state (even when this state is painful) and thus basically re-

[80] S. Freud, *The Resistances to Psycho-Analysis, SE XIX*, p.216.

[81] S. Freud, *The Claims of Psycho-Analysis to Scientific Interest, SE XIII*, p.182

[82] S. Freud, *Three Essays on the Theory of Sexuality, SE VII*, p.168.

[83] S. Freud, *Instincts and Their Vicissitudes*, pp.121-122.

[84] S. Freud, *Three Essays*, p.168.

[85] S. Freud, *Beyond the Pleasure Principle, SE XVIII*, p.56.

sists the formation of an ego (in narcissism).[86] An important motive for this re-formulation of the drives after the introduction of the concept of narcissism was to reaffirm a fundamental drive dichotomy as opposed to Jung's monistic libido theory. Even though Freud himself already acknowledged that his theory of the death drive wass highly speculative – the death drive is "dumb" and can only be presupposed in the various amalgams of the drives.[87] Yet we should be careful not to regard Eros and Thanatos as metaphysical principles that build the muster for a philosophy of life that can compete to Jung's "message of salvation". Eros and Thanatos are drives, psychical representative of bodily urges and it is there-fore no surprise that a biological theory (A. Weismann) is called upon to prove the death drive.[88]

In *Project for a Scientific Psychology* and in later texts the main sys-tems and mechanisms of the psychical apparatus are called primary systems or processes that have to be distinguished from secondary processes indicating the censoring moral and intellectual systems. In *Formulations on the Two Princi-ples of Mental Functioning* (1911) Freud reinterprets these processes by means of their main mechanisms, the pleasure principle and the reality principle. The latter does not indicate an adaptation by the individual to "reality" (real life cir-cumstances), but refers to the control over reality in order to gain "assured pleasure at a later time".[89] By thinking, fantasying and remembering children create insight into reality for the purpose of employing outside reality to satisfy their need for pleasure. "Actually the substitution of the reality principle implies no deposing of the pleasure principle, but only a safeguarding of it."[90] In other words, the censoring function of the secondary processes takes care of the grad-ual discharge of unpleasure and thus ensures pleasure. Here we see important effects of Freud's analyses of the psychical apparatus: logical thinking or moral behaviour is not simply conscious capacities that one acquires in the process of adapting or adjusting to outside reality. Thought processes first of all aim at making satisfaction possible. Freud's later pleas for science over religion (in *The Future of an Illusion*) could be interpreted in this light: religion only prom-ises illusionary satisfaction in an after-life whereas science can offer "real" sat-isfaction in this life.

This train of thought on the pleasure and reality principle is continued in *The Ego and the Id* (1923). Next to the first topic model Freud launches a structural second topic model introducing the concepts of id (drives) and super-ego into Freudian vocabulary – the ego had always been present. The superego

---

[86] Idem, pp.36f. See also J. Laplanche, J.-B. Pontalis, *Vocabulaire de la psychanalyse*, *Vocabulaire de la psychanalyse*, Presses Universitaires de France, Paris, 1967, p.372.
[87] S. Freud, *The Ego and the Id, SE XIX*, chapter IV; S. Freud, *The Economic Problem of Masochism, SE XIX*, pp.159ff.
[88] S. Freud, *Beyond the Pleasure Principle*, pp.45-50.
[89] S. Freud, *Formulations on the two Principles of Mental Functioning, SE XII*, p.223.
[90] Idem. See also J. Laplanche, J.-B. Pontalis, *Vocabulaire de la psychanalyse*, p.336.

is regarded a mostly unconscious part of the ego. It is an "expression of the most powerful impulses and most important libidinal vicissitudes of the id".[91] Simultaneously it represents that which is "higher" in man throughout history: religiosity, morality and social feeling.[92] The superego is not only the repressive power against the id, but also casts the drives in a concrete, ideal form.[93] The superego is the concrete form in which the drives can find satisfaction, the inner norm that defends from being overwhelmed by the id. The id wants satisfaction always and unlimited; the superego's demand is to gain pleasure by desiring and being something/someone specific.

To summarize, the conflict between drive and morality cannot simply be equated with a classic model on body and soul (consciousness). A moral character can repress, but only by deriving the strength to repress from the drives itself. Conscious thought processes are necessary, not in order to intellectually reflect on the drives and hence to distance from them, but in order to discharge tension *in* the thought process. It means that the moral character, the ego, cannot indicate a consistent or autonomous conscious subject. The ego itself is a composition in conflict.

Freud's narcissism theory (1914) makes perfectly clear that the ego is a construct. Narcissism is "the libidinal complement to the egoism of the instinct of self-preservation".[94] It is a general human developmental stage in which egoism (ego drive) comes to completion meaning that the ego drives are taken up libidinously, i.e. an individual experiences himself as a single bodily unit and makes himself into a love object.[95] The first experience of an own identity is not an experience of having a body, but of being a body. This "identification" with a bodily image of oneself is the ground model of what Freud would now call the "ego ideal", a self image of what a person wants to be and against which he measures himself. This ideal places high demands on the ego and is the motor behind repression. The critical agency which measures the ego against the ego ideal is conscience. This narcissistic stage indicating the object relation with oneself is *sine qua non* for later object relations that are formed along the lines of object love and identification. The ego ideal will then be personified by oth-

---

[91] S. Freud, *The Ego and the Id*, p.36.

[92] Idem, p.37.

[93] In fact, this recalls an old notion in Freud's thought. We have already seen (in chapter 1) that enforced morality could not sufficiently explain unpleasure or the sense of guilt. If the libido were strong enough, morality could be overcome. This old clinical idea is reflected in Freud's formulations of the origin of the superego.

[94] S. Freud, *On Narcissism: An Introduction, SE XIV*, pp.73-74.

[95] J. Laplanche, J.-B. Pontalis, *Vocabulaire de la psychanalyse*, pp.261-263; P. Vandermeersch, "Het narcisme. De psychoanalytische theorie en haar lotgevallen", in J. Huijts (ed.), *"Ik zei de gek". Tussen zelf-ontkenning en zelf-verheerlijking*, Uitgeverij Ambo, Baarn, 1983, pp.31-56.

ers and internalized to give conscience content. In other words, the conflict between drives and morality is not primarily a conflict between sexuality and internalized censorship – in narcissism, in the "sexual" relation with a bodily image of oneself, the ego ideal is erected and the foundations for conscience and morality are laid.

The ego is what Freud in his earliest writings indicated as moral character and it represents what he will later in *The Ego and the Id* describe as "reason and common sense".[96] Yet, Freud also repeats that the ego is a narcissistic construct with a physical surface. "The ego is first and foremost a bodily ego", that is to say, "the ego is ultimately derived from bodily sensations". It is surface both of mental life and of the "apparatus".[97]

In Freud's late writings on sexuality, especially on female sexuality, the biological rock upon which psychoanalysis is build is again made explicit. From the 1920s on Freud engages in discussions with a younger generation of psychoanalysts (such as Melanie Klein) on issues such as the female Oedipus complex and the pre-oedipal foundations of conscience and sense of guilt.[98] Freud is forced to think beyond the world of the boy and his father in order to formulate the psychical development among girls. His strategy can be summarized as follows: he defends the Oedipus complex with an appeal on the anatomical differences between men and women.[99]

To conclude this paragraph: the psychic conflicts of man result from and are situated in the unity of "body and soul". The unconscious is the missing link that, contrary to the Romantic tradition, is not a cultural and individual "mystical"[100] reservoir of unknown innate potentialities, but a realm where bodily mechanisms and drives struggle and merge with thought processes – the theory of the superego underscores this.

This model of conflict in unity causes a fundamental problem in Freudian thought as he principally is unable to make a distinction between a physiological and psychological vocabulary and thus tends to reduce psychical experiences to physiological mechanisms. Such a tendency to reduction can, for example, be found in *Totem and Taboo* and *Moses and Monotheism* when he flirts with Lamarck's theory on the inheritance of psychic dispositions in order

---

[96] S. Freud, *The Ego and the Id*, p.25.

[97] Idem, p.26

[98] Important publications in the debate between Freud and to so called London School are M. Klein, "Early Stages of the Oedipus Complex", in *Love, Guilt and Reparation and Other Works, 1921-1945*, R.E. Money-Kyrle (ed.), Hogarth Press, London, 1975, pp.186-198; E. Jones, "The Origin and Structure of the Super-Ego", in *International Journal of Psychoanalysis* 7 (1926), pp.303-311; E. Jones, "Fear, Guilt and Hate", *Papers on Psycho-Analysis*, Baillière, London, 1950, pp.304-319; S. Isaacs, "Privation and Guilt", in *International Journal of Psychoanalysis* 10 (1929), pp.335-347.

[99] For example in S. Freud, *Female Sexuality. SE XXI*, pp.225-243.

[100] S. Freud, *The Claims of Psycho-Analysis to Scientific Interest*, p.178.

to explain the transition of the sense of guilt in religious tradition. Yet, when we would only focus on such justified critique we would miss the fundamental issues that are at stake when we consider religion. Firstly, when we accept the idea that man is a bodily being whose psychic life largely depends on his bodily experiences, the logics of religions, philosophies of life and belief systems are probably less rational and reasonable as theologians would like them to believe. The "higher" thoughts in man would actually be far more "lower" than we think.[101] In other words, Freud opens up a realm of unconscious motives to which religion relates, but is often unwilling or unable to consider. Secondly, we should also take into account the fact that in Freudian anthropology man cannot be called *homo religiosus*, that is to say, there is no innate religious potentiality nor is there a natural intuition of the divine. Like the enlightened civilized bourgeois citizen every religious person is basically an instinctual animal apparatus: under the ego, under the surface of consciousness, reason and moral respectability one stumbles upon the chaotic world of the id, the human perversion of the drives aiming at satisfaction. Religiosity is thus the product of socialization. In religion human nature is processed, i.e. repressed, expressed and diverted, veiled and staged.

1.6 Projection and sublimation

In his early writings Freud saw projection as the primary defence mechanism active in paranoia and anxiety neurosis[102], two derivatives from his early ideas on hysteria and obsessional neurosis. Desire releases a self-reproach which is repressed by externalization. There is a "refusal of the belief in the self-reproach" and in instead a belief in the reproaches of another emerges through projection. These reproaches are considered a threat and this causes anxiety/paranoia.[103]

The projection mechanism was thus situated, but not defined or explained. When Freud stated in *The Psychopathology of Everyday Life* that most modern religions were "psychology projected in the external world"[104] no clearly defined mechanism was thus referred to. This one rather vague statement however did tempt Freud's early followers to apply the concept of projec-

---

[101] Compare S. Freud, *The Ego and the Id*, p.26.
[102] For example S. Freud, *Draft H. Paranoia, SE I*, pp.206-212; S. Freud, *On the Grounds for Detaching a Particular Syndrome from Neurasthenia under the Description "Anxiety Neurosis", SE III*, p.112. See also J. Jeremias, *Die Theorie der Projektion im religionkritischen Denken Sigmund Freuds und Erich Fromms*, Oldenburg, 1978, pp.42-48.
[103] S. Freud, *Draft K*, p.227.
[104] S. Freud, *The Psychopathology of Everyday Life, SE VI*, p.258.

tion in their attempts to explain religious ideas.[105] Freud was much more re-
served. In his 1911 *Psycho-Analytic Notes on an Autobiographical Account of a
Case of Paranoia* he made his sole attempt to elaborate upon the projection
mechanism. The point of departure was the homosexual desire of the paranoid
Schreber that was countered with contrast-desire: "I do not love him – I hate
him". This contrast-desire is processed by the mechanism of projection: "I do
not love him – I hate him – because he hates me". Projection is thus merely responsible for the symptom of the paranoia, namely the delusion of persecu-
tion.[106] It is thus no longer a defence mechanism (against self-reproach) but a
mechanism of symptom formation (delusion).[107]

In *Totem and Taboo* Freud argues that in animism projection is a very
primitive mechanism constituting a philosophy of life before the development
of abstract language made possible another relation with the external world.[108]
Primitive man imagines that something outside himself is taking place which
had previously been only an internal experience. This is not to say that reality is
projection. We are not dealing here with the creation of reality but with the development of a primitive (pre-religious) philosophy of life. The term projection
refers to the creation of meaningful relations between the internal and external
world, before abstract language makes possible to create meaning in a symbolic
way.

In Freud's fantastic hypothesis on the origins of culture and religion in
Totem and Taboo the concept of projection is carefully avoided. This care can
be understood when we consider this text as answer to Jung. Jung had argued
that religion is in essence a systematic organization designed to process both
unconscious conflicts and the accumulation of libido via projection to the external world.[109] Hence, Jung could claim that Christianity was a useful religion resolving inner conflicts (actual sin is forgiven and atoned for) and offering a

---

[105] For example O. Rank, *The Myth of the Birth of the Hero, and other Writings*, P.
Freund (ed.), Vintage Books, New York, 1959, p.10; O. Rank, *Die Lohengrinsage. Ein
Beitrag zu ihrer Motivgestaltung und Deutung*, Deuticke Verlag, Leipzig/Vienna, 1911,
pp.132-133; A. Storfer, *Zur Sonderstellung des Vatermordes. Eine rechtgeschichtliche
und völkerpsychologische Studie*, Deuticke Verlag, Leipzig/Vienna, 1911, p.2.

[106] S. Freud, *Psycho-Analytic Notes on an Autobiographical Account of a Case of Paranoia, SE XII*, p.63.

[107] As in *Formulations on the Two Principles of Mental Functioning* perception is thus
not the key concept in man's relation with reality. In paranoia the delusion is a symptom, an attempt to restore the relation with reality after the breakdown of the actual
structuring processes, the libinal relation with reality. J.-M. Quinodoz, *Reading Freud.
A Chronological Exploration of Freud's Writings*, Routledge, London/New York, 2005,
p.105.

[108] S. Freud, *Totem and Taboo*, p.64.

[109] C.G. Jung, *Transformations and Symbolisms of the Libido*, pp.63-64.

framework for imagination through projection. Freud opposes this "message of salvation"[110] with his focus on the sense of guilt and morality in religion.

In the Schreber case Freud wrote that the term projection required further thorough analysis, yet the scheduled article on the matter was never published.[111] In his later writings on religion the concept of projection is not mentioned.

In *Three Essays* sublimation is defined as the diversion of the sexual instinctual forces from sexual aims toward non-sexual aims.[112] It is introduced by Freud to indicate the normal route when taming the sexual drives in a society that demands this, and he thus situates it in between two pathological developments, perversion and neurosis.[113] Sublimation is thus first of all seen as normal reaction formation against the drives and in the service of culture. Sublimation is thus "in accordance with the general estimate that places social aims higher than the sexual ones". In other words, society's values determine whether one can speak of sublimation or not.[114]

In his study on Leonardo da Vinci Freud wrote about Leonardo's desire for knowledge as capacity for sublimation.[115] The infant's desire for knowledge first of all concerns sexual matters, says Freud, and because of this link to sexuality, the chance is high that the desire (libido) is repressed. This is what would cause neurosis. It is, however, also possible that the desire for knowledge is sublimated: the libido is then not repressed, but directed to a higher aim, intellectual work. The focus is thus on the diversion from the sexual towards intellectual activity.

In later writings such as *The Ego and the Id* this idea is repeated and a very broad and rather vague depiction of sublimation can thus make appearance – sublimation seems to indicate the desexualisation processes that cannot only be related to the transition from autoerotic object love to narcissistic self love and later identification processes, but also to every transition fom primary processes to secondary thought processes.[116] Here, the relation between sublimation and social values is no longer decisive – sublimation is situated on the level of structural transformations of erotic libido through identification and object love.

---

[110] S. Freud, *On the History of the Psychoanalytic Movement*, p.60.

[111] S. Freud, *Psycho-Analytic Notes on an Autobiographical Account of a Case of Paranoia*, p.66.

[112] S. Freud, *Three Essays*, p.178.

[113] Idem, p.165.

[114] S. Freud, *Introductory Lectures on Psychoanalysis, SE XVI*, p.345; S. Freud, *New Introductory Lectures to Psychoanalysis, SE XXII*, p.97.

[115] S. Freud, *Leonardo da Vinci and a Memory of his Childhood, SE XI*, pp.77ff.

[116] S. Freud, *The Ego and the Id*, p. 46, p.54. On the issue see also P. Moyaert, *Begeren en vereren. Idealisering en sublimatie*, SUN, Nijmegen, 2002, pp.86-90.

Due to Freud's pathological view on culture and religion as repressive morality the sublimation Leonardo is capable of is not only to be considered normal. It is in fact extraordinary. The Wolf Man case can serve as argument here. After a period of severe anxieties the Wolf Man developed an obsessional neurosis. According to Freud, the biblical stories the Wolf Man's mother told him might have allowed him to sublimate some of his fantasies.[117] Both his homosexual and masochistic tendencies could then be expressed and to a certain degree distanced from, and in this way repressed desires could be somewhat drained. "But he was unsuccessful" and the "faith of piety" was soon victorious over his "rebelliousness of critical research".[118] The Wolf Man became a victim of religion's main structures: the sense of guilt and morality. In other words, Freud suggests that sublimation is free, critical intellectual activity. But given the nature of sublimation (as mechanism in the service of taming the sexual drives) and the nature of religion (as analogous to obsessional neurosis), it is hard to see how sublimation could ever be successful. There is no way out of the pathological structures the Wolf Man is entangled in.

In later studies Freud now and again mentions sublimation in culture, art, science or religion. In *Moses and Monotheism*, for example, he related the advancement in intellectuality to sublimation, yet he does not further discuss this mechanism.[119] Hence, the issue is "poorly elaborated" upon.[120]

1.7 The Oedipus complex

When we consider the fact that Freud started analyzing patients in the mid 1880s it is astonishing that the Oedipus complex was only formulated 15 years later and only regarded a nuclear complex in the neuroses 25 years later. In fact the Oedipus complex only becomes a real key issue in Freud's writings from the 1920s and 1930s, i.e. from the moment he introduces the structural second topic model and engages in discussions with his followers on the matter.

This sketch should already give an indication of what the Oedipus complex is actually all about. It is not a term indicating the formula that a boy wants to marry his mother and kill his father. I have already argued that it was the analysis of the sense of guilt that lead Freud to formulate the complex. In *Totem and Taboo* the complex provided a scheme in which ambivalent feelings of love

---

[117] S. Freud, *From the History of an Infantile Neurosis*, pp.64-65, p.115.

[118] Idem, p.65, p.70. Compare also S. Heine, *Grundlagen der Religionspsychologie*, pp.172-173.

[119] S. Freud, *Moses and Monotheism*, p.86. See also A. Vergote, *De sublimatie. Een uitweg uit Freuds impasses*, SUN, Amsterdam, 2002, pp.202-224 (originally published as *La psychanalyse à l'épreuve de la sublimation*, 1997); S. Heine, *Grundlagen der Religionspsychologie*, pp.171-173.

[120] *La théorie de la sublimation est restée, chez Freud, peu elaborée*. J. Laplanche, J.-B. Pontalis, *Vocabulaire de la psychanalyse*, p.466.

and hate, the sense of guilt, conscience formation and identification with the father could be brought in relation. In my opinion *On Narcissism* is a further crucial text when we consider the question how the Oedipus complex could be become a key complex in Freud's work and what it actually expresses. After all,
here Freud elaborated upon identification and object love – narcissism as identification with a self-image provided the model for later identification and object
love. Here also the ego ideal and the foundations for conscience were formed.
When Freud discusses the Oedipus complex in *Group Psychology and the
Analysis of the Ego* he does so in a chapter on identification. The complex describes that the boy wants to be like his father and takes him "as his model".[121]
This identification must be differentiated from the relation to the mother who is
a sexual object for the boy. The actual Oedipus complex results from these two
relations: the identification with the father leads to the boy wanting to take his
place with his mother. Thus he saw the transition from primary identification in
narcissism to object relations as taking place via the Oedipus complex. Identification meant: I want "to be" the other. As formula this can be distinguished
from the other as a sexual object where the formula is: I want "to have" the
other.[122] The central issue expressed in the Oedipus complex is thus that man's
significant relationships with others rest upon identification. This identification
has an ambivalent nature as it combines sexual (love, admiration) and aggressive (hate, rivalry) elements. Hence the complex links identification to the sense
of guilt.

In *Group Psychology* Freud then further discussed identification as to
be distinguished from being in love and idealization (which can be appointed to
the believer's faith in religious leaders). In being in love the object is sexually
overestimated, that is to say, the object cannot be criticized and its qualities are
very highly esteemed.[123] "The object has been put in the place of the ego ideal",
and this external ego ideal is no longer an internal norm for the ego. The ego is
thus "impoverished", narcissistic libido flows to the object and the ego submits
to the elevated ideal, the other person.[124] Here lies the crucial difference between idealization and identification. In identification an object is not substi-
tuted for the ego ideal but "put in the place of the ego".[125] It thereby "enriches"
the ego.

When Freud introduces the concept of superego in *The Ego and the Id*
the Oedipus complex is discussed in the context. The superego replaces the
concept of ego ideal. It is the representative of the first object choices of the

---

[121] S. Freud, *Group Psychology*, p.105.

[122] Idem, pp.106-107.

[123] Idem, p.112.

[124] Idem, p.113. Freud elaborated here on an issue already addressed in *On Narcissism*,
the idealization of the love object. S. Freud, *On Narcissism*, pp.93-95.

[125] S. Freud, *Group Psychology*, p.114.

id[126], hence identification with a self-image and then with the father taking the mother as love object. The superego is simultaneously also a reaction formation against these choices. This is expressed in the Oedipus complex' superego individuation commandments: "You ought to be like this (like your father)" and "you may not be like this (like your father)".[127]

The superego as representative of the id's object choices and as safeguard of a narcissistic ego ideal is misinterpreted when it is equated with repressive and commanding structures. The superego is not simply the result of enforced morality, nor is it just the representative of religiosity, of morality or social feeling.[128] It is crucial in Freudian thought – and often reformulated since the 1890s – that morality cannot be solely enforced, but that it depends on an inner psychic structuralizing process. To oppose the superego (as enforced morality) to the ego (as autonomous individuality) ignores the fact that Freud regards the superego as the individuation principle within the ego. Moreover, it is crucial that the formation of the superego is linked to narcissism. It is the concrete form in which the drives can find satisfaction, the welcome inner norm that defends from being overwhelmed by the id, the safeguard of the individual's own personality and originality.[129] To give an extraordinary example: had Moses not identified with Akhenaton and his religious revolution he would not have become a great man.

The Oedipus complex signifies a structural model relating the drives to morality and tying together key concepts such as identification, object love, idealization, sense of guilt, conscience. It serves as model for interpreting the individual's relation with others and, when we take into account the paragraphs on the pleasure and reality principle, it is also linked to the individual's relation with reality. Here, the complex shows its significance in relation to religion. The complex describes concepts in their mutual structural relations that can also be found in religious language, in faith and religious behaviour.

1.8 Helplessness and illusion

In 1924 Rank published *The Trauma of Birth*, a book in which he focussed on pre-oedipal anxiety. He stated that the Oedipus complex and with it the castration complex originated from an anxiety that was related to the traumatic experience of birth.[130] It was in this context that he argued that the sense of guilt developed when the original anxiety associated with the mother's genitals was

---

[126] S. Freud, *The Ego and the Id*, p.34.

[127] Idem.

[128] Idem, p.37.

[129] A. Lambertino, *Psychoanalyse und Moral bei Freud*, Bouvier Verlag, Bonn, 1994, pp.297ff.

[130] O. Rank, *The Trauma of Birth*, Robert Brunner, New York, 1952.

attached to the father.[131] By this Rank indicated that sense of guilt should be seen as sublimated anxiety by means of projection.[132]

Freud's answer to Rank is *Inhibitions, Symptoms and Anxiety* (1926). Anxiety is a signal of approaching danger and not the manifestation of an earlier traumatic experience.[133] This danger, he says, is essentially the threat of being castrated by the father. In this way Freud was able to situate anxiety in an oedipal framework and hence he defended the Oedipus complex, the role of the father and importance of the sense of guilt.

Yet, Rank had now forced Freud to engage in the analysis of pre-oedipal developments. Freud argues that birth does have an effect on the child. Separation from the mother means that the child is now put in a situation of danger. The core of this danger is an "economic disturbance caused by an accumulation of amounts of stimulation".[134] He calls this first anxious situation "mental helplessness". It is the experience of accumulating needs and urges that the child cannot satisfy or get rid of by himself.[135] In short, the child is mentally maladapted to life and therefore completely dependent upon help from others. This mental helplessness was an important pre-oedipal motive that was processed in the Oedipus complex. *Inhibitions, Symptoms and Anxiety* thus presented a new line of approach that allowed the oedipal structures to remain central, and even to be strengthened by a powerful motive such as mental helplessness. In *The Future of an Illusion*, which can be read as a case study to his ideas on helplessness, Freud formulates this as such when he writes that "the store of religious ideas includes not only wish-fulfilments but important historic recollections. This concurrent influence of past and present must give religion a truly incomparable wealth of power".[136] In other words, religion draws its strength from helplessness and the wish for parental care as well as from recollections concerning oedipal desires and the sense of guilt that impose restrictions.

Protection is first sought with and offered by the mother. The father appears to be stronger and is then the next object from which help is sought. This

---

[131] Idem, p.19.

[132] Compare idem, pp.117ff.

[133] S. Freud, *Inhibition, Symptoms and Anxiety, SE XX*, for example p.150.

[134] Idem, p.137.

[135] Idem, p.138. This idea is already presented in *Project for a Scientific Psychology*, when Freud argued that a child is "helpless" not only because it needs others to supply needs, but first of all because the child itself is defenceless against its own primary processes, that is, the autonomous urges and discharges of unpleasure. S. Freud, *Project for a Scientific Psychology*, pp.317-318. Compare also S. Freud, *New Introductory Lectures on Psychoanalysis*, pp.87-88. On "mental helplessness" see J. Laplanche, J.-B. Pontalis, *Vocabulaire de la psychanalyse*, pp.122-123; T. Geyskens, Ph. van Haute, *Van doodsdrift tot hechtingstheorie. Het primaat van het kind bij Freud, Klein en Hermann*, Uitgeverij Boom, Amsterdam, 2003, pp.42-46.

[136] S. Freud, *The Future of an Illusion, SE XXI*, p.42.

need to defend oneself against helplessness subsequently finds its way into religious ideas, which Freud now defined in extremely limited terms: these ideas are religious "doctrines", "teachings and assertions".[137] The dogmas and religious systems of thought are embraced because and so long as they provide protection against helplessness. Primarily, these religious doctrines are "not precipitates of experience or end results of thinking: they are illusions, fulfilments of the oldest, strongest and most urgent wishes of mankind".[138]

The Future of an Illusion is a text on religion in which the subject is not primarily considered in analogy to obsessional neurosis (although Freud does define religion in its repressive doctrinal capacity) and thus the essay does not focus on the sense of guilt, superego and conscience formation or identification. Instead of analyzing the origins of and historic developments in religion this text deals with "the future" of religion. Even although Freud argued that the longing for a protecting father-God is the same as the longing for the admired primal father,[139] we should notice the difference with other approaches of religion: the complex of helplessness, need, wish and care points to another conception of religion and God (as caretaker, protector) than the approach in which the father-God was the admired rival, the brutal and strong ape man, and in which religion processed the sense of guilt.

Not only the discussion with Rank, but also a friendly debate with Oskar Pfister highly influenced the text. In *The Future of an Illusion* Pfister is not mentioned, yet there are indications in their correspondence that Freud saw his essay as a critique of Pfister.[140] In a letter Freud wrote to Pfister that his essay "has a great deal to do with you". It would reject religion "in any form and however attenuated".[141] Freud even called his essay a "declaration of war".[142]

---

[137] Idem, p.25.

[138] Idem, p.30. Freud's definition of religious doctrines as fulfilments of the oldest, strongest and most urgent wishes of humankind strongly resembles Feuerbach's 1841 depiction of faith in God, immortality and afterlife as wish-fulfilment. L. Feuerbach, *Das Wesen des Christentums*, Reclam, Stuttgart, 1994, pp.267-268.

[139] Idem, p.17, p.24. On religion as wish-illusion and as aftermath of culpability – see H. Henseler, *Religion – Illusion? Eine psychoanalytische Deutung*, Steidl Verlag, Göttingen, 1995, part I; A. Vergote, "Religion after the Critique of Psychoanalysis", in *Psychoanalysis, Phenomenological Anthropology and Religion*, J. Coveleyn, D. Hutsebaut (eds.), Leuven University Press, Amsterdam/Atlanta, 1998, pp.17-37; J.J. DiCenso, *The Other Freud. Religion, Culture and Psychoanalysis*, Routledge, London/New York, 1999, pp.47-49.

[140] W.W. Meissner, *Psychoanalysis and Religious Experience*, Yale University Press, New Haven/London, 1984, pp.73-103; P. Gay, *A Godless Jew. Freud, Atheism, and the Making of Psychoanalysis*, Yale University Press, New Haven/London, 1987, pp.75ff.

[141] S. Freud, O. Pfister, *Psychoanalysis and Faith*, pp.109-110.

[142] Idem, p.120.

In 1920 Oskar Pfister had written *Zum Kampf um die Psychoanalyse* [The Struggle for Psychoanalysis], a book on psychoanalytic method. He reasoned that psychoanalysis inevitably lead into philosophy of life as it makes claims about the nature of what is (metaphysics – metapsychology) or ought to be (ethics – therapy). Hence, psychoanalysis provides the theory and method to distinguish between true and illusionary experiences or representations and could thus contribute to defining true and healthy moral and religious personality.[143]

In *The Future of an Illusion* Freud implicitly takes a distance from Pfister's ideas on religion associated with truth and a moral ideal. All religion is considered as based on illusionary needs, wishes and desires. This radically refuted the idea that Pfister implicitly defended: there is illusionary religion and there is true healthy religion based "true" experience and "healthy" thinking. The latter type of religion would basically resemble the ideals of psychoanalysis. Of course Freud resisted the idea to compare psychoanalysis with religion – in his critique on Jung's message of salvation this had already been put forward. Moreover, Freud rejected any type of religion that would be situated beyond the border of a psychoanalytic deconstruction of religion, i.e. a type of religion that indicated that psychoanalysis was not about "remembering, repeating and working through"[144] unconscious motives such as the sense of guilt, but about defining the distinction between moral-religious truth and illusion.

In chapter 2 we will consider the debate with Pfister in more detail.

Religious doctrines are outdated illusions, says Freud.[145] In modern world only science can make human helplessness bearable.[146] Considering the idea that Christian religion is doctrinal religion and that these doctrines are "not precipitates of experience or end results of thinking" Freud could refer to studies by Theodor Reik on the origins, emergence and decline of Christian dogmas. *Dogma and Compulsion* (1927) gives evidence to that.[147] Reik focused on Christian dogmas that were formulated at the fourth-century councils, after serious conflict and debate. The source of these conflicts, according to Reik, could be traced back to the early Christians: they, beginning with Paul, built upon the revolutionary tendencies in Jesus' message and would not hesitate to replace God by Christ. In contrast there was a movement that saw Christ as the incarnation of the father-God. The compromises were written down in dogmas.[148] In

---

[143] O. Pfister, *Zum Kampf um die Psychoanalyse*, Internationaler Psychoanalytischer Verlag, Leipzig, Vienna, Zurich, 1920, pp.246ff.

[144] S. Freud, *Remembering, Repeating and Working Through, SE XII*, pp.147-156.

[145] S. Freud, *The Future of an Illusion*, chapter VII and following.

[146] Idem, pp.54-56.

[147] Th. Reik, *Dogma and Compulsion. Psychoanalytic Studies on Religion and Myths*, International Universities Press, New York, 1951.

[148] Idem, chapter II.

psychoanalytic terms this meant that the ambivalent feelings (including the sense of guilt) towards the father-God were expressed in a neurotic compromise.

It was clear to Reik that dogmas were an end product of religion. Yet, at the moment doctrine finally appeared to be solid, an inner dynamic called it into question – the underlying ambivalence returns in the form of doubt. It appeared to Reik that liberal Protestantism represented by theologians such as Pfister meant "the end of Christianity".[149] It was atheism with a thin layer of belief, or, as Freud would describe it, it was the religion of deists who "give the name of 'God' to some vague abstraction".[150] It was the dawn of dogmatic religion. The question was only which "illusion" would take its place.[151] Freud provided an answer: science.

Religious doctrines are "not precipitates of experience or end results of thinking: they are illusions, fulfilments of the oldest, strongest and most urgent wishes of mankind". Romain Rolland critically opposed to this definition of religion. In a letter to Freud he wrote: "Your analysis of religion is correct" inasmuch as religions are dogmatic systems.[152] Yet there is such a thing as a *sensation religieuse*, an "oceanic feeling" evident in every religion and every religious person. It is to be described as a directly true, inner mystic experience of participation in a religious totality, which has nothing to do with obedience to authority.

In July 1929 Freud wrote to Rolland that the oceanic feeling had been troubling him for some time and that the issue should be dealt with in an essay.[153] A short time later, he had to admit that mysticism was "foreign" to him.[154] Foreign to Freud was the conception of religion presented by Rolland (and Pfister as a matter of fact) with which he was unacquainted: religion as essentially unrelated to dogma, repressive morality or intellectuality.[155] Moreover in their religious convictions these friends favoured an anthropology in which man was *homo religiosus*, i.e. man possessed an innate capacity from which religiosity could emerge.

Civilization and Its Discontents begins with a response to Rolland. "Originally the ego includes everything, later it separates off an external world

---

[149] Idem, p.153.

[150] S. Freud, *The Future of an Illusion*, p.32.

[151] Th. Reik, *Dogma and Compulsion*, p.161.

[152] H. Vermorel, M. Vermorel, *Sigmund Freud et Romain Rolland. Correspondance 1923-1936. De la sensation océanique au Trouble du souvenir sur l'Acropole*, Presses Universitaires de France, Paris, 1993, pp.303-304.

[153] Idem, p.308.

[154] Idem, p.311.

[155] Ph. Rieff, *The Mind of the Moralist*, p.292.

from itself", says Freud.[156] A baby doesn't distinguish between inner and outer world. This distinction only gradually becomes clear as the helpless, yet narcissistic child becomes dependent on objects from the outside world that fulfil its needs (mother's breast) on the one hand and tries to separate itself from and cast out every inner source of unpleasure on the other. This gives rise to an external world that can satisfy needs while at the same time be perceived as threatening. Freud believed that infancy involved the dialectic of helplessness and need satisfaction.

Religion is a continuation of that need for satisfaction. Because the world continues to be experienced as threatening, there is continuing reason for the existence of religiosity. Although Freud sought to trace religion back to early childhood helplessness and subsequently to the need for paternal protection, he felt that the religious oceanic feeling could better be regarded as "the restoration of limitless narcissism".[157] This oceanic feeling was not linked to religion until a later stage of development.

1.9 Moses and St Paul

We thus far sketched a variety of psychoanalytic perspectives on religion, returning patterns, concepts and *Leitmotive* Freud worked on, and the influence of debates he was engaged in. But what about a personal fascination with religion? Fact is that Freud considered himself an atheist, a "godless Jew".[158] He thus considered himself a Jew. Certainly the confrontations with anti-Semitism in late nineteenth-century Vienna and in the 1920s and 1930s were an external factor that caused Freud to reflect on his Jewish identity. In the past decades several scholars have also written in Freud's fascination for the father figure of Judaism, Moses, as the result of self-analysis and/or the expression of his relationship with his own father.[159]

Freud's fascination for Moses is already expressed in his 1914 study on the Moses statue of Michelangelo.[160] He saw the statue first in 1901 and regularly visited it thereafter. Contrary to his followers who focused on Moses as mythical half-god, i.e. as a residu of primitive religion, Freud saw in the

---

[156] S. Freud, *Civilization and Its Discontents*, p.68.

[157] Idem, p.72.

[158] S. Freud, O. Pfister, *Psychoanalysis and Faith*, p.63. Also, S. Freud, *A Religious Experience, SE XXI*, pp.169-172.

[159] See for example I. Grubrich-Simitis, *Freuds Moses-Studie als Tagtraum*; Y.H. Yerushalmi, *Freud's Moses*; S. Heine, *Grundlagen der Religionspsychologie*, pp.166-178; F. Maciejewski, *Der Moses des Sigmund Freud. Ein unheimlicher Bruder*, Vandenhoeck & Ruprecht, Göttingen, 2006.

[160] On this issue see also H. Westerink, "The Great Man from Tarsus: Freud on the Apostle Paul", in *Psychoanalytic Quarterly* 76 (2007), pp.217-235; H. Westerink, "Zum Verhältnis von Psychoanalyse und Mythologie".

Michelangelo's Moses as a historic figure. Michelangelo had succeeded in expressing what Freud considered the core of Moses' personality, namely something "more than human", something that is one of man's greatest achievements, the control of one's own drives for the greater good of a higher goal.[161] In other words, Moses was one of those extraordinary men capable of sublimation of the drives in intellectuality. This aspect of the renunciation of aggressive drives had already been related to Moses by Freud via a reference to St Paul's letter to the Romans concerning religion's ability to process anti-social drives in *Obsessive Actions and Religious Practices*.[162]

In 1919 Reik deals with Judaism in *Probleme der Religionspyschologie* [The Psychological Problems of Religion] from the starting point that Freud's theories from *Totem and Taboo* should be applied on the one religion Freud had not dealt with in that book, Judaism, and on the aspect of Michelangelo's statue of Moses Freud had not analyzed namely Moses "horns" that might be the remnants of a primitive mythological past – Moses as half-god and half-totem animal. Hence, Reik reconstructs a historic development from Jewish polytheism to monotheism in which Moses is humanized.[163] An open question is still what psychological circumstances could have lead to the fact that Judaism developed into the first and strict monotheism and that lead to the idea of the Jews as chosen people.[164]

Reik, in applying *Totem and Taboo* on Judaism and the Moses figure, had raised the questions that Freud would deal with in *Moses and Monotheism*. Again Moses is regarded a historic figure with extraordinary capacities – an Egyptian prince that chooses himself a people and gives them advancement in intellectuality. Seen in this light, Freud is again fascinated by the authority of religious leadership, an interest that can be traced back to his early text on the semi-religious authority of the hypnotizer.

Moses is the great man[165] of Jewish tradition. However, here we should notice that *Moses and Monotheism*, a text Freud worked on from 1934 until 1939, is an amalgam of versions. It is mainly in the first version from 1934, later inserted in the final section of the book, that Freud presents a positive picture of Moses.[166] He is the founder of Jewish religion, the father figure who af-

---

[161] S. Freud, *The Moses of Michelangelo, SE XIII*, pp.229-234.

[162] S. Freud, *Obsessive Actions and Religious Practices*, p.127.

[163] Th. Reik, *The Psychological Problems of Religion I. Ritual. Psycho-Analytic Studies*, Farrar, Straus and Company, New York, 1946, pp.305-361.

[164] Idem, pp.360-361.

[165] S. Freud, *Moses and Monotheism*, pp.107-111.

[166] Idem, pp.105-130. The text consists of three essays. The first two were written in 1937. The third essay starts with two prefatory notes (written in Vienna and London in 1938). Idem, pp.54-58. What follows is the first part of the second version of the manuscript from 1938 (pp.59-104). Then the first version of the manuscript from 1934 is inserted (pp.105-130). The final pages are then the second part of the second version

ter he is murder the chosen people will eventually identify with.[167] Their high
moral and intellectual standards reflect Moses'. Moses imprinted certain character traits upon the Jewish people: "decisiveness of thought", "strength of will",
"energy of action", "autonomy and independence".[168]

Yet, the ambivalent feelings of sons towards their father Freud had so
often reflected upon in his writings, also characterizes Freud's own assessment
of the father of Jewish identity, i.e. his own identity as Jew. In the second version of the manuscript from 1938 Moses is no longer the great man, but the "tyrant" who forced Egyptian monotheism upon the Semitic tribes.[169] Moreover,
the greatness of Moses is deconstructed which is expressed in Freud's theory of
the two Moses figures – the Egyptian tyrant and Midianite priest who united the
Semitic tribes. The latter is the anonymous "Moses", the erased historic figure
yet actual founder of the compromise of religions Judaism is build on.

In the process of deconstructing Moses as religious father figure another
figure rose to the status of great man, the apostle Paul. In the second version of
the manuscript he is twice elaborated upon.[170] Freud's fascination for Paul runs
parallel to his fascination of Moses. In the period he analyzes the Moses statue
he also writes on Paul as the unique historic figure that continues the high religious standards of Judaism before Christianity regresses to a polytheistic, more
primitive level.[171] What Freud is preoccupied with is expressed in a letter to
Pfister: "I have always had a special sympathy for St. Paul as a genuinely Jewish character".[172]

Freud was not so much interested in Paul as founder of Christianity, as
religious leader, but in Paul's intellectual analytical capacities. In *Moses and
Monotheism* Paul is presented as a model for the psychoanalyst, the man that is
able to trace the "tragic guilt" of the Jews back to their origin by both self-
analysis and the analysis of his fellow men. He tried to liberate the Jews from
this historic burden and in doing so, making use of the historic possibilities and

---

(pp.130-137). On the genesis of the text and the amalgam of versions see I. Grubrich-
Simitis, *Freuds Moses-Studie als Tagtraum*, pp.79-103; A.F.M. Mampuys, *De ik-
splijting van de man Mozes en de inscheuring van zijn ik*.
[167] S. Freud, *Moses and Monotheism*, pp.106-115, Ph. Rieff, *The Mind of the Moralist*,
p.311.
[168] S. Freud, *Moses and Monotheism*, pp.109-110
[169] Idem, p.47.
[170] Idem, pp.86-89, pp.135-137.
[171] S. Freud, 'Great is Diana of the Ephesians', *SE XII*, 342-344.
[172] S. Freud, O. Pfister, *Psychoanalysis und Faith*, p.76. Freud writes this letter in reaction to the publication of a large article by Pfister on the apostle Paul. In this text he argues that Paul is a compulsive neurotic Jew who is then capable of a remarkable sublimation freeing himself from the guilt-laden Jewish tradition. This sublimation is
possible because of Paul's education in Hellenistic philosophy. O. Pfister, "Die Entwicklung des Apostels Paulus. Eine religionsgeschichtliche und psychologische Skizze", in *Imago* 6 (1920), pp.243-290

the religious vocabulary that stood to his aim, Paul unwillingly became the founder of a new religion. Freud could identify with Paul as analyst of the "tragic guilt". *Moses and Monotheism* shows a shift of identification from Moses to Paul. Yet, Paul is not a second Moses. Whereas Moses is the father figure[173], Paul is an intellectual brother who remembered, repeated and worked through individual and cultural history. Freud thus identifies with a religious figure that basically did what Freud did throughout his psychoanalytic career.

1.10   The inevitable sense of guilt

In both Freud's clinical writings as in his writings on culture and religion the issue of the sense of guilt is a central topic indicating the conflict between drive and morality, between man's immoral nature and a culture that stands before the impossible task to both inhibit the drives and make man happy. As far as this conflict is a cultural conflict it is an extension of psychic conflict. Freud's applications of the model of obsessional neurosis on culture and religion indicated as much. The conflict between drive and morality is an inner conflict and alternative perspectives only support this: the ideas on mental helplessness indicate that the infant is mentally maladjusted to life and needs "help" in order to drain of psychic pressure and attain satisfaction. This mental maladjustment is at the core of Freud's anthropology. The fact that the ego is not in control of the id and the superego, like the rider is not in control of the horse[174], is an expression of this. The larger part of the ego, the superego, is unconscious – the ego is merely the surface of the chaotic world that lies beneath and that actually directs our thoughts and actions. Culture and religion are supposed to control and process the unconscious impulses, yet as man is maladjusted to life, adaptation to whatever reality will ultimately fail. Therefore, culture and religion stage conflict. They process conflict by expressing it – the return of the repressed is as much apparent as the repression. Here, Freudian anthropology differs principally from later main stream psychoanalytic theories such as ego psycholog and self psychology. These latter theories stress the strengthening of the ego and the adaptation to reality as the objectives of psychoanalysis.

It is in the context of inner conflict that the sense of guilt as *the* expression of this conflict can be regarded a key concept in Freud's writings. That the sense of guilt is inevitable is not only true in the relation between individual and culture[175], but more fundamentally, it is true for "normal" mental life.

The Oedipus conflict that eventually becomes the key complex in Freud's writings indicates the structural relations between psychical topics and mechanisms. These relations are not fixe patterns, but they can vary from pa-

---

[173] S. Freud, *Moses and Monotheism*, p.110.

[174] S. Freud, *The Ego and the Id*, p.25.

[175] S. Freud, *Civilization and Its Discontents*, p.132.

thology to pathology. Here, the Oedipus complex shows to be the result of a development throughout Freud's clinical and meta-psychological writings: the analysis of the sense of guilt in obsessional neurosis leads to a differentiation in the concept of the sense of guilt in its various forms related to various pathologies. The self-reproaches Freud observed in his early writings on the neuroses will be associated exclusively with melancholia.[176] The sense of guilt in masochism will be called "need for punishment" – in masochism various types (erotogenic, feminine, moral) can be distinguished.[177] The obsessional neurosis is characterized by excessive consciousness of guilt.

Because the id and the larger part of the ego, the superego, are unconscious it is no surprise Freud introduces the concept of unconscious sense of guilt indicating an unconscious conflict between drive and morality. This unconscious sense of guilt "plays a decisive economic part" in a great number of neuroses – obsessional neurosis, melancholia, paranoia, masochism – "and puts the most powerful obstacles in the way of recovery".[178] With the latter remark Freud expresses the idea that the unconscious sense of guilt as aggression towards the ego is actually an expression of the death drive. It is thus at the heart of the negative therapeutic reaction, the painful and destructive resistance of the patient to cure.

The analyses of the inevitable sense of guilt in its various forms is what links Freud's earliest clinical observations and his oldest intuitions on the tragic struggle between drive and morality to his later metapsychological writings, the second topic model and the Oedipus complex, and his studies on culture and religion.

In this chapter I have presented my reading of Freud focusing on his writings on religion that cannot be disconnected from his others writings and his ongoing debates with others. The central questions in this study can be formulated from this reading. How did theologians read Freud? How did their theological views and interests interact with Freud's disturbing ideas on man and religion? And what is the potential of Freud's psychoanalytic theories and ideas on religion for current and future theology?

---

[176] S. Freud, *Mourning and Melancholia, SE XIV*, pp.239-258.
[177] S. Freud, *The Economic Problem of Masochism.*
[178] S. Freud, *The Ego and the Id*, p.27.

2   Theology beyond psychoanalysis

2.1 Introduction

In this chapter we will be concerned with the reception of Freud's psychoanalytic theories in German-speaking theology until the 1960s, with a special interest in the reception and non-reception of his ideas on the sense of guilt. This
will mean focusing upon individual writers as there was no broad engagement
with Freud in the theological discussions and debates of this period. There
seems to be a general disinterest other than the individual and separate elaborations on Freud by Oskar Pfister, Karl Beth, Eduard Thurneysen and Paul Tillich; these four scholars being therefore the leading figures in this chapter.

For the engagement with psychoanalysis in the field of theology it seems to
have been of the utmost importance that the Swiss minister Oskar Pfister (1873-
1956) read Freud's *The Interpretation of Dreams* in the year 1908.[1] Our investigation, however, should not begin with the moment in time that someone is impressed by the writings of someone else, as if struck by the lightning of revelation. Pfister's already existing theological views and standpoints have to be
considered: psychoanalytic theory seemed to provide just "that" which the theologian Pfister was looking for, the missing piece of a puzzle. In this chapter we
will have a closer look at his theological ideas and the way in which he interpreted psychoanalytic theories and methods. Besides, he was not the only theologian with an early interest in psychoanalysis. We should not overlook the fact
that Freud wrote his first text on religion, *Obsessive Acts and Religious Practices*, after being invited by another minister, Gustav Vorbrodt (1860-1929), to
reflect upon the subject in the first edition of a newly founded journal in the
psychology of religion, *Zeitschrift für Religionspsychologie*. From Freud's point
of view this early interest of theologians in his psychoanalytic writings, was not
something to be expected.[2] After all, he was first and foremost a clinician, an
analyst of neurotic patients. He had not yet developed a systematic theory, nor
had he shown much interest in religion. In 1907 Freud had already written a cultural study, a plea for a less strict sexual morality in society, but in this text he
showed little interest in religion. In fact, his earliest writings in applied psychoanalysis are concerned with literature and artists. In the period that concerns us
here (up to 1907/1908) *The Interpretation of Dreams* stands out as a massive
and monumental work. But again, religion plays no role of importance, except

---

[1] J. Scharfenberg, *Sigmund Freud und seine Religionskritik*, p.13; Chr. Henning, "Phönix aus der Asche. Die Wiedergeburt des Christentums aus dem Geist der Psychoanalyse bei Oskar Pfister (1873-1956)", in V. Drehsen, W. Sparn (eds.), *Vom Weltbildwandel
zur Weltanschauungsanalyse. Krisenwahrnehmung und Krisenbewältigung um 1900*,
Akademie Verlag, Berlin, 1996, pp.131-165.
[2] P.Vandermeersch, H. Westerink, *Godsdienstpsychologie*, p.137.

for some minor remarks on the dreams in the Josef saga.[3] The motives for theologians like Vorbrodt and Pfister to expect something from psychoanalysis should thus better be sought in their own theological viewpoints.

2.2 Psychology and critique of dogmatics

The interest of Pfister and Vorbrodt in psychoanalysis can be seen against the background of a key issue in late-nineteenth century theology: the status, value and meaning of subjective religious feelings and experiences, and the systematic psychological reflection thereupon. Ever since Schleiermacher had argued in *On Religion* (1799) that the essence of religion was to be found in intuition and feeling (*Anschauung* and *Gefühl*)[4], this issue of subjectivity was closely related to another key issue in theology: which method (philosophical, historic, psychological, or otherwise) was adequate for the analysis and assessment of the essence of religion. These issues played a decisive role in the emergence of a new discipline in the field of theology, viz: the psychology of religion, a field in which both Vorbrodt and Pfister can be positioned.[5]

There is a clear line from Schleiermacher to Pfister. The connecting figure is the Swiss liberal theologian Alois Emanuel Biedermann. He tried to develop a synthesis between Schleiermacher's theology and Hegel's philosophy. In his 1868 *Christliche Dogmatik* [Christian Dogmatics] Biedermann argues that dogmatics should begin with a psychological investigation of subjective religious feelings and experiences. Based on this analysis it would then be possible in metaphysics to determine the true essence of religion.[6] Pfister wrote his dissertation on Biedermann, a critical analysis of his psychology of religion. [7] Despite a critique of his starting point in Hegelian philosophy, Pfister believed that Biedermann should be praised for having brought forward the importance

---

[3] S. Freud, *The Interpretation of Dreams, SE IV*, p.97, p.334.

[4] F. Schleiermacher, *On Religion*, p.22. *Gefühl* is rightfully translated as feeling indicating a (passively) being grasped by the universe. This feeling is not be equated with emotion.

[5] Chr. Henning, "Die Funktion der Religionspsychologie in der Protestantischen Theologie um 1900", in Chr. Henning, E. Nestler (eds.), *Religion und Religiosität zwischen Theologie und Psychologie: Bad Boller Beiträge zur Religionspsychologie*, Lang Verlag, Frankfurt, 1998, pp.27-78; S. Heine, *Grundlagen der Religionspsychologie*, pp.49ff.; H. Westerink, ""Een geweldige illusie": Over de theologische achtergronden van Freuds *Die Zukunft einer Illusion*", in *Nederlands Theologisch Tijdschrift* 59 (2005/3), pp.177-194; P. Vandermeersch, H. Westerink, *Godsdienstpsychologie*, pp.102ff.

[6] A.E. Biedermann, *Christliche Dogmatik*, Reimer Verlag, Berlin, 1884. See also P. Vandermeersch, H. Westerink, *Godsdienstpsychologie*, pp.108-109.

[7] O. Pfister, *Die Genesis der Religionsphilosophie A.E. Biedermanns, untersucht nach Seiten ihren psychologischen Ausbaus*, Zürich, 1898. Also E. Nase, *Oskar Pfisters analytische Seelsorge*, De Gruyter, New York/Berlin, 1993, pp.98-103.

of the analysis of subjective religious experiences, and for having attached great value to Schleiermacher's idea of religious development and edification as an inner process in a religious person.[8]

In the period between his dissertation and his reading of *The Interpretation of Dreams* Pfister was highly concerned with the – in his view – existing gap between individual religious experience and dogmatics/metaphysics, a concern that is expressed in several writings. In a sizeable text Pfister tried to illuminate his position on metaphysics. It should be a discipline that elucidates and systematizes concepts of real and lived experiences.[9] For dogmatics this meant nothing else but a systematic reflection on religious experience. It should in the first place be "an ethics of religious personality".[10] Unfortunately dogmatics was not such a science; it was "speculative, scholastic and dead".[11] Again and again, Pfister stresses that metaphysics, theology and dogmatics should be reflections on subjective experiences and feelings aiming at true and healthy religious and moral development. He writes that the free, scientific, ethical study of faith will emerge (in the near future) and this will clarify more profoundly the traces of the living God in our souls and the figure of Christ in our lives. Yet, he does not clarify the methods and theories to be used in this reflection and edification. He only states that of the primary drives and thus a possible harmonic religious dogmatics is psychologically, logically, sociologically and epistemologically immature.[12] In this period this also applies to Pfister's own writings.

In the same period Gustav Vorbrodt voices a similar, even more radical, critique of dogmatics and metaphysics – psychology should take the place of dogmatics. The essence of Christianity is "life", but this is neglected by theologians. Therefore psychology can be fruitful in theology by reflecting upon life as it flames up in the soul, the heart, in faith and love.[13] Vorbrodt's view on psychology is a specific one. He calls it psychobiology or psychophysiology, expressing not only the unity of body and soul, but also the idea that the soul can be seen as an

---

[8] O. Pfister, *Die Genesis der Religionsphilosophie*, pp.65-66.

[9] O. Pfister, *Die Willensfreiheit: Eine kritisch-systematische Untersuchung*, Reimer Verlag, Berlin, 1904, p.268.

[10] *Unsere wissenschaftliche Glaubenslehre ist somit auf metaphysisch-spekulative Abwege geraten und hat ihre eigentliche Aufgabe, in erster Linie eine Ethik der religiösen Persönlichkeit und erst hernach Metaphysik des religiösen Bewusstseins zu sein, geradezu verleugnet.* O. Pfister, "Das Elend unserer wissenschaftliche Glaubenslehre", in *Schweizerische Theologische Zeitschrift* 4 (1905), pp.209-212 (211-212).

[11] Idem, p.212.

[12] Idem.

[13] *Jene Lebensmacht Gottes bleibt ein totes Außenweltstück der Realität, wenn sie nicht auflebt im Herzen und sich gelegentlich äußert in Glaube, Liebe oder sonst.* G. Vorbrodt, *Beiträge zur religiösen Psychologie: Psychobiologie und Gefühl*, Deichert'sche Verlag, Leipzig, 1904, p.10.

apparatus that functions in conformity with physical laws.[14] This psychobiology
is a discipline that has not yet come to full maturity. The main reason is that
thus far psychologists have failed to synthesize theories of the soul and new
theories of physiology in biology.[15]

We don't know exactly why (and what) Vorbrodt asked Freud to write
for his journal in the psychology of religion. Afterwards the cooperation was
not continued, and as far as I know, the two never met. But we can understand
why he was interested in Freud. Certainly in his early writings there is a strong
tendency to describe the psyche as an organic mechanism, a biological apparatus. This is also a characteristic of early Freudian writings. In that respect *Obsessive Acts and Religious Practices* must have been a little bit disappointing. In
the text Freud did not advocate the idea that religion or theology could be studied with the aid of physiological theories, or that "pneumagenese" was a stage
that was preceded by "biogenesis", or that faith was a stage in an "organic development".[16] Freud went no further than an analogy between compulsory acts
and religious ceremonies.

As to our topic of the sense of guilt Vorbrodt would certainly not have
agreed with the analogy. In his view the organic development of higher stages
of soul and spirit out of physiological stages was essentially nothing else but a
reformulation of the biblical notion that in faith man could be saved from the
strains of sinful flesh, and could be freed from the burden of guilt.[17]

The critiques by Vorbrodt and Pfister of dogmatics are comparable;
their ideas about the fundamental or essential status of psychology in the field
of dogmatics and the aims of this psychology are comparable: religious edification of man in healthy religiosity. However, the content and methods of these
psychologies differ. Vorbrodt is an ambassador of psychobiology. Pfister will
discover psychoanalysis. In the earliest correspondence between Freud and Pfister we find in a nutshell the issues he was most interested in: the libido theory,
anxiety neurosis and repression of sexual drives, religious sublimation, and psychoanalytic therapy as a method for "liberation".[18]

2.3 Pfister's reading of Freud

2.3.1   Anxiety and sublimation

According to Pfister the key issue in psychoanalysis is the analysis of the unconscious. Psychoanalysis had not discovered this phenomenon, but it had
found methods to make its content and structures apparent. Pfister stresses the

---

[14] Idem, pp.27-28.
[15] Idem, pp.51ff.
[16] Idem, pp.67-68.
[17] Idem, p.29, p.88.
[18] S. Freud, O. Pfister, *Psychoanalysis and Faith*, pp.15-19.

fact that the unconscious is not a disposition, but a forming, creative potency.[19] According to Pfister Freud had made a clear distinction between ego drives and sexual drives as the basic "potencies" of the psyche. However, this division is not necessary, and one could as easily speak of one drive, the libido, life force, will, life energy[20], or simply "love" (thus making an explicit connection with the Christian message of love).[21] This libido, the voluntaristic potency, is aimed at the fulfilment of an "unconscious life plan", a harmonizing of conscious and unconscious motives in an autonomous personality, an "absolute self-control".[22] Hence, the libido is not just a will, it is a will with a moral character; its goal is a moral personality.[23]

This interpretation of the Freudian libido as a formative creative power with a voluntaristic character strongly resembles the Jungian libido, and there is indeed every reason to believe that Pfister in his interpretation of the libido follows a Jungian line of thought.[24] But we should not overlook the fact that this "will" was already an issue in Pfister's work even before he had met Jung. In his 1904 *Die Willensfreiheit* [Freedom of the Will] he had argued that the will in its actual appearances is determined by both outer circumstances (such as education, social environment, cultural morality and national character, and physiological aspects)[25] and inner circumstances. Concerning the latter, a will is formed and steered by drives and feelings of pleasure and unpleasure[26], by the chain of conceptions and memories[27], and (eventually) character.[28] But within these boundaries it is possible to speak of a freedom of will. According to Pfister the will is naturally progressive, and a person will always seek to strengthen the progression. Important is the fact that outer circumstances especially can

---

[19] *Das Unbewußte sahen wir niemals als bloße Disposition, sondern stets als formende, schaffende Potenz.* O. Pfister, *Die psychoanalytische Methode. Eine erfahrungswissenschaftlich-systematische Darstellung*, Klinkhardt Verlag, Leipzig, 1921 (1913), p.45.

[20] O. Pfister, *Die psychoanalytische Methode*, p.53; O. Pfister, *Was bietet die Psychoanalyse dem Erzieher?*, Klinkhardt Verlag, Leipzig/Berlin, 1917, p.31.

[21] For example in S. Freud, O. Pfister, *Psychoanalysis and Faith*, p.18; O. Pfister, *Was bietet die Psychoanalyse dem Erzieher?*, pp.33-34.

[22] Idem, pp.9-10.

[23] Idem, p.30. We see the influence of Jung, however, we should not overlook the fact that already in his early writings Pfister favoured an "ethics of religious personality", a moral development based on real life experiences.

[24] E. Nase, *Oskar Pfisters analytische Seelsorge*, p.241.

[25] O. Pfister, *Die Willensfreiheit*, pp.29-115. See E. Nase, *Oskar Pfisters analytische Seelsorge*, pp.87ff; M. Roth, "Oskar Pfister – der Beginn einer problematischen Freud-Rezeption innerhalb der Theologie. Eine Problemanzeige", in *Praktische Theologie. Zeitschrift für Religion, Gesellschaft und Kirche* 35 (2000), pp.40-57 (44-47).

[26] O. Pfister, *Die Willensfreiheit*, pp.119ff.

[27] Idem, pp.126ff.

[28] Idem, p.136.

hinder this inclination evoking feelings of unpleasure.[29] In *Freedom of the Will* we can thus detect the contours of Pfister's later libido theory, a voluntaristic drive within boundaries that can easily lead to inhibitions of the drive.

The main discovery of psychoanalysis – and Freud had acknowledged this repeatedly – was the repression of drives and wishes. Pfister describes Freud's early attempts to connect the repression of sexual drives with real childhood experiences, but than later discovered that sexual fantasies could fulfil the same role in the aetiology of neurosis. Like Freud Pfister clearly states that repression is the result of an inner conflict. When this conflict leads to a repression of libido, all kinds of symptoms could emerge, as Freud had extensively described: sense of guilt, anxiety, aggression, depression, physical pain, etc. This simply meant that sense of guilt and anxiety were effects of repression: when libido was repressed, sense of guilt and anxiety emerged.[30] As we have seen, Freud had put it forward that aggressive sexual fantasies could trigger a sense of guilt and that in a further stage this complex of feelings would be repressed, but, like Jung, Pfister suggests that underlying such fantasies was probably already a repression of libido.[31] Here, we come across a crucial point in Pfister's reading of Freud. We will take a closer look.

Pfister took Freud's theories on anxiety neurosis as the leading model for his own pastoral psychological practice.[32] The same goes *mutatis mutandis* for his psychoanalytic writings. In his early work on neurosis Freud was particularly interested in the fact that pleasure somehow triggered unpleasure that gave strength and force to a conscience that was able to repress. We have seen that unpleasure took the form of a self reproach. This complex was then repressed. Freud's theories of anxiety neurosis and paranoia were derivatives of this theory. In anxiety neurosis and paranoia unpleasure did not take form of a self reproach, but was projected onto people in the outside world, where it took the form of a threat. Anxiety was the proper reaction to this threat. Thus the main characteristic of anxiety neurosis and paranoia was a projection mechanism as a defence against self reproach.[33]

Although we cannot be conclusive here, it seems probable that Pfister already took up this line of thought on anxiety neurosis after reading *The Interpretation of Dreams*. In passages on nightmares Freud interpreted such dreams with the help of some general remarks on anxiety neurosis. Referring to *On the Grounds for Detaching a Particular Syndrome from Neurasthenia under the Description "Anxiety Neurosis"* he writes that "neurotic anxiety is derived from

---

[29] Idem, p.134.

[30] O. Pfister, *Die psychoanalytische Methode*, pp.91-92.

[31] Idem, pp.92-93.

[32] E. Nase, *Oskar Pfisters analytische Seelsorge*, pp.236ff.

[33] S. Freud, *Draft H*, pp.206-212; S. Freud, *On the Grounds for Detaching a Particular Syndrome from Neurasthenia under the Description "Anxiety Neurosis"*, p.112.

sexual life and corresponds to a libido that has been diverted from its purpose".[34]

In another passage on the case of a nightmare he writes that "a struggle
for repression had broken out in him which had suppressed his libido and transformed it into anxiety".[35] And in yet another passage anxiety is the symptom
corresponding to repressed or inhibited libido.[36] This basic theory of anxiety
neurosis will indeed be Pfister's main model: libido is inhibited, repressed or
diverted, unpleasure is projected onto objects outside causing neurotic symptoms such as anxiety or sense of guilt.[37]

This basic model is applied in a number of case studies.[38] As we find,
for example, in the psychobiography of Ludwig von Zinzendorf. The "main motive" in Zinzendorf's religious development is the repression of sexuality, which
in this case was not only a repression of autoerotic acts (for example masturba-
tion), but a being cut off from satisfaction of the sexual drives through transference onto parents or other loved ones. His childhood years in a strict pietistic
family are of great importance here. The only possibility for him was the projection of primary components of the libido (for example homosexual and sadistic components) onto Christ. In other words, the repressed drives returned in his
orgiastic religiosity of which anxiety and aggression were key elements. The
early repression of drives prevented a normal release and thus the most perverse
components of the libido could return in his devotion.[39]

This inhibition or repression of libido can also be described as stowage
or fixation. In Pfister's view repression of the libido is indeed always the inhibi-

[34] S. Freud, *The Interpretation of Dreams, SE IV*, p.161.

[35] Idem, *SE V*, p.586.

[36] Idem, *SE IV*, p.236.

[37] Müller-Pozzi has argued that it was Pfister's "tragedy" to have formulated his revolutionary ideas in a language that is more theological than psychoanalytical, and that he
did not take into account further developments in psychoanalytic theory neglecting
Freud's theories that were formulated after 1920. H. Müller-Pozzi, "Die Tabuisierung
der Religion in der Psychoanalyse", in *Wege zum Menschen* 30 (1978), pp. 194-207
(197).

[38] Already in the case "Dietrich" from 1909 we see this model: repression of sexuality
conforms to the moral culture and the values of the parents; the projection in the outside
(devotion of the Madonna); symptoms such as compulsory acts, feelings of hate towards
love ones. E. Nase, *Oskar Pfisters analytische Seelsorge*, pp.208-332; E. Nase, ""Ein
merkwürdiger Mann"- Oskar Pfister und die Anfänge der analytischen Seelsorge", in I.
Noth, Chr. Morgenthaler (eds.), *Seelsorge und Psychoanalyse*, Verlag Kohlhammer,
Stuttgart, 2007, pp.15-33.
We should notice here that Pfister's projection theory was not solely derived from
Freud's writings. It was already a concept used by Pfister in his earlier writings, for ex-
ample: *Sühne ist eine Projektion des menschlichen Rachegefühls in die Gottheit*. O.
Pfister, *Die Willensfreiheit*, p.212.

[39] O.Pfister, *Die Frömmigkeit des Grafen Ludwig von Zinzendorf*, pp.104ff.

tion of a natural development and stowage of primitive and infantile material. Zinzendorf, unable to release his primary sexuality and projecting it on Christ, was in fact cut off from a healthy religious development. His polymorphic and perverse sexuality was at the core of his orgiastic religious fantasies. It is tragic, for instead he could have developed a healthy religiosity, sublimating his libido to a higher level. By this time Freud had hardly written upon sublimation – and in fact he never will provide a satisfying theory on the subject. In his study on Leonardo da Vinci he had written about Leonardo's astonishing capacity for sublimating his primitive drives in art and science. Pfister adds his own ideas: sublimation is also moral and religious elevation, for example in social and humanitarian practices, "the love for one's neighbour", but also in free and truthful theological and philosophical reflections.[40]

Here again it is tempting to suggest Pfister was influenced by Jung. However, these ideas on sublimation are already apparent in his writings before Jung developed his theory of the libido and its natural inclination to develop to higher levels. The motives for Pfister's specific interpretation of Freudian psychoanalysis can be found in the theological ideas we have already described: psychoanalysis seemed to provide a theory and method for reflection on individual (religious) experiences and feelings, and for the development of "an ethics of religious personality".

Sublimation is a key concept here. Psychoanalytic theory had mapped the psychical apparatus; psychoanalytic therapy could analyse and influence the unconscious, try to make the repressed conscious and thus open up new possibilities for the sublimation of libido. But when exactly do we speak of sublimation to "a higher level"? When we look at Pfister's writings the moral and religious attitudes and values are decisive. Why, for example, is Zinzendorf's religiosity not an example of a successful sublimation? His primitive and impure eroticism and the lustful religious fantasies "do not deserve the name sublimation".[41] In other words, sublimation is not defined by its mechanism, but by its goal. As a mechanism it doesn't seem distinct from projection. The difference is whether development is inhibited or takes place. To put it in a simple formula: projection is failed sublimation. For this reason Pfister can describe the devotion to the wounds and the corpse of Christ as sublimated homosexuality and sublimated necrophilia, indicating the mechanism.[42] It is actually a failed sublimation, hence projection. In other texts we find similar passages, for ex-

---

[40] O.Pfister, *Die Psychoanalytische Methode*, pp.265-266; O. Pfister, "Die Psychoanalyse als wissenschaftlicher Prinzip und seelsorgerische Methode", in V. Läpple, J. Scharfenberg (eds.), *Psychotherapie und Seelsorge*, Wissenschaftliche Buchgesellschaft, Darmstadt, 1977, pp.11-54 (50ff).

[41] *Solche unveränderte, ungereinigte Erotik, die ihrer Glut in religiösen Phantasien von Außerordentlicher Gefühlsintensität die Zügel schießen läßt, verdient den Namen der Sublimierung nicht.* O. Pfister, *Die psychoanalytische Methode*, p.265.

[42] O. Pfister, *Die Frömmigkeit des Grafen Ludwig von Zinzendorf*, p.46, p.48, p.74.

ample when Pfister describes the difference between Catholicism and Protestantism. The absolute sublimation in Catholicism with its total negation of the primary drives, shows, in a lot of historic cases of saints and monks, a failure in sublimation. In these cases religiosity is not unlike that of Zinzendorf. On the other hand, in Protestantism we find maximal sublimation with recognition of development. In this ideal we see reflected a liberal Protestant tradition starting with Schleiermacher's *On Religion*.[43]

2.3.2   A "forgotten" subject

According to Pfister, psychoanalysis does not contradict the truth claims of Christian religion, but it does deconstruct so called religious experiences to reveal them as illusionary constructs.[44] In this sense psychoanalysis is a method for distinguishing true and healthy religion from illusionary and unhealthy religion. Even stronger, religion has the ethical mission to "convert", to sublimate feelings of anxiety, hate and guilt into a religiosity of love.[45] And at the same time, true religion does not only unveil religious illusions, which he also calls religious errors, as invalid, but it also defends against regression into neurotic forms of religiosity.[46]

   The fundamental distinction between true religion and illusionary religiosity is rooted in Pfister's own earlier theological writings and his project to develop an ethics of the religious personality, a dogmatics opposed to the ones that could only build metaphysical systems without any relationship to reality, or reflect on religiosity within the narrow framework of a confession or a religious community. It was an "illusion" to suppose that dogmatics could help believers in developing true faith.[47] Pfister's decision to take anxiety neurosis as the leading model for his own psychoanalytic studies was crucial in this respect, because this model served his theological ideas and purposes very well: it provided a perfect explanation for illusionary religion as such, and a solution, a liberation into true religion.

   This did not necessarily mean that true religion was completely without anxiety or sense of guilt, but true (healthy) religion was not determined by these

---

[43] O. Pfister, *Die Psychoanalyse als wissenschaftlicher Prinzip und seelsorgerische Methode*, pp.43-54. In the correspondence of Freud and Pfister we find an echo of this historic description when Pfister writes that the Reformation is essentially an analysis of Catholic sexual repression and the anxiety neuroses caused by this repression. Freud replies that Ehrenfels was right when he called him a "Protestant in sexuality". S. Freud, O. Pfister, *Psychoanalysis and Faith*, pp.18-19.

[44] O. Pfister, *Die psychoanalytische Methode*, pp.354-355. See also H. Westerink, "Een geweldige illusie", pp.181-182.

[45] O. Pfister, *Die psychoanalytische Methode*, p.355.

[46] Idem, p.356.

[47] O. Pfister, "Das Elend unserer wissenschaftliche Glaubenslehre", p.209.

feelings, and their possible presence in true religion was thus not an issue Pfister reflected upon. He does acknowledge that civilization depends on a certain amount of repression of drives (which suggests some anxiety and sense of guilt), but his main message is that true religion is characterized by love and moral practices rooted in a free, conscious and harmonious mind.

In the early years of Pfister's specific engagement with psychoanalytic theory and method, Freud was further developing his own theories. An important reconfiguration concerns the projection mechanism in the Schreber case, where he presented projection as an attempt to restore the relationship with reality. This new definition could have forced Pfister to reconsider his own ideas on projection and sublimation, and thus on libido and repression, but it didn't. He stuck to the original meaning of projection as a defence mechanism.[48] Pfister's first reading of Freud, which evolves around anxiety, libido and sublimation, will prove decisive when we consider our topic of the sense of guilt.

Freud, in this period, published two important studies on religion: *Obsessive Acts and Religious Practices* and *Totem and Taboo*. We have seen that he took obsessional neurosis as the main model to explain religion. Pfister produces his own psychoanalytic studies on religion, yet it is striking that he hardly ever refers to these two texts. In *Die psychoanalytische Methode* [The Psychoanalytic Method] of 1913, probably the most important of Pfister's studies[49] summarizing his early psychoanalytic writings, Freud's *Obsessive Acts and Religious Practices* and *Totem and Taboo* – the first parts of the text were already published in 1912 – are not mentioned and there are no references to the sense of guilt as the crucial factor in the analogy between neurosis and religion and as the driving force in the genesis and historic development of religion and morality.[50]

The omission of reflections on the sense of guilt in relation to religion is even more remarkable when we consider the fact that Jung's *Transformations and Symbolisms of the Libido* and Freud's *Totem and Taboo* are key texts in their mutual debate on psychoanalytic theory and its applications to cultural phenomena. This debate overshadowed all other discussions and theoretical developments in the psychoanalytic movement in this period. But Pfister shows an almost naive faith in the complementary character of Jung's and Freud's theo-

---

[48] Scharfenberg is right in his conclusion that reading Pfister only gives us knowledge of the early Freud. But we have to add that it only gives us knowledge of specific theoretical elements of the early Freud. J. Scharfenberg, *Sigmund Freud und seine Religionskritik*, p.20.

[49] Freud himself called this text Pfister's most important writing. S. Freud, O. Pfister, *Psychoanalysis and Faith*, p.95.

[50] We only find references we might expect from the previous: the cannibalistic character of the Catholic Eucharist reminds us of primitive rituals such as the consummation of the totem animal; the pope rules like a harsh father. O. Pfister, *Die psychoanalytische Methode*, p.487.

ries. He does not choose a side and he does not interfere in the debate. In the correspondence between Pfister and Freud, neither *Transformations and Symbolisms of the Libido* nor *Totem and Taboo* are discussed (though we have to consider the fact that the correspondence has a lacuna between March 1913 and October 1918). Also, the sense of guilt is not a topic in the correspondence. For Pfister it remains clear that a sense of guilt is just one of the possible effects of repression, not a precondition. His reading of Freud is already fixed. Hence, the subject plays no role of importance in the reflections on true religion. In an ethics of the personality, love is the determining factor. Thus, the Freudian connection between a sense of guilt and religion is "forgotten".

Both Pfister's theological ideas and his interpretation of Freud never fundamentally changed. Whereas Freud constantly questioned his own theories and methods, thus moving forwards towards new theoretical concepts such as narcissism, death drive and a new theory on the structure of the psyche (id, ego, superego), we see in Pfister's writings a strong repetitive tendency. For example, in a text from 1923 we can read the same critique of dogmatics as was formulated twenty years earlier.[51] This repetition is understandable when we consider the fact that his enthusiasm for psychoanalysis never met the same enthusiastic response among his fellow theologians: he had thus every reason to make his mission statements over and over again. *Mutatis mutandis* we find this repetitive tendency also in his case studies. In his studies on the apostle Paul, Margareta Ebner and John Calvin we see the same structures in his interpretations as in the case of Von Zinzendorf.[52]

---

[51] O. Pfister, *Die Aufgabe der Wissenschaft vom christlichen Glauben in der Gegenwart*, Vandenhoeck & Ruprecht, Göttingen, 1923.

[52] The hysteria of the ascetic Margareta Ebner is characterized by anxiety, hallucinations, physical pain and masochistic tendencies. This anxiety, Pfister writes, is in accordance with unsatisfied (i.e. repressed) libido that is projected onto Christ. Here, true religious and moral elevation did not take place. O. Pfister, *Religiosität und Hysterie*, Internationaler Psychoanalytischer Verlag, Leipzig/Vienna/Zurich, 1928. Finally, part of the character of Calvin is described as aggressive and anxious, which becomes visible in his acts against the witches of Peney. This is an "unchristian" character trait that is unfortunately part of a personality who on all other accounts should be praised for his tremendous sublimations. O.Pfister, *Calvins Eingreifen in die Hexer- & Hexenprozesse von Peney 1545 nach seiner Bedeutung für Geschichte & Gegenwart. Ein kritischer Beitrag zur Charakteristik Calvins & zur gegenwärtigen Calvin-Renaissance*, Artemis Verlag, Zurich, 1947.
In *Die psychoanalytische Methode* we already find passages where Pfister draws his conclusions on the characters of Paul and Margareta Ebner, and explicitly mentions witch burning as a fear and hate ritual. The three studies can thus be seen as later elaborations on older ideas. O. Pfister, *Die psychoanalytische Methode*, p.231, p.265, p.354, p.485. Paul and Zinzendorf are already mentioned in *Die Willensfreiheit* (1904) for their problematic moral-religious characters. O. Pfister, *Die Willensfreiheit*, p.215.

In 1944 Pfister published *Christianity and Fear*, an extensive recapitulation of his ideas on repression, anxiety, sublimation and love in individual and social psychology, in the history of religion and in pastoral practice. In his considerations on Freud's theories of anxiety Pfister mentions *On the Grounds for Detaching a Particular Syndrome from Neurasthenia under the Description "Anxiety Neurosis"* as an important source, as the first text where Freud argued that anxiety and fear are caused by a stowage, inhibition or repression of libido.[53]

The oldest of Freud's theories on anxiety neurosis is still the basic model. Again, other types of neurosis are interpreted with this model. Thus, contrary to Freud's leading model of obsessional neurosis and the sense of guilt Pfister argues that anxiety is the key factor in the aetiology of all neuroses. The compulsory acts in obsessional neurosis for instance are essentially attempts to appease anxiety. They are reaction formations, not against the sense of guilt as Freud had argued (for example in the Wolf Man case), but against anxiety.[54] Of course in some of Freud's writings we can find an argument for the idea that anxiety is at the source of the sense of guilt. In chapter VII of *Civilization and Its Discontents* for example this is clearly expressed: a sense of guilt is either caused by fear of the aggression from an authority – which is essentially similar to fear of the loss of love – or by a later fear of the superego (which is an internalized authority).

But exactly here Freud had also turned around his theory. When anxiety about a real threat (aggression by an authority) precedes the superego, anxiety also precedes the repression of libido by the superego. Of course this idea provoked the typical Freudian question: what is the origin of this anxiety, that is, what can be such a threat that it causes anxiety? Here Freud makes clear that this threat cannot be the libido itself.[55] The answer is aggression: the authority is feared for (his) aggression, because of an original transgression against that authority. Thus, this anxiety had already a conscientious even "guilty" character. The consequence of this line of thought was that the sense of guilt was not only caused by anxiety, but that both anxiety and sense of guilt had another source: aggression. Sense of guilt and anxiety were thus placed in an ancient Oedipal framework. The conclusion was fitting: (not anxiety but) sense of guilt is inevitable.[56]

---

[53] O. Pfister, *Christianity and Fear. A Study in History and in the Psychology and Hygiene of Religion*, George Allen & Unwin, London, 1948, p.50.

[54] Idem, pp.89ff.

[55] S. Freud, *New Introductory Lectures*, p.86.

[56] In a letter Pfister points out that he does not agree with the latter line of thought. He can only agree to a death drive as a lack of life energy (libido), and besides, Freud is far too pessimistic about the hygienic possibilities of psychoanalysis in modern culture. In other words, there is no such thing is an inevitable sense of guilt. S. Freud, O. Pfister, *Psychoanalysis and Faith*, pp.130-131.

However, in *Christianity and Fear* not the complex relationship between anxiety and the sense of guilt in Freud's later writings, but the relatively
simple early model of anxiety neurosis is the framework for an interpretation of
the history of religion including, for the first time, a full account of *Totem and
Taboo* and *Moses and Monotheism*. According to Pfister primitive religion, pre-
mosaic Semitic religion, Judaism and Christianity are all essentially attempts to
defend against fear through an instinctive recovery of love.[57] However, in primitive religion the many rituals and practices also strengthened neurotic tendencies. In Judaism the message of love was overshadowed by contra productive
motives such as the wrath and fear of God, and retribution; religious ceremonies
and especially the conscientious abiding to the Law eventually gave Judaism its
obsessional character. This resulted in a general pessimism and culture of fear
characteristic of late Judaism, which was only able to cherish the message of
love in the belief in a messianic future.

Christ's message of love was the next step in this evolution of religions.
His command to love one's neighbour, oneself and God appeals strongly to a
"will", a life energy (libido), to freely realize a potential high level of religiosity
and moral acting.[58] This reconstruction of the history of religion shows a historic development, with a climax, sublimation in Christ. The message and life of
Christ is the core of Christianity, and a possible sublimation is repeated in historic figures such as the apostle Paul and Luther. In this history of religion the
sense of guilt is not a topic at all.

2.3.3 Illusions

In the first chapter of this study I have argued that Freud's *The Future of an Illusion* can be seen as a response to Pfister's ideas on psychoanalysis (meta-
psychology) as a philosophy of life. We will now take a closer look.

In Pfister's *The Struggle for Psychoanalysis* psychoanalysis describes
not only a technique that enables the analysis of unconscious motives, but aims
also at the overall theoretical knowledge to be gained from its methods (meta-
psychology). As an overall theory of the human psyche and its interactions with
reality and as a therapy which aims at a sublimation, psychoanalysis does lead
into a philosophy of life and does have something to say about the nature of
what is (metaphysics) or ought to be (ethics).[59]

According to Pfister, Freud never explicitly rejected metaphysics as a
product of illusions or as a projection of the inner psychic world onto the outer
world, nor did he ever elaborate on the issue.[60] Hence, the relation between psychoanalysis and metaphysics needs to be clarified. Referring to *Freedom of the*

---

[57] O. Pfister, *Christianity and Fear*, pp.151ff.

[58] Idem, p.176, p.193.

[59] O. Pfister, *Zum Kampf um die Psychoanalyse*, pp.246-247.

[60] Idem, p.257.

Will, metaphysics is seen here as conceptual and methodological reflection on experiences in order to make a distinction between real and illusionary experiences and in order to determine the origins and aims of the contents of experiences.[61] In this sense Freud's own meta-psychology was already metaphysical in design, says Pfister.[62]

The same goes for ethics.[63] Freud never wanted to develop an ethics of psychoanalytic therapy. But the inner conflicts of his patients were moral conflicts (between drives and morality), and in the end therapy aimed at the sublimation of the libido to a higher level of socially acceptable goals. Ethics as a science of the "ought to be", of general life goals and life norms was implicit.[64]

Pfister argues that the connection between psychoanalysis, philosophy of life, metaphysics and ethics is implicit and should be made more explicit. Psychoanalysis provides both the ideal method and theory to distinguish between true and illusionary experiences or conceptions, and the ideal method and theory for the formation of a moral and religious personality. Pfister admits that religion in orthodoxy and ritualism has often forced a repressive ethics upon people. He also agrees that religion is often dominated by an obstinate wish principle. Yet religion at its best and essentially is like philosophy, searching for truth and essence in reality, making general statements about what "is and ought to be". And even although primitive religion and mythology is coloured by anthropomorphism this search is not "illusionism". Far from it, religion is a "family member of science".[65]

We have seen that Freud defined religion as doctrine thus taking up Reik's studies on Christian dogma as applications of Freud's own ideas on the analogies between obsessive neurosis and religious phenomena. Yet, until 1927 illusion hardly played a role in Freud's writings, and even when it did, it was used as a concept to criticize a general cultural belief in progress and optimism about human nature. Now, religious doctrine is called illusion, a defence against helplessness and the expression of a wish or need for parental protection. In other words: religion is a product of a desire for love, care, safety, knowledge and comfort. Here we noticed a new perspective on religion, a perspective in which

---

[61] Idem, p.286.

[62] Idem. Pfister quotes Freud's own definition of metapsychology as *Klärung und Vertiefung der theoretischen annahmen, die man einem psychoanalytischen System zu Grunde legen könnte.*

[63] Idem, pp.291ff.

[64] Idem, p.332, p.298.

[65] Idem, pp.365-367. Religion is defined as *in Verbindung stehen des Menschen mit übermenschlichen, aber real gedachten geistigen Kraftzentern or as ein persönliches und innerliches sich Erfaßtfüllen von jenem Idealen, zugleich real gedachten Kraftzentrum, das mit dem Namen Gottes bezeichnet wird.* Idem, p.268.

the father is still the key figure, yet not as a rival who evokes aggression, but as a protecting father-God who provides care.[66]

In comparison to Freud's other writings on religion, not the Oedipal desires and annulation and repetition of an original culpable act of aggression in religion are at the centre of attention, but a desire for fatherly care and protection. The "Deed" in *Totem and Taboo* – not only the act of killing, but also the act of repetition – even seems to be at right angles with the child's helplessness, the impossibility to act. We have seen that, in the context of the debate with Rank, this new perspective was designed to strengthen his earlier perspectives and theses. Hence, the essay is not meant to present a new alternative theory of religion. In fact, Freud argues that the two perspectives are intertwined and strengthen each other.

Here, we come a across a point that Freud had already made in *Thoughts for the Time on War and Death*: belief in illusions is the opposite of the recognition of aggression and a sense of guilt as the driving forces in human nature, which means that there are aggressive wishes and desires that cause sense of guilt, and there are wishes and desires to be spared a self knowledge that confronts this aggression and sense of guilt.[67] Together, these motives give religious conceptions their strength: they are a composition of historic reminiscences and present wish illusions that deny reality. A wishful promise for the present and the future veils the repressed historic core of religion, and in addition gives a powerful motive to subject oneself to a religious tradition. "We now observe that the store of religious ideas includes not only wish-fulfilments but important historic recollections. This concurrent influence of past and present must give religion a truly incomparable wealth of power."[68]

The different perspective on religion presented in *The Future of an Illusion* has its own background in the debate with Rank and in Reik's studies on dogma. The essay is also a critique of Pfister. As we have seen, the correspondence between Pfister and Freud gives evidence of that[69] and although he is not mentioned in *The Future of an Illusion* it is clear that Freud takes his distance from Pfister's ideas on religion when he writes that religion is not the precipitate of experience or end result of thinking. Religion is instead doctrine, which means that one accepts the "teachments and assertions about facts and conditions" which one "has not discovered for oneself".[70] Doctrine is handed down

---

[66] A. Vergote, "Religion after the Critique of Psychoanalysis", pp.24ff; A. Vergote, *Religion, Belief and Unbelief. A Psychological Study*, Leuven University Press, Amsterdam/Atlanta, 1997, pp.217-218.

[67] S. Freud, *Thoughts for the Times on War and Death, SE XIV*, p.280, p.285.

[68] S. Freud, *The Future of an Illusion*, p.42.

[69] In this context, has observed that the virtual opponent in *The Future of an Illusion* has the character of a liberal, intellectual priest (someone like Pfister). Th. Reik, "Bemerkungen zu Freuds "Zukunft einer Illusion"", in *Imago* 14 (1928), pp.185-198 (187-188).

[70] S. Freud, *The Future of an Illusion*, p.25.

from generation to generation thus embedded in a tradition of and obedience to authority. This conception of religion stands opposed to Pfister's project of using psychoanalysis as a method to distinguish between true and illusionary religion, that is to say, to distinguish between religion that is based on illusionary needs, wishes and desires, and a religion that originates from "true" experiences and "healthy" thought.

As we have seen, the final part of *The Struggle for Psychoanalysis* was about the relation between psychoanalysis and philosophy of life. This concept of philosophy of life was applied to meta-psychology, and it was this application that opened the way for a further investigation on the relationship between psychoanalysis and metaphysics, ethics and (eventually) religion. In *The Future of an Illusion*, having established that religious doctrines are illusions, Freud raises the question whether all philosophies of life should now be named illusions.[71] Freud regarded psychoanalysis not to be a "message of salvation" or a new philosophy of life.[72] The main problem was the directive character of such a philosophy, which was ultimately a compelling character.

Important, and yet often neglected, is the fact that Pfister not only reacted to *The Future of an Illusion* with a critical article, but also with the republication of *Psychoanalysis and Philosophy of Life*.[73] Freud reacted a few years later in a lecture, "The Question of a *Weltanschauung*". The leading question seems to be provoked by Pfister: "Does psychoanalysis lead to a particular philosophy of life and, if so, to which?"[74] The answer is a straight "no" – psychoanalysis is an impartial science, which investigates and explains[75], whereas a philosophy of life is an illusion, a wish fulfilment. Such an illusion has a certain value, but it's not a science. In fact a science should be defended against illusionary philosophies of life, notably against the philosophy of life "religion".[76]

Veiled but unmistakably Freud reacted in his essay to Pfister's ongoing plea for psychoanalysis as theory and method that would enable distinctions to

---

[71] Idem, pp.34ff.

[72] S. Freud, *On the History of the Psychoanalytic Movement*, p.60.

[73] O. Pfister, "Die Illusion einer Zukunft. Eine freundschaftliche Auseinandersetzung mit Prof. Dr. Sigm. Freud", in *Imago* 14 (1928), pp.149-184; O. Pfister, *Psychoanalyse und Weltanschauung*, Internationaler Psychoanalytischer Verlag, Vienna/Leipzig, 1928. In an article from 1929 Pfister writes that psychoanalysis is not a philosophy of life. This had been made perfectly clear by Freud in *The Future of an Illusion*. Here it seems as if Pfister withdraws his earlier ideas on psychoanalysis and philosophy of life, however this is only appearance: Pfister never stated that psychoanalysis is a philosophy of life; he argued that psychoanalysis would lead into a philosophy of life, a specific one. O. Pfister, "Psychoanalyse und Seelsorge", in V. Läpple, J. Scharfenberg (eds.), *Psychotherapie und Seelsorge*, pp.88ff.

[74] S. Freud, *New Introductory Lectures*, p.158.

[75] Compare: "Psychoanalysis is a method of research, an impartial instrument, like the infinitesimal calculus, as it were." S. Freud, *The Future of an Illusion*, p.36

[76] S. Freud, *New Introductory Lectures*, pp.160ff.

be made between true and illusionary religion. Indeed, he was the only one in Freud's inner circle who had repeatedly written on religion as illusion. This point in itself is important, for in the secondary literature Freud is generally regarded as the critic of religion, a criticism which reaches a climax in *The Future of an Illusion*. Pfister is usually seen as the Swiss minister who reacts to Freud in *The Illusion of the Future*, defending religion against Freud's attack and criticizing his scientism. However, reality is more refined: both men criticize illusions in the name of truth, which is clearly expressed by Pfister in a creed that in his view also applies to Freud: "The truth will liberate you!"[77] His critique of religion in *The Struggle for Psychoanalysis* and elsewhere is by and large the same as Freud's. The difference is Pfister's belief in a non-illusionary true religion, religion as a philosophy of life or even a science.

When we read *The Future of an Illusion* as a critique of Pfister and when we overlook the debate that followed between Freud and Pfister we can clearly see the different views of illusion being entangled with a complex of other key issues in Freud's and Pfister's theories: the definition and possibilities of psychoanalytic theory and method, the libido theory, the "pessimistic" or optimistic view of man, aggression and the sense of guilt versus love and anxiety. In short, underlying the two texts and the debate are two variants of psychoanalysis that partly overlap, partly contradict each other.

Concerning psychoanalytic theory and method, Freud's problem with Pfister is comparable with his critique of Jung. When part of religion and ethics is "on a high level" that cannot be explained with psychoanalytic theories on sexuality and the Oedipus complex, then part of religion is *terra incognito* for psychoanalysis and important psychic motives will be obscured.[78] In the debate following the publication of *The Future of an Illusion* this Freudian line of thought is taken up by Reik in a lecture from 1928.[79] Psychoanalysis he argues has to be an empirical science which analyses the conflicts between drive and moral culture.[80] This means that the analysis of the unconscious sense of guilt in man and culture is the key issue psychoanalysis should investigate. Here, psychoanalysis is only beginning to understand a complex phenomenon that in three thousand years of history of religion and theology has been the hidden core of all dense, normative forms of religion and theology. Psychoanalysis is a science that should unveil this hidden core, not with the purpose of destroying or reforming religion, but with the aim of understanding the origins, features

---

[77] O. Pfister, "Die Illusion einer Zukunft", p.184.

[78] S. Freud, *On the History of the Psychoanalytic Movement*, p.62.

[79] Th. Reik, "Neurosentherapie und Religion", in E. Nase, J. Scharfenberg (eds.), *Psychoanalyse und Religion*, Wissenschaftliche Buchgesellschaft, Darmstadt, 1977, pp.41-53.

[80] Idem, p.42.

and effects of this unconscious sense of guilt, and thus to understand better the inner conflicts in man.[81]

In *The Future of an Illusion* this point is implicitly made in the sharp distinction between psychoanalysis as science and religion as illusion. When religion is a product of conscious experience or end result of thinking, it is highly probable that the unconscious motives will stay hidden under the surface of a religious moral system. And when psychoanalysis is a philosophy of life developing its own religious moral system, it is no longer capable of analysing impartially the deepest unconscious motives in philosophies of life or religion.[82] In this sense, Pfister's belief in a true and healthy religion is just that kind of illusion that Freud had unmasked as an attempt to be spared a self knowledge that confronts us with aggression and sense of guilt.[83]

In *The Illusion of the Future* Pfister defends his project. Religion can have a compelling repressive character, but the true Christian message is that of freedom and love, and even though this message has the form of a law, it has not the repressive character of the Mosaic Law.[84] Certainly, religion can be dominated by wish thinking, but in true religion the egoistic needs and wishes are not satisfied. The Christian message and religious ideal is quite the opposite of this egoism.[85] Pfister defends true religion as the harmonic union of faith and knowledge. Does this religion obscure the deeper unconscious motives? Pfister answers the question by arguing that in true religion love (and not aggression or the sense of guilt) is the deepest motive that was once repressed and now liberated.[86]

When Joachim Scharfenberg is right when he writes that a whole generation of theologians has only come in contact with the work of Freud through Pfister, it is hardly surprising that the sense of guilt was not the main issue distilled from these writings.[87] We know two main factors that were decisive here: the theories of anxiety neurosis and sublimation as basic models for the analysis of religiosity; and the debate on illusion, religion and philosophy of life.

---

[81] Idem, p.44.

[82] Reik presents an interesting variant of this line of thought in his lecture: he states that psychoanalysis is a science that elaborates on material that was reflected upon in the history of religion and in theology. As a science psychoanalysis can look further, deeper in the unconscious hidden truth of religion and theology. If it were not a science but philosophy of life, it would actually be nothing else but theology, a next step in the history of religion. This reversal of the statement directly applies to Pfister's project: psychoanalysis, as a method that can purify Christian religion from its illusionary elements, is part of theology, and therefore part of a repressive tradition. Idem.

[83] S. Freud, *Thoughts for the Times on War and Death*, p.280, p.285.

[84] O. Pfister, "Die Illusion einer Zukunft", p.154.

[85] Idem, pp.156ff.

[86] Idem, pp.182ff.

[87] J. Scharfenberg, *Sigmund Freud und seine Religionskritik*, p.20.

2.4 Reactions to Pfister and psychoanalysis

In an article of 1929 Pfister writes that he has been promoting psychoanalysis in pastoral care for twenty years now, albeit with little response from theologians and pastors.[88] It is indeed in the 1920s that Pfister's efforts show some result in cautious appraisal, although most responses remain critical. Scharfenberg has analysed the early responses to Freudian psychoanalysis.[89] He notices two main motives in these mainly negative responses.[90] Firstly, there is the fear that psychoanalysis deconstructs all higher moral and religious motives and values in man.[91] And secondly, there is the resistance against an ongoing process of secularization in which priests are replaced by therapists. Psychoanalysis was seen as symptom of this process.[92] In general Freud's theories on the existence of resistance or on the unconscious are not doubted.

The critique is aimed at the moral dangers of making the unconscious conscious, at the possible immorality of the analyst, and at the sublimation theory which would supposedly imply that all higher spiritual values were transformations of the sexual drives. In such a theory there was no longer a place for Christian concepts such as grace or revelation. On the other hand there was also some support: psychoanalysis is important for an "analytical pastoral care" that could help people out of their neurotic distress through a message of love; psychoanalysis provides a method for making unconscious feelings of sin and guilt conscious, which could also be the beginning of feelings of remorse and thus the beginning of a longing for salvation and reconciliation.[93]

From the very beginning of his turn to psychoanalysis Pfister had met with criticism.[94] Over the years and especially in the 1920s the critique increased. Freud's *The Future of an Illusion* certainly played a role in the responses to psychoanalysis in the field of pastoral care. For the critics it was clear that he had shown himself as an evolutionistic, naturalistic and atheistic enemy of religion. But in general the criticism of this text was certainly not pro-

---

[88] O. Pfister, "Psychoanalyse und Seelsorge", p.87.

[89] J. Scharfenberg, *Sigmund Freud und seine Religionskritik*, pp.20-25. Responses in the form of (parts of) documents can be found in J. Scharfenberg, "Die Rezeption der Psychoanalyse in der Theologie", in J. Cremerius (ed.), *Die Rezeption der Psychoanalyse in der Soziologie, Psychologie und Theologie im deutschsprachigen Raum bis 1940*, Suhrkamp Verlag, Frankfurt, 1981, documents 8-16.

[90] J. Scharfenberg, *Sigmund Freud und seine Religionskritik*, p.22.

[91] J. Scharfenberg, "Die Rezeption der Psychoanalyse in der Theologie", documents 8, 9, 10, 12.

[92] Idem, document 11.

[93] Idem, documents 11, 14.

[94] Already in 1910 Pfister had to defend psychoanalysis in pastoral care against the sharp critique (similar to other critiques of Freud in that time) by the pedagogue Friedrich Wilhelm Förster. O. Pfister, "Die Psychoanalyse als wissenschaftliches Prinzip und seelsorgerische Methode".

found.[95] In fact, the text was merely seen as a confirmation of the dangers of psychoanalysis. The arguments against psychoanalysis remained the same as before.

It seems as if this publication was only an additional argument to express concerns that already existed, and that now, in the light of Freud's new critique of religion, could be given more weight. It even remains an open question whether the critics had actually read the text. Overall it seems that they are in discussion with Pfister and indeed only knew Freud through him.[96]

After all the years of Pfister's endless efforts psychoanalysis entered the field of theology, that is to say, it entered the field of pastoral care and, incidentally, psychology of religion.[97] We have seen that Pfister's reading of Freud is a specific one. We have, for example, seen that until 1944 Pfister never showed much interest in *Totem and Taboo* nor did he recommend this text among theologians. Freud's differentiations about the sense of guilt never found its way into Pfister's writings as a means to differentiate between various possible

---

[95] J. Scharfenberg, *Sigmund Freud und seine Religionskritik*, p.21.

[96] For example J. Scharfenberg, "Die Rezeption der Psychoanalyse in der Theologie", documents 9, 10, 11, 15, 16.

[97] In Karl Girgensohn's 1921 magnum opus *Der seelische Aufbau des religiösen Erlebens* [The Psychic Structure of Religious Experience] an experimental method is used in order to determine "true" religious responses from non-religious ones. In this work Girgensohn clearly distances himself from psychoanalysis. Although he consequently speaks of a critique of Freudian psychoanalysis, it is clear that he only knows Freud through Pfister. The critique is focused, firstly, on free association as a method in psychoanalysis. This method cannot guarantee that the essential and important motives are brought to light, only that there is some chain of delusional thoughts. The second main point of critique is the libido and sublimation theory. Girgensohn does not deny sublimation in itself, but he does criticize the notion that sublimation as elevation to a higher level is restricted to the sublimation of sexual libido (as basically a physical feeling). In a broader perspective the aim is clear: having argued that the essence of religion is in "thought" and not in feelings he criticizes the idea that sublimation of feelings leads to a true (or healthy) religion. Pfister reacted with an extensive article in *Imago*, where he basically defended the libido and sublimation theory. He counterattacks the experimental method as superficial, and concludes that Girgensohn had understood virtually nothing of psychoanalysis. Here we see how not only Girgensohn's rejection of psychoanalysis, but also Pfister's sharp criticism of empirical psychology of religion cut off a more profound debate and exchange of ideas between psychoanalysis and empirical psychology of religion. K. Girgensohn, *Der seelische Aufbau des religiösen Erlebens. Eine religionspsychologische Untersuchung auf experimenteller Grundlage*, Hirzel Verlag, Leipzig, 1921; O. Pfister, "Die Religionspsychologie am Scheidewege", in *Imago* 8 (1922), pp.368-400. On Pfister and Girgensohn see E. Nase, "The psychology of Religion at the Crossroads. Oskar Pfister's Challenge to Psychology of Religion in the Twenties", in J.A. van Belzen (ed.), *Aspects in Context. Studies in the History of Psychology of Religion*, Rodopi, Amsterdam/Atlanta, 2000, pp.45-89.

forms of religiosity. These possibilities – they are no more than that – were not elaborated upon.

2.5 Karl Beth's reading of Freud

There are always exceptions that confirm a rule, and when the rule is "Freud was engaged with by theology through Pfister" there is an exception also, Karl Beth (1872-1959).[98] Beth had studied theology in Berlin where he was influenced by both Adolf von Harnack and especially by Wilhelm Dilthey.[99] Beth wrote his dissertation (published in 1898) on Schleiermacher's ethics. A Schleiermacherian line of thought is clear throughout his writings, for example when he defines the essence of religion as the intuition that totality is inspired[100], and religion as the revelation of the cohesion of individual and universe.[101]

This notion is also dominant in a book that we will discuss in more detail, *Religion und Magie* [Religion and Magic] of 1927. In the final chapter of that study he asks what might be the mutual origin of religion and magic. He argues that both originate from a symbiotic feeling in which man feels essentially united with parts of the universe or the universe in its totality. From these symbiotic feelings the fundamental attitudes towards the world and its parts develop, the conviction that there is a mutual relationship and influence on each other. This is the psychic "primal cell" from which religion and magic originate.[102]

From 1906 onwards Beth was professor in systematic theology at the Protestant Theological Faculty in Vienna. His main interests were the history of religion as the study of the objective side of religion, and psychology of religion as the study of the subjective side.[103] Throughout his writings the psychology of

---

[98] On Karl Beth see I. Noth, "Karl Beth über Religionspsychologie, Seelsorge und Freud. Zur Auseinandersetzung der Wiener Theologischen Fakultäten mit der Psychoanalyse", in *Wiener Jahrbuch für Theologie* 7 (2008), pp.313-326.

[99] Dilthey awoke in him the interest in the psychology of religion. K. Beth, "Karl Beth", in L.E. Stange (ed.), *Die Religionswissenschaft in Selbstdarstellungen*, Meiner Verlag, Leipzig, 1926, pp.1-40 (8).

[100] K. Beth, *Einführung in die vergleichende Religionsgeschichte*, Teubner Verlag, Leipzig/Berlin, 1920, p.10.

[101] K. Beth (ed.), *Religionspsychologie. Veröffentlichungen des Wiener Religionspsychologischen Forschungs-Institutes durch die Internationale Religionspsychologische Gesellschaft, Heft 1*, Braumüller Verlag, Vienna/Leipzig, 1926, "Einführung".

[102] K. Beth, *Religion und Magie. Ein religionsgeschichtlicher Beitrag zur psychologischen Grundlegung der religiösen Prinzipienlehre*, Teubner Verlag, Leipzig/Berlin, 1927, pp.397-398.

[103] We should notice here that the objective side of religion is an "inner objectivity", which means, that the objective appearance of religion in history and phenomena origi-

religion, and eventually even pastoral care, became more and more important.[104] In his later writings he tried to develop a typology of individual religiosity, for example by differentiating between a depressive passive type of personality and a "hybristic" active type.[105]

The distinction between magic and religion as two different psychological responses to the same feeling provided a basic typology here: the religious and magic man, a distinction that, through analogy, can also be found in personality types, the depressive and hybristic type.[106] This search for a typology of religiosity (in pastoral care) does certainly not mean that the religion of history was out of the picture. In his autobiography he mentions that the main problem in the science of religion is the generalization of religion, whereas different types can be distinguished: religion as expression of the psyche of masters or slaves, religion as an expression of momentous inspiration or tradition, religion as a strengthening of a normal "feeling of life" or as a sublimation of sexual processes, religion as a reaction to a unrepressed sense of inferiority and religion as victory over a sense of inferiority.[107]

Different motivations make for different religiosity, different forms of experience and expectation, resulting in specific social behaviour, convictions, and choices. And here we might find a motive for the rise and fall of different social structures in religion, or the turn to specific forms of religion, such as occultism, i.e. typology is necessary for understanding both individual religiosity and the religious mentality of a certain era.[108]

---

nates from a subjective experience or feeling. K. Beth, *Einführung in die vergleichende Religionsgeschichte*, "Vorwort".

[104] In 1922 he founded the *Forschungsinstitut für Religionspsychologie* in Vienna, and the *Internationale Religionspsychologische Gesellschaft*. In 1928 re-founded the *Zeitschrift für Religionspsychologie* and in 1931 he organized the first international conference in psychology of religion, with the key issue "psychology of unbelief". K. Beth, "Karl Beth", pp.32ff.; Chr. Henning, S. Murken, E. Nestler (eds.), *Einführung in die Religionspsychologie*, Schöningh Verlag, Paderborn/Munich/Vienna/Zurich, 2003, pp.29-31; S. Heine, *Grundlagen der Religionspsychologie*, p.43.

[105] K. Beth, "Religionspsychologie und Seelsorge", in *Zeitschrift für Religionspsychologie* 1 (1928), pp.5-25.

[106] Idem, pp.16-17. Particularly strong is the analogy between the overestimation of ones own powers in magic and the sense of superiority and belief in own powers of the hybristic "narcistic" type.

[107] K. Beth, "Karl Beth", p.33.

[108] *[Die Religionspsychologie] sollte in der Lage sein, die unterschiedlichen Entwicklungsformen individueller und kollektiver Religiosität in Geschichte und Gegenwart zu verstehen zu lehren und zu diesem Zweck eine Typologie entwickeln. Einführung in die Religionspsychologie*, p.30.

For us Beth's *Religion and Magic* is of special interest, for here we find a specific engagement with Freud.[109] The aim of this study is to understand the psyche of religious and magic man through an investigation of its primitive forms, its motivations, experiences and feelings. Beth wants to analyse "the essence of religious experience".[110] Towards this aim, the corpus of his book is a critical elaboration on the most important theories on religion and magic by that time: the theories of animism and pre-animism of Edward Tylor (in *Primitive Culture*), Frazer (in *The Golden Bough*) and the further development of these theories in, for example, Wundt's *Folk Psychology*.

Beth's main thesis is that religion cannot be deduced from magic, nor magic from animism. Instead religion and magic are two different responses to a feeling, or better a state of mind, that is pre-magic and pre-religious. Beth's elaborations on Tylor, Frazer und Wundt are interesting, because he focuses on two issues – the pillars of the animistic theory – that also play a central role in Freud's work: the dream (in *The Interpretation of Dreams*) and conceptions of death and the soul (in *Totem and Taboo*). In analysing the primitive psyche and the basic motivations and experiences that mark both the origin and the essence of religion Beth's project is familiar to Freud's *Totem and Taboo*.

Beth's critique of Tylor's animistic theory is by and large the same as Freud's critique of Wundt. According to Tylor, the dream experience of the travelling soul and the experience of death, where the soul leaves the body (or where the body is soulless), caused primitive man to assume that there is a soul that can travel, and that there is thus another place where a soul can live. In other words, through logical-causal thinking primitive man reflects on his experiences, trying to explain the world he lives in. Religion thus originates in conscious ideas, in "primitive philosophy".[111]

At this point Beth introduces Lucien Lévy-Bruhls concept of primitive mentality. Lévy-Bruhl was a French sociologist and ethnographer who was especially interested in what he called primitive mentality (*mentalité primitive*)[112] which expressed a primitive perception and experience of the world. Primitive thinking was supposed to be pre-logical (meaning that in primitive mentality

---

[109] This study is an extended version of K. Beth, *Religion und Magie bei den Naturvölkern. Ein religionsgeschichtlicher Beitrag zur Frage nach den Anfängen der Religion*, Teubner Verlag, Leipzig/Berlin, 1914.

[110] K. Beth, *Religion und Magie*, p.vii.

[111] Idem, p.9.

[112] This theory of primitive mentality was developed in *Les functions mentales dans les sociétés inférieures* (1910) and further developed in *La mentalité primitive* (1922). Beth probably only knew the first of the two texts. In *Einführung in die vergleichende Religionsgeschichte* he refers to the original French edition. In *Religion und Magie* he uses the German translation (by Wilhelm Jerusalem) from 1921, *Das Denken der Naturvölker*. On Lévy-Bruhl see P. Vandermeersch, H. Westerink, *Godsdienstpsychologie*, pp.231-232.

contradictions are not excluded[113]) and mystic (not in a religious sense, but as a concept indicating faith in forces and influences that are invisible and yet perceived as being as real as the visible[114]). This primitive mentality was dependent on and characterized by a feeling of unity or "continuum"[115] with the cosmos, which Lévy-Bruhl indicated with the concept of mystic participation (*participation mystique*).[116] This theory of primitive mentality was not just a welcome alternative to Frazer or Wundt, but also matched the theological standpoint that religion originates in an intuition of the universe, a feeling of being part of a harmonious totality.

Criticizing the animistic theory implies developing an alternative theory. As to dream theory Beth turns to Freud.[117] He argues that Freud's ideas on the dream as a wish-fulfilment, are not sufficient, because these ideas were too much focused on the pathological material that was analysed, the importance of sexuality in the dream, and the generalization of the egoistic and sexual wish fantasies as the basic model. But Freud's dream analysis does provide a good angle for determining the essence and meaning of the dream. Underlying the wish dream and other types of dreams is a more basic feeling – the same feeling that underlies religion – "the feeling of security".[118] This feeling can be interpreted as a characteristic of primitive mentality. Freud was right in suggesting that the dream is about hidden wishes: the deepest wish is being united with the cosmos or God.[119] Beth thus reverses what would have been a Freudian dream analysis: dreams of a union with God do not originate from a sexual wish, but vice versa, sexual symbolism in a dream is the expression of a wish for a union with the transcendent.

Beth has now suggested that underlying the dream is a mentality where religion also originates. The question is now how the dream can be a means to analyse the "extrasensory" of the experience of totality in primitive mentality.[120] Again, Freud provides the perspective, when he argued that the dream shows a conflict between drive and morality. According to Beth this morality or *Ethos*

---

[113] L. Lévy-Bruhl, *Les functions mentales dans les sociétés inférieures*, Alcan, Paris, 1922, p.79. Compare: *prélogique, c'est-à-dire indifférente le plus souvent à la contradiction*. L. Lévy-Bruhl, *La mentalité primitive*, Presses Universitaires de France, Paris, 1947 (originally 1922), p.85.

[114] L. Lévy-Bruhl, *Les functions mentales dans les sociétés inférieures*, p.30. L. Lévy-Bruhl, *La mentalité primitive*, p.14.

[115] L. Lévy-Bruhl, *Les functions mentales dans les sociétés inférieures*, p.109.

[116] The main characteristic of primitive mentality is: *tous impliquent une 'participation' entre les êtres ou les objets liés dans une représentation collective*. This is called *la loi de participation, le principe propre de la mentalité 'primitive'*. Idem, p.76. Compare L. Lévy-Bruhl, *La mentalité primitive*, pp.17-18.

[117] K. Beth, *Religion und Magie*, pp.18ff.

[118] Idem, p.22.

[119] Idem, pp.26-27.

[120] Idem, p.29.

originates from two sources, firstly, through interiorising family- and moral culture, and secondly, from an innate unconscious psychic source, a "disposition" that is seen as a capacity for moral thinking and feeling, a capacity for the interiorization of moral ideas and principles .[121] The conflicts mostly appear when moral culture collides with the drive. But this conflict can be overcome when the two sources of *Ethos* (from outside) fuse. Through this fusion man will be able to penetrate deeper in his unconscious.[122] When this happens, there can be a censor in the dream which not only implies a restriction of immoral/amoral dreams (such as a murder without shame or sense of guilt) but also the possibility of a "concentration" on the deepest inner wishes.[123] In other words, through an internalized *Ethos* man can be guided towards his innermost and deepest religious wish of "hearing God's voice in one's soul".[124]

We should notice here that Beth positions himself in the romantic tradition of Von Hartmann, and with the idea of an unconscious from which consciousness emanates. Here we find the reason why Beth rejects Freud's observation that the dream is often a digestion of experiences from the previous day.[125] In his interpretation of dreams Freud stuck too much to the superficial analysis of the interaction between conscious and unconscious. From this Beth is able to cut off the idea that the dream is the wish fulfilment of a previous conscious or "real" wish, for example the wish to kill the father. Under the model of conflict lies the model of harmony. In this analysis Freud's Oedipal dream and its sense of guilt are implicitly regarded as not essential to dreams, because of the connection with the empirical, the sensory and conscious.

Beth had stated already that religion is essentially an intuition of the extrasensory. In *Religion and Magic* he investigates this in primitive religion, for example in totemism. He argues that totemism is a religion that is dominated by the social structure and strength of the clan.[126] Robertson-Smith's thesis of the totem meal and its application in *Totem and Taboo* are rejected with the simple remark that it is "a fable".[127]

We know that the thesis of the totem meal was a crucial argument in *Totem and Taboo* and Beth now seems to cut off a further elaboration on this

---

[121] Idem, p.34; K. Beth, "Der Josephkomplex", in K. Beth (ed.), *Religionspsychologie. Heft 2*, pp.156-198 (188).

[122] *Dieser Verschmelzungsprozeß vertieft die Lebensauffassung des Menschen von der bewußten in die unbewußte Sphäre.* Idem, p.189.

[123] Idem, p.190.

[124] Idem, p.196.

[125] Idem, pp.183-184.

[126] K. Beth, *Religion und Magie*, p.311.

[127] Idem, p.318. According to Beth, there is no evidence that this meal was a general custom (not all totem animals were edible). See also K. Beth, "Die Religion im Urteil der Psychoanalyse, Sigmund Freuds Kampf gegen die Religion", in *Zeitschrift für Religionspsychologie* 2 (1929), pp.76-87 (85-86).

topic. However, the following pages of *Religion and Magic* are of some interest. Instead of the totem meal, Beth elaborates on the totem feast, a ritual where the totemists drink their own blood and spill it on the ground.[128] This ritual must be seen as a fertility ritual to strengthen the power of the totem clan that is believed to be the original power of the primal fathers. Here, Beth argues, we see the early stages of sacrifice. Essentially, sacrifice is not about guilt and reconciliation, but it is aimed at strengthening the mystic union with the extrasensory-divine. In this sense, totemistic ritual and the earliest forms of sacrifice show a very early development out of primitive mentality: the rituals aim at a restoration of the primitive symbiosis of man and cosmos, which indicates that there had already been a first split between an individual ego and cosmos.[129]

It is interesting to notice here that Beth in his analysis of the totem feast and primitive sacrifice comes actually very close to the theories about the totem meal. Freud had argued that the totem meal was first of all a communion of believers and their gods.[130] The meal served the clan as a whole, or in psychoanalytic terms, the mutual identification of the clan members with each other and their totem animal was strengthened.[131] The crucial step for Freud was then to argue that the totem animal was actually a father substitute. This step leads to the well known thesis of patricide, sense of guilt and commemoration. Beth's reconstruction of the totem feast leaves out the element of the killing or eating of the totem animal. Instead he stresses the mutual identification as restoration of primitive symbiosis. Underlying the feast is thus a harmonic union with nature, not a repressed and commemorated guilty act.

In naming the totem meal theory "a fable", Beth draws a sharp line with a theory that is quite similar to his interpretation of the totem feast. It is clear that he distances himself from Freud in order to put forward his own ideas on primitive mentality and the essence of religion.

In *Religion and Magic* Freud's dream theories serve as an important argument against the theories of Tylor, Frazer and Wundt: not in logical-causal thinking, but in unconscious motives the essence and origin of religion must be sought. Contrary to Freudian thought these motives are not related to unconscious conflicts or to a sense of guilt. These issues belong with the superficial analyses of psychoanalysis. Underlying religion are what Rolland would have called "oceanic feelings". Beyond *Totem and Taboo* and its deconstruction of religion as collective neurosis lies the true essence of religion in mystic participation.

---

[128] K. Beth, *Religion und Magie*, pp.322f.

[129] Idem, p.328. The reference to Robertson-Smith, Freud,and the elaborations on the totemist ritual of drinking and spilling blood and sacrifice, are not in the first version of 1914. Compare *Religion und magie bei den Naturvölkern*, pp.199-201 and *Religion und Magie*, pp.318-326.

[130] S. Freud, *Totem and Taboo*, p.136.

[131] Idem, pp.137-138.

In an article on Freud's *The Future of an Illusion*, in which Beth sharply attacks Freud's attempt to "destroy" religion, we can recognize the concern for the mystic essence of religion that cannot be reduced to a simple wish, need or pathological construct. Freud, says Beth, failed to produce a phenomenology of religiosity and religion that would have enabled him to deal with the underlying essence of religiosity and religion, i.e. the feeling for the totality of being. Hence, Freud failed to analyze religion and instead mistakenly took one of its forms (dogma) as object of enquiry.[132]

Interesting is Beth's argument that Freud not only in *The Future of an Illusion*, but especially in *Totem and Taboo*, failed to show how the god idea could emerge both in history as well as in the individual mind. The step from the primal murder and its psychic after-effects (identification, sense of guilt) to the god idea is an "immense step" that cannot be explained by psychoanalysis. Freud in fact presumes the god idea he is willing to prove. In other words, from the primal deed and its correlating psychic motives religion cannot be explained. What is at least failing here is a teleological aspect of the human mind that produces religious ideas, says Beth.[133] With introducing this teleological aspect and the formation of ideas, Beth is well aware that his anthropology is fundamentally different from the one presented by Freud. Moreover, *Totem and Taboo* was dominated by a critique on teleology (Jung) and the primacy of ideas (Wundt).

2.6 Dialectic theology and psychoanalysis

Pfister's efforts to promote psychoanalysis in theology met with relatively little response. In the 1920s there was a cautious reception of Freudian thought against the background of a general critical attitude. Freud's own critique of religion was a factor of importance of course, but developments in theology were at least equally decisive: with the emergence of dialectic theology in the early 1920s the theologian's interest in the human sciences including psychology and psychoanalysis faded. After an era dominated by liberal theology, Schleiermacher's subjectivism and flirtations with the human and natural sciences, theology sought to return to its core business: the proclamation of the revealed Word of God.[134]

---

[132] K. Beth, "Die Religion im Urteil der Psychoanalyse", pp.79-81.

[133] Idem, pp.85-87. Also, I. Noth, "Karl Beth über Religionspsychologie, Seelsorge und Freud", pp.322-326.

[134] In *Die Mystik und das Wort* (1924) Emil Brunner opposes dialectic theology to a theology based on the "application of general scientific views and methods", in short "theology as science of religion", "philosophy of religion" or "psychology of religion". He distances himself from those who "fabricate new religions" that serve "the needs of European intellectuals". E. Brunner, *Die Mystik und das Wort*, Verlag Mohr, Tübingen, 1924, pp.1-2, 26, 32ff. In a further elaboration he calls Schleiermacher's definition of

In his study of Calvin, Pfister criticizes the "Calvin renaissance" in the work of Karl Barth (1886-1968) and Eduard Thurneysen (1888-1977), the regression of theology to the ideas of the intolerant and anxious Calvin, and the ecclesiastic criteria for pastoral care – *extra ecclesiam nulla salus*.[135] But here we should add: this is a rearguard action. By then, dialectic theology was already dominant, and Pfister was an almost isolated relic of an old liberal theology (and of the old Freudian movement).

Barth's rejection of experience as the basis of faith and his attempts to unravel theology and anthropology are important for his view of psychoanalysis. In the second edition of *Der Römerbrief* [Letter to the Romans] from 1922, when reflecting on the god-man dichotomy he sharply rejects human experience as the source of knowledge of God.[136] Such an experience can only be more or less "sexually coloured identification forms and fusion processes" in which man and animal characteristics are elevated as experiences of God.[137]

In the idea that faith should be opposed to every attempt to reach to God by means of human capacities – an opposition that can be described as faith versus religion[138] – not only Pfister's concept of sublimation is implicitly rejected, but in fact every psychoanalytic theory, Freudian and Jungian. Implicitly, for a most striking fact in Barth's writings is the absence of psychoanalysis. In *Die kirchliche Dogmatik* [Church Dogmatics] there are minor remarks on

---

the essence of religion as feeling and intuition psychologism, that is, the divine is seen as being based on and realized in a psychic mode or function. In further reflecting on the psychology of religion, Brunner argues that this discipline need not necessarily be psychologism, when it is practiced as an auxiliary science "observing and describing psychic reflexes". Psychologist of religion should be aware of the fact that studying these "reflexes" does not imply studying faith itself: faith, as knowledge of being united with God "because God wants it and says so", is opposed to any religious experience. Idem, pp.179ff.

[135] O. Pfister, *Calvins Eingreifen in die Hexer- und Hexenprozesse von Peney 1545*, p.161.

[136] In the first part of his church dogmatics Barth states that the relation between man and God is initialized by God, that is, his Word is preached and the hearer can know and understand this Word. How man exactly experiences or should experience this revealed Word is not a question, because every limitation in this respect would imply that the revealed is dependant on specific psychic capacities. Thus faith should not be regarded as a "historic-psychological determined religious experience" which would imply that faith was an "actualization of a general apparent religious psychic capacity". K. Barth, *Die kirchliche Dogmatik I,1*, §6,1, §6,2. *Die kirchliche Dogmatik* was published at Evangelischer Verlag, Zollikon-Zurich, 1932-1967.

[137] K. Barth, *Die Römerbrief*, Theologischer Verlag Zürich, Zurich, 1976, p.25.

[138] K. Barth, *Die kirchliche Dogmatik I,2*, §17,2.

Freud's outdated theory on sexuality[139], but more significant is Barth's silence on psychoanalysis in general.[140]

We certainly do not have to conclude from this that Barth was uninterested in man's inner life or that he was totally unacquainted with psychoanalysis.[141] De Quervain mentions two main reasons for Barth not elaborating upon psychoanalysis. Firstly, there is the fact that Barth was fully concentrated on his theological project and took the liberty not to "fight wind mills".[142] Secondly, Barth did not view man in his psychic or historic development (or evolution) but in his existence before God (with either faith or religion).[143] I will add one further reason: from his theological point of view it is of secondary importance which anthropology should be "chosen": whether the anthropology of Schleiermacher is preferred or "a contemporary such as from Heidegger" is not decisive. A critical distance should instead be preferred towards any anthropology that in principle excludes God. Freud is thus not a "conversation partner" for theology.[144]

In general we can say, that it is only after the Second World War that the tide somewhat turns. Not so much in the work of Barth, but in the writings on pastoral care of his friend Thurneysen. In his 1946 *Die Lehre von der Seelsorge* [The Doctrine of Pastoral Care] pastoral care is seen as a sub-discipline of practical theology, a discipline reflecting on the art of preaching and hearing.[145] It is defined within these parameters as "having the same content as the public preaching of God's Word, but now in a private setting".[146] Pastoral care is regarded as a means to bring the individual into contact with God's Word and into the community of believers.[147]

---

[139] Idem, *III,4*, §54,1.

[140] P. de Quervain, *Psychoanalyse und dialektische Theologie. Zum Freud-Verständnis bei K. Barth, E. Thurneysen und P. Ricoeur*, Verlag Hans Huber, Bern/Stuttgart/Vienna, 1977, p.22; Chr. Henning, "Zankapfel Psychoanalyse. Ein Rückblick auf das gespannte Verhältnis von evangelischer Theologie und Psychologie im 20. Jahrhundert", in Chr. Henning, E. Nestler (eds.), *Religionspsychologie heute*, Lang Verlag, Frankfurt, 2000, pp.67-102 (69).

[141] In the period Barth was still a minister in the Reformed church of Safenwil (Switzerland) one of his friends was Ewald Jung, a nephew of Carl Gustav Jung and one of the members of the psychoanalytic movement in Zurich. Barth was even analysed – in one evening – by Ewald. Idem, pp.22-24.

[142] K. Barth, *Die kirchliche Dogmatik III,4*, §54,1.

[143] P. de Quervain, *Psychoanalyse und dialektische Theologie*, pp.28-29.

[144] K. Barth, *Die Kirchliche Dogmatik I,1*, §6,2.

[145] E. Thurneysen, *Die Lehre von der Seelsorge*, Theologischer Verlag Zürich, Zürich, 1994, pp.9-10. A good introduction to Thurneysen's theories on pastoral care can be found in K. Winkler, *Seelsorge*, De Gruyter, New York/Berlin, 2000, pp.28-45.

[146] E. Thurneysen, *Die Lehre von der Seelsorge*, p.13.

[147] Idem, pp.26ff.

It is indeed a "bringing back": Thurneysen calls the pastoral conversation a "battle against sin". At stake is man's soul – the battlefield – that is, man's physical and psychic existence before God. It is in the context of this "battle" that he writes pastoral care cannot do without some knowledge of psychology and pathology.[148] Why? The first reason is in the relation between "illness and sin", that is, psychic illness as a symptom of sin. The example Thurneysen presents is neurasthenia in the late nineteenth century as a symptom of secularization.[149] Understanding the symptom is an advantage in the "battle"; it is a vulnerable spot, so to speak. The second reason is linked with the first: modern man is neurotic; secular psychotherapies have become popular. Many people that pastors meet in pastoral conversation have a history of psychotherapeutic or psychiatric treatment, which means that they are not a *tabula rasa*, but have already developed a specific self-understanding and expression thereof. The pastor will have to make a translation, which means he has to understand the language of the "symptoms" in order to be able to point to the underlying sin.

When Thurneysen in a chapter on the relation between pastoral care and psychology further reflects on the content of the pastoral conversation the two above mentioned reasons for having knowledge of psychology and pathology are taken up again.[150] A certain knowledge of psychology is necessary in order to successfully preach the Word. In this sense, psychology is an auxiliary science in pastoral care. To be more precise, psychoanalysis is the auxiliary science Thurneysen has in mind.[151]

Why psychoanalysis? Why not some other psychology? The main reason Thurneysen mentions is the "dimension of the unconscious". Psychoanalysis has made this dimension into its subject of analysis and in doing so it has shown that the old psychology focusing on the conscious capacities of thought, will and feeling is outdated. The "dimension of the unconscious" with its unknown depths is important for another reason: it is opposed to a materialistic view of man reducing the soul to the realm of the physical.[152]

Thurneysen admits that Freudian psychoanalysis with its "naturalistic-mechanic thought" is problematic, but Jungian psychoanalysis is in fact a worse option. His "mystic philosophy of life" and his theories of projection and of the divine as being equal to man's soul should be rejected.[153] Instead, Thurneysen

---

[148] Idem, pp.57, 114ff.

[149] Idem, pp.73-77.

[150] *Indem aber der Seelsorger sich diesem Gebiete zuwendet, findet er es bereits besetzt, bearbeitet und durchdrungen durch eine bestimmte, gerade der Erforschung dieses Innenlebens sich widmende Wissenschaft, die Wissenschaft der Psychologie.* Idem, p.174.

[151] Idem, p.187.

[152] In the next chapter we will see that this argument had already been an important argument in the earliest engagement with Freud in the Netherlands.

[153] Idem, pp.189-191.

argues that psychoanalysis is basically a form of "descriptive phenomenology", that is, a science that should confine itself to the observation and analysis of phenomena without formulating an all-embracing philosophy of life.[154]

After having discussed the relation between pastoral care and psychology Thurneysen continues elaborating on the relation between pastoral care and psychotherapy. He takes up his earlier remarks on the connection between neurosis and sin.[155] The psychiatric or psychoanalytic theories of the aetiology of neurosis are of no interest to the pastor. The important thing for him is to see the analogies between psychoanalysis as a theory of man's inner ruptures focusing on the conflicts between drives and morality to which man is unfreely subjected, and the Paulinian view of man (torn between desire and spirit) as depicted in his letter to the Romans. The pastor should point at the underlying sin, translating the modern idiom into the biblical.

Such a translation always implies a clear distinction from psychology or psychotherapy. Neurosis is not sin, but points at sin. It is its symptom. Another example of such a distinction can be found in Thurneysen's reflections on psychotherapy: psychotherapy aims at curing a patient (through a talking cure); pastoral care aims at the salvation of man (through preaching the Word). In short, the alleged analogies make psychoanalysis and psychotherapy the ideal auxiliary sciences offering profound knowledge of human nature, but at the same time a critical distance should be maintained: the philosophies of life as presented in psychoanalysis and psychotherapy should be rejected. And although a modern psychoanalytic idiom can be translated in the language of faith, Thurneysen wants to make certain that faith and the Word cannot be re-translated into a psychoanalytic idiom.

Scharfenberg has uttered a cynical critique against Thurneysen arguing that he only incorporated psychoanalysis into his theories on pastoral care for strategic reasons.[156] Thurneysen wanted to use the popularity of psychoanalysis for his own purposes and used this theory as a resource of ideas that showed analogies with the language of faith. At the same time he tried to keep a distance from the critical potential of psychoanalysis.

One might call this attitude arbitrary[157] or ambivalent.[158] One might also point at historic developments that make this "ambivalent" relation between psychoanalysis and dialectic theology understandable: on the one hand, developments in psychoanalysis moving away from a Freudian naturalistic theory and from Pfister's translation of theology in psychoanalytic idiom[159] towards a

[154] Idem, p.181.

[155] Idem, pp.198ff.

[156] J. Scharfenberg, *Sigmund Freud und seine Religionskritik*, pp.25-26.

[157] Idem.

[158] P. de Quervain, *Psychoanalyse und dialektische Theologie*, p.39.

[159] E. Thurneysen, *Die Lehre von der Seelsorge*, p.178. See also Chr. Henning, "Gescheiterte Beziehung? Ein Einblick in das Verhältnis von Theologie und Psychologie in

Jungian "theistic" theory, and on the other hand, developments in dialectic theology moving away from Barth's uncompromising views on human experience.[160] All this however does not answer the question why Thurneysen turned to psychoanalysis in particular.

So, what are the reasons? First of all, the dimension of the unconscious had important advantages in different directions. It could be opposed to a materialistic view of man in which the "soul" was simply reduced to physical processes. More importantly psychoanalysis had made this dimension of the unconscious the subject of analysis and in doing so it has shown that the old psychology focusing on the conscious capacities of thought, will and feeling is outdated.

Thurneysen thus actually presents psychoanalysis as a critique of those theologians who supposedly wanted to found theology and faith on specific human capacities. The dimension of the unconscious had a third important advantage. It pointed in the direction of an underlying sin presented as a "reality" in man. The unconscious with its hidden depths was a perfect theory to veil some problems this concept of sinfulness of man might raise in modern times. For what is sin when, for example, neurosis is its symptom? Is it purely spiritual or does it also have a physical dimension? After all, sinfulness has to do with man's physical and psychic existence before God.

It is also possible to look at Thurneysen's turn to the unconscious from another perspective: what if there isn't an unconscious? Modern science has anatomized and analysed the physical and psychic (that is, conscious) dimensions of man extensively. There was no place for sin in these findings. The concept of unconsciousness with its hidden and principally unknown depths is a concept that enables Thurneysen to speak of an all-underlying real sin like a perverted blueprint avoiding a naturalistic critique.

A second advantage of psychoanalysis as an auxiliary science in pastoral care is the connection that psychoanalysis had made between the rise of neurosis in modern era and secularization. In other words, it had suggested a connection between health and social-religious cohesion. In *The Future Prospects of Psychoanalytic Therapy* Freud had indeed suggested a relation between neurosis and secularization. In this text he had argued that psychoanalysis "destroys illusions", that is, the illusion of the high moral standards of modern society, the illusion that "this society" is superior, whereas psychoanalysis points at necessary "changes in our culture" for the sake of "our descendants". In other words, psychoanalysis implies a critique of modern society and aims at other social structures.

Of course, Freud had specific ideas in this respect. We remember his pleas for a more sexually liberated morality in *"Civilized" Sexual Morality*.

---

der Zeit zwischen 192 und 1960", in *Praktische Theologie. Zeitschrift für Religion, Gesellschaft und Kirche*, 35 (2000/2), pp.85-97 (94).
[160] P. de Quervain, *Psychoanalyse und dialektische Theologie*, pp.44-46.

Thurneysen may well have ignored this liberal plea, but he did notice that psychoanalysis in "destroying illusions" had something in common with dialectic theology and its critique of modern society and search for a new social cohesion.[161]

As to the sense of guilt there are no elaborations on this issue in Thurneysen's discussion of psychoanalysis. The neurotic ruptures of psychic life are regarded as analogous to the ruptures in man's sinful existence. From Freud we know that the sense of guilt is the key issue in these psychic conflicts. Thurneysen stresses neurosis as symptom of sin. Consequently, sense of guilt is a symptom of sin. It is therefore not quite as inevitable as Freud thought, because sin can be forgiven, and from this "maybe" psychic life might be healed, and a new "wholeness of personality" be restored within the boundaries of normal human psychic life.[162]

2.7 Paul Tillich's reading of Freud

The key difference between a liberal theologian like Pfister on the one hand and dialectic theologians on the other is expressed in the words of Paul Tillich (1886-1965): "theology moves back and forth between two poles, the eternal truth of its foundation and the temporal situation in which the eternal truth must be received. Not many theological systems have been able to balance these two demands perfectly. Most of them either sacrifice elements from the truth or are not able to speak of the situation".[163]

The German-American theologian Tillich himself has tried to find this "balance" in his writings. The final pages of this chapter will be devoted to his work. Although he migrated to the United States in 1933 where he had a post at the Union Theological Seminary in New York and was later a professor at the universities of Harvard and Chicago, he is generally considered to be one of the most important German theologians of the past century.

---

[161] We should not overlook the fact that Thurneysen saw pastoral care as a means of church discipline. E. Thurneysen, *Die Lehre von der Seelsorge*, §2. One of the old critiques of Schleiermacher's religion as feeling or intuition of the universe, was the neglect of social cohesion. What remained was merely – in William James phrase – "varieties of religious experience".

[162] Idem, p.205, p.211, p.213. Dorothee Hoch, a student of Thurneysen, did elborate on the issue of the sense of guilt in relation to reconciliation. She argued that (Jungian) psychoanalysis helps to make unconscious sense of guilt conscious, i.e. helps man to realize his guilty (and sinful) nature. This recognition of guilt is the premise for reconciliation. Thus recognition of guilt contributes to maturation processes and the wholeness of personality. D. Hoch, "Vom Umgang mit Schuld. Geschichte einer Tagung", in *Wege zum Menschen* 32 (1980), pp.239-253.

[163] P. Tillich, *Systematic Theology, Vol. I*, University of Chicago Press, Chicago, 1967, p.3.

Paul Tillich's *Systematic Theology* (published in three volumes in 1951, 1957 and 1963) can be seen as an attempt to interpret and retranslate Christian concepts by using philosophical concepts, eclectically derived from various philosophically traditions (most importantly Thomism).[164] These philosophical or more precisely ontological concepts are not used to replace one outdated metaphysical "system" by another, but they are "products of a critical analysis of experience" which means that they cannot form a "static and unchangeable structure" (for, experiences changes depending on place and moment in time). Yet they can be called "a priori", because these ontological concepts are "present whenever something is experienced".[165]

The backbones of his systematic theology are the concepts of essence and existence. In Tillich's view God does not "exist". He "is".[166] He calls this essence "the true and undistorted nature of things". This "logical ideal" is to be reached by "abstraction", that is to say, the logical deduction that everything we experience as untrue and distorted is already valued in the light of the true and the undistorted in the intuitive experience of the "immediate awareness of something unconditional".[167] At this point, it is important for us to notice that there is no "proportion or gradation between the finite and the infinite. There is an absolute break, an infinite "jump"."[168] In other words, whatever the mecha-

---

[164] D.F. Dreisbach, "Essence, Existence, and the Fall: Paul Tillich's Analysis of Existence", in *Harvard Theological Review* 73 (1980/2), pp.521-538 (521-523). On Tillich and Thomism see R.R.N. Ross, "The Non-Existence of God: Tillich, Aquinas, and the Pseudo-Dionysius", in *Harvard Theological Review* 68 (1975/2), pp.141-166.

[165] P. Tillich, *Systematic Theology, Vol. I*, p.166.

[166] Idem, p.204f. Here we should notice Tillich's criticism of Christian theism and super-naturalistic conceptions of God. In Tillich's view theistic conceptions of God are bound to a subject/object dichotomy which he wants to overcome by pointing towards God as "ultimate reality". The Christian theistic God is nothing else but what Freud had called the elevated father, that is, the human projection of an image of God to which it can relate as subject to object. This projection is part of existence not of essence. The theistic image of God is further characterized by strong authoritative features related to what Tillich called "the bad conscience" which has its correlate in Freud's superego. On this subject see P. Homans, "Towards a Psychology of Religion", in P. Homans (ed.), *The Dialogue between Theology and Psychology*, The University of Chicago Press, Chicago/London, 1968, pp.53-81.

[167] P. Tillich, *Systematic Theology, Vol. I*, p.41.

[168] Idem, p.237. In *Biblical Religion and the Search for Ultimate Reality* (1955), Tillich describes the search for ultimate reality as a "deeper entering of levels": if we enter the levels of personal existence which have been rediscovered by depth psychology we encounter the past, the ancestors, the collective unconscious, the living substance in which all living beings participate. In our search for the "really real" we are driven from one level to another to a point where we cannot speak of level any more, and where we must ask for that which is the ground of all levels". This is the "jump": from the levels to what lies beyond it, "being-itself". P. Tillich, *Biblical Religion and the Search for Ultimate Reality*, University of Chicago Press, Chicago, 1955, p.13.

nism of deducing essence from existence, it is not by sublimation as a mechanism indicating religious and moral elevation to a higher level in a Pfisterian sense of the word, that man will be able to make this "jump".[169]

The distinction between essence and existence is fundamental in Tillich's theological views. Whereas the philosopher is focused on his object "objectively", with "pure reason" penetrating the structures of being and reflecting on his own philosophical assertions, the theologian is "existentially" involved in his object with "passion, fear, and love", focusing on the manifestation(s) of what "concerns him ultimately", longing and searching for a "new being" that is no longer estranged from his essence.[170] "The state of existence is the state of estrangement", Tillich writes, indicating that the Fall meant the estrangement from man's essence, that is, being created after God's image.[171] The essence however is not lost from sight. Man remembers it, and it is dreamt of, longed for, asked for.[172] The more man acknowledges his existence as finite and estranged, the stronger his "ultimate concern" about being and meaning, his longing for participation in the Divine Life (or the New Being as it is manifest in Jesus the Christ).[173]

Existence, estrangement, sin ... ultimate concern begins where indifference about one's existence ends and man discovers his finite and estranged existence. Freudian psychoanalysis is par excellence the analysis of human sinful existence in modern idiom. Hence, in his later writings Tillich regards psychoanalysis an important auxiliary science in theology, like in Thurneysen's views on pastoral care strictly partitioned from theology, philosophy of life or pastoral care.[174] But unlike Thurneysen he does not stress the usefulness of psychoanalysis as a vehicle against subjectivism or materialism, or as means to talk about sin. Tillich values psychoanalysis for having "rediscovered" the full depth and meaning of the theological concept of sin in the first place.[175]

---

[169] P. Tillich, *Systematic Theology, Vol. II*, pp.3-4.

[170] Idem, *Vol. I*, pp.18-24.

[171] Man's estrangement moves in three directions: estrangement from God as the ultimate ground of being, from fellow man, and from ourselves. Idem, *Vol. II*, p.44. On essence as *Imago Dei* see H. Anzenberger, *Der Mensch im Horizont von Sein und Sinn. Die Anthropologie Paul Tillichs im Dialog mit Humanwissenschaften (Rupert Riedl, Erich Fromm und Viktor E. Frankl)*, EOS Verlag, St.Ottilien, 1998, pp.86ff; T.D. Cooper, *Paul Tillich and Psychology. Historic and Contemprary Explorations in Theology, Psychotherapy, and Ethics*, Mercer University Press, Macon, 2006, pp.17-21.

[172] P. Tillich, *Systematic Theology, Vol. II*, pp. 22, 33.

[173] Idem, *Vol. I*, p.177, *Vol. III*, p.405.

[174] Chr. Henning, "Zankapfel Psychoanalyse", pp.79-82.

[175] *Es kann kein Zweifel darüber bestehen, dass Existentialismus und Tiefenpsychologe von unendlichem Wert für die Theologie sind. Beide Bewegungen haben zunächst der Theologie etwas in Erinnerung gerufen, das ihr immer hätte bewusst bleiben müssen, das sie aber aus dem Gedächtnis verloren oder verdrängt hat (...) der Selbstzerstörung des Menschen in seiner Entfremdung von seinem essentiellen Sein.* P. Tillich, "Die theo-

Psychoanalysis has shown sin is more than just immoral acts; sin is a fundamental estrangement from essence, says Tillich. It has depicted the "demonic structures" that determine our thoughts and acts. Thus, it has proven man's absolute freedom to be an illusion (just like existentialist philosophers had done[176]) for in man consciousness is not the determining element.[177] As a therapeutic method psychoanalysis has resisted moralism and shown the true meaning of grace by not primarily judging patients according to their acts or imposing a change in moral behaviour, but by simply accepting them.[178] Hence, the acceptance of patients in psychotherapy has opened our eyes to the "motherly" characteristics of God replacing the classic image of the threatening Father God.[179]

This line of thought is also apparent in *Systematic Theology*. In a chapter on the characteristics of man's estrangement and sin Tillich elaborates on the "classic" Christian equation of sin and *concupiscentia*. "The doctrine of concupiscence – taken in its all-embracing sense – can be supported by much material and deeper insights from existentialist literature, art, philosophy, and psychology".[180] Freud's theory of the libido has contributed to a "rediscovery of the Christian view on man's predicament".[181] He has shown man's unlimited desire "to get rid of his biological, especially sexual, tensions and to get pleasure from the discharge of these tensions".

This insight culminates in the theory of the "death instinct" which Tillich prefers to translate as a "drive for death". It is the desire of man to get rid of himself as a constant source of unpleasant tensions. Here, Freud has been able to fully grasp man's estrangement. But Tillich adds: "Freud did not see that his description of human nature is adequate for man only in his existential predicament but not in his essential nature".[182] In this case, libido as concupiscence

---

logische Bedeutung von Psychoanalyse und Existentialismus", in *Gesammelte Werke, Band VIII*, Evangelisches Verlag, Stuttgart, 1970, pp.304-324 (313).

[176] Perry has argued that Tillich regarded Freudian psychoanalysis as entangled with the existentialist movement of the nineteenth and twentieth century: both movements protested against a "philosophy of consciousness" and described human nature not with abstract theories, but in concrete terms, uncompromisingly honest about man's tragic predicament. J.M. Perry, *Tillich's Response to Freud: A Christian Answer to the Freudian Critique of Religion*, University Press of America, Lanham/New York/London, 1988, pp.13ff.

[177] P. Tillich, "Die theologische Bedeutung von Psychoanalyse und Existentialismus", p.314.

[178] Idem. Compare P. Tillich, "Der Einfluss der Psychotherapie auf die Theologie", in *Gesammelte Werke, Band VIII*, pp.325-335 (328-329).

[179] Idem, p.328.

[180] P. Tillich, *Systematic Theology, Vol. II*, p.52.

[181] Idem, p.53.

[182] Idem, p.54. At this point Tillich criticizes Freud for having disregarded the limitations of psychoanalysis as a science. Freud's pessimism about culture and his reduction

only wants pleasure, but the love that marks man's essential nature, whether it is called *eros*, *philia* or *agape*, wants participation. The partition between the psychoanalyst and the theologian is clear: beyond Freud's pleasure principle lies true love.

Tillich's interpretation of the Freudian concepts of libido and death drive can be criticized. Not only because Freud identified his concept of libido with Plato's *Eros*, and not with concupiscence, but more important is the fact that the death drive was not a concept introduced to rename the sexual drives. As we have seen, the death drive is introduced to indicate a source of unpleasure "beyond the pleasure principle". The concept of the death drive in Freud's writings has thus a speculative almost enigmatic character, a theoretical construction with hardly any clinical evidence. However, when we look at Freud's applications of the concept one thing is clear: it is connected with aggression and sense of guilt.

The death drive is thus destructive, which includes self-destruction. However, this self-destruction should not be interpreted in terms of a drive for death, but basically as a destruction of any "positive" change in identity formation. Hence, its clinical expression was found in the negative therapeutic reaction, the "destruction" of progress in therapy.

In my opinion, Tillich's interpretation of the Freudian concepts of libido and death drive as descriptions of the full meaning of estrangement and sin are moulded by his theological views on sin and estrangement in the first place. Sin and estrangement are essentially self-destructive. Originating from man's hostility towards God (the Fall) man's existence is marked by "hostility against man as combined with his distorted desires".[183] An important element in Tillich's view of existence should be added here: man in his existence is finite, condemned to exclusion from eternal life, and it is this finitude that makes him ultimate concerned about his life which will lead to the opposite of self-destruction, namely self-affirmation.[184] The combination of these elements – self-destruction, finitude and distorted desire – as characteristics of sin determines Tillich's interpretation of mutual connections and interdependencies between the Freudian concepts of the pleasure principle, libido and death drive as self-destruction.

According to Tillich, the Fall, "the transition from essence to existence results in personal guilt and universal tragedy".[185] Man's hostility is man's own

---

of religion to (for example) projection or wish illusion, are actually expressions of faith but not the results of scientific analysis. In other words, Freud ignored his own philosophical or theological presuppositions in his psychoanalytic theories. J.M. Perry, *Tillich's Response to Freud*, pp.40ff.

[183] P. Tillich, *Systematic Theology, Vol. II*, p.45.

[184] P. Tillich, *The Courage to be*, Yale University Press, New Haven/London, 2000, pp.21ff. (originally published in 1952).

[185] P. Tillich, *Systematic Theology, Vol. II*, pp.44-45.

act. He is responsible for it and hence guilty. Guilt is "a factor which separates man from God".[186] Man's guilt in estranged existence is inevitable and this fact alone is reason enough to call man's existence "tragic". Although Tillich in his considerations on hostility, guilt and tragedy does not directly refer to Freud's writings, we should notice that these concepts are closely related in his major studies on culture and religion. However, at this point the earlier remarks made by Tillich can be repeated: Freud depicted existence, not essence. Freud could not see the full meaning of atonement and salvation: the possibility of reconciliation and regeneration.[187]

Taking this into consideration and given the fact that Tillich's theology focuses on man's ultimate concern with his life and his longing for participation, existential anxiety plays a more fundamental role than guilt itself. Especially in *The Courage to be* of 1952 is this issue reflected upon. Anxiety is described as finitude experienced as one's own finitude.[188] It has three forms: anxiety of death, of meaninglessness and of guilt and condemnation.[189] Tillich is discussing the ontology of anxiety which should not be confused with the pathology of anxiety.[190] Again a sharp partition is made. Freud was absolute right in arguing that anxiety was the product of inner conflicts between structural elements of the personality.

Psychoanalysts have elaborated on anxiety, but have not been able to point out convincingly a "basic anxiety". Each psychological explanation points to symptoms and psychic structures, but the lack of distinction between existential and pathological anxiety has made it impossible for depth-psychologist to present a convincing theory. Hence, "only in the light of an ontological understanding of human nature can the body of material provided by psychology and sociology be organized into a consistent and comprehensive theory of anxiety".[191]

Having stated this Tillich turns the positions around: from an ontological point of view he interprets neurotic anxiety as "existential anxiety under

---

[186] Idem, p.170.

[187] Tillich defines salvation as "the act of cosmic healing" by the God, "the reestablishment of a whole that was broken, disrupted, disintegrated". The main difference between salvation and (therapeutic) healing is the cosmic and eternal character of salvation as opposed to the temporal and existence-bound character of healing. What is the object of salvation? Tillich calls it "cosmic guilt", which is not the same as an individual sense of guilt, because it precedes the individual: cosmic guilt is sin against and estrangement from essence. This idea of cosmic guilt implies a critique of the (Protestant) emphasis on personal guilt and moral responsibility. K. Grau, *"Healing Power" - Ansätze zu einer Theologie der Heilung im Werk Paul Tillichs*, LIT Verlag, Munster/Hamburg/London, 1999, pp.71-100.

[188] P. Tillich, *The Courage to be*, p.35.

[189] Idem, p.45.

[190] Idem, pp.64ff.

[191] Idem, p.65.

special conditions": "Neurosis is the way of avoiding non-being by avoiding be-ing"[192], meaning that the neurotic has a strong self-affirmation, but in a reduced mode namely through not affirming anxiety and finitude. He thus remains es-tranged from his essence.

Again we notice the same structure in Tillich's use of psychoanalysis: it has "rediscovered" the meaning of anxiety for theology, but was unable to point out the basic underlying ontological structures. This structure is apparent when-ever Tillich discusses psychoanalysis. I will shortly give two more examples. The first one is in Tillich's depiction of faith as an "act of the whole person". Psychoanalysis has shown the depths of this person depicting its structures, su-perego and ego, consciousness and unconsciousness. But again: the whole per-son is more than its parts. It is beyond the depictions presented.[193] A second ex-ample is Tillich's discussion of psychological projection theories.[194] Theologians must face the fact that man projects elements of "existence" on the divine, but psychoanalysts such as Freud should acknowledge that "projection is always projection on something", and this "something" is not itself a projection.

At first sight Tillich's view of and use of psychoanalytic theory in theology seems more affirmative towards these theories than Thurneysen's. However, we also noticed the sharp partitioning of realms. So how can we assess Tillich's view of Freudian psychoanalysis? The main problem in my opinion is Tillich's claim that psychoanalysis rediscovered the true meaning of "forgotten" theo-logical concepts and his actual interpretation of psychoanalysis. For when this claim is just one might expect a more profound analysis of Freud's writings on man's nature and "existence".

From Freud's point of view psychoanalysis did indeed discover some-thing "forgotten" in the history of religion, namely the origin of religion and its most important effect/motive the sense of guilt. Paul had "rediscovered" it, Ref-ormation theologians maybe, Goethe and Freud certainly. In Freud's view the belief that religion could offer salvation from the "demonic structures" of exis-tence would be an illusion. Religion merely cultivated those structures in an ambivalent manner, negatively in its dogmatic and repressive tendencies, posi-tively in providing structures for sublimation.

But this was not the main issue picked up by Tillich. For him this redis-covery of sin was the forgotten connection between the libido and the death drive, between desire and self-destruction. And beyond or behind these drives?

---

[192] Idem, p.66.

[193] P. Tillich, "Wesen und Wandel des Glaubens", in *Gesammelte Werke, Band VIII*, pp.111-196 (114-115).

[194] P. Tillich, *Systematic Theology, Vol. I*, p.212; P. Tillich, "Psychoanalyse und Religi-on. Zum gleichnamigen Buch von Erich Fromm", in *Gesammelte Werke, Band XII*, Evangelisches Verlag, Stuttgart, 1971, pp.333-336.

In Freud's view the drives were the mental representatives of bodily urges and needs.

In Tillich's theology we must make a "jump" from the drives towards a theological concept, the true centre of man, the *Imago Dei* or what is left of it. In other words, Tillich ignores the biological element in Freudian psychoanalysis. The correlation between Freud's drives and the concepts of sin and estrangement implies an abstraction of Freudian theory. The crucial point here is that Tillich could only see human nature in an estranged relation to its essence or ultimate ground, whereas Freud primarily related the basic psychic structures and mechanisms to the realm of the physical.

As a consequence the awareness of finitude and identity are differently valued. In Freud's view our identity, that is to say, the specific finite person that "I am", is primarily based on bodily experiences, physical unity in narcissism, identification with oneself and others, and from thereon being able to say "this is who I am". The finitude given with identity is not only a disturbing awareness; on the contrary, it can give the enjoyment of being someone unique. In other words, finitude does not necessarily result in an anxious longing, in an ultimate concern about being, but is a source for enjoyment. Whereas Tillich can only regard this enjoyment as concupiscence or hubris, in Freud's view the self-affirmation of being a finite person with its own identity is no reason for "ultimate concern" at all. Freudian psychoanalysis confronts with tragic human nature, and avoids a "jump" into an illusionary world.

Tillich's reading of Freud is moulded by his theological ideas of sin and estrangement from being, and his project of pointing out the correlations between drive and sin. There is another point to be noticed: Tillich's reinterpreting of psychoanalysis from an ontological point of view. This is for example the case when he defines neurosis (as the way of avoiding non-being by avoiding being) from his ontological position, or when he argues that the pleasure principle is only valid in "sick" life.[195]

The effect of reading Freud from a theological perspective and reinterpreting his theories ontologically, is that Freudian psychoanalysis loses its critical potential like a wasp that has lost his sting. Tillich's partition of realms enables him to use psychoanalysis as a science reflecting on human nature, but obstructs a critical interference with theology itself. Christian Henning has called this a "tendency towards hierarchization"[196]: in theology the essential is what ultimately concerns man, whereas other sciences should restrict themselves to the realm of the existential; in pastoral care the salvation of every man (given estranged existence) is at stake, whereas psychotherapy is confined to the realm of the pathological ill without being able to "cure" the fundamental (onto-

---

[195] P. Tillich, *Systematic Theology, Vol. III*, p.56.
[196] Chr. Henning, "Gescheiterte Beziehung?", p.95.

logical) structures of human being.[197] In other words, psychoanalytic therapy can only cure the pathological symptoms of estrangement. (The difference between Tillich and Thurneysen is not as big as we might have thought.)

Despite the correlations between psychoanalysis and theology, psychoanalysis' realm is strictly confined to the existential, more precisely to the realm of the analysis of pathologies and the development of therapeutic methods. Hence, it seems that faith as the non-pathological relation between man and the Ultimate is not a subject in psychoanalysis. Exactly here the sting is lost: psychoanalysis is useful for theology, but it seems it cannot critically question theology, for example by asking "what is the psychological content and meaning of Tillich's "jump" from existence or essence, or from anxiety to courage?" Neither can it question the status of theological thought itself: on the level of ontological constructs psychic motives are not involved.

2.8 Comparison and preliminary conclusion

Pfister, Beth and Tillich: it is important to notice that engagement with Freud was mainly by theologians who were deeply influenced by Schleiermacher, theologians whose writings evolve around the essence of religion, its subjective content (feeling, intuition, experience, existence), and the methods to obtain knowledge of it. Their theological standpoints serve as the framework for the reception of psychoanalytic theory and method. But we should add "to a certain extent".

For, in the writings of Pfister the analysis of true and healthy religion is outside the objectives of psychoanalysis. Psychoanalysis is basically a method to liberate neurotics from their inhibitions. True religion is not a subject of psychoanalysis. In fact the elevation of the libido means that true religion is elevated above the field of psychoanalytic practice, and above possible critique or deconstruction.

In Beth's writings there is not a true religion elevated above the psychoanalytic realm: it is underlying it. Here, Freud's psychoanalysis did not dig deep enough; he stuck too much to analysis of the conflicts between the unconscious and the conscious-sensory. Underlying the complexes he described, are deeper complexes, deeper wishes, and eventually the harmonic world of primitive mentality, intuition and totality.

---

[197] *Die existentiellen Strukturen des menschlichen Daseins können auch mit noch so vollkommenen Techniken nicht geheilt werden. Hier kann nur Erlösung helfen. Natürlich kann auch der Psychotherapeut, geradeso wie jeder Freund, wie Vater und Mutter oder ein Kind, zum Werkzeug der Erlösung werden. Aber das geschieht dann noch nicht in seiner Eigenschaft als Psychotherapeut mit Hilfe seiner Heilkunst, denn diese Erlösung erfordert die Heilung des Zentrums der Person.* P. Tillich, "Die theologische Bedeutung von Psychoanalyse und Existentialismus", p.313.

In Tillich's writings, Freud did dig deep enough, so deep that he redis-covered the meaning of sin, and yet not deep enough to go beyond the realm of existence. Underlying and "beyond" human existence is an ultimate ground that is man's ultimate concern. Freud shows us, to put it in terms of the Heidelberg Catechism, our "misery", but "salvation" is beyond his reach.

Thus, in the writings of Pfister, Beth and Tillich, we find a similar structure: psychoanalysis is a method to grasp the essence of religion or at least points in its direction, but the essence of religion itself lies beyond the realm of psychoanalysis. The only ones who could avoid this "paradox" were dialectic theologians who simply ignored psychoanalysis or eventually used it as an aux-iliary science in pastoral care.

In the writings of Pfister and Beth Freud's theories on aggression and the sense of guilt in religion were neglected for basically a simple reason: ag-gression and sense of guilt did not belong to the essence of religion. The theo-logical conviction that the essence of religion is a harmonious essence is deci-sive here. This is clear in their readings of *Totem and Taboo*. In Pfister's writings its absence is striking until finally it is taken up in his account of the historic evolution of anxiety and sublimation in Judeo-Christian religion. The central thesis of *Totem and Taboo* does not fit in the frame.

In Beth's text on religion and magic the thesis of the totem meal is eas-ily put aside as a fable, and with it Freud's thesis of aggression, sense of guilt and commemoration, in order to push forward to the true historic essence of re-ligion. Although it is never expressed explicitly, it is clear that Freud's theories of aggression, conflict and the sense of guilt in religion were basically unac-ceptable for theologians who believed in the harmony of man, religion and real-ity.

Comparing Beth and Tillich we have seen the importance of the concept of participation in their writings. In the next chapter we will see the importance of this concept in relation to the reception of Freud's writings in the Nether-lands. Han Fortmann (see next chapter) has argued that the concept of participa-tion in Tillich's theology strongly resembles Lévy-Bruhl's concept of mystic participation in primitive life.[198] Indeed, when Tillich writes that the individual participates in his world like a "leaf participates in the natural structures and forces which act upon it and which are acted upon by it" we might be tempted to identify Tillich's participation with mystic participation.

But we should be careful here. Tillich regards participation as underly-ing "the category of relation as a basic ontological element". In other words, the concept is not used to characterize primitive mentality, but functions as an onto-logical concept that "guarantees the unity of a disrupted world and makes a uni-

---

[198] H.M.M. Fortmann, *Als ziende de Onzienlijke. Een cultuurpsychologische studie over de religieuze waarneming en de zogenaamde religieuze projectie, deel I, 1. Freud, Marx, Jung-referaat, 2. Kritiek op de grondbegrippen*, Uitgeverij Gooi en Sticht, Hil-versum, 1981, p.536.

versal system of relations possible", including – and this is essential – the relation between a finite existing person and the God who "is".[199] Unlike Lévy-
Bruhl, and Beth for that matter, Tillich is not interested in presenting an anthropology based on primitive man's perception of the world, but in retranslating
Christian concepts in philosophical (ontological) concepts. Ultimately the concept of participation indicates an individual fulfilment, an "essentialization" or
identification with Divine or Eternal Life.[200]

Nevertheless, Fortmann has a point, an important point for it shows
similarities between Beth, Tillich and – as we will see – Fortmann himself: the
theological search for an underlying "essence" or "participation", an "inner-
worldly-transcendence", an ultimate ground of ultimate concern or deepest wish
beyond all wishes, outside the realm and reach of a critical discipline focusing
on inner psychic motives and structures that underlie religious representations.
Moreover these motives and structures indicated struggle and conflict as expressed in Freud's thought on the drives, the inevitability of the sense of guilt or
mental helplessness. In Freudian anthropology man is mentally maladjusted to
live harmoniously in his environment.

Freud analysed the modern subject in the modern world. Theologians
ask the question what lies beyond and underneath this modern subject and this
world, an essence of religion that is endangered by modern enlightened thought
and needs to be "saved". In doing so – and certainly when they call upon
Schleiermacher – what binds them is a romantic vision of religion. Romantic it
is, in the sense that religion is regarded as some sort of intuitive participation in
a meaningful coherence or totality that is lost sight of in the development of
modernity and nostalgically longed for.

---

[199] P. Tillich, *Systematic Theology, Vol. I*, p.177. In an article of 1955 Tillich elaborates
on the concept of participation. He argues that the concept plays an important role in
phenomenology, but on the level of a subject-object dichotomy and the reflection on
understanding an object. According to Tillich "participation precedes objectivation",
that is, the encounter between oneself and others precedes the separation of subject and
object. For example: an infant experiences friendliness or hate in an encounter before he
can recognize the participant in the encounter as his father or mother. Hence, participation "underlies the subject-object structure of finitude". P. Tillich, "Participation and
Knowledge", in *Main Works, Vol. 1: Philosophical Writings*, G. Wenz (ed.), De
Gruyter, New York/Berlin, 1989, pp.382-389.
[200] P. Tillich, *Systematic Theology, Vol. III*, pp.406ff.

3   Phenomenology of religion and the reception of Freud

3.1 Introduction

In this chapter we deal with Freud's reception in the Netherlands, both its early prelude and actual reception from the 1930s onwards, notably in the context of an interest in psychology in the phenomenology of religion. We will focus on the so called "projection debate" in the1950s and 1960s that was of profound influence in the interpretation of Freudian psychoanalysis and its reception in Dutch psychology of religion, pastoral theology and mental health up until current discussions on giving meaning (*zingeving*).

I will present this reception as a continuing intellectual line of debate and thought in which early points of view (such as Rümke's ideas on man as *homo religiosus* and Van der Leeuw's thoughts on the totality of meaning and mystic participation) became and still remain important issues. The projection debate will be crucial here as it eventually leads to a reading of Freud as a projection theorist, a rejection of his "theories" of religious projection, and a later revaluation of the projection mechanism in *zingeving*, but without a return to or reappraisal of Freudian psychoanalysis.

In these developments the topic of the sense of guilt as the dominant issue in Freudian thought on religion though not absent is of minor importance. Hence, in this chapter we will see how important elements in Freudian thought were not recognised. In the final chapter of my study I will show in what way the forgotten Freudian issue of sense of guilt might be of importance in current debates in the psychology of religion, pastoral theology and mental health on *zingeving*.

Unlike the developments in German theology interest in psychology and psychoanalysis in Dutch theology did not primarily emerge in liberal theology, but in the orthodox environment of reformed (*gereformeerde*) dogmatics. In the last quarter of the nineteenth century a strong orthodox movement in the Reformed church closely related with a political movement provoked a schism. It is in these orthodox circles that the importance of psychoanalysis was first noticed.

In 1884 the *Vereeniging tot Christelijke Verzorging van Geestes- en Zenuwzieken in Nederland* [Association for Christian Care of Mentally Ill and Neurotics in the Netherlands] was founded.[1] This association in turn founded several institutions and strived for its own chair in psychiatry at the newly es-

---

[1] On this Association see J.M.W. Binneveld, "De ontwikkeling van de institutionele zorg voor krankzinnigen in Nederland in de 19de eeuw", in *Een psychiatrisch verleden. Uit de geschiedenis van de psychiatrie*, J.M.W. Binneveld et al. (eds.), Uitgeverij Ambo, Baarn, 1982, pp.94-119.

tablished Free University, with the aim of developing a Christian (*gerefor-meerde*) counterpart to medical materialism in psychiatry.

In 1907 Leendert Bouman (1869-1936) became the professor in psychiatry that had been sought.[2] Bouman was not a theologian but a psychiatrist, who was willing to fit the Christian profile of the chair, albeit with reservations as he was sceptical about the possibilities of a Christian psychology or psychiatry. Whereas others in the Association saw, for example, degeneration as a synonym for original sin, or regarded the bible as a fitting instrument for cure[3], Bouman believed that theological terminology could not easily be translated into psychological terms, or vice versa. Albeit with hesitation because of its mechanistic and deterministic view of the human psyche, he showed an early interest in psychoanalysis as an alternative for a "psychology without a soul".[4] In several articles he defended psychoanalysis[5], and hence, Pfister mentioned him as an example of the positive international responses to psychoanalysis.[6] By that time however he had become much more interested in the phenomenological psychology of Karl Jaspers.

Bouman's most important student and his later successor was the psychiatrist Henricus Cornelis Rümke (1893-1967). Rümke was one of the first to discuss psychoanalysis and religion. A positive attitude towards religion is the starting point in his 1939 *Karakter en aanleg in verband met het ongeloof* [Character and Temperament in Relation to Unbelief] in which he opposes Freud's negative opinion of religion.[7] Rümke argues that unbelief is a developmental disorder.[8] Normally there would be a development of trust in life in which religion plays a natural role: religion is essentially "being a meaningful

---

[2] I. Bulhof, "Psychoanalysis in the Netherlands", in *Comparative Studies in Society and History* 24 (1982), pp.572-588; I. Bulhof, *Freud en Nederland. De interpretatie en invloed van zijn ideeën*, Uitgeverij Ambo, Baarn, 1983, pp.144-164; J.A. van Belzen, "Leendert Bouman (1869-1936) en de gereformeerde psychiatrie", in *Maandblad voor de geestelijke volksgezondheid* 43 (1988), pp.817-836.

[3] Lindeboom believed that the bible was full of knowledge about body and soul, sickness and cure. Reading the bible was like "being guided through the halls of an immense hospital". Idem, p.820.

[4] Idem, p.821.

[5] For example L. Bouman, "De Psycho-Analyse van Freud", in *Psychiatrische en Neurologische Bladen* 16 (1912), pp.346-363. In this article Bouman presents an outline of Freudian psychoanalysis focusing on clinical perspectives and the dream theory. There are no references to Freud's writings on culture and religion.

[6] O. Pfister, *Zum Kampf um die Psychoanalyse*, p.6.

[7] H.C Rümke, *Karakter en aanleg in verband met het ongeloof*, Uitgeverij Ten Have, Amsterdam, 1939. On the text see J.A. van Belzen, *Rümke, religie en godsdienstpsychologie. Achtergronden en vooronderstellingen*, Uitgeverij Kok, Kampen, 1991; J.A. van Belzen, *Psychologie en het raadsel van de religie. Beschouwingen bij een eeuw godsdienstpsychologie in Nederland*, Boom, Amsterdam, 2007, pp.151-171.

[8] H.C. Rümke, *Karakter en aanleg*, pp.7ff.

part of totality", a totality that serves as the "ultimate ground" and as a life-directive that "demands obedience and recognition of guilt".[9]

From this starting point in which man is regarded to be *homo religiosus* Freud is criticized.[10] According to Rümke, Freud had stated that God is the "projection" of a life-long longing for care and solidarity that was experienced in earliest childhood.[11] (The sense of guilt appears when and where this solidarity is – inevitably – disturbed.) However, true belief should be distinguished from this infantile, neurotic belief, characterized by a fixation on parental images.[12] The God-father-idea is not the projection of the child-father-relationship, but *vice versa*; the child knows of a child-father-relationship through an ideal-typical relation to God.[13] In other words, religion originates from an "idea", a primal belief that in later life can take the distorted form of neurotic belief.[14] Freud only deserves credit for having thoroughly depicted these neurotic forms.[15]

Rümke is the only connecting figure between the earliest interest in psychoanalysis in the context of a theological position and further developments. Before the Second World War there was hardly any interest on the part of theologians in Freudian psychoanalysis, yet the engagement with Freud by theology after the war was marked by earlier developments. Unlike developments in German theology psychoanalysis was not first recognised in practical and pastoral theology – the writings of Pfister were hardly known in the Netherlands – but in the phenomenology of religion, in the writings of students of Gerardus van der Leeuw (1890-1950), professor in the history of religions at the theological faculty in Groningen.

---

[9] Idem, p.13.

[10] Idem, pp.43ff.

[11] *God is de projectie van het immer levend verlangen naar deze geborgenheid.* Idem, p.44. Clearly, this is a specific interpretation of *The Future of an Illusion*: in this text Freud never stated as such that religion is a projection of a longing for care. In Rümke's text projection is used to indicate that man projects the image of the real father on God in such a way that the image of God is pictured after the image of the father. When in later life these "paintings" are removed, the "real" unknown God (the totally Other) comes to the surface (the God that had always been there as primal ground for "primal faith"). Idem, pp.50-51.

[12] In fixation (or identification) as a mechanism in the formation of neurosis we see a clear influence of Jungian psychoanalysis. Van Belzen has shown that Rümke was particularly influenced by Alphonse Maeder, psychiatrist in Zurich and former assistant of Jung. J.A. van Belzen, *Rümke, religie en godsdienstpsychologie*, pp.45-47, 143-152.

[13] H.C. Rümke, *Karakter en aanleg*, p.48.

[14] Idem, pp.48-51.

[15] *Freud beschrijft feitelijk onecht geloof. (...) Telkens zal blijken dat vele van de door Freud waargenomen psychologische verhoudingen het geloof verhinderden in plaats van geloof te doen ontstaan. Zoo helpt ons Freud bij het vinden van de determinerende factoren van "het ongeloof".* Idem, p.52.

Van der Leeuw stood in a Dutch tradition of phenomenological approaches to the study of the history of religion.[16] Concerning his interest in psychology two important lines can be detected.

In the first place there is the influence of the writings of Lévy-Bruhl on primitive mentality.[17] In several writings Van der Leeuw elaborated on this concept[18], and even when Lévy-Bruhl in his later writings partially seemed to revise his theories Van der Leeuw still uncritically accepted them.[19] Primitive mentality was in the first place a mentality, "a structure of our mind"[20], characterized both by a way of thinking that was pre-logical and by a mystic participation in which the world was perceived as a "continuum", a harmonious totality. In Van der Leeuw's interpretation primitive mentality is – much stronger than in Lévy-Bruhl's writings – a general anthropological structure for primitives as well as modern man. According to Van der Leeuw mystic participation was the essence of primitive as of modern religion. It is the "unity of subject and object, God and man, the primal identity that is so often desired as ultimate identity".[21] The aim of the phenomenology of religion should be to understand this essential structure of religion (through the analysis of empirical data), not only to further develop the science of religion, but also as a critical theory of modern secularized society detached from its primitive nature as *homo religiosus*.[22] As in Beth's *Religion and Magic* Lévy-Bruhl's theories serve as an alternative to an

---

[16] G.A. James, *Interpreting Religion. The Phenomenological Approaches of Daniël Chantepie de la Saussaye, W. Brede Kristensen, and Gerardus van der Leeuw*, The Catholic University of America Press, Washington, 1995; A.F. Molendijk, *The Emergence of the Science of Religion in the Netherlands*, Brill, Leiden/Boston, 2005, pp.41ff.

[17] W. Hofstee, *Goden en mensen. De godsdienstwetenschap van Gerardus van der Leeuw*, Uitgeverij Kok, Kampen, 1997, p.240.

[18] G. van der Leeuw, *La structure de la mentalité primitive*, Alcan, Paris, 1928; G. van der Leeuw, *De primitieve mensch en de religie*, Uitgeverij Wolters, Groningen/Batavia, 1937, chapter 3. See also H. Kippenberg, *Die Entdeckung der Religionsgeschichte. Religionswissenschaft und Moderne*, Beck Verlag, Munich, 1997, pp.255-258.

[19] L. Leertouwer, "Primitive Religion in Dutch Religious Studies", in *Numen. International Review for the History of Religion* 38 (1991), pp.198-213 (203-204, 210); W. Hofstee, *Goden en mensen*, pp.207-237.

[20] G. van der Leeuw, *La structure de la mentalité primitive*, p.27. Van der Leeuw mentions several elements in the theory on primitive mentality that resemble psychological phenomena. Firstly, there is the dominant presence of affections and imagination in the perception of reality. Secondly, this mentality was collective, based on mutual sympathy, i.e. on identification. Thirdly, certain features of primitive mentality, such as the belief in the travelling soul or in several souls in one person, showed similarities to psychiatric phenomena such as schizophrenia. And lastly, primitive thinking in general showed similarities with dreaming.

[21] G. van der Leeuw, *De primitieve mensch en de religie*, p.171.

[22] W. Hofstee, *Goden en mensen*, pp.233-234.

"evolutionistic" causal explanation of religion (as for example presented in the writings of Tylor and Frazer).

In the second place, there is the hermeneutical tradition that starts with Schleiermacher, and that was further developed and deepened by Wilhelm Dilthey and further elaborated upon by scholars such as Karl Jaspers[23] and Ludwig Binswanger[24]. Their ideas on hermeneutics as empathetic understanding (*einfühlend Verstehen*) deeply influenced Van der Leeuw's phenomenological method of *Nacherleben* and *Einfühlung*.[25] The most important precondition for this empathic understanding was, as Van der Leeuw had already put forward in his inaugural lecture in 1918, that all religions "originate from the same functioning of the human mind" and that they can be studied as "a psychological unity".[26] Hence, empathetic understanding was the psychological method necessary for the understanding of primitive mentality and participation. This psychological method[27] in his phenomenology is not a fixed scientific method – it is itself in constant further development into a deeper understanding of both object and subject. This process Van der Leeuw calls "the broadening of the ego"[28] –

---

[23] Jaspers had argued that psychology should be psychology of understanding and he had used the concept of empathetic understanding to indicate the method for understanding an object in its coherence. In his view psychoanalysis was also a psychology of understanding, but it had made the mistake of going beyond the reasonable limits of understanding, in trying to explain human nature by reducing it to general structures with the character of a myth. K. Jaspers, *Allgemeine Psychopathologie*, Springer Verlag, Berlin/Göttingen/Heidelberg, 1959 (1913), p.253, pp.261ff, pp.450ff.

[24] Binswanger was a colleague of Jung, but more interested in Freud's psychoanalyis than in Jung's. In his earlier writings, notably in his 1922 *Einführung in die Probleme der allgemeinen Psychologie* he tried to develop a phenomenological psychology along the lines of Dilthey in which also elements of psychoanalysis could be taken up. Although he expressed his admiration for Freud's psychoanalysis, he also criticized its shortcomings: psychoanalysis was too much focused on explaining the structures of the psyche with a speculative theory of unconscious drives, whereas psychology should be aimed at understanding the psyche (or subjectivity) in its coherence and unity of experiences. L. Binswanger, *Einführung in die Probleme der allgemeinen Psychologie*, Springer Verlag, Berlin, 1922.

[25] See G. van der Leeuw, "Über einige neuere Ergebnisse der psychologischen Forschung und ihre Anwendungen auf die Geschichte, insonderheit die Religionsgeschichte", in *Studi e materiali di storia delle religioni* 2 (1926), pp.1-43 (4-8).

[26] G. van der Leeuw, *Plaats en taak van de godsdienstgeschiedenis in de theologische wetenschap*, Uitgeverij Wolters, Groningen, 1918, p.5.

[27] G. van der Leeuw, "Strukturpsychologie und Theologie", in *Zeitschrift für Theologie und Kirche* 9 (1928), pp.321-349; G. van der Leeuw, "Über einige neuere Ergebnisse der psychologischen Forschung und ihre Anwendungen auf die Geschichte"; G. van der Leeuw, *Phänomenologie der Religion*, Mohr Siebeck Verlag, Tübingen, 1933, Epilogemena.

[28] G. van der Leeuw, "Über einige neuere Ergebnisse der psychologischen Forschung", pp.25-26.

the more one understands oneself, the more the art of understanding can be further developed. To indicate there is a limit to empathetic understanding, Van der Leeuw speaks of an *epoche* – the phenomenologist experiences and understands structures of meaning, coherences of meaning, but does not pretend to have an ultimate understanding of reality or the truth.[29] However clear this limit might seem, the broadening of the ego not only brings a better understanding of phenomena, but also opens up a subject for the revelation of truth: beyond the understandable (for the phenomenologist) there is a last "totality of meaning" in which all human understanding is taken up in a "being understood by God".[30] Phenomenology of religion was thus ultimately a person-bound discipline circling around the inner contact of the researcher and religious phenomena. It was not about "objective" observation or scientific explanation, but about a subjective structuring of phenomena in order to participate in a religious totality of meaning.

3.2 The first study of Freud and religion

Van der Leeuw's interest in psychology as a method of understanding and as reflection on primitive mentality is clear.[31] Jaspers and Binswanger had argued that Freud had made important contributions to the field of a psychology of understanding. These two factors were the main premises for an engagement with Freud's reception by theology in the Netherlands, not by Van der Leeuw himself, but by his students. In 1933 Coenraad Liebrecht Tuinstra (1901-1993) obtained his doctorate with a dissertation on the symbol in psychoanalysis.[32]

The aim of his dissertation was to investigate the meaning and value of psychoanalytic studies of symbols for theology. According to Tuinstra, psychoanalysis is a psychology that "attempts to understand the hidden causes of uncomprehended phenomena".[33] Phenomena that seem meaningless and deviant in reality and that have the form of a symptom, can be understood in their own

---

[29] G. van der Leeuw, *Phänomenologie der Religion*, p.640.

[30] In this theological position and conviction we find the deepest source of Van der Leeuw's notion of primitive mentality. L. Leertouwer, "Primitive Religion in Dutch Religious Studies", p.204.

[31] In an international context Van der Leeuw could be considered a psychologist of religion. In a letter (12-12-1928), for example, Karl Beth asks whether Van der Leeuw would like to consider becoming a member of the editorial board of *Zeitschrift für Religionspsychologie* together with scholars like Jung and Wobbermin. Also in other letters from Beth to Van der Leeuw, the latter is considered a scholar in the psychology of religion contributing to the field with articles and lectures. *Brieven van Karl Beth aan Gerardus van der Leeuw. 1921-1938*, University Library Groningen, unpublished.

[32] C.L. Tuinstra, *Het symbool in de psychoanalyse. Beschrijving en theologische critiek*, H.J. Paris, Amsterdam, 1933.

[33] *Het psychoanalytisch onderzoek poogt de verborgen oorzaken van onbegrepen verschijnselen te verstaan.* Idem, p.21.

hidden unconscious reality, for "behind the uncomprehended phenomena lies a reality" in which the phenomenon is a part of an "organic connection". The aim of psychoanalysis is to understand this unconscious reality behind the symptom, to give the phenomenon its place in that reality, thus reducing the tension between the two "realities".[34] In this unconscious reality the phenomenon is not a symptom anymore, but a symbol, i.e. a meaningful sign of the libido.[35]

To understand what Tuinstra is describing here, we should first notice the influence of Van der Leeuw and Lévy-Bruhl on the notion of primitive mentality: the idea of an organic world or totality that lies hidden in man. This is combined with an interpretation of psychoanalytic theory and method in which Tuinstra reads Freud through Jung. Especially concerning the unconscious, the libido and symbolization he follows a Jungian line of thought.[36] The most important feature of this combination of theories is the idea that there is an unconscious reality in man that in its origin lies "beyond the historic".[37]

An important influence on Tuinstra is also Ernst Cassirers *Philosophie der symbolischen Formen* [Philosophy of Symbolic Forms], 1923-1929.[38] In this study Cassirer had argued that thought and knowledge are not based on immediate and clear data that can be observed in and derived from reality, but on mediation through symbolic forms.[39] According to Cassirer, historically, mythical thinking lies at the origin of symbolic forms.[40] The most elementary form of mythical thinking could be found in totemism, in the historic stage of development that was characterized by a sense of communion.[41] In the historic development from mythological thinking to religion, the mediative character of symbolic forms is the key to understand this evolution: in cults, sacrifice, prayer, etc, the purpose is a sense of community, a being united with God.[42] We

---

[34] Idem, pp.24-25.

[35] Idem, pp.51-52.

[36] Idem, pp.26-74. Concerning symbolization Tuinstra focuses on *Transformations and Symbolisms of the Libido* where Jung had argued that in the process of the desexualization of the libido man has a natural inclination towards finding symbolic analogies for this libido, analogies that are produced by fantasy. Here lies not only the origin of myth and religion, but also of a broadening of conscience, which lead to all kinds of discoveries (also technical) in the evolution of mankind.

[37] Idem, p.13.

[38] Idem, p.6ff., pp.134ff.,

[39] E. Cassirer, *Philosophie der symbolischen Formen. Erster Teil. Der Sprache, Gesammelte Werke 11*, C. Rosenkranz (ed.), Meiner Verlag, Hamburg, 2001, p.4. The aim of his study was to present a systematic outline of different symbolic forms in order to gain insight into the way human understanding functions. Idem, pp.16-17.

[40] E. Cassirer, *Philosophie der symbolischen Formen. Zweiter Teil. Das mythische Denken, Gesammelte Werke 12*, C. Rosenkranz (ed.), Meiner Verlag, Hamburg, 2002, Vorwort.

[41] Idem, pp.205ff.

[42] Idem, p.259.

will not go into further detail here. For us it is important to notice that Tuinstra read Cassirer's ideas on mythological thinking and totemism as being in concordance with Van der Leeuw, Lévy-Bruhl and psychoanalytic theory (Jung).[43]

This theoretical framework determines Tuinstra's reading and evaluation of Freud's *Totem and Taboo*. He gives a lengthy description of this text focusing on the reconstruction of the origin of religion, but without elaborating on its meaning for Christianity.[44] In his evaluation of the text several possible points of critique are discussed. One is the Oedipus complex. According to Tuinstra, Freud's Oedipus complex was an important discovery, because it shows important psychic structures, the meaning of the relation between child and parents. The emphasis here is on structure, the child-parent relation is a symbolic form.[45]

Another point of discussion is the identity of the totem as father. Tuinstra argues that in primitive mythological thinking the "family" is often the symbolic form that expresses the relationship with the totality of nature. The problem with *Totem and Taboo* is that Freud considers these family relations to be real historic relations. It would have been better, had he spoken of "images" of family members.[46] The next point of discussion is the totem meal. Tuinstra defends Freud's interpretation of the totem meal as far as it is similar to the interpretation of Cassirer: it is about a communion with the father-god and it is the origin of sacrifice.

The fundamental problem in these points of discussion is again the real historic event. Tuinstra's critique is mainly pointed at this thesis. As to the sense of guilt, a general critique applies: it can only be as meaningful as Freud suggests when we take the remorse of the sons for real.[47] But this should not be done. Thus Tuinstra does not take up Freud's ideas on the sense of guilt as a dominant unconscious motive in religion, but simply ignores the issue, turning to Jungian thought on the importance of innate structures and their symbolic expressions.

In his description of *Totem and Taboo*, Tuinstra did not mention Freud's ideas on the primitive core of Christianity. In the final chapter of his

---

[43] Cassirer was influenced by Lévy-Bruhl, but also the connection with Freud's *Totem and Taboo* could be made through Cassirer: he provides an interpretation of the totem meal in which the meal functions as a medium for the community of the clan with its totem-god, which is, in Cassirer's version, essentially the primal father. Idem, p.267.

[44] C.L. Tuinstra, *Het symbool in de psychoanalyse*, pp.75-90.

[45] Idem, pp.113-114.

[46] Idem, pp.115-117. The critique of Freud's reconstruction of primal historic events is justified and is in fact in congruence with general criticism of the text. The fact that Freud returned to the "real events" of the seduction theory instead of emphasizing the role of fantasy (the death-wish against the father), is highly problematic and can, in my opinion, only be understood as an attempt to formulate a clear alternative for Jung.

[47] Idem, p.119.

dissertation we learn why. Here Tuinstra is no longer the phenomenologist or psychologist describing and analysing psychoanalysis, but – "without warning"[48] – a theologian. The critique of psychoanalysis is suddenly much sharper, focusing not only on *Totem and Taboo* and *The Future of an Illusion*, but especially also on Reik's writings on Christian dogma. In Freudian psychoanalysis Christianity is regarded an obsessional neurosis and wish illusion, says Tuinstra.[49] The main underlying problem is that Freud regarded Christianity as comparable to other religions and mythologies. It was just "a system next to other systems", which undermined the truth claims of Christianity.[50]

Tuinstra now states that Christianity is a religion of revelation which gives it a unique character. The message is obvious: the psychoanalytic critique of religions does not touch the essence of Christianity. Only to a certain extent is Christianity comparable to other religions: in the Gospel we may find symbolic forms that are comparable to symbolic forms in other religions. In these forms we meet man in his longing for God. But whereas in myths and in primitive religions the same never ending courses of nature (of life and death; of longing for God) are symbolically expressed without being redeemed, in Christianity Jesus Christ is a person with the character of a symbol functioning as a mediator between world and God. It is this revelation that makes Christianity incomparable.

After having compared the function of the symbol in psychoanalysis and mythology, and after having argued that Freud's interpretation of primitive religion can be defended, the aim of the final chapter is to make a clear distinction between the realm of psychoanalysis and mythology on the one hand, and Christianity on the other. Myth is "pious fraud" presenting an "illusionary reality".[51] In short, Tuinstra read *Totem and Taboo* on primitive religion and mythology as a psychologist/phenomenologist – descriptive with a careful positive evaluation: for the theologian there was no danger in a psychoanalytic interpretation of primitive religion when Christianity was a religion of a different and unique order.

3.3 Fokke Sierksma and the turn to psychoanalysis

Fokke Sierksma (1917-1977) was one of the most talented of Van der Leeuw's students. In 1950 he obtained his doctorate with a dissertation called *Phaenomenologie der religie en complexe psychologie* [Phenomenology of Re-

---

[48] Sierksma sharply criticizes Tuinstra for this change of perspective from psychology to theology "without warning", suddenly using revelation as a theological argument against psychoanalysis. F. Sierksma, *Freud, Jung en de religie*, Uitgeverij Van Gorcum, Assen, 1951, pp.154-155.

[49] C.L. Tuinstra, *Het symbool in de psychoanalyse*, pp.185-192.

[50] Idem, pp.206-207.

[51] Idem, p.230.

ligion and Complex Psychology] which was published under the title *Freud, Jung en de religie* [Freud, Jung and Religion] a year later. Sierksma's starting point is that the phenomenology of religion ought to establish contact with psychoanalysis. The reason for a more profound interest of phenomenologists in psychology lies in the fact that the phenomenological method of empathic understanding calls for a profound reflection on the nature of man, and thus tends towards a philosophical anthropology.[52] Psychology's own development originates from philosophical reflections on the soul, "loosing the soul" in empirical formalistic research and than rediscovering the soul in the psychology of Jaspers and in psychoanalysis. Jung especially, Sierksma argues, has been able to use a phenomenological method in order to bring together psychic phenomena in a coherent meaningful structure.[53] So here we find two disciplines that share the same method and the same objective: a theory of the human subject.

Before presenting an introduction in the "phenomenology" of Jung Sierksma dedicates a chapter to Freud. Because Freud's "causal-mechanic" psychology is aimed more at explaining than understanding it seems not very "useful" for phenomenologists. For them reductionism explains nothing, "it explains away".[54] The problem with Freud's reductionism is not the method of explaining itself, but the fact that he studied man "between bios and psyche" arguing that drives are fundamental and that "everything that is layered above the level of the drives" is an "epiphenomenon". Here the phenomenologist has to conclude that the difference between the two phenomena of bios and psyche simply does not allow a theory of the singular reality of the drives, and that a theory of the drives and its "epiphenomena" ignores the autonomy of different layers of the psyche.[55] In short, Freudian psychoanalysis is a simplifying theory neglecting the stratifications of the psyche and the diversity of phenomena.

In this comparison between phenomenology and psychoanalysis Sierksma opposes Freudian psychoanalytic reductionism to a phenomenology and psychology that acknowledge primitive mentality. Of course he acknowledges that both Jung and Freud have shown that modern man "lives on a primitive basis".[56] The problem with the Freudian concept of the primitive is "the cult of the object".[57] Freud's primitivism is nothing else but the association of primary drives that are aimed at objects in the outside world and the first "dis-

---

[52] F. Sierksma, *Freud, Jung en de religie*, p.15.

[53] Idem, pp.21ff. Jung's depth psychology is thus presented as an alternative basis in religious studies, instead of Jasper's empathic understanding as a method that can only understand and not explain. J. van Iersel, *Wetenschap als eigenbelang. Godsdienstwetenschap en dieptepsychologie in het werk van dr. F. Sierksma (1917-1977)*, Uitgeverij Dora, Rosmalen, 1991, p.38.

[54] F. Sierksma, *Freud, Jung en de religie*, p.97.

[55] Idem, pp.104-105, pp.163-164.

[56] Idem, p.165.

[57] Idem, p.169.

torted" Oedipal conceptions of love objects, father and mother. This cult of the object could allegedly even explain primitive man's mentality and society.

Opposing this notion in Freud's thought Sierksma elaborates on primitive mentality as described by Van der Leeuw: in primitive man there is a constant transgression between inner and outside world. Prohibitions are formed without the influence of frustrating outside objects: the taboo is an inner prohibition, a "sacrifice" made with the aim of transforming something natural into something supernatural. Modern man, modern mentality, on the contrary, is characterized by a struggle for life, a constant anticipating of and reacting to objects from the outside that are either threatening or providing/nourishing. In other words, Freudian psychoanalysis had tried to analyse and explain primitive mind by means of a modern theory characterized by modern mentality.

For Sierksma it is clear that Freud thus built a pessimistic anthropology marked by a deep a sense of the distorted human soul. This pessimism and the "cult of the object" made him ignore primitive mentality, the original, possible and future completeness of man, just like he had explicitly rejected oceanic feelings as a source of religion. As to the sense of guilt the consequences are clear: it is an element of Freud's reductionism and the application of a modern theory of the struggle for life onto primitive mentality.

In the final chapter of his dissertation Sierksma elaborates on the relation between Jungian psychology and phenomenology arguing that Van der Leeuw's phenomenogical method of empathetic understanding and broadening of the ego points in the same direction as Jung's integration and individuation process, viz: the realization of the self.[58] Ultimately this means a restoration of primitive mentality in order to bridge the gaps of modernity: between subject and object, conscious and unconscious, ratio and belief, in order to attain human completeness. Freud was convinced of the deep ruptures in human life and in his thought these gaps and ruptures are made absolute.[59] Instead Sierksma argues that this conclusion of the incompleteness of man is the point where a descriptive anthropology should evolve into what he names a "projectional anthropology"[60], a design of a future ideal for man.

Despite the fact however that primitive mentality is a key issue in this dissertation it is clear that Sierksma is in search of a phenomenological method that not only focuses on understanding, but also on explanation. Jung is called upon as an alternative to Lévy-Bruhl and Jaspers.[61] In the background there is a specific objective: that the phenomenology of religion should emancipate itself from theology. Sierksma not only pleads for a distancing from Barthian theol-

[58] Idem, pp.214ff.
[59] Idem, pp.206-207.
[60] Sierksma speaks of *ontwerpende antropologie* which is translated by himself in the English summary as "projectional anthropology". Idem, p.233.
[61] W. Hofstee, *Goden en mensen*, p.236.

ogy[62], but in fact from every phenomenology of religion including Van der Leeuw's that was developed within a theological framework. Phenomenology of religion should free itself from this burden with the help of a depth psychology that would enable explanation and understanding, and that promises a coherent understanding of religion, individual and society without the aid of theological discourse.[63]

3.4 The projection debate

It is fair to say that the reception of psychoanalysis in theology and religious studies after the Second World War was determined by the so called projection debate.[64] This debate started with the publication of Simon Vestdijk's 1947 essay *De toekomst der religie* [The Future of Religion] and ended with Han Fortmann's *Als ziende de Onzienlijke* [Envisioning the Invisible] from 1964-1968. In between the central figure in the controversy was Sierksma. His defence of Vestdijk's essay against the criticism of theologians was the main reason that the debate did not ebb away in the late 1940s, but continued until the late 1960s as a central debate in the field of the science and psychology of religion.[65]

3.4.1   A religion without God

Simon Vestdijk (1898-1971) was probably the most important Dutch novelist in the mid-twentieth century. In the period around the Second World War one of his main interests was religion. Of special interest is *De vuuraanbidders* [The Fire Worshippers], written in 1944 and published three years later in 1947. This novel is situated in the Dutch War of Independence (1568-1648). The central figure is a young Contra-remonstrant Calvinist man who is at first extremely intolerant of Remonstrant Calvinists.[66] After debates on religious matters with

---

[62] F. Sierksma, *Freud, Jung en de religie*, pp.19ff.

[63] J. van Iersel, *Wetenschap als eigenbelang*, pp.43-48.

[64] An overview on this debate is presented in R. Nauta, *Ik geloof het wel.Godsdienstpsychologische studies over mens en religie*, Uitgeverij Van Gorcum, Assen, 1995, pp.24-28; J.A. van Belzen, *Psychologie en het raadsel van de religie*, pp.177-193, pp.217-231.

[65] Van de Breevaart has presented an outline of the projection debate. Counting the contributions to the controversy in different periods, the number of contributions in the period 1948-1951 is sixty; in the period 1952-1959 fifty; in the period 1960-1972 forty. J.O. van de Breevaart, *Authority in Question. Analysis of a Polemical Controversy on Religion in the Netherlands, 1948-1998*, Uitgeverij Eburon, Delft, 2005, Chapter I.

[66] The terms Contra-remonstrant and Remonstrant refer to the two religious parties in the Netherlands that in the first decade of the 17th century quarrelled over the doctrine of predestination. The dispute had a political dimension which almost caused civil war. At the Synod of Dordrecht (1618-19) the Remonstrant party and their teachings were condemned.

several other persons, love affairs and, most importantly, his experiences as a
soldier during the siege of Heidelberg and of the atrocities of the war, he loses
his faith in God and develops his own "religiosity" in *een godsdienst zonder
God*, a religion without God.[67] Religious intolerance in combination with orthodox Calvinism is a central topic of the novel. The novel is interesting for another reason, for since Contra-remonstrant religiosity is marked by a deep sense
of sin and guilt in combination with a strong belief in predestination, this also
became an important element in the work.[68]

The key issues in *The Fire Worshippers* can also be found in Vestdijk's
essay published in the same year, *The Future of Religion*. The starting point of
which is a distinction between three types of religion that function as psychological personality types in which the religious ideal of "the natural complete
man or natural complete humanity"[69] is pursued. In what Vestdijk calls the
"metaphysical type" complete man is envisioned as a transcendent reality. In
this metaphysical type of religion an ideal is projected on the transcendent.[70]

This projection is in the first place the transformation or recreation of
subjective intra-psychic elements into an objectively experienced reality.[71] In
this general definition Vestdijk is not applying the psychoanalytic concept of
projection, but defines it by reference to Kant and his reflections on human
cognition and subjective perception.[72] Images of reality are created because of
certain "emotions, needs and drives, dislike and inclination, dream and reflection, anxiousness and self-interest".[73] Projection is thus common and necessary.

---

[67] *Wat ik, in ogenblikken van zelfbezinning, zocht was: een godsdienst zonder God, -
deugdzaamheid, goedheid des harten, liefde, opofferingsgezindheid, ja vroomheid, zonder God.* S. Vestdijk, *De vuuraanbidders. Roman uit de tachtigjarige oorlog, deel 3,*
Nijgh & Van Ditmar, Den Haag, 1985, p.543.

[68] Guilt is a theme in many of his novels and also in some of his essays. In 1944, for example, he had written an essay on the sense of guilt in the writings of Dostoyevsky just
like Freud had done fifteen years earlier. In comparison to Freud Vestdijk attempts to
broaden the perspective not only focusing on the "facts" (and their explanation) in *The
Brothers Karamasov* and Dostoyevsky's personality, but comparing basic motives - the
"typical experience" - in both his novels and his personal experiences (in order to understand his work). Sense of guilt is such a motive. S. Vestdijk, "Het schuldprobleem
bij Dostojewski", in *De Poolse Ruiter. Essays*, Uitgeverij Bert Bakker, Den Haag, 1958,
pp.76-88.

[69] S. Vestdijk, *De toekomst der religie*, Uitgeverij Meulenhoff, Amsterdam, 1975,
pp.29-30. Vestdijk defines religion as a desire for and pursuit of unity, totality or *To-
talsinn* referring to the phenomenological tradition. Idem, pp.11-12.

[70] Idem, p.63.

[71] *Projecteren is het omvormen of herscheppen van subjectieve of intrapsychische ele-
menten tot een subjectief bepaalde, zij het ook allerminst als subjectief ervaren werkelijkheid.* Idem, p.64. See also J.O. van de Breevaart, *Authority in Question*, pp.125ff.

[72] S. Vestdijk, *De toekomst der religie*, pp.64-65.

[73] Idem, p.66.

There are Freudian elements in his further elaborations on the concept of projection, for example when he speaks of projection as a defence mechanism.[74] More importantly, there are Jungian elements in Vestdijk's concept, notably in the idea of projection as a mechanism involved in the pursuit of totality.[75] But Freud and Jung are never explicitly referred to when he elaborates his analysis of the concept.

Although metaphysical projection as the belief in supernatural beings can be found in most religions it is especially dominant in Christianity. Vestdijk is particularly interested in what he calls "the absolute projecting man – the dogmatic".[76] This "type" is no longer capable of acknowledging the subjective motivational origin of his projections. Instead he can only view the transcendently "real" without "the core of his personality" being involved.[77] Subjective elements, such as doubts or fears, are denied and "projected" onto others: their doubts become the object of religious intolerance. This intolerance which is according to Vestdijk "so characteristic for Christianity" is the main objection against the metaphysical type.[78]

When we bear in mind *The Fire Worshippers* with its depictions of the belief in predestination, sin, God's omnipotence and religious intolerance, Vestdijk seems to have orthodox Calvinism in mind when he depicts the metaphysical type. This becomes especially clear in his discussion of sin and guilt. His interpretations of Christianity and biblical texts focus on the issues depicted in his novel: predestination, original sin, sin as guilt, salvation, atonement. Here, Vestdijk argues, guilt is everywhere, "human life is guilt".[79] Being severely isolated as against his fellow man, intolerant towards others, treating and using people as "dead objects"…, the metaphysical type is socially guilty. There is only one way out, to project this guilt onto God which doesn't mean that God is guilty, but that man is guilty before God, i.e. projection as a defence mechanism: man's own guilt is projected outside himself and returns as a reproach

---

[74] Idem.

[75] Idem, p.159.

[76] Idem, pp.77-78.

[77] Idem, pp.80ff. Vestdijk depicts him – the type is "masculine" – in his development: in his earliest childhood he lives in an emotional symbiotic totality with the parents. As he grows up he becomes detached from this totality and aware of his isolation as an individual. His religious aim is to regain this totality, but "he is not a saint" and "he is reasonable". "He stays where he is", only capable of projecting his ideal in the transcendent. This man is not capable of really getting emotionally involved with his fellow man outside his small familiar circle, and his isolation is characterized by severity. Towards the transcendental this man also stands isolated, for the God he believes in functions not only as ideal, but, more importantly, makes him constantly aware of his fundamental incompleteness (sin). For a religious and moral development this is catastrophic. For this reason Vestdijk speaks of a disintegrated religiosity.

[78] Idem, pp.93-95.

[79] Idem, pp.236ff. Also J.O. van de Breevaart, *Authority in Question*, pp.142ff.

from God to man. The advantage of this projection is the confirmation of the
individual in his disintegration: he can stay where he is.[80]

As to salvation and atonement Vestdijk calls this the "capitalist aspect
of the metaphysical interpreted guilt problem": make someone suffer (Christ, a
workman) to pay one's own debts. What, finally, is the future of religion? Vestdijk proposes the metaphysical type as a stage in religious development that
grows into a combination of a social and mystical type of religion, more con-
cretly, a combination of Socialism and Buddhism. In the latter, subjective projection is fully acknowledged and denounced. Hence, as the critics observed,
Vestdijk aims at "a religion without God".[81]

Vestdijk's essay contained a critical analysis of Christianity in general
and Calvinism in particular focusing *inter alia* on intolerance, sin and guilt in
relation to personality types and psychological development. It was a clear
questioning of the status of traditional dogmatics and a plea for another type of
religion in a new era. One might expect a further debate on these issues. In that
case discussing guilt and sin would have been inevitable. However such a discussion was not provoked by the essay.

Outlining the early theological critique it is clear that the main issue in
the controversy in response to *The Future of Religion* was projection.[82] This
eclipsed all other themes. A main reason for not discussing Vestdijk's elaborations on sin and guilt in relation to a disintegrated personality type or in relation
to Christianity and intolerance was surely the fact that his ideas on disintegration and guilt depended on the concept of projection. A firm and strategic critique of this mechanism would thus render the rest of the essay harmless.

Behind this there is a more fundamental reason to focus on the issue of
projection. Vestdijk had thematized a problem in Van der Leeuw's phenomenology: the psychic motives of the metaphysical type that projects totality in
front of him. It could be read as a deconstruction of Van der Leeuw's ideas on
broadening of the ego and growing understanding of the "world". Indeed Van
der Leeuw was one of the scholars who sought to sharply refute Vestdijk's essay as a phenomenological failure, the work of an "intellectual" who doesn't
ask questions of ultimate meaning.[83] In his analyses of the disintegrated metaphysical type and his depictions of guilt, sin and intolerance Vestdijk had shown
himself to be a modern reductionist without any sense for mystic participation

---

[80] Vestdijk argues that sexuality had become the most prominent sin in Christianity because of disintegration. In sexuality as sin disintegration is confirmed: our "erotic debt"
to fellow man, i.e. love, is not settled. "sexuality [as sin] is not guilt in a positive sense,
but guilt in a negative sense: it hinders us to do something we should do." S. Vestdijk,
De toekomst der religie, pp.240-241.

[81] J.O. van de Breevaart, *Authority in Question*, pp.146.

[82] Idem, pp.118-150.

[83] F. Siersksma, *Tussen twee vuren. Een pamflet en een essay*, Uitgeverij De Bezige Bij,
Amsterdam, 1952, pp.125-127.

or religious commitment, just like Freud.[84] Sierksma gives a clear indication about the general reaction to Vestdijk: "his scientific hypothesis fell in the hands of persons who not studied religion, but wanted to defend Christianity".[85]

Looking back the "opportunity" to debate sin and guilt in the Reformed tradition seemed there, but these issues were not the key problems in the debate that followed. Instead it was about a clash of anthropologies that either were immanent in or could be synthesized with Van der Leeuw's ideas on empathetic understanding, search for meaning and participation or, as against this, a view of man characterized by conflict, eccentricity, tragic struggle and helpless attempts to regain an ever unstable control over life. In his project of emancipating phenomenology of religion (science of religion) from theology and distancing himself from Van der Leeuw, Sierksma will associate Freud with the latter view and this will be a decisive moment in the reception of Freud in Dutch theology.

3.4.2   *Homo proiiciens*

After the initial critical reviews and Vestdijk's replies, Sierksma took the initiative of defending him against fellow theologians. This ultimately led to the publication of *De religieuze projectie* [The Religious Projection] in 1956. This was Sierksma's declaration on the nature of projection in the midst of the controversy. But there are more reasons why Sierksma had to write this study.

One reason had already been announced in his dissertation. Both psychology and the phenomenology of religion tended towards a philosophical anthropology. The first ideas of such anthropology had already been ventilated, but a systematic outline had not been presented. In *The Religious Projection* this anthropology is presented, namely by bringing in Helmuth Plessner's *Die Stufen des Organischen und der Mensch* [The Gradation of the Organic and the Human], 1928.

Another major reason for writing on projection was Sierksma's awareness that projection was a key issue in the phenomenology of religion as developed by Van der Leeuw.[86] When a phenomenologist used a method of interpre-

---

[84] One of the strategies in the many critical reviews was to argue that Vestdijk was a reductionist who could be situated in a tradition of firm critiques on religion – Feuerbach, Nietzsche, Freud. Indeed, Freud was mentioned in *The Future of Religion*, albeit solely in connection to sexuality. But the fact that Vestdijk had developed a "psychology" and that Freud was a known critic of religion was probably enough reason for associating Vestdijk with Freud. That the title of the essay seemed to refer to *The Future of an Illusion* did the rest.

[85] F. Sierksma, *De religieuze projectie. Een antropologische en psychologische studie over de projectie-verschijnselen in de godsdiensten*, Uitgeverij Meulenhoff, Amsterdam, 1977, p.162.

[86] Idem, pp.107-134.

tation through empathic understanding, i.e. an affective intuitive method, the question could be raised how this understanding could or should be distinguished from projection. The projection mechanism and the phenomenological method of empathic understanding were situated in the same affective entanglement of subject and object. Van der Leeuw himself had made this problem explicit when he argued that there was no "outside" position from which the world or the "self" could be understood.[87] Understanding phenomena was eventually the same as understanding the subject's own structuring of reality. *The Religious Projection* is a thorough refutation of Van der Leeuw's phenomenological method that was too much focused on the empathic self-expression of the researcher and had too little of a scientific basis.

Sierksma argues that projection is always the subjective component in perceptual activity.[88] To understand the typical human features of subjectivity in perception Sierksma takes up Plessner's distinctions between the centricity of animal life in their natural environment and human eccentricity.[89] Humans, like animals, as far as they "are" a body with senses and instincts, live centric in their environment being able to create a world in which they can easily orientate themselves.[90] But unique to humans is their ability to objectify the world, to take a distance from the world in which they live, and create an image of the world, i.e. to make a distinction between subject and object.[91] In this sense man lives "eccentricly"; he can experience himself as being in the centre from an "objective" position. Being both centric and eccentric implies that "he knows that the world is actually different from how it is perceived".

---

[87] In a 1941 anthropological study Van der Leeuw's starting points – referring to Plessner amongst others – are reflections on the relation between man and world addressing the problem that understanding the world (as object) is actually nothing else but understanding the structures man implanted onto the world in order to understand it. That means, that man only understands himself, i.e. his thought constructions and perceptions of the world. In other words, he understands the "echo" – one might say, projection – of himself. G. van der Leeuw, *Der Mensch und die Religion. Anthropologischer Versuch*, Verlag Haus zum Falken, Basel, 1941, chapter 1.

[88] F. Sierksma, *De religieuze projectie*, p. 64. *De eenheid in de verscheidenheid der projectie-verschijnselen is het feit, dat de mens weet, dat zijn eigen waarnemingen zo goed als die van andere levende wezens een wereld scheppen, die niet samenvalt met de wereld-los-van-die-waarnemingen.* Idem, p.7.

[89] H. Plessner, *Die Stufen des Organischen und der Mensch. Einleitung in die philosophische Anthropologie*, De Gruyter, Berlin/New York, 1975, pp.309ff.

[90] F. Sierksma, *De religieuze projectie*, p.20. Apparently Sierksma had a profound interest in animal psychology and spend a lot of time in the Zoological Laboratory in Leiden observing the behaviour of sticklebacks. L. Leertouwer, "Primitive Religion in Dutch Religious Studies", p.208.

[91] F. Sierksma, *De religieuze projectie*, pp.21-22.

Man knows he is projecting – he is *homo proiiciens* – and he knows he has to de-project in order to know the world as it really is.[92] The key issue is no longer the relation between primitive mentality and modern mentality, but non-projection (in earliest childhood), projection and de-projection.[93] The theory of eccentricity and projection is a further step in an intellectual development away from Lévy-Bruhl's mystic participation, Van der Leeuw's phenomenological method of empathic understanding, theology in general, and also Jung's ideas on archetypes.

Sierksma now takes up elements of Freudian psychoanalytic theory in his anthropology. Psychoanalysis has shown that man lives partly self-conscious, partly unconscious. This implies conflicts: man is naturally neurotic, always desperately seeking a balance between unconsciousness and conscious-ness, drive and mind, centricity and eccentricity, subjectivity and objectivity.[94] The content of this balance differs, for it depends on the culture a person lives in and the cultural patterns that structure man's life and enable him to feel se-cure.[95] This balance is however fundamentally problematic: "man is an animal thrown out of his balance"; he has lost centricity and the accuracy of animal in-stincts is replaced by feelings of helplessness that can only be overcome as far as he is able to control himself and the world from an eccentric position.[96] This, according to Sierksma, is the core of Freud's conception of the projection of the sense of guilt as a defence mechanism: an attempt to regain control over inner life.[97] Helplessness is thus the dominant motive for the development of cultural systems of which religions are also a part. Such a system provides stability and security.[98]

Sierksma's project of an "anthropological broadening and deepening of the projection problem"[99] implied discussing the issue of religious projection

---

[92] Idem, pp.25-26.

[93] This is exactly what Sierksma aims at and admired in Vestdijk: a theory of religion, not based on or culminating in a Christian perspective, but a theory of religion based on a mechanism that could be found in all religions, even that religion which, because of its atheistic nature, had always posed a problem in the study of religions, Buddhism. Idem, p.175.

[94] Idem, pp.44-45.

[95] Idem, pp.46, 51ff. *Cultuur is een evenwichtstoestand, een status quo tussen de mens en de natuur, of hij nu op die natuur stoot in zijn buiten- dan wel zijn binnenwereld.* Idem, p.54.

[96] Idem, pp.70ff.

[97] Idem, p.59.

[98] Compare: "Both animals and man need fixed points by which they can orient them-selves and 'know where they are'. Man too needs security, something to hold on to." F. Sierksma, *The Gods as we shape them*, Routledge, London, 1960, p.28.

[99] "Sierksma stripped the concept of projection of its association with pathology and il-lusion and placed it in the wider framework of perception." J.A. van Belzen, "Between

beyond Freud's clinical perspectives. Religious projection is a form of common projection, subjectifying a hidden aspect of reality when objectifying fails to control reality.[100] It is the humanization of a mystery – transcending the soul into the unknown, only in order to find oneself back in a new unstable balance.[101] This control over reality is necessary because of the "uncanny" character of religion and revelation.[102]

Religion is defined here as the notion that "there is something" and when this something reveals itself, it is the disruptive experience that there is more out there than the "stable" perceived world. Religious experience and religious projection are thus defined in relation to the eccentric structures of man and his desire for the "stability of a spirited coherence".[103]

Because of the inevitable separation of subject and object Sierksma finishes his book with a plea for de-projection as it is found in Buddhism, a religion that like a science is "the last step out of humanity's childhood, out of a world where mind-created figures populated a metaphysical heaven and hell".[104] Man is so firmly rooted in his modern (secularized) world that a return to participation in a primitive totality or a broadening of the ego in order to understand essence is – tragically – no longer possible.

The last pages of *The Religious Projection* were devoted to Freud and his pioneering ideas on projection and to Buddhism as a "scientific" religion unveiling illusions. It was a provocation as well as a challenge for theologians to respond.

Feast and Famine. A Sketch pf the Psychology of Religion in the Netherlands", in *International Journal for the Psychology of Religion* 4 (1994) pp.181-197 (190).

[100] F. Sierksma, *De religieuze projectie*, p.156.

[101] Idem, pp.157-158. According to Sierksma, Barthian theologians have ignored the psychological fact that man believes in "the totally Other" as far as he can make the Other familiar. In this sense Barthian theology is strictly theoretical; the "Other" is not something man can actually belief in. Or in other words, Barthian theologians radically deny projection.

[102] Idem, pp.140ff. Although Sierksma does not directly refer to Freud, it is my opinion that Sierksma's ideas on the uncanny (*Unheimlichkeit*) of the mystery, the horror of something disruptive suddenly appearing and disappearing, are influenced by Freud's *The Uncanny*.

[103] Idem, p.144.

[104] Idem, pp.175-177. We should notice here that Jung held similar ideas on de-projection. In the context of discussing Eastern religions such as Buddhism and Hinduism in *Psychologie und Religion* Jung argues that in individual development towards becoming "self" (as the sum of conscious and unconscious phenomena) the illusionary anthropomorphic projections of gods and demons should be "taken back". This deprojection would bring back the projected elements of the soul to their psychic origin. C.G. Jung, *Psychologie und Religion*, in *Gesammelte Werke. Band 11*, Rascher Verlag, Zurich/Stuttgart, 1963, pp.1-117 (90-93).

3.4.3   Envisioning the Invisible

"We will have to consider theoretical atheism – Marx and Freud – as the effect of a structure of consciousness and hence ask ourselves why atheism cannot but regard God as a fiction, a creation of man out of need, in short as a projection. The projection theory is the outcome of a change in our structure of consciousness, which one can provisionally indicate as the separation of subject and object". "The subject of this study is the projection theory as manifestation of our one-sided scientific culture."[105]

These are sentences from the introductory chapter of Han Fortmann's *Envisioning the Invisible* in which he puts forward the main hypothesis of his study, namely that projection theory as a manifestation of a specific scientific culture is not useful as a theory to understand religious perception.

In 1956 the psychologist and Catholic priest Fortmann (1912-1970) became professor in the general and comparative psychology of culture and religion at Nijmegen University. In his writings from the 1950s onwards he stresses that the Catholic Church's weakest point, despite its message of "salvational love", was its pastoral care for individuals.[106] Fortmann detects a growing distance between the official teachings of the church and pastoral practice.

In his view theology has a lot to gain from the human sciences, from psychotherapy and psychology as auxiliary sciences. He argues that therapy can be a first step towards "salvation", towards "moral and religious growth", stressing the difference between a mature religiosity and religion as the projection of infantile needs.[107] This is an important distinction, because Fortmann will not deny the projection mechanism as such. His criticism is aimed at "projection psychologists" who claim that all religion and belief in God is merely projection.

In his refutation of psychoanalytic projection theory in general, and of Vestdijk's and Sierksma's theories in particular[108], Fortmann finds his alternative for the "one-sided scientific culture" in the writings of the German theologian Romano Guardini and his ideas on religious experience in the modern world. Religious experience originates where man experiences his world as contingent, incomprehensible, unknown and opaque. This experience does not evoke a religious experience of the transcendent as a "nature reserve for God"

---

[105] H.M.M. Fortmann, *Als ziende de Onzienlijke, deel I*, pp.28, 29.

[106] H.M.M. Fortmann, "De verlossende liefde", in *Heel de mens. Reflecties over de menselijke mogelijkheden*, W. Berger (ed.), Uitgeverij Ambo, Baarn/Bilthoven, 1972, pp.17-28.

[107] Idem, pp.23ff.

[108] P. Vandermeersch, H. Westerink, *Godsdienstpsychologie*, p.258.

outside this world[109], but as an inner-worldly transcendence.[110] Guardini had shown that modern man has lost the ability to intuit the spiritual in the physical, and had become merely a spectator of himself and the world. He had also shown that the subject-object dichotomy is modern, and with it the perception of the world as either objective (rational scientific) or subjective (projection of needs, wishes, affects). Guardini further tried to depict an alternative in religious experience as the existential experience of inner-worldly transcendence, of a deeper mystery and meaning of life beyond the worldly contingencies. In religious experience one thus finds what the projection theorists neglected: "that seeing is a response to the fact that there is something to see".[111]

Fortmann's refutation of the projection theory is laid down in the more than 1200 pages of *Envisioning the Invisible* published in the period 1964-1968.[112] The first part of his study is a descriptive analysis of "theories in which religion is treated as projection" including those of Freud, Vestdijk en Sierksma.[113] In his description of Freud's projection theory he starts off with projection as a defence mechanism as in Freud's early clinical writings on anxiety neurosis and paranoia. Here projection is expressed by Freud in rather general terms, says Fortmann.[114] A first broadening of the concept of projection is detected in *Totem and Taboo*.[115] Here, according to Fortmann, the mechanism is

---

[109] Fortmann is both criticizing Catholic Neo-Scholasticism with its abstract Thomistic theology, and Barthian theology and its attempt to separate theology from psychology and mythology running the risk of widening the gap between theology and modern man.

[110] H.M.M. Fortmann, *Als ziende de Onzienlijke, deel I*, pp.312-313. Also: *[De wereld] blijkt innerlijk begrensd en eindig en niet autonoom te zijn. Overal waar eindig zijn is, is grens. (…) Langs deze innerlijke grens der dingen, aan de andere zijde ervan, loopt de transcendentie, de "plaats van God". En deze transcendentie kunnen wij, modernen, "lebendig erfahren". Wanneer ik deze begrensdheid immers aanvaard en wil erkennen, ervaar ik ook haar betekenis, haar uitdrukkingskracht, haar vermogen om te verwijzen naar de Andere. Deze echte grens is als de huid van ons lichaam: "Sie admet, fühlt, übersetzt von der einen Seite auf die andere".* Idem, p.311.

[111] Idem, p.411.

[112] Van Belzen has rightfully argued that Fortmann's study can hardly be regarded as a unity. There is a clear shift of interest from the projection theory (volume 1) to the problem of religious perception and the field of mental care (volume 2). In general I agree with his depiction of the book as both high point and low point: *het betoog is niet te volgen: het is overladen, men ziet door de bomen het bos niet meer, het zijn teveel pagina's. (…) Buitendien klinkt zijn inhoudelijke antwoord op de projectieproblematiek uiterst zwak.* J.A. van Belzen, *Psychologie en het raadsel van de religie*, p.224, pp.225-226..

[113] H.M.M. Fortmann, *Als ziende de Onzienlijke, deel I*, p.30.

[114] Included here is Fortmann's interpretation of the Schreber case: projection is not (as Freud argued) an attempt to reconstruct a relationship with the outside world, but it is still a defence mechanism as in earlier writings. Idem, pp.35-36.

[115] Idem, pp.38ff.

taken out of its context in the interpretation of pathologies and applied to the sphere of normality and the construction of reality.

As to the belief in God or gods Fortmann has to admit that Freud seldom speaks of projection. Nevertheless, he finds enough reason to suggest that Freud explained the belief in God "along similar lines": Christianity is the effect of father projection. *The Future of an Illussion* is interpreted from this perspective.[116] In short, religious projection is the creation of beings that are either identical to ourselves (for example the belief in the demons in animism) or serve as a correlate for our needs (for example the belief in God).[117] The core of Freud's writings on religion is thus the projection theory.[118]

After having described Freudian, Marxist and Jungian projection theories, part two of the first volume of *Envisioning the Invisible* is devoted to a "critique of the basic concepts". Fortmann attempts to develop a synthesis of the different versions of "the projection theory" looking for general underlying structures. In his view, the Freudians and Jung basically held the same theory: an inner subjective perception is replaced by "something" outside the subject that is objectively perceived. In other words the basic concepts are: subjective versus objective, and inner versus outer.[119]

Another general feature of projection is in its aim: projection is either a defence mechanism (for example against helplessness or self-reproach), or an attempt to continue or restore a state of unity.[120] As to the latter aspect of the projection theory Fortmann notices that Jung had related this state of unity to

---

[116] *Wortel van alle religie is de "Vatersehnsucht" schrijft Freud in Totem und Tabu. Het geloof in een God is evenals het geloof in het noodlot een vaderprojectie. In Die Zukunft einer Illusion zoekt hij de bron van die projectie in de menselijke hulpeloosheid.* H.M.M. Fortmann, *Als ziende de Onzienlijke. Een cultuurpsychologische studie over de religieuze waarneming en de zogenaamde religieuze projectie, deel II, 3a. Geloof en ervaring, 3b. Geloof en geestelijke gezondheid*, Uitgeverij Gooi en Sticht, Hilversum, 1981, p.284.

[117] Idem, *deel I*, p.323. Compare: *Freud schreef, dat projectie een primitief mechanisme is en normalerwijs het grootste aandeel heft in de opbouw van onze wereld.* Idem, p.363.

[118] We should notice here that Fortmann does not consider *Moses and Monotheism*. There are no elaborations on the "projection" of the Moses character on Yahweh, nor on Judaism as religion based on longing for the father. We cannot be sure about the reason for this omission, but it is clear that Fortmann interpreted *Moses and Monotheism* primarily as a study of the sense of guilt, repression and anti-Semitism. Idem, *deel II*, pp.291ff.

[119] Idem, *deel I*, p.359. Concerning the question of what is projected he detects two basic ideas: projection is either projection of inner psychic elements or structures (for example hate or reproach), or projection of its correlates (such as father projection as correlate to one's helplessness). Idem, pp.361-363.

[120] Idem, pp.363-367.

Lévy-Bruhl's concept of mystic participation.[121] From this synthesis the key concepts that should be critically reviewed are distilled: projection in relation to the separation of subject and object (inner and outer world), in relation to the unconscious and to participation.

As to the subject-object dichotomy Fortmann first argues that the projection theory is not based on the experience of projection – this mechanism is unconscious, and scientifically hypothetical – but on specific philosophical notions.[122] The basic idea is that of the existence of one objective reality that can only be subjectively perceived. This idea is paradoxical and thus "foolish".[123]

Another problem with the projection theory is the choice of the object of projection: why does someone project his feelings onto one particular object, and not onto another? The only answer can be that this particular object already had a meaning: the affect is elicited by the nature of the object.[124] He stresses that in phenomenology subjectivity is not an isolation of consciousness, but "transcendence", an elevation of the self towards the world, a being part of a coherence of meaning.[125] This coherence is not a projection; it is given with the objects that show themselves (as they really are). The world is not subjective-unreal as the projection psychologists thought, but real in its appearances.[126] Here Fortmann defends Van der Leeuw against Sierksma.

In Fortmann's view, the projection theory cannot be saved with an appeal to the unconscious. For, what is the status of an unconscious mechanism? Does it exist somewhere hidden under a surface? We have already seen the problem this question refers to, when Freud thought of the possibility of unconscious sense of guilt, or in general, when he spoke of unconscious facts, systems and mechanisms.[127] According to Fortmann, the unconscious is a result of abstract thinking originating in nineteenth century philosophy, a Romantic myth rather than a psychoanalytic fact. "What Freud called 'the dynamic unconscious' does not exist".[128] It is not a hidden entity or "thing" in man; it has no psychic reality.[129]

Projection is subscribing subjective "processes" to objects which means identification or participation with the outside world. Not only Jung, but also

---

[121] Idem, p.366.

[122] *Zowel het werk van Freud als dat van Sierksma is doortrokken van een zeer bepaalde wijsgerige opvatting over het bewustzijn (een innerlijk met inhouden) en over de verhouding tussen subject en object, nl. als principieel van elkaar gescheiden.* Idem, p.375.

[123] Idem, p.373, p.377.

[124] Idem, p.378.

[125] Idem, p.381.

[126] Idem, p.384.

[127] On the reality character of the unconscious as an apparatus between body and consciousness see A. de Block, *Vragen aan Freud. Psychoanalyse en de menselijke natuur*, Uitgeverij Boom, Amsterdam, 2003, pp.23-37.

[128] H.M.M. Fortmann, *Als ziende de Onzienlijke, deel I*, p.445.

[129] Idem, p.457.

Van der Leeuw had taken up the concept of participation with reference to Lévy-Bruhl. Hence, Fortmann gives an extensive introduction to Lévy-Bruhl and of the main critical points made against his theory of primitive mentality and mystic participation. This participation should not be interpreted as the effect of projection (or identification), but as the awareness of coherences and relations between "things". The primitives were not yet isolated subjects that projected, but they had knowledge of their world (objects) in which they lived and were integrated.[130]

Fortmann further continues discussing the role of the symbol as a most important "form of knowing" the unknown that cannot be captured in rational concepts, i.e. the primitive participation in "everything that lies before the disunity and isolation of the subject".[131] It is what, according to Fortmann, Paul Ricoeur had called a "second primitivity" as a new openness and spontaneity towards the world.[132]

In his discussion of Lévy-Bruhl Fortmann refutes the critique by Sierksma of the concepts of mystic participation and primitive mentality, and of Van der Leeuw's search for totality of meaning in a modern secularized world.

3.4.4   Han Fortmann's reading of Freud

When Fortmann sums up the first volume of *Envisioning the Invisible* he writes: "our aim was to save perception, especially the primitive, naive, spontaneous perception. I must admit, that I made this effort in order to save the faith of believers, but also the vision of poets."[133] We might add that Fortmann did more than just trying to save primitive perception. He also "saved" religious partici-

---

[130] Idem, pp.516-517.

[131] *Primitief is alles wat nog voor de gespletenheid en het isolement van het subject ligt.* Idem, p.552. This primitivity is not only found in primitive society, but also in the bible and in the Middle Ages.

[132] Idem, p.547. In his 1965 *L'interprétation* Ricoeur had introduced the concepts of first and second naivety. First naivety was for example indicated by Lévy-Bruhl and Van der Leeuw as an immediate participation in a divine reality. This immediate participation is no longer accessible for modern man, but as phenomenologists of religion had argued, there was the possibility of understanding this reality in the revelation of the Sacred. In hermeneutics this teleological perspective should be combined with Freud's archaeology relating religion to unconscious motives. This means that belief cannot emerge intact from the confrontation with psychoanalysis. Freud's critique of religion will separate idols (illusions) from symbols, and a second naivety can only be possible when it integrates this critique. Fortmann's interpretation of second naivety as openness beyond Freudian thought is thus problematic. P. Ricoeur, *Freud and Philosophy: An Essay on Interpretation*, Yale University Press, New Haven/London, 1970, part 3, chapter 4.

[133] H.M.M. Fortmann, *Als ziende de Onzienlijke, deel II*, p.31.

pation, religious experience, the symbol and even phenomenology.[134] In this project Freud was read as a projection theorist, a positivist without any sense for religious experience or participation in a totality of meaning.

There are obvious problems when Fortmann tries to establish a synthesis between Freud, Jung and Sierksma (and others) as projection psychologists. For example: is Freud's psychoanalysis a theory of perception, comparable to Sierksma's? The answer is a straight no. As for example the Schreber case had shown, and as Freud had argued in *Formulations on the Two Principles of Mental Functioning* our relationship with reality is not based on perception, but on (narcissistic) identification and the libidinal relations with reality.[135] As to Freud and Jung we have already seen that their anthropologies are incompatible, and that their ideas on for example projection, identification and primitivity are hardly comparable.

A major problem with calling Freud a projection psychologist is the simple fact that the concept of projection does not play an important role in either Freud's clinical and meta-psychological writings, or in his writings on religion. Freud had called religion "psychology projected in the external world" (in *The Psychopathology of Everyday Life*), but afterwards projection was only further elaborated upon in *Totem and Taboo* in the context of the belief in demons in (pre-religious) animism, but not in the context of advanced religions.[136] In *The Future of an Illusion* and in *Moses and Monotheism* the concept of projection is absent.

Already in 1966 Antoine Vergote voiced the critique of Fortmann that reading Freud's writings on religion from the perspective of projection meant that the actual structuralizing processes in religion were lost from sight, covered up by a "pseudo-scientific fantasy" having no substance apart from a few infantile motivations.[137] Indeed, considering Freud's writings on religion as the work of a projection psychologist means neglecting the fact that in Freud's writings affective relations to the world or to specific objects can be described in a range of terms all describing different structures and mechanisms: identification, idealization, sublimation, transference, etc. We might even add the general processes of fantasy and thought, for the reality principle is a continuation of the pleasure principle, and underlying abstract thinking are libidinal relations with reality.

---

[134] *De fenomenologische antropologie ontkent het uitgangspunt, dat door de projectie-psychologen wordt ingenomen: de scheiding tussen subject en wereld. Zij beschouwt met Binswanger die scheiding als "Krebsübel aller Psychologie".* Idem, *deel I*, p.381.

[135] P. Vandermeersch, *Unresolved Questions in the Freud/Jung Debate*, p.218.

[136] S. Freud, *Totem and Taboo*, pp.64-65. See also A. Vergote, "Projection and Intolerance versus Symbolization", in *Psychoanalysis, Phenomenological Anthropology and Religion*, pp.87-101 (92).

[137] A. Vergote, *Religionspsychologie*, Walter-Verlag, Olten/Freiburg, 1970, pp.244-247.

For Fortmann Freud is a projection psychologist and his writings are interpreted from this perspective. Fortmann elaborates for example on the connection between primary narcissism and magic in animism as described in *Totem and Taboo* as an attempt to master reality, through what Klein had later called "projective identification".[138] He goes on to discuss the Oedipus complex as a further reflection of the ambivalent nature of the longing for the father: "the father does not only protect, but also demands".[139] The rebellion triggered by these demands in response, ultimately leads to a sense of guilt. According to Fortmann, here we find the reason for Freud's preoccupation with the sense of guilt in religion: it was a further elaboration of the question "what is projected in religion". The answer is not only the longing for the father, but also sense of guilt. "Sense of guilt and the projection thereof onto others are a key problem in Christianity."[140]

Freud's ideas on the sense of guilt as a key issue in religion were essentially a further elaboration on projection, says Fortmann. This is the reason why Freud thought religion was structured as obsessional neurosis: it was an attempt to find a compromise between ambivalent feelings (desire and sense of guilt) projected in religion. In other words, from the "idea" of projection Freud's writings on religion got their content. We should notice however that in fact Freud's clinical analyses of the sense of guilt in his earlier writings provided the structures for applied psychoanalysis. Sense of guilt was not a topic in his writings on religion because of earlier basic ideas on religion, namely religion as projection, but, on the contrary, Freud was primarily interested in religion because of its analogies with clinical pathological phenomena.

In the final part of his study on mental health Fortmann discusses issues such as sense of guilt, dogma and authority, and sexuality. These issues are not randomly chosen. They reflect important issues debated upon within the Catholic Church during the 1950s and 1960s.[141]

---

[138] H.M.M. Fortmann, *Als ziende de Onzienlijke, deel II*, p.285.

[139] Idem, p.286.

[140] Idem, p.291.

[141] The issues of sexuality and authority were key issues in the changing mentality of the 1960s in general, but certainly also in the Catholic Church in the period of and after the Second Vatican Council (1962-1965). P. Vandermeersch, H. Westerink, *Godsdienstpsychologie*, pp.242-245. The topic of (pathological) sense of guilt was put on the agenda in the 1950s. In a speech addressed to an international conference on psychotherapy in 1953 pope Pius XII had admitted that religiosity in some cases could be marked by an irrational pathological sense of guilt. In his view, psychoanalysis could be an auxiliary science, though limited, to "cure" this sense of guilt, or better, to make possible a healthy religious sense of guilt. This speech opened up new perspectives on the relationship between psychoanalysis, psychotherapy and religious mental care. J. Scharfenberg, "Die Rezeption der Psychoanalyse in der Theologie", document 22.

After Fortmann has argued that psychologists should not "explain away" God as a projection and should "limit themselves to the study of empirical factors" and the description of religious behaviour[142], he states that Freud has depicted the "immature" and pathological (neurotic, projectional) forms of religion rather convincingly.[143] Pathological elements in religious behaviour are of course key issues in mental health and religious psycho-hygiene and Freud's writings are very useful in gaining insight into these issues.

Here we recognize Fortmann's basic distinction between mature and immature religion, and psychology as an auxiliary science of "salvation". Such a mature religion is no longer based on infantile needs and wishes, but on a search for God for his own sake.[144] This mature religion had always been there, albeit hidden under a surface of aberrations. It is the pastoral project for the future to free this religion from its (historic) burden.[145]

As to our topic of the sense of guilt, Freud had argued, according to Fortmann, that "religion was an attempt to resolve the problem of guilt". This starting point indicates a specific interpretation, for as we have seen, Freud also argued that the sense of guilt is cultivated in religion. It is not simply resolved, but returned to.

This tendency to redeem the sense of guilt is opposed, especially in Christianity, by overzealous moralism and dogmatism and changing "guilt" into "sin", says Fortmann.[146] At this point it is important to notice that in Fortmann's view the superego is a "representative of all restrictions imposed from outside". The superego "aims at sheer conformity with collective norms".[147] This interpretation of the superego is linked with the projection mechanism. The ego trying to defend itself against the demands of the superego, projects the superego onto God. Significantly he calls this superego-morality "immature and pathological".[148] Again, we must notice that this is a very specific interpretation of Freud fitting Fortmann's theological ideas and aims as well as his basic assumption that Freud is a projection psychologist.

What does guilt or sense of guilt mean? Fortmann asks the question, but from his perspective it is difficult to formulate an answer. He tries to establish a general definition of the sense of guilt in such a way that it is understandable as an effect of a repressive morality (superego) and as an affect that needs to be

---

[142] H.M.M. Fortmann, *Als ziende de Onzienlijke, deel II*, pp.56-57.

[143] Idem, p.399.

[144] Idem, p.451.

[145] Idem, pp.580ff.

[146] Idem, p.456.

[147] Idem, p.459. This notion has immediate consequences for practical theology: the sense of guilt is evoked by moralist preaching, not by "accepting" preaching. This acceptance means: accepting that man is a being in development that can only further mature when he is able to lovingly accept his incompleteness. Idem, p.479.

[148] Idem, p.459.

projected. He must admit though that this general definition is hard to find in Freud's writings. Instead Freud speaks of remorse, moral masochism, the need for punishment, unconscious sense of guilt, discontent and conscience anxiety. In short, the concept seems diffuse and does not allow of a general definition.

"From Freud I cannot get any clarity", Fortmann writes.[149] The problem he faces and is unable to solve is the fact that Freud made differentiations in the concept of the sense of guilt. It is true that these differentiations make it impossible to give a compact definition of a general concept of the sense of guilt. From his early writings onwards Freud had been analysing self-reproaches in various pathologies, which inevitably led to differentiations in the concept according to its function in the mechanisms and structures of pathology. It was in this context that Freud had introduced the concept of projection as a defence mechanism in anxiety neurosis and paranoia.

Fortmann's perspective is the projection of the sense of guilt in religion and the superego as representative of parental, cultural or religious morality. From this perspective it is indeed impossible to get a grip on the various forms of the sense of guilt. To name just one example: self-reproaches in melancholia. They hold no relation to projection and are not directly evoked by cultural or religious morality. To conclude, Fortmann's perspective is too narrow to acknowledge the full complexity of Freud's analyses of the sense of guilt.

3.4.5   Evaluation and influence of the projection debate

The projection debate was a strictly Dutch controversy. It can be situated in the context of a Dutch phenomenological tradition and the approaches of Van der Leeuw. Yet, underlying the debate were questions that point towards a broader context. The first and most obvious one is the fact that the controversy was also a debate about the relation between psychoanalysis and theology. In what way and to what extent could psychoanalysis contribute to theology? Or was psychoanalysis nothing else but a critique of religion? How should the writings of Freud be read and valued? These questions were certainly not typically Dutch. In the previous chapter we have already seen how these questions were also dominant in the reception of psychoanalysis in theology and religious studies in the German-speaking world.

This brings me to a second issue: reactions to Barthian theology. Sierksma's scientific objective of a philosophical anthropology for both phenomenology and psychology were certainly motivated by the fact that he felt the scientific "objective" study of religion was being endangered by developments in theology, viz: the emergence of Barthian theology. Viewed from this perspective the debate can be situated in a broader international context.

---

[149] Idem, p.454.

A third motive that should be noticed can be found in the objectives of Fortmann: his aim to bridge the gap between the official teachings of the church and pastoral practice, and to save religion in a disintegrated world. Embracing psychology and psychotherapy as auxiliary science and technique was a way to establish this. It is a motive that could already be found not only as early as in Pfister's or Bouman's interest in psychoanalysis, but also in the writings of Van der Leeuw.

Fortmann's *Envisioning the Invisible* would determine the views about Freud of many theologians for a long period. One might even say until today.[150] Sierksma remained an isolated figure (in his many conflicts), his approach was not further developed by students. Fortmann on the contrary had several sympathizers and students who pursued academic careers and who would be important scholars in the field of psychology of religion, pastoral theology and spiritual care. Jaap van Belzen has rightfully argued that Fortmann belonged to a generation of theologians who were convinced that the church should pay a lot more attention to the believers, who struggled with their faith in a modern world and a cold church.[151]

Jan Weima (1926-), one of Fortmann's students, should be mentioned here. He was not a theologian, but a psychologist and sociologist who was asked in 1964 by Fortmann to become his assistant. In 1977 he was appointed professor in psychology of religion at the University of Tilburg. Jan van der Lans (1933-2002) must also be named, a theologian and psychologist, assistant of Fortmann in the late 1960s. In 1987 he became professor in the psychology of religion in Nijmegen. Given these careers it is already obvious that Fortmann's agenda would be influential. The key concept in this agenda was religious experience.

In his 1981 study on the psychology of religious (especially mystical) experience, *Reiken naar oneindigheid* [Reaching for Infinity] Weima discusses the

---

[150] *Het godsdienstpsychologisch onderzoek dat sinds het aantreden van Han Fortmann op deze universiteit [Nijmegen] verricht is, heeft bij voortduring de grenzen van de kerkelijke instituties opgezocht. Het werk van Fortmann, Weima, Berger, Van der Lans en Van Uden, maar ook het onderzoek dat ik zelf met collega's heb verricht, wordt gekenmerkt door een zoeken naar religiositeit op onverwachte plaatsen. Een zoeken naar de verborgen psychologische kern, gedragen door Fortmanns roep om een herstel van de religieuze ervaring.* J. Janssen, "Aan de onbekende God. Reiken naar religie in een geseculariseerde cultuur", in J. Janssen, *Religie in Nederland: kiezen of delen?*, KSGV, Tilburg, 2007, pp.103-142 (114).

[151] J.A. van Belzen (ed.), *Van gisteren tot heden. Godsdienstpsychologie in Nederland. Teksten I*, Uitgeverij Kok, Kampen, 1999, pp.16ff. Theologians like Fortmann, Heije Faber, Willem Berger and Coen van Ouwerkerk all studied psychology mainly with the objective of using their practical-relevant psychological knowledge in pastoral theology. They all became professors in their field.

unconscious in the context of religious experience: religious experiences seem
to bring man into contact with unconscious layers of the soul. Because psychoanalysis "discovered" the unconscious, Freud and Jung are discussed.[152] In
Weima's depiction of psychoanalysis the writings of Freud are not referred to.
Instead he strictly follows Fortmann's critical analysis of the concept of unconsciousness in *Envisioning the Invisible* focusing on the problematic reality character of the unconscious, its contents and mechanisms, in both the writings of
Freud and Jung.

According to Weima, the psychoanalytic concept of the unconscious is
not very useful for the study of religious experience. But given the fact that this
concept has gained importance in popular literature and has become part of everyday language, he decides to use the concept anyway, although this does not
imply the "choice for a psychoanalytic theory of the subject". There are two
main reasons why psychoanalysis is not a useful theory in the study of religious
experience. The first reason is Jung's theory that every experience of the divine
always is an experience of psychic contents projected into the world surrounding us.[153] The second reason is Freud's rejection of oceanic feelings as primal
religious experience.[154]

According to Weima, Freud argued that oceanic feelings were a regression to earliest childhood experiences when there was not yet a separation between inner and external reality. Further development can be characterized by
the separation of subject from objects. In short: "originally the ego enclosed
everything; later the external world is separated from the ego". The need for this
regression can be explained by means of feelings of helplessness and fear resulting in a longing for the fatherly protection. In short, psychoanalysis only reduces religious experience to either projection or the need for fatherly protection. We are back to Fortmann's main criticisms against psychoanalysis.

The influence of Fortmann can also be found in the work of Jan van der Lans.
Jacques Janssen, his colleague in Nijmegen, wrote in a biographical sketch that
Van der Lans in many ways "followed the agenda" of Fortmann. His project of
saving religion and religious experience by searching for a second primitivity in
a modern secularized world was continued by Van der Lans. Key concepts in

---

[152] J. Weima, *Reiken naar oneindigheid. Inleiding tot de psychologie van de religieuze
ervaring*, Uitgeverij Ambo, Baarn, 1981, pp.93-104.
[153] We should notice here that Weima does not interpret Freud's and Jung's theories as
two conflicting theories, but instead regards Jungian psychoanalysis as further elaboration on Freudian concepts. The theory of archetypes is for example a further elaboration
of Freud's ideas on "archaic rests".
[154] Idem, pp.73-80.

his work are: "experience, myth, giving meaning (*zingeving*), and again experience".[155]

Indeed his writings bear the marks of Fortmann. When for example elaborating on the disappearance of the mythical-religious world view in modernity Van der Lans describes mythical thinking in terms of participation, a world of unity without separation between nature and culture, subjective and objective reality.[156] He even explicitly refers to Lévy-Bruhl and Van der Leeuw as scholars who reflected on "mythical consciousness", a synonym for primitive mentality.[157] Opposed to this mythical consciousness is our modern rationalized world with its divisions into domains: inner subjective reality, inter-subjective reality (collective norms, ideas and values) and the world of the physical objects. This "lost" mythical consciousness should be rediscovered as a religious ideal in everyday life and in the longing for the *Deus absconditus*.[158] Here psychologists of religion have a task by reflecting on religious experience and giving meaning to life.

Van der Lans makes perfectly clear that psychologists of religion should first of all study religious experience as a form of human behaviour, which doesn't have to lead into conflicts with theological interpretations unless the psychologist judges that these experiences "are nothing but hallucinations or fantasies". But such a judgement is not for a psychologist to make: he "cannot know whether supernatural factors play a role".[159] Freud is criticized here for having reduced religious experience to basic needs, illusions and fantasies, and having rejected them as infantile and pathological.[160]

In these basic ideas we clearly hear the echo of Fortmann, even although the concept of projection is not explicitly mentioned. The latter fact is not unimportant, for Van der Lans makes an interesting move towards psychoanalysis. Although Freud strongly rejected "religious imagination" as pathological and contrary to rational logic[161], since the 1970s there is a turning of the tide. Psychoanalysts have developed new theories of symbolization, narcissism and imagination in which these mechanisms do not indicate infantile behaviour,

---

[155] J. Janssen, "Ten geleide", in J. van der Lans, *Religie ervaren. Godsdienstpsychologische opstellen*, KSGV, Tilburg, 2006, pp.7-15. "Experience" comes first, because of Van der Lans' dissertation on religious experience and meditation from 1978, and last, because of the theme of his valedictory lecture in 1998: religious experience.

[156] J. van der Lans, "Geloven: een kwestie van fantasie. Een godsdienstpsychologische bijdrage aan een hedendaagse verantwoording van het godsdienstige geloven", in Idem, pp.52-71.

[157] Idem, p.58. Compare also J. van der Lans, *Religieuze ervaring en meditatie*, Uitgeverij Benschop en Thissen, Nijmegen, 1978, pp.38ff.

[158] J. van der Lans, "Geloven: een kwestie van fantasie", p.65.

[159] J. van der Lans, "Religieuze ervaring en meditatie", in *Religie ervaren*, pp.16-34 (20-21).

[160] J. van der Lans, "Geloven: een kwestie van fantasie", pp.64, 68-69.

[161] Idem, p.64.

but are interpreted as aiming at finding meaning in life. Freud's theories are not abandoned but corrected in new psychoanalytic theories, such as object relations theory.[162] The influence of developments in German pastoral psychology can also be recognised.[163]

New psychoanalytic theories have opened up possibilities for scientific reflection on the role of fantasy and imagination in religion as a means to give meaning to life. "Faith", Van der Lans concludes, "is an affective relationship with an object that can only be grasped in images." "Nobody has ever seen God. But when I detect the feeling in myself that there is someone who speaks to me, I cannot do anything else but form an image with the help of my imagination. For a modern anthropology of faith this seems to me of extreme importance."[164] He adds that it is important for believers to be conscious of the fact that these images of the divine are not the same as the imagined, and that the symbol is not identical to the symbolized. When this consciousness is lost religion becomes dogmatism and fundamentalism (in which the symbol is taken as a "real" object).[165] Finally, according to Van der Lans, this role of imagination and fantasy in religion has a liberating effect: it elevates us above everyday reality and liberates from fear.[166] Key elements from Fortmann's views on religious perception in a modern world, participation, and the salvational character of religion,

---

[162] Idem, p.66. When Van der Lans speaks of a turning of the tide in psychoanalysis he often refers to the writings of the Dutch-American psychologist of religion Paul Pruyser and his reflections on Donald Winnicott's object relations theory and the key concept of transitional experience. It is interesting to notice that Pruyser's writings were already received in the Netherlands even before he wrote his major studies on creative imagination in religion. Fortmann "introduces" him in the second volume of *Al ziende de Onzienlijke*. Together with Berger Pruyser published a book in 1970, *Wat doen we met ons geloof?*, "What do we do with our Faith?".

[163] J. van der Lans, "In de spiegel van de mythe herken ik mijzelf", in *Religie ervaren*, pp.35-51 (46-48); J. van der Lans, "Geloven: een kwestie van fantasie", pp.64-66. Already in his dissertation on religious experience and meditation Van der Lans mentions the writings of Fritz Meerwein and Joachim Scharfenberg on narcissism (see next chapter) as important corrections in psychoanalytic theory for a positive interpretation of religious experience. Religious experience is no longer regarded as a regression to infantile feelings, but an "experience of solidarity". J. Van der Lans, *Religieuze ervaring en meditatie*, p.14, p.22.

[164] J. van der Lans, "Geloven: een kwestie van fantasie", p.67.

[165] Idem, p.68

[166] Idem, p.69. This elevation above everyday one-dimensional (rational-technical) life is also expressed in the definition of religious experience in Van der Lans' dissertation. Religious experience is considered as "a special way of perceiving in which reality is differently approached in comparison to everyday life, on a different level of consciousness which enables the discovery of new meanings of objects, that were otherwise not considered". Interesting is the fact that religious experience is regarded to be a "perception". This can be associated with projection which after all was also considered as a perception. J. Van der Lans, *Religieuze ervaring en meditatie*, p.43.

can thus be recognized in Van der Lans' ideas on religious experience, mythical consciousness and "meaning" (as an ideal coherent meaning in life), and the liberating character of faith.

An interesting question is "what happened to projection?" In an article on religiosity and fantasy from 1986 Van der Lans (and his co-author) speaks of a "revaluation of imagination in the domain of religion" inspired by new psychoanalytic theories.[167] This revaluation is opposed to Freud's rejection of a positive meaning for religious imagination, when he, according to Van der Lans, saw religion as nothing else but an infantile fantasy, illusion and projection.[168] Hence, the concept of projection reappears in the guise of imagination, fantasy and "giving ultimate meaning", in the mental activity of making an image of an object one cannot know otherwise, and in the subjective meaning-giving structuring of the world.[169]

This revaluation of projection among scholars influenced by Fortmann is certainly inspired by the writings of Heije Faber, for it was Faber who had already in the late 1960s and early 1970s described the positive meaning of projection in faith development.[170] In *Geloof en ongeloof in een industrieel tijdperk* [Belief and Unbelief in an Industrial Era] Faber discusses the cultural change from a civil society to an industrial society in terms of a change in authority structures and a decline of paternalism.[171] Traditional superego structures are decon-

---

[167] J. van der Lans, L. Vergouwen, "Religiositeit en fantasie. Een beschouwing over onderzoeksgegevens omtrent het omgaan met religieuze beelden", in J.A. van Belzen, J. van der Lans (eds.), *Rond godsdienst en psychoanalyse. Essays voor dr. Arnold Uleyn*, Uitgeverij Kok, Kampen, 1986, pp.88-101 (89).

[168] Idem, p.88, p.95.

[169] This line of thought can also be found in the writings of Jacques Janssen. He has argued that Freud should be criticized for having reduced religion to illusion. This is however not the final word. In the 1960s Freud was reappraised for having criticized the neurotic unhealthy forms of religion. In the 1970s psychoanalysts indicated the positive functions of illusion: illusions are not only inevitable, but even wholesome. J. Janssen, "De terugkeer van God in de psychologie. Het voordeel van illusie", in J. Janssen, *Nederland als religieuze proeftuin*, KSGV, Nijmegen, 1998, pp.61-71.

[170] On Faber and projection see J.A. van Belzen, *Psychologie en het raadsel van de religie*, pp.294-298.

[171] An important reference in the context of cultural change is Alexander Mitscherlich's *Auf dem Weg zur Vaterlosen Gesellschaft* from 1963, a socio-psychological study on the evolution of culture strongly inspired by Freud's cultural writings and by Erikson's theory on stages of development. In this study Mitscherlich proclaimed the end of an era characterized by father authority, obedience, guilt and superego functions. A. Mitscherlich, *Auf dem Weg zur Vaterlosen Gesellschaft. Ideen zur Sozialpsychologie*, Piper & Co. Verlag, Munich, 1969.

structed and replaced by an emphasis on individual faith.[172] In this process the father God image has been unmasked as a projection of infantile wishes.[173] But this decline of religion and paternalistic structures should not be seen as merely negative, for it opens new possibilities for faith.[174]

In his 1972 *Cirkelen om een geheim* [Circling around a Secret] this is elaborated upon.[175] In this major study Faber starts with a critique of Freud and Jung arguing that the first basically regard "the religion" as "collective imma-turity".[176] Such a generalization shows that Freud had little "empathetic under-standing" of individual religiosity due to the fact that he didn't "participate".[177] In the second part of his depictions of psychological and psychoanalytical theo-ries on religion – originally called "turn of the tide" – Faber focuses on Rümke and Erik H. Erikson.[178] Rümke is important for arguing that man is *homo re-ligiosus* and that unbelief is in fact a developmental disorder. This, according to Faber, is an important turn of the tide towards new psychoanalytic theories. He even considers Rümke's idea of an "ultimate ground" as a forerunner of "basic trust".[179] The latter term is a key concept in the writings of the American psy-chologist and psychoanalyst Erikson.[180] According to Faber, Erikson's study of

---

[172] H. Faber, *Geloof en ongeloof in een industrieel tijdperk. Een verkenning*, Uitgeverij Van Gorcum, Assen, 1969, pp.9-13.

[173] Idem, pp.17-19.

[174] Idem, pp.37ff. Like Scharfenberg, Faber agrees with Barth and Bonhoeffer that a clear distinction should be made between religion and faith. See next chapter.

[175] The English translation of this book is simply *Psychology of Religion*. The teleology expressed in the original Dutch title is therefore lost. Literally the title means "circling around a secret" in which the word "geheim" – secret – has the double meaning of "hidden" and "mystery". In the final chapters of his book Faber makes clear that a cul-tural change and "evolution" from primitivity to maturity in which religion is more and more "spiritualized" can be clearly seen in the decline of "the old pattern" (paternalistic tradition, the father God image), but that the "new society" has not yet been realized. Modern believers thus find themselves on a quest towards an era of "unity of the world" and "freedom, peace, love, work and community". This is not only "hidden" in the fu-ture, but also envisioned in the Gospel, the inspiring "mystery" that keeps man going. H. Faber, *Psychology of Religion*, SCM Press, London, 1976, pp.319-325.

[176] Idem, p.86.

[177] Idem, p.85. Here we see that Faber is also rooted in a Dutch phenomenological tradi-tion.

[178] Already in *Geloof en ongeloof in een industrieel tijdperk* Faber had mentioned Rümke and Erikson as important scholars offering promising perspectives for rethink-ing religiosity in an industrial age. H. Faber, *Geloof en ongeloof in een industrieel tijd-perk*, pp.36-37, p.114.

[179] H. Faber, *Psychology of Religion*, p.75-76.

[180] Faber is especially impressed by Erikson's study *Young Man Luther. A Study in Psy-choanalysis and History* (1958). Idem, pp.94-126. In his writings Erikson focuses atten-tion on the development of the ego in relation to social reality (and religion as part of it) that can either inhibit or support the development of identity. This is the central idea in

Luther and his theory of developmental stages shows that basic trust as a starting point for further development and the internalization of the father-son relation are "essential elements" in individual development.[181] In other words, "we
get the impression that primitive infantile feelings can develop into more mature
ones".[182]

This calls for a new view of projection: the projection of feelings onto
God "always play their part at a certain moment in the relation to the God in
whom a person "believes" in the framework of his pattern of upbringing and
culture". These feelings can be infantile, "but they can also (in spite of what
Freud says) have a mature character, albeit within a prevailing cultural pattern."[183] This includes the notion that a believer acknowledges that he cannot
believe beyond the limits of the specific personal form this belief has taken
throughout development and in time (an acknowledgement that evokes religious
tolerance). This is why faith is always "circling around a secret".[184]

In the mid 1980s this line of thought is again taken up by Faber.[185] In an
article on the meaning of psychoanalysis for religion he detects a clear shift of
attention in psychoanalysis from a Freudian emphasis on Oedipal structures towards an emphasis on pre-Oedipal developments focusing on the mother-child
relation.[186] He detects a clear shift towards the self psychology of Erikson and
Heinz Kohut[187], and to object relations theory. Faber mentions other scholars in

---

Erikson's famous study *Young Man Luther*, a study that focuses on the importance of
the period of adolescence. In later theoretical writings this stage is regarded by Erikson
as a crucial stage in developing a self-identity. The theory of the life stages is developed
in *Identity, Youth and Crisis* (1968). On Erikson see T.H. Zock, *A Psychology of Ultimate Concern*; S.A. Mitchell, M.J. Black, *Freud and Beyond. A History of Modern Psychoanalytic Thought*, Basic Books, New York, 1995, pp.142-149.

[181] H. Faber, *Psychology of Religion*, pp.120-121.

[182] Idem, p.278.

[183] Idem.

[184] Scharfenberg has criticized this concept of "secret". In his view it is the product of
thinking too much in terms of "empirism", i.e. in terms of the specific historic and individual forms of faith. According to Scharfenberg, a theory of the symbol that presents
dissolving horizons between experiences of people throughout and in time (see next
chapter) would be a good alternative. J. Scharfenberg, "Religionspsychologie nach
Freud", in *Wege zum Menschen* 27 (1975), pp.433-448 (440).

[185] H. Faber, "Zicht op de structuur van de godsdienstige ervaring: twee boeken", in *Nederlands Theologisch Tijdschrift* 36 (1982), pp.311-331; H. Faber, "Een nieuwe kijk op
projectie als godsdienstig verschijnsel", in *Nederlands Theologisch Tijdschrift* 39
(1985), pp.110-127.

[186] H. Faber, "De betekenis van de huidige psychoanalyse voor het inzicht in religie", in
J.A. van Belzen, J. van der Lans (eds.), *Rond godsdienst en psychoanalyse*, pp.9-22.

[187] Probably Faber was inspired by Scharfenberg (see next chapter) to study Kohut.
Scharfenberg had presented a lecture on Kohut on the first symposium for European
psychologists of religion in Nijmegen (1980). J.A. van Belzen, *Psychologie en het
raadsel van de religie*, p.297.

this field such as Paul Pruyser and Ana-Maria Rizzuto. Central in their theories is the idea of "transitional objects which create an intermediate area of experience, through which the experience of religion becomes possible".[188]

According to Faber the object relations theory can help us to understand the structures of religious experience, that is to say, "the belief that ultimate reality can be called upon [by us, H.W.] and that the other opens the way [for us, H.W.]".[189] This "other" is on the one hand the "matrix of empathy", the continuation of basic trust in adult life which shared with fellow man (concrete, in communities).[190] On the other hand it is God, "the called-upon" who "objectifies this [ultimate, H.W.] reality for us". This "sheds new light on the problem of projection". Object relations theory shows that projection is not just an "infantile" mechanism, "but a structural precondition for mature basic trust".[191] Projection is not an infantile mechanism in which illusionary images are created, but primarily a mechanism that is part of basic trust[192], that is to say, a positive anticipation of the existential confrontation with the limitations of life.[193]

Here we see, as later in the writings of Van der Lans, how projection is revalued in connection with new psychoanalytic theories that were welcomed as an alternative to Freud's, and that also seemed to correspond with the focus (since Fortmann) on the structure of religiosity and religious experience.

I will not further pursue the analysis of current discussions on religion as "meaning giving", on imagination and fantasy in the psychology of religion,

---

[188] Idem, pp.17-18.

[189] Idem, p.20.

[190] Here we see how Faber synthesizes the concept of basic trust (self psychology/object relations theory) with the concept of empathy (Rogers, clinical pastoral movement).

[191] Idem; H. Faber, "Een nieuwe kijk op projectie als godsdienstig verschijnsel", pp.118-119.

[192] Faber argues that projection functions on different levels. Projection as a mechanism in basic trust is original in comparison to the projection of the father image on God. This basic trust (or in Kohut's words a "matrix of empathy") is described as a participation in a "sense of we". Idem, pp.123-124.

[193] Idem, p.121. Compare: *Wanneer dit [het openstellen voor "groei" in onszelf, H.W.] zo is, betekent dit dus: dat wanneer wij in staat zijn onze relatie tot de moeder (of vader) in de vorm van beelden op de basis van het zijn, op het Zijn zelf als onafhankelijk van ons, dus op God te projecteren, wij een "echte", bevrijdende godsdienstige ervaring hebben*. In this quotation we can notice the influence of Tillich (God as essence, *Zijn*). Real religious experience and faith are not to be found in the projection of parental images (as in theism) but in a projection as a envisioning of the existential in relation to essence. The "key word" here is presence (or participation), that is, "being there with and for the other through the Other, the holy Presence". This is what Weima had called "reaching for Infinity". H. Faber, "Zicht op de structuur van de godsdienstige ervaring", p.328, p.330.

and on pastoral theology and spiritual care in the Netherlands.[194] However, one observation can be made: the central problem in Fortmann's *Envisioning the Invisible* may not have been overcome. The general concept of projection as used by Fortmann covered and veiled a broad variety of mechanisms, structural and libidinal relations between subjects and objects. We will return to this issue in the final chapter.

To conclude, not only was the projection debate typically Dutch, but also some of the important issues debated upon in Dutch psychology of religion and pastoral theology in the following decades are to a certain extent moulded by the key concepts and ideas from this projection controversy: the subject-object dichotomy, participation and primitive mentality, the subjective processes that structure a coherent meaningful reality. Given this historic background and the influence of Fortmann on a new generation of psychologists in religion and pastoral theologians we can at least partly understand the – typically Dutch – focus on religious experience and the positive function of imagination, fantasy or giving meaning in contemporary literature in the field of psychology of religion, pastoral theology, spiritual care and sometimes beyond these disciplines.[195]

Van der Lans was a leading figure in putting these issues on the agenda.[196] As to Freud, the Fortmann tradition can be summarized in two

---

[194] Key publications in psychology of religion on this issue are M.H.F. van Uden, "Tussen zingeving en zinvinding. Onderweg in de klinische godsdienstpsychologie", in J.A. van Belzen (ed.), *Op weg naar morgen. Godsdienstpsychologie in Nederland. Teksten II*, Uitgeverij Kok, Kampen, 2000, pp.114-133; H.A. Alma, *De parabel van de blinden. Psychologie en het verlangen naar zin*, Humanistics University Press, Utrecht, 2005; T.H. Zock, *Niet van deze wereld? Geestelijke verzorging en zingeving vanuit godsdienstpsychologisch perspectief*, KSGV, Tilburg, 2007.

[195] An echo of the previously described debate and discussions can be heard in systematic theology. In Anton Houtepen's major study in theological anthropology he asks whether the religious dimension of humanity is not a human construct in the search for meaning. In other words, "is not everything men states about God and his relation to God a projection, imagination, metaphor, born out of a desire for a trustworthy Father and a caring Mother?" He calls this in short "the projection thesis". This thesis can be found in the writings of Feuerbach, Marx and Freud, but also in contemporary systematic theology. Houtepen is in debate here with Harry Kuitert who in his study of man's religiosity had argued that "religion is a human construct", i.e. the product of imagination - which doesn't rule out the possibility of "transcendence as experience". Religious imagination is itself a "mystery", a putting into words, a creation of meaning, and in this act inevitably transcendence is involved (transcendence as an inner-worldly experience of "something" (or "it") that is not of this world. A. Houtepen, *Uit aarde, naar Gods beeld. Theologische antropologie*, Uitgeverij Meinema, Zoetermeer, 2006, pp.36-38; H. Kuitert, *Voor een tijd een plaats van God. Een karakteristiek van de mens*, Uitgeverij Ten Have, Baarn, 2002, p.106, pp.119ff., pp.131ff.

[196] T.H. Zock, *Niet van deze wereld?*, pp.21-22, p.27. J.A. van Belzen, "Religie, zingeving, spiritualiteit: waar gaat godsdienstpsychologie eigenlijk over?", in J. Janssen,

words: critical distance. In an intellectual line of thought from Rümke and Van der Leeuw up to the present discussions about *zingeving* the key issues are man's natural inclinations towards giving ultimate meaning and to proceed in a process of "broadening of the ego" and growth in coherent understanding. It is a discourse on *homo religiosus* who through self-transcendence is taken up in a totality of meaning experienced in and despite a modern secularized world. In this line of thought Freud is not only regarded as the projection theorist who deconstructs self-transcendence and imaginary world views, but also the psychoanalyst who presents an anthropology that cannot be synthesized with a perspective on mystic participation as the transgression of life's contingencies or subject-object dichotomy.

Concerning the sense of guilt we can conclude that in the whole projection debate and its after-effects it was not a dominant issue. The focus of attention was on projection and later on imagination and "giving meaning", i.e. on theories concerning the subject's structuring of a worldview. The emphasis was thus on (re)constructing religion and religiosity in a modern secularized world, an objective that was already present in the writings of Van der Leeuw.

The question that should be raised is whether the positively reassessed projection mechanism in discussions on *zingeving* suffices for a full analysis of the way individuals structure their relation with reality and the divine, or that Vergote is right after all when he stated that reading Freud's writings on religion from the perspective of projection meant that the actual structuralizing processes in religion were lost from sight. From Van der Leeuw via Fortmann until Van der Lans the emphasis was on perception: understanding the object as it shows itself; religious experience as the response to the fact that there is something to see; giving meaning as the structuring of perceptions in a coherent world view. The status of perceptions was discussed by Freud in his major contribution to a theory on projection, the Schreber case, yet exactly there he already pointed out that man's relation to reality is not based on perception, but on libidinal relations. In that direction we find the actual structuralizing processes of which the sense of guilt is then a structural element. Despite the fact that Dutch psychologists of religion were clearly interested in the specific characteristics of inner-worldly religious experience, religious world views and ultimate meaning systems, the moment Freud was rejected as just a projection theorist, the Freudian questions on how the subject relates to reality were lost from sight. We will return to this issue in the final chapter.

M.H.F. van Uden, H. van der Ven (eds.), *Schering en inslag. Opstellen over religie in de hedendaagse cultuur*, KSGV, Nijmegen, 1998, pp.207-224 (215).

4 On dialogues, debates and rediscoveries

4.1 Introduction

In this chapter we will focus on the engagement with Freud in theology and religious studies in the German-speaking world from the 1960s until the present
day. Our starting point will be the writings of Joachim Scharfenberg (1927-
1996), who was from the 1960s onwards a leading figure in pastoral psychology
advocating the dialogue between theology and psychoanalysis.[1] His writings
will serve as the guideline and point of reference in further discussion on various issues and developments in the dialogue between theology (both Catholic
and Protestant) and psychoanalysis from the 1960s until the present day. Further
we will discuss the reception of Freud in exegesis and biblical hermeneutics,
and the "rediscovery" of Freud's *Moses and Monotheism*.

    Our special attention will again concern the engagement with Freud's
ideas on the sense of guilt. We will see that an advocated debate on the "guilt
problem" in pastoral psychology did not take place. Instead there was a turn towards other fields of attention (narcissism) and a general shift from Freudian
psychoanalysis towards new and seemingly more constructive (less critical)
psychoanalytic theories. Incidental studies from both Catholic and Protestant
theologians on the guilt problem did appear, and we will discuss them. Here we
will see clear denominational differences between Catholic and Protestant approaches to the issues of the sense of guilt and narcissism. In recent years the
guilt problem seems to reappear in pastoral psychology in the context of discussions on responsibility and conscience formation. The "guilt problem", first associated with outdated traditional religion, reappears as an issue in the context
of a return of religion in the public domain and a general concern about a disin-
tegrating "guiltless" society.

There is a tendency in the writings of Joachim Scharfenberg to argue that the
dialogue between practical theology and the human sciences (psychoanalysis)
started late in German-speaking theology because of the dominance of dialectic
theology in general and Thurneysen's theories on pastoral care in particular.[2] In

---

[1] According to Scharfenberg pastoral psychology is a concept on the boundary of pastoral care and psychology. J. Scharfenberg, *Einführung in die Pastoralpsychologie*,
Vandenhoeck & Ruprecht, Göttingen, 1985, p.13. In general we can say that pastoral
psychology is a discipline seen either within or underlying practical theology, that develops theories on the integration of psychological or psychotherapeutic ideas and experiences in pastoral care.
[2] J. Scharfenberg, *Religion zwischen Wahn und Wirklichkeit. Gesammelte Beiträge zur
Korrelation von Psychoanalyse und Theologie*, Furche-Verlag, Hamburg, 1972,
pp.127ff. Not only Thurneysen is regarded as a towering figure in the landscape of theories on pastoral care. We should also mention Hans Asmussen and his study *Die Seel-*

for example the preface of his 1972 *Seelsorge als Gespräch* [Pastoral Care as Conversation] Scharfenberg writes that practical theology was like Sleeping Beauty only just awoken by a kiss. Whether the prince was the clinical pastoral training or psychoanalysis would be for future historians to decide.[3] The metaphor suggests that after an initial interest by theologians in psychoanalysis (Pfister) dialectic theology smothered the dialogue. Even the cautious attempts – in the 1950s and the early 1960s – by a new generation of practical theologians to explore psychoanalysis were not free from the burden of dialectic theology – essentially psychoanalytic conversational techniques were only used as a tool to create a conversation on sin and guilt.[4] Scharfenberg thus presents himself as one of the first critics of what he calls a "superseded patriarchical structure" in pastoral conversation.[5]

In fact Pfister had been an isolated pioneer and by the time of his death another "pioneer"[6] had already started writing on pastoral care in relation to psychoanalysis (or depth psychology): Otto Haendler (1890-1981).[7] In the 1950s the subject of his main publications is the dialogue or correlation between theology and Jungian psychoanalysis. The central idea in his writings is that both theological anthropology and psychoanalysis are concerned with the integration of consciousness and unconsciousness so enabling a person to accept his life by removing inhibitions and liberating the natural possibilities of the human psyche.[8] Haendler regards the problem of guilt as the fundamental problem of

---

sorge (1933). He is often criticized by Scharfenberg in one and the same breath as Thurneysen. See for example J. Scharfenberg, "Seelsorge und Beichte Heute", in *Wege zum Menschen* 24 (1972), pp.80-90.

[3] J. Scharfenberg, *Seelsorge als Gespräch. Zur Theorie und Praxis der seelsorgerischen Gesprächsführung*, Vandenhoeck & Ruprecht, Göttingen, 1991, Vorwort (originally 1972). Elsewhere Scharfenberg speaks of an "iron curtain" that was raised between theology and psychoanalysis for more than two decades. J. Scharfenberg, "Die Rezeption der Psychoanalyse in der Theologie", p.262.

[4] J. Scharfenberg, *Seelsorge als Gespräch*, p.18.

[5] Idem, p.25.

[6] Scharfenberg and Winkler consider Haendler a practical theologian "who was ahead of his time", that is, he was a pioneer for pastoral care in dialogue with psychoanalysis. O. Haendler, *Tiefenpsychologie, Theologie und Seelsorge. Ausgewählte Aufsätze*, J. Scharfenberg, K. Winkler (eds.), Vandenhoeck & Ruprecht, Göttingen, 1971, Vorwort.

[7] For biographical data see K. Voigt, *Otto Haendler – Leben und Werk. Eine Untersuchung der Strukturen seines Seelsorgeverständnisses*, Peter Lang, Frankfurt et al., 1993.

[8] Idem, p.248. An example can be found in an article on religious projection of 1954. Projection seen positively – in congruence with Pfister's concept of sublimation – is directed at truth, more precise the God-father-image of the New Testament. However, this positive projection can be inhibited by unconscious projections of infantile father-images on God (fixations). This means that projections should be "managed and purified". This process of purification and correction aims at a deeper experiencing of God. O. Haendler, "Unbewußte Projektionen auf das christliche Gott-Vaterbild und ihre seelsorgerische Behandlung", in *Tiefenpsychologie, Theologie und Seelsorge*, pp.11-47.

human existence.[9] His concept of existence bears the markings of Tillich's influence.[10] Existence is described as "being there" in relation to God who "is" as creator, essence and meaning of man's existence.[11] This existence is marked by guilt, that is to say, by the very fact that (through the Fall) man has become what he is.[12] Here the limits of pastoral care and psychotherapy become clear, for only as far as guilt is related to acts of injustice or inner psychic conflicts can pastoral care and psychotherapy help overcoming feelings of guilt.[13] Existential guilt cannot be overcome with these methods. In pastoral care and psychotherapy aiming at liberation from guilt, man can only be guided to the "edge" of existence. At that point a person will not only fully realize his guilt-existence, but also his being accepted by God as a new trust and faith that gives freedom.[14]

In Haendler's writings on the correlation between Jungian psychoanalysis and pastoral care Freudian psychoanalysis does not play an important role. Nevertheless this chapter on the "rediscovery" of Freudian psychoanalysis in German-speaking theology in the 1960s should start here for a simple reason: Haendler's plea for a fundamental dialogue between psychoanalysis and pastoral care on key issues such as guilt.

4.2 Joachim Scharfenberg

4.2.1   The critique of religion and the purification of faith

Scharfenberg argued that the early cautious attempts by a new generation of practical theologians to explore psychoanalysis were not free from the burden of dialectic theology.[15] But was his work free from this burden? In his 1985 *Ein-*

---

[9] O. Haendler, "Schuldverhaftung und Schuldlösung in Theologie und Psychologie", in *Tiefenpsychologie, Theologie und Seelsorge*, pp.72-100.

[10] Haendler and Tillich had already met in their youth and over the years a friendly contact remained. Haendler considered his theological thoughts very near to Tillich's. K. Voigt, *Otto Haendler*, pp.95ff.

[11] O. Haendler, *Grundriss der Praktischen Theologie*, Alfred Töpelmann Verlag, Berlin, 1957, pp.317-318.

[12] O. Haendler, "Schuldverhaftung und Schuldlösung in Theologie und Psychologie", p.83.

[13] Idem, pp.91-94.

[14] Idem, pp.84ff.

[15] Scharfenberg studied theology and psychology. He was one of the first Europeans to conclude a training program in clinical pastoral education in the United States. From 1953 until 1963 he worked as a minister and hospital pastor. In the period 1956-1961 he was trained in psychoanalysis by Carl Müller-Braunschweig and others. From 1971 onwards he was professor in Practical Theology at the University of Kiel. An introductory article in Scharfenberg's ideas is H. Wahl, ""Zwischen" Theologie und Psychoanalyse: Joachim Scharfenbergs Impulse für die Religions- und Pastoralpsychologie", in

führung in die Pastoralpsychologie [Introduction to Pastoral Psychology] he writes that he chose "religion as a profession" in order to "help people". His additional choice to train in psychoanalysis was evoked by an experience in the hospital. After he had taken a confession and forgiven the sins of a female patient he noticed that her feelings of guilt had not diminished. He also found out that she confessed to about thirty other pastors, all of whom were unable to help her. At that point he decided to become a psychoanalyst.[16]

Scharfenberg was moulded by dialectic theology and his pastoral methods in his early years as a minister and pastor were marked by the Thurneysen-model of confession and absolution of sin and guilt. This legacy from the past was not completely thrown overboard in his later theoretical work. Although he writes that the extreme distinction between religion and faith Barth made cannot be defended, his turn to psychoanalysis is made "in the name of faith". Freudian psychoanalysis is called upon as a *Fremdprophetie*, an instrument of "purification of different forms of Christian faith"[17] in order to make "Christian symbols understandable" again. It is a *Fremdprophetie* against outdated Christian metaphysics and ethics: "Religion must go down in order for faith to stand up".[18]

In this context we can also situate Scharfenberg's interest in Pfister.[19] He is presented as an important inspiration for the dialogue between psychoanalysis and theology.[20] The influence of Pfister on Scharfenberg can be detected not only when he opposes outdated abstract theology to experienced faith, but especially when unhealthy illusionary religion is placed in opposition to true healthy faith.[21] Freudian psychoanalysis thus comes in as a tool to purify

---

Wege zum Menschen 49 (1997), pp.439-458. For biographical data see J.A. van Belzen, "Reflections on the Passing Away of a Trailblazer: Joachim Scharfenberg, 1927-1996", in *The International Journal for the Psychology of Religion* 7 (1997), pp.53-55.

[16] J. Scharfenberg, *Einführung in die Pastoralpsychologie*, p.15.

[17] J. Scharfenberg, *Sigmund Freud und seine Religionskritik*, p.154.

[18] J. Scharfenberg, *Einführung in die Pastoralpsychologie*, p.215; J. Scharfenberg, "Die Rezeption der Psychoanalyse in der Theologie", pp.262-263, pp.311-313.

[19] Chr. Henning, "Oskar Pfister – der Beginn einer problematischen Freud-Rezeption innerhalb der Theologie", pp.51-54. See also M. Klessmann, *Pastoralpsychologie. Ein Lehrbuch*, Neukirchener Verlag, Neukirchen, 2004, p.97; I. Noth, "Seelsorge zwischen Erinnern und Vergessen – Zur Einseitigkeit des Dialogs mit der Psychoanalyse", in I. Noth, Chr. Morgenthaler (eds.), *Seelsorge und Psychoanalyse*, pp.9-14 (10).

[20] J. Scharfenberg, *Sigmund Freud und seine Religionskritik*, pp.13-20. The attempts to revive an interest in Pfister's writings by republishing (parts of) his texts can be found in J. Scharfenberg, "Die Rezeption der Psychoanalyse in der Theologie" and in E. Nase, J. Scharfenberg (eds.), *Psychoanalyse und Religion*.

[21] *Es könnte sein, daß Freuds Kritik in Wahrheit mithilft, den Glauben von den Verzerrungen seines pathologischen Doppelgängers zu befreien.* (The pathological alter ego of faith is obsessional neurosis.) J. Scharfenberg, *Sigmund Freud und seine Religionskritik*, p.156.

religion and extract a mature form of faith characterized by a healthy developed libido (love), freedom and growth in knowledge.[22]

Here we can detect the same concerns underlying Scharfenberg's position as those in the writings of Fortmann, Faber and others, as described in the previous chapter. Theology and the church have become estranged from modern believers. But unlike developments in the Netherlands the new strategies and ideas formulated by Scharfenberg in the critique of outmoded theology and in the new alternative theories and movements did not go hand in hand with an anti-Freudian attitude. In German pastoral psychology, psychoanalysis and the new methods of pastoral counselling could even to a certain extent be synthesized.[23] In Scharfenberg's writings on pastoral conversation for example we can clearly see a focus on Freud's theories of transference and counter-transference[24], but also of Rogerian empathic understanding as non-directive attitude in conversation.[25]

This synthesis of different elements from different psychological schools (or philosophies) not only meant elements from other psychologies could be taken up in a basically Freudian theory. In Scharfenberg's writings we can clearly see a shift of attention from an emphasis on Freud's critique of religion in the 1960s and early 1970s towards the self psychologies of Erikson and Kohut.[26] In my opinion the shift must be understood as a move from an empha-

---

[22] Idem, p.180.

[23] The foundation of the *Deutsche Gesellschaft für Pastoralpsychologie* ("German Association for Pastoral Psychology", 1972) by both psychoanalytic oriented theologians and clinical pastoral oriented theologians is an indication that on an institutional level different schools in pastoral psychology could cooperate. M. Klessmann, *Pastoralpsychologie*, pp.644ff.

[24] For example J. Scharfenberg, *Sigmund Freud und seine Religionskritik*, pp.114ff.; J. Scharfenberg, "Übertragung und Gegenübertragung in der Seelsorge", in E.R. Kiesow, J. Scharfenberg (eds.), *Forschung und Erfahrung im Dienst der Seelsorge. Festgabe für Otto Haendler zum 70. Geburtstag*, Vandenhoeck & Ruprecht, Göttingen, 1961, pp.80-89.

[25] J. Scharfenberg, *Einführung in die Pastoralpsychologie*, p.70. From the early 1940s onwards the American psychologist Carl Ransom Rogers (1902-1987) had developed a therapeutic method characterized by a non-directive attitude of the therapist: the so called client-centered therapy. The therapist, or better counsellor, should try to identify with the client through an empathic understanding of the client's self understanding through which the therapist will be able to mirror the feelings of the client thus enabling a situation in which the client can understand and accept him/her self better. C.R. Rogers, *Client-centered Therapy. Its current Practice, Implications and Theory*, Houghton Mifflin, Boston, 1951, ch.2.This therapeutic theory was to become the theoretical backbone of what was already established before the Second World War as clinical training for theology students.

[26] In *Sigmund Freud und seine Religionskritik* and *Religion zwischen Wahn und Wirklichkeit* Freud's psychoanalytic theories are central in Scharfenberg's reflections. In his later *Einführung in die Pastoralpsychologie* Freud is hardly elaborated upon and instead

sis on the psychoanalytic critique of religion towards an accent on psychoanalytic contributions towards the maturation of faith.

Christian Henning has argued "in the writings of Scharfenberg faith is situated within the boundaries of psychoanalysis".[27] Scharfenberg however preferred to speak of a "correlation" between psychoanalysis and theology following in Tillich's footsteps. He stresses his critical potential: the exposure of individual and collective "instutional profanities" and "moral perversions"[28] and, affiliated to this, Tillich's method of correlation between psychoanalysis and theology as a critical alternative for Barthian pastoral care with its equation of conversation and preaching[29] and its emphasis on the confession of the sense of guilt as the sole precondition for absolution.[30]

Most importantly he agrees with Tillich on the correlation between psychoanalytic and theological anthropology. According to Scharfenberg, the key anthropological notions in Freud's writings are those of "conflict" or "ambivalence" between delusion, fantasy and wish on the one hand and reality on the other hand, the conflict between "progression" and "regression", and between "autonomy" and "participation".[31] In Freudian psychoanalysis these conflicts are expressed and structured in the two basic psychic complexes, the narcissistic and the Oedipal conflict. Conflict is also the subject in pastoral care, that is to say, theories of pastoral care and theological anthropology "describes man in conflict".[32] Psychoanalysis offers the paradigmatic structures for understanding human existence and describing such anthropology.

Freud did more than just depict the tragic struggle of Eros and Thanatos, says Scharfenberg, he also pointed towards a solution in "love". A Pfisterian line of thought can be detected here when the conflict in man is not only to be regarded as an existential suffering but also as a "potential", a possibility

Kohut, Erikson and Pfister are mentioned in the context of Scharfenberg's paradigms. J. Scharfenberg, *Einführung in die Pastoralpsychologie*, pp.33-43.

[27] Chr. Henning, "Oskar Pfister – der Beginn einer problematischen Freud-Rezeption innerhalb der Theologie", p.54.

[28] J. Scharfenberg, *Sigmund Freud und seine Religionskritik*, pp.33-34.

[29] J. Scharfenberg, *Seelsorge als Gespräch*, p.10.

[30] J. Scharfenberg, "Bewußtwerdung und Heilung bei Johann Christoph Blumhardt", in F. Wintzer (ed.), *Seelsorge. Texte zum gewandelten Verständnis und zur Praxis der Seelsorge in der Neuzeit*, Kaiser Verlag, Munich, 1985, pp.175-190 (176).

[31] *Freuds Psychoanalyse steht und fällt mit der Vorstellung vom innerpsychischen Konflikt. (...) Wirklichkeit gibt es für ihn nur in der Lebensvolle Spannung zwischen zwei Polen.* J. Scharfenberg, *Sigmund Freud und seine Religionskritik*, pp.84-85 (also pp.30-31, p.39, p.41). See also J. Scharfenberg, H. Kämpfer, *Mit Symbolen leben. Soziologische, psychologische und religiöse Konfliktbearbeitung*, Walter-Verlag, Olten/Freiburg, 1980, pp.171-181.

[32] J. Scharfenberg, *Einführung in der Pastoralpsychologie*, p.52. Compare K. Winkler, *Seelsorge*, p.8; I. Karle, *Seelsorge in der Moderne. Eine Kritik der psychoanalytisch orientierten Seelsorgelehre*, Neukirchener Verlag, Neukirchen, 1996, p.73.

for a positive change. Scharfenberg speaks of a "broadening of possibilities" through sublimation that overcomes the existential limitations of life.[33] Sublimation is described as the process of transforming the aggressive (anti-social) drives in social and community-building inclinations, i.e. the strengthening of Eros against Thanatos in the service of shared values.[34] Such sublimation is possible with "the help of biblical symbols and stories".[35]

The aim of pastoral care is "healing through love"[36] or in more psychotherapeutic terms "healing as ego-integration".[37] Religious symbols have a crucial function in this process from conflict to integration, for in these symbols inner experiences and conflicts can be expressed and worked through.

Paul Ricoeur's Hegelian interpretation of Freud with an emphasis on the sublation (Aufhebung) of conflicts is an important point of reference here.[38] According to Scharfenberg, the symbol is a substitute expressing a hidden meaning that, because a symbol binds emotions, not only encloses this hidden meaning but is also meaningful in itself.[39] Symbols evoke a "liberating experience" when they bring about "dissolving horizons" between a "system of mean-

---

[33] J. Scharfenberg, Einführung in der Pastoralpsychologie, pp.196-197.

[34] J. Scharfenberg, Sigmund Freud und seine Religionskritik, pp.164-165.

[35] J. Scharfenberg, Einführung in der Pastoralpsychologie, p.182.

[36] Sein [Freuds, H.W.] gesamtes Lebenswerk konnte er unter dem Stichwort "Heilung durch Liebe" verstehen und unterbringen. J. Scharfenberg, "Beiträge zu einem neuen Freud-Bild", p.460.

[37] J. Scharfenberg, H. Kämpfer, Mit Symbolen leben, p.156. Ego-integration is seen by Scharfenberg as "identity formation". Although the formula Heilung als Ich-Integration seems be derived from the psychoanalytic writings of Wolfgang Loch (W. Loch, "Heilung als Ich-Integration", in Zur Theorie, Technik und Therapie der Psychoanalyse, Fischer, Frankfurt, 1972, pp.135-155) Scharfenberg in his elaborations on the concept of ego-integration from the early 1970s onwards follows a line of thought in congruence with self psychology: identity is not just the sum of childhood identifications (Freud), but a life-long process in which the ego integrates old and new "identification fragments". J. Scharfenberg, Religion zwischen Wahn und Wirklichkeit, pp.39-45; J. Scharfenberg, "Identitätskrise und Identitätsfindung im psychoanalytischen Prozeß", in Wege zum Menschen 24 (1972), pp.241-252.

[38] P. Ricoeur, Freud and Philosophy; J. Scharfenberg, H. Kämpfer, Mit Symbolen leben, pp.127-131, p.173, p.197.

[39] Idem, p.63. Scharfenberg indicates four functions of biblical symbols. The first function is articulation of inner conflicts through biblical symbols which implies the possibility of taking a distance from the immediate inner conflict. Second, symbols enable a person to accept inner conflicts. Third, biblical symbols make possible the articulation of one's own inner conflicts. Fourth, symbols open up the possibility of integration of diverging inner forces. Idem, p.157. The "ultimate" biblical symbols are Jesus Christ who is described by Scharfenberg as the symbol of an integrated self, and the cross as a symbol of integration. Idem, pp.156-157; J. Scharfenberg, Einführung in die Pastoralpsychologie, pp.223-224.

ing" and "everyday experience".[40] Some important preconditions underlie this function of the symbol. The first is the principle of "anthropological constancy".[41] The inner conflicts of contemporary man that can be described according to narcissistic and Oedipal structures have their correlates in the conflicts and ambivalences as expressed in biblical symbols or depicted in biblical stories.

The backbone for this principle is Scharfenberg's reading of Rudolf Bultmann.[42] His notion of an existential interpretation of the kerygma[43] is valued by Scharfenberg as a "change of paradigm" as it opened up the possibility of a correlation between biblical, theological and psychoanalytic anthropology, because in biblical myth the same human psychic conflicts are expressed as are present in the reader.

In the 1960s the symbol does not yet play an important role in Scharfenberg's writings. Only from the 1970s onwards does this issue become more and more central in his writings.[44] The reason for this can be found in developments in psychoanalytic theories of the symbol. Crucial here is Alfred Lorenzer's 1970 *Kritik des psychoanalytischen Symbolbegriffs* [Critique of the Psychoanalytic Concept of "Symbol"]. Lorenzer had rightfully argued that Freud had restricted the formation of symbols to the realm of the unconscious primary

---

[40] J. Scharfenberg, H. Kämpfer, *Mit Symbolen leben*, pp.157-158.

[41] *Es scheint so etwas wie "anthropologische Konstanten" zu geben, die dafür sorgen, dass der Abstand überbrückbar wird, dass Menschen sich mitsamt ihren Konflikten wieder finden können in religiösen Symbolen und deren konfliktbearbeitendes Potential für sich selbst entdecken.* J. Scharfenberg, *Einführung in die Pastoralpsychologie*, p.93. See also I. Karle, *Seelsorge in der Moderne*, p.92.

[42] J. Scharfenberg, *Einführung in die Pastoralpsychologie*, pp.185ff.

[43] Bultmann had criticized liberal theology for having "reduced" Christ to the historic Jesus and his moral acts and character. Instead he focuses on the proclamation (kerygma) of Christ. The main problem in understanding this proclamation was the fact that biblical language is mythological language (for example in stories about miraculous events) that is no longer understandable for modern man. Hence, he calls for a demythologization as a deconstruction of the idea that biblical language presents "facts". Instead, he argued that biblical language should be interpreted anthropologically or existentially, that is, biblical language should be seen as expression of man's understanding of the world in which he lives and of himself in a particular manner, for Jesus proclaimed the Kingdom as a future act of God which appeals to the reader/listener in the here and now to examine himself from this perspective, and (ultimately) to obediently accept the Word of God as truth and guideline. In other words, existential interpretation was about understanding the other in order to understand oneself. G.W. Dawes, *The Historical Jesus Question. The Challenge of History to Religious Authority*, Westminster John Knox Press, Louisville/London/Leiden, 2001, pp.248-296.

[44] D. Seiler, "Symbol und Glaube", in I. Noth, Chr. Morgenthaler (eds.), *Seelsorge und Psychoanalyse*, pp.82-94 (85-86).

processes, i.e. the symbol as symptom of the repressed.[45] The main new paradigm Lorenzer now formulated was that the formation of symbols was not limited to the primary processes, but on the contrary, mainly situated on the (various) level(s) of secondary processes. In short, the formation of symbols is a function of the ego.[46] Symbols are not representations of the repressed, but, on the contrary, have the function of bringing unconscious material to the level of conscious perception and expression. Hence, the symbol is important for the – liberating – expression of deeper layers of the psyche. Regression is now seen as a de-symbolization to the level of what Lorenzer calls cliché formation (primary process)[47], a level which is also the realm of the neurotic.[48]

In *Mit Symbolen leben* [Living with Symbols], 1980, this theory is taken up as leading theory and applied in the field of theology.[49] What was meant as a meaningful symbol can take the form of cliché when Christian tradition becomes rigid. At those moments religious critique is needed in order to revive the symbol.[50] For indeed, as long as there is neurotic regression the symbol will not come to its full creative power.[51] After the Freudian critique of religion the symbol becomes a key issue in Scharfenberg's writings because of its constructive potential – (re-)establishing the connection between symbolic meaning systems that stem from Christian tradition and individuals or groups in their maturation process.[52]

4.2.2 Reading of Freud

Different elements of Scharfenberg's reading of Freud have already been mentioned and necessarily so, because his theological views are strongly intertwined with his psychoanalytic views. This correlation between psychoanalysis and theology means a constant shift from one discourse to the other. That faith can

---

[45] A. Lorenzer, *Kritik des psychoanalytischen Symbolbegriffs*, Suhrkamp Verlag, Frankfurt, 1970, p.27. Also, H. Wahl, *Glaube und symbolische Erfahrung. Eine praktisch-theologische Symboltheorie*, Herder Verlag, Freiburg, Basel, Vienna, 1994, pp.198-221, pp.412-424.

[46] Idem, p.65. The unconscious is now regarded as merely a reservoir of material with an affective charge. Idem, p.72.

[47] Idem, p.110.

[48] Idem, p.105.

[49] J. Scharfenberg, H. Kämpfer, *Mit Symbolen leben*, Kapitel II.

[50] Idem, p.72. Here we should notice a difference between Lorenzer and Scharfenberg. Whereas Lorenzer clearly states that the differentiation between lower and higher levels of cliché and symbol formation does not imply a value judgement, Scharfenberg's application of these theories does imply such a judgement.

[51] See also J. Scharfenberg, "Between Mythology and Symptomatology. Thoughts on the Psychology of Symbols", in J.A. van Belzen (ed.), *Hermeneutical Approaches in Psychology of Religion*, Rodopi, Atlanta/Amsterdam, 1997, pp.233-240 (239).

[52] H. Wahl, ""Zwischen" Theologie und Psychoanalyse", p.455.

be situated within the boundaries of psychoanalysis and that theology is integrated in psychology, as Henning argued[53], is one side of the correlation. From the analysis of Freud's writings Scharfenberg is able to point out the basic structures and content of faith. However, his reading of Freud – even his decision to become a psychoanalyst – is also situated within a theological project, namely the critique of an outdated theology, thus aiming at a maturation in faith which is then again translated into psychoanalytic idiom as a critique of superego structures – *Entautorisierung*[54] – and de-neurotization, and ego-integration as a further indication of maturation. In the following paragraphs we will see how Scharfenberg uses his method of correlation and its shifts of perspective in his reading of Freud.

Scharfenberg's starting point is that a theologian should be careful and critical in his reading of Freud. The engagement with Freud (until 1968) shows that theological view points strongly determine the interpretation of his writings. Whoever reads Freud should read "the whole of Freud as a historic phenomenon", because his thoughts are in a "constant process of change". One should "describe lines of development". From thereon it is possible to find elements or lines of thought that are "fruitful" in contemporary theology.[55] This first of all means reading Freud "as a child of the 19th century" and trying to establish the roots of his ideas in the books that he read and admired: Goethe, Plato, Shakespeare, the books on classic mythology and on history, and Multatuli, who provided Freud with the formula so important in his later work "Eros and Ananke, love and reality".[56] Also Freud's scientific roots are described with a focus on his rejection of metaphysics and on his empirical attitude.[57] Finally Freud's personal fascination for Jewish identity is considered.[58] Here in a nutshell some themes that are central in the developments in his writings on religion are already present.

---

[53] Chr. Henning, "Oskar Pfister – der Beginn einer problematischen Freud-Rezeption innerhalb der Theologie", p.54.

[54] J. Scharfenberg, "Narzißmus, Identität und Religion", in *Psyche. Zeitschrift für Psychoanalyse und ihre Anwendungen* 27 (1973), pp.949-966 (950). In his writings on narcissism, as we will see, Scharfenberg follows a line of thought "in the footsteps" of Erikson and especially Kohut. The influence of Scharfenberg and Kohut can be noticed in, for example, an early article by Thomas Auchter on love in Freud's writings and its relevance for theological reflections on love for fellow men. Th. Auchter, "Psychoanalytische Überlegungen zum Thema Liebe", in *Wege zum Menschen* 27 (1975), pp.137-150.

[55] J. Scharfenberg, *Sigmund Freud und seine Religionskritik*, p.38.

[56] The word ἀνάγκη means necessity or life fate, but is translated by Scharfenberg as reality. Idem, pp.50-51. Freud had expressed his admiration for Multatuli on several occasions.

[57] Idem, p.54.

[58] Idem, pp.58-66.

Reading Freud as historic phenomenon also implies reading Freud in debate. Scharfenberg depicts Freud's discussions and quarrels with Breuer, Fliess, Adler and Jung in order to the show the principle points of view in Freud's line of thought such as the genetic development of sexuality, the critique of physical explanations and the emancipation of a psychological perspective, dualism instead of monism, (individual) history versus un-historic unconsciousness.[59] In these debates crucial elements in the further development and "progress" of Freud's thought can be seen, notably, that "unconsciousness means regression and being bound to the past; consciousness and interpretation liberates for the future".[60] The correlation with a critique of outmoded theological constructs should not be overlooked.

Reading the whole of Freud does not only mean interpreting his theories, but includes analysing his therapeutic practice. Freud's writings on culture and religion cannot be disconnected from "the heart of his work" which is therapy. Scharfenberg argues that Freud in his therapeutic practice went through a development from suggestion in hypnosis via "interrogation" and cathartic method towards the "talking cure" as the conversation between equal partners in which the method was based on the transference and counter-transference mechanism: interpretation situated in interpersonal dynamics.[61]

The first time Freud had elaborated on the mechanism of transference was in the Dora case, the case characterized by mutual reproaches by Dora and her father and attempts to gain Freud's sympathy. Transferences "are new editions or facsimiles of the impulses and fantasies which are aroused and made conscious during the progress of the analysis; but they have this peculiarity, which is characteristic for their species, that they replace some earlier person by the person of the physician".[62] This replacement or "repetition of "infantile images""[63] mainly concerned Oedipal structures. Freud discovered that transference was a general mechanism in the relation of patient and therapist. Hence, he also had to assume counter-transference, the transference of affects (provoked by a patient) of the therapist on the patient.[64] Working through these repetitions in order to "lay open a way into the future"[65] was now the core activity in the

---

[59] Idem, pp.67-98.

[60] Idem, p.98.

[61] Idem, pp.109-114.

[62] S. Freud, *Fragment of an Analysis of a Case of Hysteria, SE VII*, p.116.

[63] J. Scharfenberg, *Sigmund Freud und seine Religionskritik*, p.116.

[64] Idem, p.118. Compare S. Freud, *The Future Prospects of Psychoanalytic Therapy*, pp.144-145. A short definition is: Transference is the attitude of the analysand towards the analyst based on former relations with others; counter-transference is the reaction this attitude evokes in the analyst. P. Vandermeersch, H. Westerink, *Godsdienstpsychologie*, p.306. Compare also J. Laplanche, J.-B. Pontalis, *Vocabulaire de la psychanalyse*, p.103.

[65] J. Scharfenberg, *Sigmund Freud und seine Religionskritik*, p.117.

analysis. This working through was a matter of interpretation, not suggestion or force.[66] According to Scharfenberg, therapy aims at freedom which is a further indication of the ego's power over infantile unconscious ideas and affects.[67]

Another point Scharfenberg focuses on is Freud's idea that the neurotic suffers from his reminiscences. According to Scharfenberg this means that a neurotic is incapable of accepting himself as a historic being, that is, as a time continuum.[68] Here also therapy aims at freedom now described as liberation from reminiscences and repetition. But what exactly is liberated? In Scharfenberg's reading of Freud the answer is "love". "Only love" is capable of changing reality in such a way that the wish-reality dichotomy does not lead to regression into psychic conflicts.[69] In short, Freud's therapeutic aim was to liberate from neurotic symptoms and conflicts through love.

In his chapter on therapeutic practice Scharfenberg tries to establish correlations with facets of theology. The possible correlations with pastoral conversation are not elaborated upon, but correlations with Bultmann's theological hermeneutics. The issue is the demythologization of theological language and the turn towards anthropology and existentialism, towards proclamation as making the structures of man's existence explicit and conscious in order to keep positive possibilities of existence (such as love, trust and goodness) open for the future. Before being able to point out these correlations, a depiction of Bultmann's hermeneutic approaches is inserted as an "excurse" in the chapter on Freudian therapy.[70] This excurse is more than a depiction inserted to make certain correlations plausible. Bultman's ideas are also used to raise some questions that serve as a guideline for an analysis of Freudian therapy. The correlations later established are evoked by this strategy of questioning Freud through Bultmann. We are confronted here with a recurring problem in Scharfenberg's reading of Freud. After having criticized those theologians who read Freud from a theological perspective he presents his study as a reading of the whole Freud

---

[66] Idem, p.119.

[67] Idem, p.120.

[68] Idem, pp.129-130.

[69] Idem, p.130.

[70] J. Scharfenberg, *Sigmund Freud und seine Religionskritik*, pp.100-109. The main correlations are: firstly, the avoidance of mythical language in the sense of avoiding talking on the level of facts and, instead, the focus on language in which the structures of existence can be made understandable. Secondly, both Freud and Bultmann focus on man as a historic being and on the possibility of human freedom and love. Thirdly, the correlation of transference and counter-transference as a mechanism and method to turn regressive tendencies round into progressive possibilities on the one hand, and a biblical hermeutics focusing on working through existential structures and opening up the realm of faith (love, trust, goodness) on the other hand. In short the correlation between human beings as "living human documents" and texts. J.A. van Belzen, "Reflections on the Passing Away of a Trailblazer", p.53.

"from his own presuppositions".[71] From thereon he wants to extract relevant issues for theology. Yet, concerning therapy Freud is read from the perspective of a theologian. And this is crucial, because in this chapter Scharfenberg points out that Freudian psychoanalysis is essentially "healing through love", a love with its correlate in a language of faith. Only from this perspective can Freud's critique of religion be made fruitful for theology.

Scharfenberg's reading of Freud's writings on religion[72] is based on two premises: Freud's writings on religion cannot be harmonized, but can only be understood within the development of his oeuvre; Freud's critique of religion is not aimed against theology or faith, but against the "outer religious forms" (ritual, dogma).[73] According to Scharfenberg, critique of religion aimed against its outer forms is already apparent in Freud's article on the analogies between obsessional acts and religious ceremonies.

The analogy between obsessional neurosis and religion is also taken up in *Totem and Taboo*. Here Freud focuses his attention on two problems in particular: the fact that people accept moral prohibitions without conscious motivation and the sense of guilt as part of human existence.[74] The quest for the origins of these phenomena lead back to primal events and childhood, back to the ambivalent feelings toward the (primal) father. For Scharfenberg the main questions *Totem and Taboo* raises are whether a moral law without motivation can claim general acknowledgement, and whether ritual can free us from the sense of guilt.[75]

A different perspective on religion is presented in *The Future of an Illusion*. The analogy with early childhood experiences is dominant, but now Freud focuses on the relation between wish (pleasure principle) and reality (reality principle): does one hold on to illusionary wishes; what are the possibilities for development towards the acceptance of reality (or "maturation towards reality")?[76] This question did not only evoke Freud's plea for a rational scientific world view, but also led to a concise analysis of human existence in *Civilizations and Its Discontents*. Here, Scharfenberg argues, Freud formulates an alter-

---

[71] J. Scharfenberg, *Sigmund Freud und seine Religionskritik*, p.6.

[72] The following section is based on Scharfenberg's *Sigmund Freud und seine Religionskritik*. A summary can be found in J. Scharfenberg, *Religion zwischen Wahn und Wirklichkeit*, pp.77-96 and in J. Scharfenberg, "Sigmund Freud", in W. Schmidt (ed.), *Die Religion der Religionskritik*, Claudius Verlag, Munich, 1972, pp.9-17

[73] J. Scharfenberg, *Sigmund Freud und seine Religionskritik*, p.137.

[74] Idem, p.142.

[75] Idem, p.145.

[76] Idem, pp.145f. Scharfenberg's interpretation of Freud's reality principle not as a continuation of the pleasure principle, but as an adjustment to outside reality, seems to be inspired by either Jung or Erikson.

native for science as a life goal: love, i.e. Eros which is in full struggle with Thanatos.[77]

Finally, there is *Moses and Monotheism*, a study on the "historic truth" of religion. According to Scharfenberg, Freud focuses his attention on man as a historic being whose inner life is moulded by his socio-historic context, that is, the historic development in the tension between regression ("return of the repressed") and progression ("advancement in intellectuality"). As a "prophet" Freud analyses his own tradition in order to find a revolutionary solution in St Paul's interpretation of the Golgotha tragedy.[78]

Scharfenberg's starting point in the further analysis of Freud's critique of religion is the following: Freud confronts religion because in its manifestations known to him it fails to accomplish the task for which it is actually there.[79] Religion is unable to accomplish its task – moral insistence and education, and comfort – without degrading the value of life, thus creating a delusional world view and inhibiting intelligence.[80] Scharfenberg will argue that Freud only confronted religion in its "pathological" manifestations. The first aspect of religion Freud questioned was "taboo obedience".[81] In *Totem and Taboo* he deconstructs both primitive taboo and the Kantian categorical imperative because of its unmotivated authoritative superego.

We should notice that Scharfenberg here and elsewhere regards the superego primarily as "historic results of historic forces", that is to say, the "parental forces" with which one identifies.[82] Hence, the superego is "the result of reality experience". At stake is thus the individual "autonomy versus the outside world".[83] Freud's project of "maturation towards reality" implies the replacement of "blind obedience" to authority by individual "existential responsibility".[84] Instead of taboo obedience moral decisions should be based on individual assessment.[85] But how is this transition made? Key concepts are freedom, sublimation and love.[86] Freedom means a therapist or pastor does not take on the role of authority figure, but instead, creates a sphere of open dialogue in which moral decisions can be made without force. The sublimation of aggression components of the libido towards higher goals, such as knowledge or friend-

---

[77] Idem, pp.148-149.

[78] Idem, pp.150-154.

[79] *Er* [Freud, H.W.] *kämpft nicht gegen die Religion, weil er gegen sie rebelliert, sondern weil sie ihm in den Gestalten, in denen er sie kennen gelernt hatte, nicht das zu leisten vermag, wofür sie eigentlich da ist.* Idem, p.155.

[80] Idem, p.156.

[81] Idem, pp.156-168. See also Chr. Henning, "Oskar Pfister – der Beginn einer problematischen Freud-Rezeption innerhalb der Theologie", p.52.

[82] J. Scharfenberg, *Sigmund Freud und seine Religionskritik*, p.160.

[83] J. Scharfenberg, *Religion zwischen Wahn und Wirklichkeit*, p.38.

[84] J. Scharfenberg, "Beiträge zu einem neuen Freud-Bild", p.454.

[85] J. Scharfenberg, *Sigmund Freud und seine Religionskritik*, p.162.

[86] Idem, pp.163ff.

ship, is advocated by Freud. Love as life goal means that the focus of attention in an "art of life" is satisfaction and happiness from loving and being-loved.[87] Eros and Ananke, love and reality, capture Freud's psychoanalytic ideals. Although Freud did not realize it, these psychoanalytic ideals were merely variants of the Christian message, says Scharfenberg.[88]

The second aspect of religion criticized by Freud is "pious delusion".[89] Those perceptions that are not related to reality are called delusional. In Freud's writings on religion this theme is elaborated upon in his analyses of mythology and mythological thinking in analogy with dream and symptom analysis. Crucial here is the idea that in mythology the symbol is taken literally, and exactly this element makes mythology unrealistic/delusional. Myths must be interpreted, like dreams, in order to find their underlying "truth".

Finally, Freud criticizes infantile wishful thinking as comfort.[90] In his search for "truth" in religion Freud discovered not only regression, the return of the repressed and the sense of guilt cultivated in religion (*Totem and Taboo*, *Moses and Monotheism*), but also progression in the form of wish illusions about the future. He advocated the idea of acknowledging "Ananke, the merciless reality". Doing so implied being free from wishful thinking. According to Scharfenberg, Freud was unable to see his ideals, Eros and Ananke, realized in faith. And yet this is what he now puts forward: the "truth" in religion is faith characterized by freedom of responsibility through assessment, freedom from delusion and acceptance of reality, and freedom from a-historic unmotivated metaphysics or dogmatics.

4.2.3   De-authorization and assessments

In Scharfenberg's theological project Freud's critique of religion is used as an instrument for the "de-authorization of patriarchal structures"[91] or a replacement

---

[87] This issue is elaborated upon in Scharfenberg's article on narcissism. Both psychic development and reality demand that narcissistic self-love is transformed into object-love

[88] "Diskussion" (H. Zahrnt – J. Scharfenberg), in H. Zahrnt (ed.), *Jesus und Freud. Ein Symposion von Psychoanalytikern und Theologen*, Piper & Co Verlag, Munich, 1972, pp.117-118.

[89] J. Scharfenberg, *Sigmund Freud und seine Religionskritik*, pp.168-176.

[90] Idem, pp.176-180.

[91] J. Scharfenberg, "Narzißmus, Identität und Religion", p.950. In this context Scharfenberg points towards his major inspirations in religion critique: Roy Stuart Lee, Paul Tillich and especially Peter Homans. In *Theology after God* Homans had argued that with "the collapse of transcendence" in the death-of-God-theology the old Protestant anthropology focusing on "self-limitation" had also collapsed. This "crisis of conscience" should be the starting point for a new theological anthropology characterized by "self-completion". P. Homans, *Theology after Freud*, pp.160ff.

of a "severe unquestioned superego" by an individually formulated "norm".[92] Modern man doesn't need a fatherly pastor who represents "decrepit patriarchical structures" and uses conversation for proclamation.[93] In Scharfenberg's view superego structures are associated with enforced structures. These structures can be opposed to an ego-integration process that implies the formulation of an individual norm.

From a strictly Freudian point of view this division between superego and an individual norm, an ego conscience, cannot be defended. In the first part of our study we have seen that in Freudian thought superego and conscience formation is closely related to narcissism. The superego is not just a representative of outside authorities and the result of moral enforcements, but much more importantly an advocate of the id and the result of identifications through which a person can establish an identity. The superego is the individual norm in the first place.[94] Guided by the pleasure principle it represents to us who we are, who we want to be and what we concretely desire. The ego is merely reason and deliberation. As to the autonomy of the ego Freud would say it is an illusion.

Scharfenberg's reconstruction of Freud's thought is presented firstly as a critical and deconstructive attitude towards superego structures and moral-religious authority enforced upon people, and secondly as a "prophecy" of freedom and love. In this reconstruction certain elements in Freud's writings are underestimated or even disregarded. First of all there is Freud's fascination for authority. In his writings there certainly is a development from suggestion in hypnosis via interrogation towards a therapy in which transference and counter-transference are the key mechanism and method. But this transition is not a de-authorization. In fact in all three methods the therapist is a father figure, albeit that there is shift from enforcing authority to receiving authority. To put it in Lacanian terms: the therapist is always *le sujet supposé savoir*, the analyst who knows "more" than his client.[95] This authority is a crucial element in psycho-analytic practice[96] which is apparent when Freud describes how transference can change into falling in love which means that an analyst runs the risk of being idealized as love object. Probably, Freud argues, this falling in love is an attempt to question the authority of the analyst. The only response can be that the analyst sticks to his authority, i.e. his function to understand and interpret "the truth".[97] This is an important point, for when Scharfenberg argues that pastoral

---

[92] J. Scharfenberg, "Narzißmus, Identität und Religion", p.961.

[93] J. Scharfenberg, "Seelsorge und Beichte heute", p.85, p.90.

[94] On this issue see A. Lambertino, *Psychoanalyse und Moral bei Freud*, pp.297ff.

[95] P. Vandermeersch, H. Westerink, *Godsdienstpsychologie*, pp.310-312.

[96] Laplanche and Pontalis suggest that transference implies regarding the analyst as authority. J. Laplanche, J.-B. Pontalis, *Vocabulaire de la psychanalyse*, p.497.

[97] S. Freud, *Observations on Transference-Love, SE XII*, p.164.

care is a free conversation between equal partners that could also be described in Rogerian terms of empathy he neglects the analyst's "knowledge".[98]

Not only in psychoanalytic practice is authority important. Throughout Freud's writings you find a fascination for authorities and "great men" that in different ways express a "historic truth", men that embody a nuclear element of a tradition that is still profoundly influential on people including Freud himself (Moses, Paul, Goethe). Scharfenberg undervalues this life-long fascination for authority in relation to tradition. In my opinion this is related to the fact that he regarded "tradition" as outdated and instead focused on reviving Christian symbols. Yet, exactly concerning symbols one might raise the question whether the existential meaning of symbols can be detached from an alleged outdated tradition or whether it does need an authoritative tradition in order to function meaningfully.

Another problematic point in Scharfenberg's reconstruction of Freudian thought concerns Eros. He puts forward the concept almost as a shibboleth and in such a way that it can function as a correlate to Christian love. In *Civilization and Its Discontents* Freud does argue that civilization shows a constant struggle between Eros and Thanatos. Civilization is also a "process" serving Eros which binds people together.[99] Scharfenberg strongly emphasizes this point in his reading of Freud. Two remarks should be made here.

Firstly, this binding of people brings us not only back to the problem of authority and tradition as indicated above, but also to the Oedipal relations that serve as the models for future identifications and object choices. We are in the heart of Freudian thought again including his ideas on the sense of guilt. Associating Eros with Christian love seems to elevate the binding of people above this level of struggle and ambivalence. Hence, whereas Freud associates this struggle with repression and an inevitable return of the repressed, Scharfenberg focuses on progression and the sublation (Hegel) of conflict.[100]

Secondly, Eros and Thanatos as drives are speculative conceptual constructs that as such are not distinctively and in a pure form present in human re-

---

[98] Scharfenberg does criticize Rogerian conversation methods when he argues that Rogers is too optimistic about man's ability to overcome his own resistance in a free conversation with an empathic pastor. In other words, in Rogerian pastoral care the unconscious motives will not be expressed. Psychoanalytic techniques are therefore important, that is to say, the analysis of the transference of images on the pastor. Scharfenberg does not say that a pastor has an authority because he "knows more", but focuses solely on the parental images that are transferred onto him. J. Scharfenberg, *Seelsorge als Gespräch*, pp.115-119.
[99] S. Freud, *Civilization and Its Discontents*, chapter VI.
[100] Already in his first book Scharfenberg calls upon Ricoeur's Hegelian reading of Freud arguing that Freud, although his works points towards "freedom, sublimation and love", was unable to depict a solution for the struggle and ambivalence of feelings related to the Oedipus complex. J. Scharfenberg, *Sigmund Freud und seine Religionskritik*, pp.161-163.

lationships.[101] In fact, from a clinical perspective, there are hardly arguments for assuming that these drives as such exist. As soon as drives are related to objects relations are ambivalent. There is always a sadistic component in the sexual drive, and hence in "love".

Thirdly, there is Freud's critique of the Christian ideal to love one's fellow man: we can love the ones that love us; we cannot and should not love the ones that hate us. In Scharfenberg's work the concept of Eros is a pivot the enables him to associate Freudian and Christian thought, yet without making explicit that its meaning shifts when it is taken out of the "horizontal" psychoanalytic discourse into another, "vertical", register.[102] His reading of Freud is not just based on Freud's own presuppositions, but also on an a priori decision to present the whole of Freud in correlation with a theological project. This has consequences for the interpretation and meaning of psychoanalytic concepts.

In the final chapter we will return to the issue of the relation between therapy and pastoral care. As to our topic of the sense of guilt, it is striking that, though it was a key issue in Freud's writings on religion and culture and in his ideas on identity formation, it is not a key issue in his writings on Freud's critique of religion. In Scharfenberg's project of the purification of faith, the inevitability of the sense of guilt in both religion and Freudian thought seems to constitute a problem that has yet to be resolved.

4.2.4   Beyond the guilt principle?

"The guilt problem"[103] is at the heart of Scharfenberg's theological project. We have seen that he regarded his decision to become a psychoanalyst as evoked by a pastoral experience in which the sense of guilt was the major issue. The decision to become a psychoanalyst was thus elicited by an experience that could be characterized as the failure of dialectic theology in the field of pastoral care. When Scharfenberg argues that the movement in practical theology towards the human sciences in 1960s can be seen as a response to outdated theologies and church practice he also notices the hesitation of some of his colleagues, especially those who stuck to the idea that pastoral care was about the confession of guilt and absolution. The reason for this sentiment could be found in the "monopolization of the problem of guilt" in the Christian doctrine of justification. This is the "heart" of Christian theology and thus of Christian identity, but from the 1960s on also one of the "spear points" of critique. Can the traditional view of guilt be part of contemporary and future theology, or does it definitely belong

---

[101] S. Freud, *The Ego and the Id*, chapter IV.

[102] See H. Henseler, *Religion – Illusion?*, pp.80-81.

[103] J. Scharfenberg, *Religion zwischen Wahn und Wirklichkeit*, p.189.

to a "culture of guilt" that now seems to characterize a past stage in cultural development?[104]

At this point we can again ask the question whether Scharfenberg's thought was not also deeply influenced by dialectic theology. We have seen that Thurneysen basically regarded neurosis, and thus the neurotic sense of guilt, as symptom of sin. Pastoral care was not only about confessing sin and guilt, and absolution, but was also supposed to have an effect on neurotic structures. The healing work of God's love created the possibility for psychic healing by overcoming the inner ruptures and restoring the "wholeness of personality". These latter ideas resound in Scharfenberg's ideas on "healing through love" and healing as ego-integration.

In his attempt to find a solution for the problem of guilt in theology and pastoral care Scharfenberg starts off with Freud's observation that a sense of guilt was characteristic of all neuroses, and that repression of drives increased the sense of guilt. According to Scharfenberg, the "law" behind this phenomenon is the child's basic amorality, the enforcement of morality by the feared parents, and the development of an ambivalent attitude towards them. Only in a further development is the superego erected through identification. Here the internalization of psychic conflicts takes place, and aggression is now aimed against oneself.[105] According to Scharfenberg, Freud noticed that his secularized and neurotic patients were also a product of culture dominated by religion that had influenced socialization processes for centuries by demanding repression and a sense of guilt. Freud found a solution for the problem of the sense of guilt by making the unconscious conflict conscious. In short, the solution was found in the strengthening of the ego through which "the conflict between the drive impulses of the id and the real outside world can be brought to a better solution than provided by repression", because "possibilities of sublimation" could be opened up.[106] The question is whether this solution can also be applied to religion.

According to Scharfenberg, Freud's writings on the cultural superego indicate that there is a parallel solution possible in both individual neurosis and in culture. For although the overall impression from Freud's ideas on the sense

---

[104] Idem, pp.189-190. The concept of "culture of guilt" is a reference to Alexander Mitscherlich's *Auf dem Weg zur Vaterlosen Gesellschaft*. In this socio-psychological study strongly inspired by Freud's cultural writings and by Erikson's theory on the stages of development Mitscherlich not only analyses but also welcomes – as the title already suggests – a cultural development ("evolution towards consciousness" or "emancipation") from a society characterized by father authority and obedience with an emphasis on conscience and superego functions towards a society that is psychologically characterized by an integration of drive, conscience and ego.

[105] Idem, p.190f.

[106] Idem, p.193.

of guilt is that these feelings are inevitable, psychoanalytic theory has been further developed. The inevitability of a sense of guilt was questioned in 1960s,
mainly because the further development of culture seems to open up the perspective of socialization without an emphasis on guilt.[107] In response to this
Scharfenberg detects two reactions. First, there is an even stronger emphasis on
the sense of guilt and sinfulness in some of the writings of representatives of
dialectic theology, and second, the total deconstruction of traditional theology
and liquidation of superego and guilt structures in the death-of-God-theology.[108]

Basically, Scharfenberg now argues for a critical position in-between
these two radical positions.[109] He puts forward the idea of cultural development
arguing that just as the classic era was dominated by the id-function and the pu-
ritan bourgeois society by the superego-function, so will contemporary and future society will be dominated by the ego-function. That means that the problem
of guilt belongs to a developmental stage (in the individual and) in Western culture. He points out that in contemporary critical theology this developmental
change can be noticed.[110] Guilt no longer has a prominent place in a "changing
psychic situation".[111] In short, "the monomaniac emphasis on the guilt-
absolution relation" is criticized. The formulation of alternatives remains a task
for the present and the future.[112] In Scharfenberg's discussion of the sense of
guilt outdated patriarchal and superego structures are seen as a developmental
stage that should be carefully reflected especially in religious pedagogy.[113]

---

[107] Idem, p.196.

[108] The death-of-God-theology was a (small) theological movement (with a climax in
the 1960s) sharply criticizing traditional theological conceptualizations. Such a critique
could already be found in the writings of Bultmann (demytholization) and Tillich (God
as non-existent – essence), but was radicalized in this movement.

[109] Idem, p.203.

[110] Amongst others he refers to the writings of Dorothee Sölle and to Kurt Niederwimmer's study of Jesus from 1968 (see 4.4). In their writings Scharfenberg detects alternative bible interpretations criticizing traditional dogmatic issues and opening up possibilities for faith beyond morality and guilt. Idem, pp.205-206.

[111] J. Scharfenberg, "Seelsorge und Beichte heute", p.87.

[112] This line of thought is taken up by Christian Link in his analysis of Freud's ideas on
the sense of guilt in culture and religion and some elaborations on the possibility of a
"beyond sense of guilt" in religion. Link argues with Scharfenberg that for the future of
religion solving the guilt problem is crucial. That is to say, either religion will stay illu-
sionilary attached to its traditional moral standpoints believing that conscience formation is still its task in a changing society, or religion will survive the "death of God and
modernize towards a realistic faith in freedom and clear engagement wherever humanity
is threatened". Chr. Link, *Theologische Perspektiven nach Marx und Freud*, Kohlhammer Verlag, Stuttgart, 1971, pp.99-117.

[113] Idem, pp.207-208. The statement on pedagogy is almost similar to what Vestdijk had
argued 20 years earlier in the Netherlands.

This line of thought was clearly situated in the context of the 1960s, the critique of (parental) authority and the expectation that an old era (culture of guilt) had passed and a new era had begun. It was the period of the secularization theories developed by sociologists on the passing away of traditional religion in Western culture, theories that are now under question, because of the return of religion in the public domain. From a contemporary point of view Scharfenberg's association of guilt with a past era or cultural developmental stage is thus no longer very satisfactory.

We cannot criticize Scharfenberg for being a child of his time, but we can say that this association of guilt with a past era did not contribute to a further debate on "the guilt problem". We will see – which is in fact in line with Scharfenberg's thought – that the issue of the sense of guilt reappears in current discussions on ego conscience formation and responsibility. But what is lacking here is a thorough analysis of the still present positive or negative influences from traditional Christian concepts of modern man. The starting point has become the idea that we no longer live in a culture of guilt but in a culture of narcissism. The idea that superego obedience belongs to the past and that we live in a cultural era in which we are freely responsible for our own destiny seems almost to have become paradigmatic in German pastoral psychology. Guilt and the sense of guilt are thus issues in so far as they are related to the new culture in which we are supposed to live. Yet, the Freudian analysis of guilt structures throughout history, its conscious but mostly unconscious influence, its various guises and solutions, has not lost its relevance when we consider the possibility that (traditional) religion did not simply disappear, but returns in new forms. The question is thus not whether guilt belongs to a past culture or not, but how and which elements from traditional religion have returned in new religious forms such as fundamentalism, New Age spirituality or other and everyday kinds of ritualization.

4.2.5   Influence of Scharfenberg

Given the fact that Freudian psychoanalysis in the 1960s was still "tabooed" by theologians Scharfenberg's study of Freud's critique of religion and its possibilities to rethink faith was a "guiding" study for scholars in the field of pastoral psychology.[114] His study made it possible to re-evaluate Freudian psychoanalysis – to a certain extent. Scholars such as Dietrich Stollberg, Klaus Winkler, Richard Riess and Michael Klessmann who were/are representatives of the clinical pastoral counselling movement could now integrate elements from Freudian psychoanalysis into their theories.

---

[114] M. Klessmann, *Pastoralpsychologie*, p.112.

In an article on conscience Stollberg, for example, elaborates upon Freud's model taking Scharfenberg as his guide.[115] The ego is seen as a "intra-psychic organ of responsibility and independence".[116] In an immature state however it can become dependent on superego obedience. Psychoanalytic therapy then aims at further maturation of "ego-freedom" as the liberation from infantile regressive forces towards love as the life-goal.[117] From thereon Stollberg differentiates between superego conscience and ego conscience, a differentiation that will become a dominant issue in debates to come (see below).

Klessmann, a student of Stollberg, further elaborates on this line of thought arguing in his dissertation from 1980 that Freud's ideas on psychic structures (ego, superego, id) are still important for reflections on faith, for they are the starting point for further theoretical developments in ego psychology and self psychology.[118] According to Klessmann, it was an achievement of Scharfenberg to show the importance of Freud's critique of religion. However, Freud's conflict models cannot point out "the integrative potentials of religion and faith" beyond the model of conflict.[119] In Freudian thought religion is "superego religion" that inhibits the maturation of the individual. Via ego psychology Klessmann turns to the self psychology of Erikson and his ideas on the positive function of religion and social structures in reaching the possibilities for the development of identity (ego-integrity).

Similar lines of thought can be found in writings of Winkler, a student of Haendler and one of the founding fathers of German pastoral psychology. In an article of 1981 he argues that Scharfenberg deserves full credit for having shown that Freud's critique of religion is a challenge for theologians and for Christian faith.[120] Winkler detects two reactions to this Freud-Renaissance in theology. First, there are scholars like Helmut Harsch and René Goetschi (see next paragraph) who seem to be concerned that the influence of psychoanalysis could be a levelling out of norms, and who are apparently afraid that the sense of guilt is no longer at the heart of theological anthropology. Second, there is the broad tendency in pastoral psychology – including Winkler himself – to

---

[115] D. Stollberg, "Das Gewissen in pastoralpsychologischer Sicht", in *Wort und Dienst. Jahrbuch der Kirchlichen Hochschule Bethel* 11 (1971), pp.141-158.

[116] Idem, p.150.

[117] Idem, pp.150-151.

[118] M. Klessmann, *Identität und Glaube. Zum Verhältnis von psychischer Struktur und Glaube*, Kaiser Verlag, Munich, 1980, p.12.

[119] Idem, p.22. In later wrings Klessmann has repeated this point of critique of Freud. The issue is thoroughly discussed in his magnum opus. Here, ego psychology and self psychology are theories developed upon Freud's second topic model (ego, superego, id), focusing on ego formation, and showing that "man can act reasonably and conflict free". M. Klessmann, *Pastoralpsychologie*, pp.118-139, pp.491ff.

[120] K. Winkler, "Ich- Und Über-Ich-Problematik im Umgang mit Normen", in E. Hölscher, M. Klessmann (eds.), *Grundmuster der Seele. Pastoralpsychologische Perspektiven von Klaus Winkler*, Vandenhoeck & Ruprecht, Göttingen, 2003, pp.65-79 (68-69).

move beyond Freud towards ego psychology and self psychology, theories in which the superego is no longer predominant, but the ego and the self. To summarize: *Wo Über-Ich war, soll Ich werden.*[121]

Scharfenberg certainly also had an influence on the next generation of scholars in the psychology of religion and practical theology who took Freudian psychoanalysis as paradigm. Heinz Müller-Pozzi's 1975 *Psychologie des Glaubens* [The Psychology of Faith] and Hans-Günter Heimbrock's 1977 *Phantasie und Christlicher Glaube* [Fantasy and Christian Faith] are two clear examples of studies that take their starting point from Freud's critique of religion. The aim of the study by Swiss psychoanalyst Müller-Pozzi is a critical examination of the dialogue between psychoanalysis and theology and its possibilities for the future. Scharfenberg's study of Freud's critique of religion is regarded as "programmatic" – it convincingly shows the potential of Freudian thought as a critique of infantile and illusionary forms of religiosity and on outdated superego structures.[122]

But this religion critique is not yet a "psychology of faith". Such a psychology lies beyond Freud. In the course of his study it is clear that this "beyond" is found in new psychoanalytic perspectives offered by ego psychology, self psychology and object relations theory, and by the writings of Ricoeur and Lorenzer on hermeneutics and the symbol. The theologian Heimbrock takes a similar position towards Freud's critique of religion. He argues that the dialogue between theology and psychoanalysis should be continued beyond Freud's critique of religion. The revival of this critique could be situated in the cultural context of the 1960s in the critique of manifestations of a cultural superego; however it hardly contributed to a better understanding of religiosity in a "fatherless society".[123] There is thus a need for further theoretical development in order to rethink faith in a new cultural environment.

Scharfenberg's influence can also be noticed in theological anthropology. This is especially evident in Jürgen Moltmann's 1973 *Der gekreuzigte Gott* [The Crucified God]. Moltmann clearly points out that theological anthropology can only be constructed in dialogue with anthropology as such and with Freudian psychoanalysis.[124] In the chapter devoted to Freud references to Freud's

---

[121] R. Riess, "Zeit der Schuldlosen? Zur Zukunft einer Illusion", in R. Riess (ed.), *Abschied von der Schuld? Zur Anthropologie und Theologie von Schuldbewusstsein, Opfer und Versöhnung*, Kohlhammer Verlag, Stuttgart/Colone/Berlin, 1996, pp.74-94 (87).

[122] H. Müller-Pozzi, *Psychologie des Glaubens. Versuch einer Verhältnisbestimmung von Theologie und Psychologie*, Kaiser Verlag, Munich, 1975, p.110.

[123] H.-G. Heimbrock, *Phantasie und Christlicher Glaube. Zum Dialog zwischen Theologie und Psychoanalyse*, Kaiser Verlag, Munich, 1977, p.13.

[124] J. Moltmann, *Der gekreuzigte Gott. Das Kreuz Christi als Grund und Kritik christlicher Theologie*, Kaiser Verlag, Munich, 1973, p.268. Moltmann does not present an argument for his choice of anthropology. However, in the course of his chapter on this

own writings are hard to find. Instead, the text is almost solely based on *Sigmund Freud and his Religion Critique*.[125] This means that Freud's critique of religion is presented as a critique of the manifestations of religion, not on its faith core. Freud is a "bulldozer making way for the Gospel".[126] The psychoanalytic critique of religion can be used to "negate the negative" – a reference to Scharfenberg Hegelian reading of Freud – that is to say, the delusional and illusionary constructions in religion, and thus free faith from its caricatures. Religion characterized by regression is unable to perform its task of "bringing people to maturation".[127] This religion of regression is characterized by guilt, anxiety and apathy.

In Moltmann's theology the crucified God saves us from such religion of regression by "breaking the spell of the superego" and liberating from infantile "longing for powerful idols". This God opens up a dimension of humanity marked by "suffering and love", a transcription of Ananke and Eros.[128] In this context Moltmann discusses "the guilt problem". The problem is related to Oedipal structures in religion. Christian faith should be "purified from Oedipal religion", and the "symbol of the cross should be purified from Oedipal motives", for at the cross the guilt problem and obsessional repetition have been conquered. He continues arguing that Freud advocated a victory of the reality principle over the pleasure principle as an acceptance of the reality of human existence, suffering, death and love, which is vital for the constitution of a mature ego and faith that is characterized not by wishful thinking but true hope.[129]

Moltmann's dialogue with Freudian psychoanalysis does not have the form of an engagement with Freud, but with Scharfenberg. The latter's ideas on de-authorization, maturation, love, reality, and freedom are magnified and integrated in a theological perspective. Consequently, it is hard to see how Moltmann's depiction of psychoanalysis can still be called Freudian. His ideas of the victory in faith over the "Oedipal situation", sense of guilt, aggression (hate), anxiety, apathy, and over the pleasure principle, can find no substantial support in Freud's writings.

---

subject it becomes clear that his reading of Freud-Scharfenberg perfectly fits his theology as sketched in the previous chapters.

[125] Idem, pp.268-292.

[126] Idem, p.274.

[127] Idem, p.277.

[128] Idem, p.280, p.283.

[129] Idem, p.p.285ff. Because of Moltmann's focus on omnipotence, "idols", weakness and humility, Heimbrock has argued that in Moltmann's text actually the importance of the concept of narcissism was implicitly discovered. H. Heimbrock, *Phantasie und Christlicher Glaube*, pp.114-132.

4.3 The guilt problem

4.3.1   Debate on narcissism and guilt

In *Das Schuldproblem in Theologie und Tiefenpsychologie* [The Guilt Problem in Theology and Depth Psychology] of 1965 Helmut Harsch writes that considering the guilt problem and the relation between theology and psychoanalysis is paradoxical. Where the two disciplines are nearest to each other the greatest differences appear.[130] The main reason for this is to be found in the fact that guilt is at the heart of Protestant theological anthropology and that psychotherapy is regarded as a rival in absolution. Apparently guilt is a spear point of theology and thus a "problem" in its relation with psychoanalysis.

In his study on "the guilt problem" Harsch analyses the various formulations of guilt that are apparent in theology and in psychoanalysis. From his analysis he concludes that the differences between views on guilt and the sense of guilt are difficult to overcome. Yet he also points out the possibility for dialogue when both theology and psychoanalysis discuss guilt and the sense of guilt on an anthropological level, that is, when they discuss the question "what is man?".[131]

In this discussion both theology and psychoanalysis should review their own positions critically. Psychoanalysis ought to consider man's relation with the transcendent as at the heart of the guilt problem. In other words, it should commit itself to a biblical-theological anthropology that is broader than a strict "immanent" anthropology. On the other hand, theology should consider a new foundation for anthropology, namely the "concrete constitution of man".[132] This is clearly a critique of dialectic theology. Harsch's study is basically an attempt to open a fruitful conversation between theology and psychoanalysis on guilt and the sense of guilt, a conversation that both in psychoanalysis and theology opens a new perspective on the concepts of sin and grace as ultimate "realities" in existence.[133] Obviously Harsch is concerned that in a changing cultural and theological climate the sense of guilt and sin will disappear from the heart of theological anthropology. This determines his reading of Freud.

The first point Harsch stresses in his discussion of Freud's theories on the sense of guilt is his rediscovery of the issue in his later writings. Conse-

---

[130] *Es ergibt sich daher die paradoxe Lage, daß Theologie und Tiefenpsychologie im Schuldproblem, wo sie von der Sache her gesehen einander am nächsten kommen, noch am weitesten voneinander entfernt sind.* H. Harsch, *Das Schuldproblem in Theologie und Tiefenpsychologie*, Quelle & Meyer, Tübingen, 1965, p.14.

[131] Idem, p.176.

[132] Idem, p.177.

[133] Idem, p.16, p.179. Here we se the same concern expressed as in writings of other theologians previously discussed (Fortmann, Scharfenberg): the concern about the loss of connection between theology/church and modern man.

quently, in his reconstruction of the sense of guilt Freud's earlier formulations on the issue are either neglected or interpreted in the light of later texts. According to Harsch it is Freud's accomplishment to have reduced psychic life to a "dynamic interaction of two energies (love and death drive) that emanate and are managed by three topics (id, superego and ego)".[134] The guilt problem is nothing else but the expression of this libido-death drive dichotomy.[135] From thereon he discusses the ego and superego formation emphasizing the identification with parental authority, the meaning of the Oedipus complex and the individual development as a repetition of a phylogenetic example. The conflict between drives is thus a repetition of an "eternal conflict".[136]

In Harsch's view Freud was aware that the "old problem of good and evil returns in the Eros-Thanatos dichotomy" as a "metaphysical aspect" in his theory.[137] Although Freud is regarded as a positivist whose theories are bound within the limits of a mechanistic world view and a theory of sexuality, it is also clear that in his fascination for religion this limitation could not be maintained: "The "religious" in religion would not in the end let itself be repressed".[138] Freud's "heavenly forces" replaced good and evil (that is to say, God and sin), and the tragic obsessional character of the sense of guilt strongly resembles the Christian concept of original sin. A conversation between psychoanalysis and theology could start from this point, although there are of course differences, most importantly the fact that in the bible guilt is regarded as sin, whereas Freud does not speak of guilt, but the sense of guilt.

Consequently, solutions to the guilt problem are differently formulated: the Christian solution is forgiveness, reconciliation and "new obedience and self responsibility" whereas Freud's solution is a maturation of the individual, says Harsch.[139] Exactly on this point theology has much to gain from psychoanalysis when it is able to use psychoanalytic theory to re-establish a connection between sin and the physical world of drives and senses. Salvation should be seen as a process of individual change in terms of maturation. In short, psychoanalysis can be an auxiliary science in pastoral care aiming at bringing people into contact with God.

---

[134] Idem, pp.69-70.

[135] *Dieser Kampf zwischen Lebens- und Todestrieb ist für Freud der wesentliche Inhalt des Lebens überhaupt, und es wird uns nicht verwundern zu hören, daß (...) das Schuldproblem auch nichts anderes ist als ein Ausdruck dieses Gegensatzes von Eros und Thanatos.* Idem, p.74.

[136] Idem, p.79.

[137] Idem, p.73.

[138] *Das "Religiöse" in der Religion, der vertikale Bezug des Menschen zu einem Absoluten, ließ sich aber auf die Dauer nicht völlig verdrängen. Es trat, wenn auch chiffriert, immer deutlicher hervor.* Idem, p.93.

[139] Idem, pp.94-95.

This study of Helmut Harsch is the first major study that focuses on the sense of guilt as a key issue in a wished-for dialogue between theology and psychoanalysis. But were guilt and the sense of guilt heavily debated in this period? Was there a dialogue as Harsch hoped there would be? As Scharfenberg already pointed out guilt as a key element of dialectic pastoral care was one of the spear points of critique. However, in 1978 he writes that in European theology there has been a long silence concerning the issue of guilt. The reason for this silence is the fact that guilt had become an enigmatic existential concept in dialectic theology. Theologians were not willing to discuss this key concept in their theology with those who questioned the concept from a psychoanalytic point of view.[140]

This critique of unwilling dialectic theologians is only one side of the coin. Christian Link has argued that Scharfenberg's uncritical attitude towards Freud made an open dialogue with theology problematic from the start.[141] This is indeed true in general and hence also for the topic of the sense of guilt. Concerning this specific problem Wolfhart Pannenberg writes that Scharfenberg has "clouded normal feelings of guilt and sense of guilt" in his attempts to deneuroticize religion. In his plea for faith as freedom and autonomy he neglected the necessity of a sense of guilt for a normal awareness of norms and rules.[142]

Indeed, this is to an extent apparent in Scharfenberg's writings. His project is not aimed at developing new theories of guilt that are acceptable for modern theology and man, but at resolving "the problem". Guilt and the sense of guilt are part of a stage and period that through maturation should be outgrown. In a purified faith characterized by freedom and the autonomy of the ego the sense of guilt seems not to play an important role. Associated with superseded patriarchical structures in theology and pastoral practice guilt and a sense of guilt are not major issues in the theories of the new movements in pastoral psychology.[143]

To my knowledge there is only study elaborating on guilt in psychoanalysis from a dialectic theological point of view in critical debate with Scharfenberg: Heide-Linde Bach's unpublished dissertation on the theological-

---

[140] J. Scharfenberg, "Zur Deutschen Ausgabe", in E. Stein, *Schuld im Verständnis der Tiefenpsychologie und Religion*, Walter-Verlag, Olten/Freiburg, 1978, p.9.

[141] Chr. Link, *Theologische Perspektiven nach Marx und Freud*, p.80.

[142] W. Pannenberg, *Anthropologie in theologischer Perspektive*, Vandenhoeck & Ruprecht, Göttingen, 1983, p.280.

[143] *Mutatis mutandis* the same goes for writings in the field of clinical pastoral counselling. In the writings of Dietrich Stollberg guilt and the sense of guilt are seen as elements of a pastoral care characterized by confession and absolution. Criticizing this practice Stollberg focuses on pastoral conversation as a conversation not on how people ought to be, but on who people are given the all-embracing love of God. This conversation is seen as a conversation beyond norms and discipline, and beyond good and evil. It is a conversation on the personal creed of people at a certain point in their development. K. Winkler, *Seelsorge*, pp.46ff.

soteriological implications of Freudian and Jungian psychotherapy. She sharply criticizes Scharfenberg's ideas on healing as ego-integration. She argues that already in his early work Freud is convinced a patient cannot heal himself through ego-strengthening or self-knowledge, but needs someone from outside to show the unconscious truth.[144] In his later work the emphasis is on the inevitability of death and the sense of guilt. Stronger than ever Freud emphasizes that there can be no healing of the subject by the subject. The refusal to regard psychotherapy as a "message of salvation" is radicalized; psychotherapy can only confront the patient with his own conflicts in order to reconcile him with himself.[145] In short that means guilt recognition as the "utopia of a healed free human subject".[146]

According to Bach, at this point Freud's anthropology is quite similar to that of the apostle Paul's (and Luther's anthropology). But whereas Freud is unable to point out a salvation beyond guilt recognition – even though he did believe that man needs someone else to "heal" – Paul could in his message of salvation in Christ.[147] From this position the German pastoral care movement in general and Scharfenberg in particular[148] are criticized. Their ideas on the correlations between psychoanalysis and pastoral psychology on healing find no support in Freud's work. He only confronts with the fragmented psychic life of human beings, and with the inevitability of guilt. His psychotherapy is an "endless analysis", because there is no resolution, no definitive healing, no ego-integration, and since his theories are atheistic there is no salvation. The objective of the pastoral care movement – healing through ego-integration or self-realization – can thus find neither support in Freudian psychoanalysis nor in the Paulinian tradition (including Lutheran anthropology). They confuse psychoanalytic *Heilung* (healing as guilt recognition) with *Heil* (salvation)[149] thus making "the degree of psychic maturation" the criterion for Christian "healthy" faith. Instead of focusing on Freud's pessimistic anthropology and the inevitability of guilt they focused on his critical potential for deconstructing traditional religion.[150] Scharfenberg *cum suis* thus ignored the fact that the guilt problem

---

[144] H.-L. Bach, *"Heilung und Heil, Heilung und Erlösung". Eine Untersuchung der theologisch-soteriologische Implikationen der Seelenheilkunde nach S. Freud und C.G. Jung*, Munster, 1980, p.38, p.52.

[145] Idem, pp.66-69, p.122.

[146] Idem, p.124.

[147] Idem, pp.126-129, pp.434-440, pp.444ff. Here we can recognize the Thurneysen model: Freudian psychoanalysis confronts us with the sinfulness of human nature and need for salvation.

[148] Idem, pp.360-367.

[149] Idem, p.602.

[150] Idem, p.443.

cannot be resolved in ego-integration, but only in an "eccentric ego" that responds to a "saving divine Thou".[151]

A dissertation debating the guilt problem with Scharfenberg.... A broad discussion on the issue in pastoral psychology and/or between psychoanalysts and theologians proved to be difficult. That doesn't mean that there was a general silence on closely related issues. At about the same time Thomas Auchter argued that in the past decade there had been a broad discussion among German psychoanalysts on the superego in relation to narcissism.[152] In the German journal *Psyche* several articles had been devoted to this issue discussing superego formation and questioning the concept in an era of cultural change.[153] The psychoanalyst Fritz Meerwein had argued in 1971 that at heart of the Freudian psychology of religion is superego formation.[154] In his analysis of this formation Meerwein focused his attention not on Oedipal structures but on narcissism and the formation of the ego ideal. He turned to the writings of Jeanne Lampl-De Groot who had argued that the ego ideal is essentially a formation that provides satisfaction, whereas the superego is a formation of restriction and prohibition.[155] Meerwein's next step was a turn to the theories of Kohut on narcissism and its progressive development. This shift from Oedipal to pre-Oedipal developments implies a shift of attention away from the sense of guilt and superego formation towards pre-Oedipal issues such as separation and fantasies of omnipotence. This article is the start of a "narcissism debate"[156] in the 1970s in pastoral psychology.

Scharfenberg was among the first to participate in this debate on narcissism in theology. He also turned to Kohut.[157] Why this turn to Kohut? Accord-

---

[151] Idem, p.367

[152] This discussion among German psychoanalysts on the topic of narcissism can be seen as part of broad international debate on this matter starting in the 1960s with the attempts by a new generation of psychoanalysts such as Kohut to reformulate narcissism in such a way that it met the aims of a changing society in which the development of the self was already declared holy. On this issue see E. Zaretsky, *Freuds Jahrhundert. Die Geschichte der Psychoanalyse*, Zsolnay Verlag, Vienna, 2006, pp.436-447.

[153] Th. Auchter, "Zum Schuldverständnis in der Psychoanalyse im Alten und Neuen Testament", in *Wege zum Menschen* 30 (1978), pp.208-224 (208). Auchter refers to articles by H. Lincke (1970), H. Lowenfeld and Y. Lowenfeld (1970), B. Grunberger (1974), S. Goeppert (1975), J. Cremerius (1977, 1977).

[154] F. Meerwein, "Neuere Überlegungen zur psychoanalytischen Religionspsychologie", in E. Nase, J. Scharfenberg (eds.), *Psychoanalyse und Religion*, pp.343-369.

[155] The article Meerwein is referring to is J. Lampl-De Groot, "Ich-Ideal und Über-Ich", in *Psyche* 17 (1963), pp.321-332.

[156] Th. Auchter, "Zum Schuldverständnis in der Psychoanalyse im Alten und Neuen Testament", p.208; H.-G. Heimbrock, *Phantasie und Christlicher Glaube*, p.95.

[157] J. Scharfenberg, "Narzißmus, Identität und Religion". The influence of Scharfenberg and Kohut can be noticed in, for example, an early article by Thomas Auchter on love

ing to Kohut narcissism is not a developmental stage that passes into object love as Freud thought, but a seperate psychic structure that has its own development.[158] In Kohut's theories this maturation process of (desexualized) narcissism is strongly emphasized. In this process libido and aggression are seen as derivatives. The Oedipus complex with its conflicts is thus seen as a stage of minor importance.

Although Scharfenberg certainly does not disregard Freud's Oedipus complex and the conflicts that it expresses he does take up Kohut's theory as a welcome alternative for the Freudian connection between narcissism, superego and identification with parental authorities. In other words, Kohut's theories on narcissism and identity formation are welcomed in the project of de-authorization and critique of superego structures. He provides a theory that enables us to rethink identity and ego formation without an emphasis on the sense of guilt. Thus instead of a dialogue on sense of guilt Scharfenberg engages in an alternative debate.

The narcissism debate was first of all a psychoanalytic debate on new narcissism theories, and thus – given the fact that there was a dialogue between theology and psychoanalysis – the debate also had a theological branch. Here also new narcissism theories – especially Kohut's – and their value for theology (psychology of religion, pastoral psychology) were debated. The journal *Approaches to Man* was twice devoted to the subject, the first time in 1977 and later in 1981. The most important monographs in the context of this debate were made by Heinz Müller-Pozzi and Hans-Günter Heimbrock.

Müller-Pozzi argues that the writings of Meerwein and Scharfenberg on narcissism are important initiatiatives in the psychology of religion towards a further and better understanding of religion and faith.[159] Not withstanding Freud's ignorance towards oceanic feelings narcissism is a promising issue for the study of religiosity.[160] In an article on the origin and essence of the God-idea Müller-Pozzi applies Kohut's theories of narcissism and the self in an analysis of the biblical myth of paradise and the Fall.[161]

---

in Freud's writings and its relevance for theological reflections on love for one's fellow men. Th. Auchter, "Psychoanalytische Überlegungen zum Thema Liebe".

[158] For a comprehensive analysis of Kohut's theories on narcissism see S.A. Mitchell, M.J. Black, *Freud and Beyond*, pp.149-169.

[159] H. Müller-Pozzi, *Psychologie des Glaubens*, pp.129ff.

[160] Müller-Pozzi mentions three developments in Freudian psychoanalysis that are important for the psychology of religion. First, there is the turn from a conflict psychology towards a psychology of the whole individual in ego psychology. Second, the new theories of narcissism that open up the possibility of rethinking religion and faith in relation to the pre-Oedipal. Third, the revisions in the theory of symbols by Ricoeur and Lorenzer are mentioned. H. Müller-Pozzi, "Die Tabuisierung der Religion in die Psychoanalyse", pp.201-202.

[161] According to Müller-Pozzi, paradise describes the stage of primary narcissism in which the man-child lives in symbiosis with his environment. The Fall is interpreted as

Heimbrock also elaborates on the new narcissism theories in his study of the role of narcissistic fantasy in faith.[162] In the introduction he points out that the issues of fantasy and creativity as elements in faith and religiosity have emerged out of the ashes of traditional religious and cultural superego structures. Theology as "critical reflection on faith" has the task of reflecting on "progressive ego fantasies" or else will run the risk of a "regression" into the identity crisis that is related to the breakdown of traditional structures.[163] Heimbrock focuses on "progressive" issues. Freud's ideas on fantasy are presented as initiatory ideas on a topic further theoretically developed by others. He depicts Freud's dream theory in which fantasy is basically seen as wish fantasy[164], then continues with an analysis of *Formulations on the Two Principles of Mental Functioning* in which he stresses that Freud situated fantasy between pleasure and reality, or between imagination and reality.[165] In Freud's second topic model (ego, superego, id) fantasy is situated between id and ego.[166]

From Heimbrock's analyses we might expect elaborations on psychic conflicts between pleasure and reality, unconsciousness and consciousness, or drive and morality (primary and secondary processes). Consequently we might expect a connection with the sense of guilt, a connection that was made by Freud in his study on the pleasure principle and reality principle when he associated fantasy with the sexual drive and with death wishes against the father.[167] But Heimbrock focuses on another issue, namely the relation between fantasy and sublimation in Freud's writings on art (especially his study of Leonardo da Vinci).[168] This relation is regarded as the most fruitful for further elaborations on fantasy and faith. Does all this imply that guilt is "explained away"? According to Heimbrock, a theology that focuses on the dynamics of fantasy does not deny or ignore the importance of superego structures, but merely points out other "sectors" as equally or more important for religiosity. Guilt can be a topic

---

a story of necessary individuation. The God-idea emerges in this process as a longing for symbiosis which can be a healthy and creative force when at least reality is not lost from sight. In other words, the God-idea, that is to say, faith, emerges as a heritage of the illusionary world of primary narcissism. H. Müller-Pozzi, "Gott- Erbe des verlorenen Paradieses. Ursprung und Wesen der Gottesidee im Lichte psychoanalytischer Konzepte", in *Wege zum Menschen* 33 (1981), pp.191-203.

[162] In the preface to Heimbrock's study Scharfenberg writes that narcissism is a very promising issue for the analysis of religiosity. J. Scharfenberg, "Vorwort", in H.-G. Heimbrock, *Phantasie und Christlicher Glaube*, p.7.

[163] H.-G. Heimbrock, *Phantasie und Christlicher Glaube*, pp.13-14.

[164] Idem, pp.28-35.

[165] Idem, pp.36-41

[166] Idem, pp.42-46.

[167] S. Freud, *Formulations on the Two Principles of Mental Functioning*, p.225.

[168] H.-G. Heimbrock, *Phantasie und Christlicher Glaube*, pp.57-67.

in this "sector" when one considers a distinction between "superego guilt" and "ego guilt" (moral responsibility as an ego-function).[169]

The narcissism debate in the 1970s is important for the engagement with Freud for several reasons. Firstly, in the context of our study of Freud and the sense of guilt we notice a shift of attention from Freud's critique of religion as an instrument to criticize patriarchical superego structures towards ego psychology, self psychology and object relations theories that seem promising for further constructive theorizing on the nature of faith. In the 1970s when new psychoanalytic theories emerge and are integrated into the dialogue between psychoanalysis and theology Freud is more and more regarded as merely an initiator in new "sectors". As Müller-Pozzi writes, pastoral psychology and the psychology of religion could move beyond Freud thanks to Freud. Secondly, the narcissism debate in the 1970s effected a lasting interest in the issue of narcissism in pastoral psychology and pastoral care and evoked a continuing discussion on conscience formation. We will discuss these two issues in the next paragraphs. Thirdly, as Klessmann has argued, the dialogue between psychoanalysis and theology was important for developments in theological anthropology.[170] He explicitly mentions Pannenberg's 1983 *Anthropologie in theologischer Perspektive* [Anthropology in Theological Perspective]. Another example is an article by Gunda Schneider-Flume from 1985.

In my opinion Pannenberg's reading of Freud in his study of theological anthropology can be situated in the narcissism debate. In a part called "Estrangement and Sin" the Freudian critique of religion is seen as a symptom of estrangement in religion itself. The fact that Freud could criticize a "form of religion" that was solely concerned with "another world" instead of "this world" is a sign that theology itself had become detached from religious consciousness.[171] Consequently, the critique does not involve authentic religion.[172]

In this context he discusses Freud's superego and conscience formation as an introjection of the "authority of society". The sense of guilt is the tension between ego and superego. This theory should be criticized, says Pannenberg, but is important, for it makes churches aware that they have "a liberating function for the formation of conscience", that is to say, conscience should be thought of as "autonomous conscience based on an understanding consent of coherence of meaning of the social world" by self-conscious free individuals, instead of conscience as introjected authority.[173] Consequently, the sense of

---

[169] Idem, pp.94-95.

[170] M. Klessmann, *Pastoralpsychologie*, p.116.

[171] W. Pannenberg, *Anthropologie in theologischer Perspektive*, p.272.

[172] *Diese authentische Gestalt der Religion wird von der durch Marx und Freud vorgetragenen Religionskritik nicht erreicht. Nur die Verfallsform der Religion verfällt der Religionskritik.* Idem, p.273.

[173] Idem, pp.298-299.

guilt should be redefined. It is "the expression of estrangement of the ego from the self".[174]

To understand what Pannenberg means by this we have to look at his reading of psychoanalytic theories of ego and identity formation. He argues that Freud formulated a "double concept of ego".[175] It was grounded in primary narcissistic self love and at the same time based on the ego ideal that originates from identification with parental expectations. As we have seen Freud explained the ability to identify with others through narcissistic identification with an image of oneself. But Pannenberg's starting point is the meanwhile widely spread conception that the superego is solely based on identification with outside authorities. From that starting point he criticizes Freud for not satisfactory explaining how the ego can emanate from narcissistic ego.[176] A solution is provided by ego psychology and self psychology – there must be an innate ego-core or self, next to the Id and the drives, that is not dominated by the sexual impulses and the pleasure principle. Identity formation is now a development in the direction of ego-integration or ego-synthesis. For a theological anthropology this solution to a Freudian problem is "perhaps the most important contribution" made by psychoanalysis.[177] We will not discuss further Pannenberg's elaborations on ego and self. It suffices to say that the sense of guilt can now be seen as the expression of tension between ego and self in the process towards integration.

Gunda Schneider-Flume writes that the narcissism debate gave important new impulses to the psychology of religion. Religion and faith were no longer bound to Oedipal structures and authority, but related to narcissistic issues such as self, fantasy and omnipotence. For theological anthropology this was important, because issues such as self love, love for one's fellow man and love for God could now be more thoroughly analysed from a psychoanalytic perspective.[178] According to Schneider-Flume Freud's anthropology had little potential for a theological anthropology that regards man as constituted in history with God, whereas his starting point is an ego that has to constitute its relations with the world all by itself.[179] The theories of Kohut are a more promising

---

[174] *So gesehen stellt sich das Schuldbewußtsein als zugespitzter Ausdruck der Entfremdung des Ich vom eigenen Selbst dar.* Idem, p.278.

[175] Idem, pp.186-187.

[176] *Allerdings konnte Freud die Mechanik dieses Prozesses nicht voll aufhellen, weil der genetische Übergang vom narzisstischen Ich zum Real-Ich als Zensurinstanz nicht befriedigend geklärt wurde.* Idem, p.193.

[177] Idem, p.194.

[178] G. Schneider-Flume, "Narzißmus als theologisches Problem", in *Zeitschrift für Theologie und Kirche*, 82 (1985), pp.88-110 (99-100).

[179] Idem, p.93. In her 2004 *Grundkurs Dogmatik* Schneider-Flume comes to a somewhat different assessment of Freud. Kohut's narcissism theory plays no role of importance – in her later writings Schneider-Flume clearly distances from theological discourses on self-realization etc. that, based on self psychology, disregard the nature of the man-God

starting point for theological reflections, because here the self is regarded as primarily passive and constituted by an empathetic outside world (mother). In short, the self is "not an achievement, but a gift".[180] At that point Kohut's narcissism and theological anthropology meet.

Schneider-Flume's concern is not a theological anthropology that focuses on ego-integration eventually in order to grasp a totally of meaning as in the writings of Pannenberg, but, quite on the contrary, she argues against an innate ego-core or self and turns to Kohut in order to argue that identity and various forms of love are constituted in its history with God. This interpretation of Kohut against Freud is remarkable in itself[181], but at least it shows that Kohut's theories on narcissism as a corrective on Freudian psychoanalysis found its way in different positions into the field of theological anthropology.

Given these general and dominant developments we might ask whether the guilt problem was thoroughly discussed in the 1970s. There were indeed some major studies on the sense of guilt in the field of the dialogue between psychoanalysis and theology, though not in the context of a mutual debate.

The first "classic" monograph[182] is René Goetschi's 1976 *Der Mensch und seine Schuld* [Man and his Guilt]. Written from a Catholic perspective the sense of guilt is discussed in relation to theological notions of guilt and sin. But a debate between psychoanalysis and theology is not the only issue, for Goetschi also raises the question whether modern people who lost a sense of guilt and sin haven't also lost an "essential dimension of Christian existence".[183] Hence, he starts his study with a discussion of the concepts of guilt and sin in theology. Then he discusses the three classic psychoanalytic positions: Freud, Adler, and Jung. After that he turns to a broad variety of scholars such as

---

relationship. Instead Freud is elaborated upon as critic of religious illusions ("cheap" comfort; omnipotence fantasies). Taking up Ricoeur's and Scharfenberg's ideas on Freudian critique of religion as purification of illusionary faith (sublation of illusionary wishes), she now argues that Freud's critique of religion can be helpful to reach a better insight in the core of Christian faith: participation in a history with God. This implies a critique of Freud's thought on reality (Ananke) which excludes God as life giving Creator. G. Schneider-Flume, *Grundkurs Dogmatik. Nachdenken über Gottes Geschichte*, Vandenhoeck & Ruprecht, Göttingen, 2004, chapter 8.

[180] Idem, p.96.

[181] Schneider-Flume's interpretation of Freud's anthropology as primarily monadic in comparison to Kohut's concept of the self as constituted by an empathic environment, is very problematic. In general we can say that the opposite is actually the case: Kohut's self is an innate monadic core, whereas in Freud's view man establishes an identity through identification and interaction with the outside world.

[182] K. Winkler, *Seelsorge*, p.352 (footnote)

[183] R. Goetschi, *Der Mensch und seine Schuld. Das Schuldverständnis der Psychotherapie in seiner Bedeutung für Theologie und Seelsorge*, Benziger Verlag, Zurich/Einsiedeln/Colone, 1976, p10.

Binswanger, Victor Frankl, Igor Caruso, Gion Condrau and Martin Heidegger who are all discussed under the heading "anthropological psychotherapy".[184]

Goetschi turns to the latter theories, because here a clear distinction can be made between pathological conscience formation in which conscience is totally dominated and inhibited in its maturation process by the superego (neurotic or bad conscience) and an "existential", "ontological", "autonomous" or "personal" conscience which is rooted in transcendence and which even can be named an "organ of transcendence".[185] This distinction between two forms of conscience "corresponds" to different forms of the sense of guilt.[186] Hence, in these psychologies "theology finds a recognizable world view".[187] Or in other words, pope Pius XII was right in arguing for a differentiation between a pathological and an existential sense of guilt.[188] Anthropological psychotherapy, consequently, no longer aims at simply releasing man from the sense of guilt, but at differentiating between pathological and existential forms, releasing us from the first and enabling us to courageously accept the second.[189] This guilt recognition is a precondition for the possibility of absolution presented in the confession of sins in a church context.

This concise outline indicates in what context Freud was to be read. According to Goetschi, Freud first of all considers the sense of guilt from the perspective of his clinical experience with neurotic patients. It is for this reason he starts his critical discussion of psychoanalysis with Freud's early writings on hysteria and its inner conflicts.[190] (Certainly this is a strong point in Goetschi's text, for not often is the issue sense of guilt traced back into the early stages of

---

[184] What is indicated by Goetschi as anthropological psychotherapy is generally known as existential or personalistic psychoanalysis. On these schools see J.-B. Fages, *Geschichte der Psychoanalyse nach Freud*, Ullstein Materialien, Frankfurt/Berlin/Vienna, 1981, pp.179-195.

[185] R. Goetschi, *Der Mensch und seine Schuld*, p.294, p.296.

[186] Idem, p.299.

[187] Idem, p.294.

[188] In his introduction Goetschi refers to a speech made by pope Pius XII in 1953 on this matter. His position on the relationship between psychotherapy and theology is taken as a guideline in the study. Idem, pp.11-13. The position of the pope, in short, was the following: there was no doubt that an unhealthy sense of guilt existed which ought to be treated in psychotherapy, but therapist should not touch upon a healthy religious sense of guilt (or sense of sin). P. Vandermeersch, H. Westerink, *Godsdienstpsychologie*, p.243. Another important reference for Goetschi is Martin Buber. Buber had written a text in which he sharply distinguishes between the neurotic sense of guilt as studied by Freud and an "existential guilt" (presented as a "fact" in the relation between individual and world) of which an "authentic sense of guilt" is the expression. R. Goetschi, *Der Mensch und seine Schuld*, pp.231-232; M. Buber, *Schuld und Schuldgefühle*, Verlag Lambert Schneider, Heidelberg, 1958, pp.12-22.

[189] R. Goetschi, *Der Mensch und seine Schuld*, p.325.

[190] Idem, pp.43-49.

psychoanalytic theory.) After hysteria he continues with elaborations on Freud's differentiations between various pathologies and, in correspondence, various forms of feeling of guilt.[191] These elaborations are not intended to show that various forms of the sense of guilt demand different treatment in either psychotherapy or pastoral care, but are presented as further developments of a theory that is based on a fundamental misconception, namely that all feelings of guilt are related to pathological moments and structures.[192] That is to say, the sense of guilt is essentially regarded as originating from abnormally strong drive impulses and the severe influence of parental authorities that culminate in the pathological structures of the Oedipus complex.[193]

The core of Goetschi's reading of Freud is the theory of conscience and superego formation. The pathological context has already been indicated, and is increased by the fact that Freud's starting point in discussing conscience and superego formation is narcissism, which is in itself also a pathological phenomenon, because narcissism is basically an infantile attachment to fantasies of omnipotence and to self-love.[194] Narcissism further implies a splitting of the ego into an ego and an ego ideal which is then later renamed as superego. Again this splitting indicates a pathological structure in which the sense of guilt describes the tension between ego and superego.[195] It is from this perspective that Freud discussed conscience which in his theories is regarded as being completely overshadowed or occupied by the superego. In other words, a normal psychic phenomenon such as conscience is described by its pathological characteristics, whereas in a normal development or "maturation process" the dominance of an infantile superego is overcome when it is detached from a "personal" conscience.[196]

Goetschi's project is one of marking the boundaries between psychotherapy and theology/pastoral care clear by means of a distinction between an unhealthy and a healthy sense of guilt. The critique of Freud is severe though – like the pope – Goetschi admits that Freud presents a thorough depiction of pathological structures and developments. From this perspective his critique of certain forms of religion should also be taken at heart.[197] On this point his posi-

---

[191] Idem, pp.49-56.

[192] Ultimately this line of thought culminates in a formula: *Von Geburt an hat das Kind "das Bedürfnis, geliebt zu werden, das den Menschen nicht mehr verlassen wird". Schuldig fühlt sich, wer nicht geliebt wird. Und wer nicht geliebt worden ist, ist auch selber unfähig zu lieben – und wird deswegen auch unter Schuldgefühlen zu leiden haben.* Idem, p.93.

[193] Idem, p.356.

[194] Idem, p.59.

[195] Idem, p.63.

[196] Idem, p.360.

[197] *Ohne Zweifel hat die Kirche vielfach einen moralischen und religiösen Infantilismus begünstigt durch eine übertriebene Kasuistik und einen mehr oder weniger bewussten Legalismus.* Idem, p.360.

tion is comparable to that of Scharfenberg. In Goetschi's view however all theoretical issues in Freudian psychoanalysis are situated in the context of pathologies and consequently his position offers no leads for further knowledge of existential conscience and the existential sense of guilt. In this respect the
narcissism theory brings no solution either. Goetschi thus turns to "anthropological psychotherapy".

We find the clear influence of Goetschi in a study of anxiety and guilt in
depth psychology and theology by Marianne Hartung. She claims to finally
open the discussion on the guilt problem as had been wished for by Scharfenberg.[198] But before the dialogue actually starts she turns to Goetschi and his
reading of Freud. Both anxiety and the sense of guilt are studied from the analysis of neurotics, "sick people", whereas for theologians anxiety and guilt are existential.[199] The only thing theologians can learn from Freud is that not every
sense of guilt refers to existential guilt. Freud helps to draw a clear line between
the healthy and unhealthy forms of sense of guilt and to make good assessments.[200] The "by far largest discrepancy" between Freudian psychoanalysis
and theology is found in the theories on conscience formation.[201] Here Freudian
conscience is seen as originating in a narcissistic personality through both inner
(drive) and outer (enforced morality) forces.[202] From this view man's further
maturation into autonomy and responsibility which is regarded as the heart of
theological anthropology, is unthinkable.[203] Theology has thus more to gain
from Jungian depth psychology and other psychoanalytic theories that regard
the superego as a stage that can be overcome in a maturation process of conscience formation. Whereas Scharfenberg in the late 1960s and early 1970s intended an equal dialogue between Freudian psychoanalysis and theology, ten
years later the Catholic theologian Hartung pleas for a "critical corrective" from
the perspective of theology, especially with regards to Freud.[204]

An important issue in Goetschi's study is the question of whether religiosity "needs" a degree of the (normal) sense of guilt. In Catholic theology
this was an issue heavily commented upon during and since the 1950s.[205] A de-

---

[198] M. Hartung, *Angst und Schuld in Tiefenpsychologie und Theologie*, Kohlhammer
Verlag, Stuttgart, 1979, p.108.

[199] Idem, pp.111-113.

[200] Idem, pp.113-114. Hartung speaks of Freud's "unreal sense of guilt" as opposed to
real existential guilt.

[201] Idem, p.114.

[202] Idem, p.31, p.115.

[203] Idem.

[204] Idem, pp.134-135.

[205] Illustrative are the discussions around Angelo Hesnard's *Morale sans peché* (1954).
The French psychoanalyst Hesnard had argued that the sense of guilt including religious
motivated guilt feelings could have such an overwhelming effect upon people that they
preferred not to act instead of running the risk of making a mistake. The book was heavily debated by catholic theologians who feared that catholic morality was endangered.

piction of debates on the relation between guilt, penitence and confession is presented by Goetschi and includes scholars such as Karl Rahner and Josef Ratzinger. Goetschi agrees with Ratzinger that modern man who has lost his sense of guilt and lives his life in "self-importance" should "convert". Here we find a motive for a sharp critique of narcissism, not only in Goetschi's study, but also in some other Catholic studies on this topic. In their 1982 *Das Böse* [Evil] Albert Görres and Rahner define evil in terms of "that what man's conscience forbids him" and in terms derived from Freud's writings: evil as a wish for omnipotence, an illusionary belief in a false ego ideal, self love or plain egoism.[206] This characteristic of evil is opposed to man as a responsible being, consciously aware of duties, values and life goals of oneself and others.[207] Certainly this conscientiousness should not be confused with superego severity. "The actual conscience" is "moral reason".[208] Rahner takes it as a sign of modern times that people do not feel responsible anymore, and do not accept their guilt.[209] Self confrontation and remorse, which presupposes a sense of guilt, are thus wished for.[210] Though Freud of course never proclaimed that self love or narcissism were evil Görres and Rahner use psychoanalytic theory to make this claim.[211] Here, psychoanalysis is not so much seen as an auxiliary theory (or set of theories), but merely as a reservoir of concepts that can be used descriptively in theological discourse.

Goetschi's study can be situated in a Catholic debate on the demarcation between psychoanalysis and theology, between an unhealthy and a healthy sense of guilt in a cultural era of narcissism.[212] Contrary to developments in Protestant pastoral psychology where narcissism was more positively valued as a crucial element in identity formation and as an alternative to a traditional emphasis on superego structures and the sense of guilt, Goetschi (and other Catho-

---

P. Vandermeersch, "The Failure of Second Naiveté. Some Landmarks in the History of French Psychology of Religion", in J.A. van Belzen (ed.), *Aspects in Contexts*, pp.235-279 (240ff).

[206] A. Görres, K. Rahner, *Das Böse. Wege zu seiner Bewältigung in Psychotherapie und Christentum*, Herder Verlag, Freiburg/Basel/Vienna, 1982, p.25, pp.41-43, p.215

[207] Idem, p.76.

[208] Idem, p.79.

[209] Idem, p.204.

[210] Idem, p.215, p.221.

[211] Idem, pp.25ff., pp.76ff.

[212] Another example in this context is a study by Werbick of guilt experience. He argues that whereas psychoanalysis aims at resolving the pathological forms of sense of guilt, theology should aim at a "rehabilitation" of a sense of guilt, not in order to strengthen superego again, but to question a self image characterized by a firm belief in psychic maturity and autonomy repressing the inevitable dark sides of humanity. In this context a sense of guilt can be made fruitful for a true maturation of the subject as a religious and social (morally conscious) being. J. Werbick, *Schulderfahrung und Bußsakrament*, Matthias-Grünewald-Verlag, Mainz, 1985, pp.11-19.

lic theologians) regard narcissism as unhealthy and focus on a differentiation between a healthy and an unhealthy sense of guilt. A healthy sense of guilt is then regarded as in conformity with tradition; guilt acceptance is processed in religious tradition (confession, absolution).

Another classic study on the guilt problem is Bernard Lauret's 1977 *Schulderfahrung und Gottesfrage bei Nietzsche und Freud* [Experience of Guilt and the God Question in the Writings of Nietzsche and Freud]. The French Protestant theologian Lauret wrote this dissertation as a student of Pannenberg in Munich, but his background is still reflected in his use of French secondary literature. Lauret's starting point is that the sense of guilt can be situated in a process of identity formation, that is to say, the sense of guilt as a moment in identity formation can either inhibit or enhance this process.[213] In general the (existential) experience of guilt points to a disturbance in the relation with reality as not being conscious (through illusionary wishes) of one's position in the world, that limited "space" in which man can pursue his specific desires and participate in a totality of meaning.[214] In theological discourse this is expressed in the idea that guilt is seen as the "failure of identity" and the perversion of the totality of the meaning of creation.[215]

A sense of guilt is a crucial moment in identity formation for it marks the point where illusionary narcissistic totality of meaning is given up and replaced by a more realistic experience of meaning through identification with the father figure. But does this imply that Freud has an open mind towards the totality of meaning?[216] According to Lauret, psychoanalysis as a therapeutic method points towards "meaning", i.e. it aims at a "practical theory of healthy human integrity, that is, man as not being overpowered by either his drives or the outside world, but as being actively adjusted to reality and capable of achievements."[217] The goal of psychoanalysis is "strengthening of the ego" which includes an "ego-synthesis".[218] Lauret admits that the term "identity formation" (or terms derived from this concept) is not found in Freud's writings, but actu-

---

[213] B. Lauret, *Schulderfahrung und Gottesfrage bei Nietzsche und Freud*, Kaiser Verlag, Munich, 1977, pp.13-14.

[214] Idem, p.16, p.263. *Die Schulderfahrung hat ihren Ort in der Identitätsbildung zwischen Nicht-Identität und Identität, insofern diese Identitätsbildung durch die Sinnerfahrung (zwischen Unsinn und Sinntotalität) vermittelt wird.* Idem, p.16. The idea of a "totality of meaning" is derived from Ricoeur and Lauret's teacher Pannenberg.

[215] Idem, p.15.

[216] Idem, pp.16-18. Lauret argues that contemporary theology has the obligation to formulate a theory of salvation, not from the perspective of the "question of guilt", but from the perspective of the "question of meaning" (which will imply a reconfiguration of the guilt concept). Idem, p.21.

[217] Idem, p.242. This formulation is largely inspired by the ideas of Erikson and Loch (*Heilung als Ich-Integration*).

[218] Idem, p.243.

ally derived from Erikson's self psychology and Heinz Hartmann's ego psychology.[219] These psychologies are indeed partly the guiding psychoanalytic theories in his reading of Freud, and given this fact it will be no surprise that the synthesized ego is also named "self".[220]

Freud's theory of drives makes the sense of guilt inevitable as long as a person is submitted to these drives.[221] However there seems to be a possibility of resolving the sense of guilt in the Oedipus complex. Through identification and superego formation there is a possibility of distancing oneself from the drive conflict and from imaginary wishes. In other words, the sense of guilt can be corrected through identification as a means to strengthen the ego and overcome the drive dichotomy.[222]

So far the key concepts are identification and reality as a meaningful "space". In a chapter on the coherence of meaning in psychoanalysis it becomes clear what Lauret means by these concepts.[223] The psychoanalytic theoretical framework is mainly derived from Jacques Lacan's psychoanalytic thought. According to Lacan (see next chapter) the crucial moment in identity formation is the transition from the imaginary order into the symbolic order, a transition marked by the end of primary narcissistic desire for the mother through the "Name-of-the-Father".[224] The subject's relation with the symbolic order is char-

---

[219] Idem, pp.245-246. Heinz Hartmann was a student of Anna Freud. He would become the founding father of ego psychology (until today the most dominant psychoanalytic school in the United States). His starting point was not the Freudian idea of conflict between pleasure and reality, but the idea that man was designed to fit into his environment. Conflict free ego capacities are seen as potentials for an adaptation to reality and for the development of identity. In this process sexual and aggressive drives are not channelled through sublimation, but through neutralization by the strength of the ego. In therapy this was central: strengthening the ego in order to neutralize the drives and conflicts. S.A. Mitchell, M.J. Black, *Freud and Beyond*, pp.34-38.

[220] For example B. Lauret, *Schulderfahrung und Gottesfrage bei Nietzsche und Freud*, p.319.

[221] Idem, p.249.

[222] This is why in psychotherapy the mechanism of transference and countertransference is crucial: it offers the possibility of correction of earlier identifications. Idem, pp.288-289.

[223] Idem, pp.267-289.

[224] Lacan's plea for a *retour à Freud* is primarily motivated by a critique of ego psychology and the idea that psychoanalysis should aim at strengthening an autonomous ego capable of adaptation to societal norms. Lacan stresses the fact that the subject is organized in structures over which it has no control. Hence, the ego is never a "self" (as an essence, or true ego) but a "function" in a structure. The imaginary order is the first important structure in which the ego originates through mirroring, through identification with an image. In the symbolic order the dual relationship of the imaginary is exchanged for a triangular Oedipal structure. (In the next chapter we will further discuss Lacan.) Ph. van Haute, *Against Adaptation. Lacan's "subversion" of the subject*, Other

acterized by Lauret as a "participation in a meaningful structure that organizes the unconscious forces in the service of social communication".[225] He further argues that within this structure a person cannot produce the totality of meaning out of itself, because the experience of meaning and the formation of identity is now dependant on its position in a social structure. "A subject cannot find its identity in itself, because it is contingent"[226] and yet the totality of meaning is life's "telos". Psychoanalysis has to keep open this perspective, or otherwise a subject would – tragically – only be conditioned by his drives.

Lacanian thought is by now dominant in Lauret's depictions of the sense of guilt and identity formation (through identification).[227] The picture presented is that feelings of guilt are situated on the level of imaginary desire and aggression, whereas this guilt can be resolved through the symbolic function of the father. It is for this reason that Lauret argues that psychoanalysis aims at coherence and strengthening the ego. This coherence is first of all provided by the symbolic order (reality), now interpreted by Lauret as "tradition" which provides a coherence of meaning. Parallel Lauret argues that the different psychic structures should be regarded as ego-functions and integrated in a self (otherwise the different structures would remain alienated and conflicted). Freud did not pursue this line of thought, and this is why the sense of guilt, as an issue marking the tension between structures, between "wish" and "reality", was such a dominant issue in his writings (on religion).[228]

In the final chapter of his elaborations of Freudian psychoanalysis Lauret again turns to the Oedipus complex and the sense of guilt in Freud's writings on religion.[229] The main problem in Freud's critique of religion, according to Lauret, is that his plea for an adjustment to reality (renunciation of drives, submission to the name of the father) is combined with the negation of reality (religion as imaginary wish-fulfilment). In other words, Freud suggests that religion is important in overcoming imaginary desires, but at the same time Freud can only regard religion as an imaginary construct.

Is Freud's critique of religion justified? According to Lauret, Freud only criticized private neurotic religion, whereas we consider "biblical" religion at least to be a religion that provides an open coherence of meaning that does not imply the denial of human contingency and reality.[230] In an open coherence of

---

Press, New York, 2002; P. Vandermeersch, H. Westerink, *Godsdienstpsychologie*, pp.249-255, pp.269-271.
[225] B. Lauret, *Schulderfahrung und Gottesfrage bei Nietzsche und Freud*, p.280.
[226] Idem, p.284.
[227] For example see idem, pp.315-317, pp.335ff..
[228] Idem, pp.317-320.
[229] Idem, pp.335-375.
[230] Idem, pp.363-366. For example: *Die Religion selber – wir sprechen hier von den biblischen Religion – kritisiert durch ihren Propheten die illusorische Sehnsucht nach*

meaning wishes would not just be illusionary, but realistic as "a longing for meaning, an intentional relatedness to the world". In other words, Freud neglected the fact that longing for the father doesn't necessarily lead to imaginary wishful thinking, but instead to "opening the realm of reality as open totality of meaning".[231] It is here that a theology of sin meets psychoanalysis in a structural resemblance: from failure of identity, through the name of the father to totality of meaning in which "realistic" wishes and desires are preserved and further identity formation is made possible. The final part of the study is devoted to this issue.

In conclusion we can say that Lauret tries to resolve the guilt problem by pointing out potentials within Freud's psychoanalytic theory to overcome the sense of guilt. In order to establish this he turns to Hartmann and Lacan. The experience of guilt is now situated in an identity formation process on the level of imaginary and conflicting wishes; both ego-integration and the symbolic order are presented as respectively goal and realm in which the guilt problem can thus be resolved.

As already mentioned, this study is highly interesting because of the various scholarly traditions it tries to synthesize. But here is also a major weakness, for Lacanian psychoanalysis and ego psychology – two clearly opposed theories – are combined. From ego psychology the idea of ego-integration, ego-strengthening and adaptation to reality are taken up as the innate goals of identity formation and resolving the guilt problem. A meaningful coherence of life seems to imply such an ego-integration.[232] In this process of integration psychic conflicts are neutralized.[233] The Freudian emphasis on unconscious conflicts, the return of the repressed or the disturbing presence of the drives is left behind (situated on an imaginary level), and a more positive view on man is advocated. From Lacanian psychoanalysis thus only the imaginary and symbolic order are taken up and interpreted in such a way that it fits the identity formation process. The symbolic function of the father is strongly stressed and identity formation is situated in a specific symbolic space in which desires and wishes can be considered realistic, thus keeping open the possibility of a totality of meaning.

Sicherheit oder eine Gottesvorstellung, die die Realität verstellt: Kritik des Gottesglaubens ohne Gerechtigkeit und Nächstenliebe. Idem, p.366.

[231] Idem. In the next chapter we will see that Vergote voices a similar critique of Freud: Freud only saw religion as an imaginary construct and neglected the fact that religion is a symbolic order.

[232] Idem, p.320. Compare: *Schulderfahrung und Sündenbegriff sind dann* [wenn die Nicht-Identität oder Nicht-Integrität als die realistische Kehrseite der Selbsttranszendenz verstanden wird, H.W.] *im Prinzip als realistischer Ausdruck dafür zu begreifen, dass der Mensch noch nicht identisch ist mit der Idee seiner Bestimmung.* W. Pannenberg, "Aggression und die theologische Lehre von der Sünde", in *Zeitschrift für Evangelische Ethik* 21 (1977), pp.161-173 (165-166).

[233] B. Lauret, *Schulderfahrung und Gottesfrage bei Nietzsche und Freud*, p.330.

Can these views be synthesized? Problems arise when Lauret writes about reality. It is presented as symbolic order, meaningful coherence and tradition, but reality is also discussed in relation to the reality principle as opposed, according to Lauret, to the pleasure principle (Freud), and discussed in the context of an adaptation to reality (Hartmann).[234] The situation becomes more obscured when Lauret speaks about reality from a theological perspective as a social reality (in which one loves one's neighbour and does justice) and "the reality of God".[235] Certainly these "realities" are not exactly one and the same.

More fundamental even, problems arise concerning the subject. From the perspective of ego psychology and self psychology the subject can (and must) be integrated in a coherence dominated by the ego or self. However, from a Lacanian point of view this goal is nonsense: the subject is always contingent and divided in itself. It is mentally not equiped to adapt to reality nor can such adaptation be the goal of psychoanalysis. In Lacanian thought – as we will see in the next chapter – the transition from the imaginary to the symbolic order cannot be regarded as a de-conflictualization. In fact, guilt as expression of a conflict between desire and Law, is not situated on the imaginary level, but on the symbolic level as it is related to the father introducing the Law. In my view Lauret unjustly interprets Lacan's symbolic order as an adaptation to reality in which the imaginary conflicts can be resolved. In Lacanian thought the subject's contingency always implies inner conflicts and the impossibility of integration. In fact, arguing that in the symbolic order there can be some kind of participation in "totality of meaning" is, from a Lacanian perspective, an imaginary wish that rejects the symbolic.

Meanwhile – certainly in comparison to Scharfenberg – the father and tradition make reappearance. Freud's sense of guilt is neutralized in the process of ego-integration. Within a theology of meaning sin and guilt are no longer related to subjective feelings, but have a "trans-individual meaning", namely the failure of identity. Being conscious of this failure is the basis for an awareness of life's *telos*. In short, man is designed to reach his destiny – something that Freud did not fully comprehend. But then again, underlying this design are two conflicting psychologies.

4.3.2   Narcissism

Protestant scholars in pastoral psychology and theological anthropology enthusiastically engaged in ego psychology and especially self psychology. Kohut's narcissism theory was seen as highly promising for theology. A more critical

---

[234] Idem, p.330.
[235] Idem, p.414.

point of view is taken by the Catholic theologian Heribert Wahl in a 1985 study entitled *Narzißmus?* [Narcissism?][236]

Wahl presents a concise description of the Narcissus myth and of Freud's theories of narcissism[237], though the larger part of his study concerns Kohut's theories of narcissism.[238] After a descriptive analysis Kohut's theories are severely criticized from an object relations theory point of view. Kohut has reduced the constitution of the subject, the origins, developments and object relations to an "autistic narcissistic monad"[239], a theory in which Freud's primary narcissism is made absolute. We will not discuss Wahl's study in detail, because strictly speaking this is not a study of Freud and Freudian theory. Interestingly however Wahl's critique of Kohut calls for certain though limited reappraisal of Freud. For although Freud's theories of narcissism show a basic "misunderstanding" of the Narcissus myth and an uncritical belief in a blissful primal state of self love, his narcissism theories also point to other elements to be considered next to primary narcissism (such as object relations and moral points of view – egoism and altruism).[240]

It is because of this possible reappraisal of Freud's narcissism theory that the Catholic theologian Herman van de Spijker wrote a study of Freud's narcissism theory.[241] A paradigmatic concept in this study is "narcissistic competence", a concept that is not found in Freud's writings, but that could, according to Van de Spijker, be derived from them. It is defined as the individual's competence throughout the development of its life and in its differing relations with different people, in balancing benevolence and active morality between love for one's fellow man and self love.[242] The main part of the study concerns Freud's theory narcissism in its development from 1910 onwards.[243] This development can be described as a development from narcissistic incompetence towards narcissistic competence.[244]

---

[236] H. Wahl, *Narzißmus? Von Freuds Narzißmustheorie zur Selbstpsychologie*, Kohlhammer Verlag, Stuttgart/Berlin/Colone/Mainz, 1985, pp.9-1.

[237] Idem, pp.19-30.

[238] Idem, pp.63-182

[239] Idem, p.193. Compare H. Wahl, *Glaube und symbolische Erfahrung*, pp.101-103.

[240] H. Wahl, *Narzißmus?*, pp.29-30.

[241] H. van de Spijker, *Narzisstische Kompetenz – Selbstliebe – Nächstenliebe. Sigmund Freuds Herausforderung der Theologie und Pastoral*, Herder Verlag, Freiburg/Basel/Vienna, 1993, pp.24-25.

[242] *Narzisstische Kompetenz ist die Fähigkeit und die Zuständigkeit eines Menschen, durch die Entwicklungen des Lebens hindurch und in den verschiedensten Begegnungen mit und Beziehungen zu Menschen jeder Sorte gekonnt, wohlwollend und wohltuend zwischen Nächstenliebe und Selbstliebe zu balancieren.* Idem, p.26, p.280.

[243] Idem, pp.97-280.

[244] In Freud's earliest writings narcissism is, according to Van de Spijker, primarily regarded "negatively" with an emphasis on pathological disposition, fixation and regression (Schreber). In his next phase Freud differentiates between primary and secondary

Van de Spijker's study is a balancing act. Searching for an optimum of narcissistic competence he is trying to formulate what Freud could not: a balance that is undisturbed by ambivalences of love and hate. It is therefore significant that Freud's critical analysis of the biblical commandments to love one's fellow man and one's enemy are only concisely depicted by Van de Spijker, but not discussed in its implications.[245]

In Wilhelm Meng's study of narcissism the concept is also related to "art of life" and a competence to receive and to give love.[246] In Meng's discussion of Freud's narcissism theory Van de Spijker's study serves – to a certain extent – as a guide line.[247] The Protestant Meng starts off from Freud's theory of primary and secondary narcissism, but then turns to Kohut in order to argue that object love doesn't originate from primary narcissism (as Freud thought). Kohut's sharp distinction between the development of object love and narcissism is taken up.[248] Here, both object love and self love can come to full maturity without a necessary negative influence from one on the other in for example the case of loss of a love object which can lead to melancholic self reproaches.

Such a turn to Kohut is not new for us, and indeed Meng writes that his theories have found a broad reception in theology[249] and that the importance of his narcissism theory for religious practice supporting the development of both the self and object love in a "culture of narcissism" (see next paragraph) has been recognized by scholars such as Scharfenberg.[250] Schneider-Flume's point that Kohut's theory can be related to a theological anthropology situating the subject's position in a history of divine love (God as "cosmic object") is taken up by Meng.[251] Hence, the development of the self, the maturation of the ego and the "health" of the individual can be brought into relation with the God-idea as an "emancipatory impulse" towards "realistic utopias".[252] The commandment to love one's neighbour does not have to be related to superego laws, but is now a logical result of the fact that the subject was loved (mother, God). Self love and love for one's neighbour thus develop hand in hand.

---

narcissism. The second topic is valued positively by Freud, because it is related to the formation of an ego ideal, idealization and sublimation. However, Freud's view of man is basically negative and the danger of regression or perversion is always there. Eventually – notably in *Civilization and Its Discontents* – narcissism can be related to what Freud called the "art of life" which he envisioned in the lives of great men such as Leonardo da Vinci: the perfect balance between love for one's fellow man and self love.

[245] Idem, pp.244-248.

[246] W. Meng, *Narzißmus und christliche Religion. Selbstliebe – Nächstenliebe – Gottesliebe*, Theologischer Verlag Zürich, Zurich, 1997, pp.384-385.

[247] Idem, pp.50-67.

[248] Idem, pp.81ff.

[249] Idem, p.88, p.213.

[250] Idem, pp.192-193.

[251] Idem, p.235.

[252] Idem, p.231.

In Monika Hoffmann's 2002 study of self love this line of rethinking self love and love for one's fellow man is continued from a Catholic perspective. In a concise discussion of theoretical developments concerning the issue she regards Freud's narcissism theory as primarily limited to the realm of psychopathology.[253] Instead of turning to Kohut's theories she takes Otto Kernberg's narcissism theory, which was developed in critical dialogue with Kohut, as her starting point. Whereas Kohut had stressed the internal development of narcissism, Kernberg focuses on the interaction between narcissism and object love for the constitution of healthy self love. Basically this means a return to Freudian psychoanalysis.[254] In his return to Freud and his criticism of Kohut Kernberg interprets primary and secondary narcissism respectively as normal narcissism in childhood development and pathological narcissism. In other words, narcissism is adult life in considered pathological by definition.

Hoffmann takes up this point arguing for a sharp distinction between self love and narcissism.[255] In the final part of the study Hoffmann argues that self love implies love for one's fellow man and love for God. Her next step is to argue that self love is a fundamental principle in an ethics of virtues. Her view on narcissism is particularly negative.[256]

Meng's study of narcissism is a relatively late example of a Protestant view on an issue discussed already in the 1970s. Kohut's thought is again dominant: through narcissism man can engage autonomously and responsibly in relation to his fellow man. Outdated superego structures and the sense of guilt can thus be avoided. The Catholic discussions about the sense of guilt and narcissism have – roughly speaking – another perspective and objective. Here the scheme was as introduced by Pius XII: the distinction between a healthy and an unhealthy sense of guilt, later extrapolated to the issue of narcissism and elaborating on the distinction between narcissism and self love (Hoffmann) or an attempt to formulate a healthy narcissism in narcissistic competence (Van de Spijker). The objective seems to be to formulate a healthy sense of guilt and self love in correspondence with religious tradition. In Protestant pastoral psychology *au con-*

---

[253] M. Hoffmann, *Selbstliebe. Eine grundlegendes Prinzip von Ethos*, Schöningh Verlag, Paderborn/Munich/Vienna/Zurich, 2002, pp.43-50.

[254] Kernberg's sharp criticism of self psychology is an expression of his basic psychoanalytic ideas formulated in the 1970s. The psychoanalyst Otto Kernberg tried to combine Freud's drive theory and second topic model with object relations theory and Kleinian thought. The central dynamic struggle is between love and aggression. S.A. Mitchell, M.J. Black, *Freud and Beyond*, pp.172-180; E. Zaretsky, *Freuds Jahrhundert*, pp.447-448.

[255] M. Hoffmann, *Selbstliebe*, pp.83ff.

[256] Interestingly, there is a parallel in Catholic theology in the Netherlands. In Leon Derckx's 2006 study of cardinal sins in a culture of narcissism clearly narcissism as a pathological self overestimation is regarded as the main cardinal sin. L. Derckx, *Wrok & begeerte: Een pastoraal-psychologisch onderzoek naar de praktijk van hoofdzonden in een cultuur van narcisme*, Uitgeverij Damon, Budel, 2006.

traire tradition is criticized and the ego maturation processes are strongly stressed. Despite the fact that Protestant and Catholic scholars reacted to each other in these studies of narcissism, the denominational differences in perspectives and objectives were not made explicit.

Both Catholic and Protestant scholars though do agree on a fundamental interpretation of narcissism: the issue is treated in the context of a moral evaluation of self love and love for one's fellow man; egoism versus altruism. But is this the core of Freud's narcissism theory? According to Freud narcissism is not simply self love. It is essentially the libidinal relation with one's own body as *the* constitutive moment in the development of the ego. It is true that this first identification with an image of oneself – "this (body) is who I am" – is the basis for later identifications and object relations. However, the focus on the latter issue, i.e. on the moral implications of narcissism, neglects this essential element in the narcissism theory: a person is first of all a body.

4.3.3   Conscience beyond superego

In the 1990s it appeared that the issue of guilt definitely belonged to a past era, a Christian "culture of guilt" which in "silence has been bid farewell".[257] But did it? We have seen that Scharfenberg and others detected this "silence" where a wished for debate on the problem of guilt should have taken place. Moreover, the most important issue in the debate between psychoanalysis and (Protestant) theology in the 1970s is narcissism (which is also an important issue in the studies by Goetschi and Lauret on sense of guilt). This debate is the starting point of another issue that becomes dominant in the 1980s and especially in the 1990s: conscience formation and the acceptance of societal norms.

The narcissism debate in Protestant pastoral psychology was characterized by the incorporation of new psychoanalytic theories in the debate between psychoanalysis and theology in order to establish coherent theories on identity and faith formation beyond the Freudian critique of religion. In ego psychology and self psychology this identity formation (as ego-integration, etc.) was already related to theories of conscience formation. All these theories implied in one way or another critique of Freud's emphasis on the Oedipus complex as a structure of closely related mechanisms and topics such as aggression, superego, sense of guilt, identification, and the father as authority.

The exact content and meaning of this complex had always been an issue of debate especially in discussions between Freud and the London School. Klein was amongst the first to argue that conscience formation and the sense of guilt emerged out of aggression and privation. Others further elaborated on this domain – pre-Oedipal developments – that was thus opened up. Hence, already during Freud's life time we see the first contours emerge of new psychoanalytic

---

[257] R. Riess (ed.), *Abschied von der Schuld?*, p.7.

theories that determine further developments in the Anglo-American psycho-analytic movements that eventually also became dominant in the dialogue be-tween psychoanalysis and theology in the 1970s. In 1971 the psychoanalyst Hans-Günter Preuss describes how in ego psychology "moral responsibility" is rediscovered. Where the superego's demand for obedience was, "responsible ego" should be. In this development he notices that ego psychology draws near towards Protestantism with its emphasis on salvation through personal faith, and not through moral obedience.[258] Our findings on Protestant and Catholic studies thus far seem to prove his opinion right.

In an article of 1981 Winkler describes how this turn to ego psychology and self psychology was already related to the problem of conscience formation and societal norms from the very start. Hartmann's theories on the conflict free ego capacities, adaptation to reality and neutralization of the drives by the strength of the ego was essentially about finding a balance between drive, con-science and reality. This implied rethinking the mutual influences between sub-ject and society. It was thus important that Hartmann had published his book *Psychoanalysis and Moral Values* (1960) in a German translation (1973), a study in which a subject's moral development is described: the subject is first dominated by enforced norms through the superego, later – after a period of in-ner conflicts – through an autonomous judgement function of the ego. This moral development is characterized by a movement from submission to norms to an adaptation of norms by a strong ego that is capable of neutralizing de-mands from drives and superego: a "conscience beyond superego".[259] There is thus an immediate connection between ego formation, conscience formation and a relation to the norms of society.[260] The writings of Erikson on identity formation in a socio-historic context including cultural norms and values point in the same direction of a distinction between "moral conscience and a later ethical inclination".[261]

---

[258] H.-G. Preuss, *Illusion und Wirklichkeit*, pp.123-124.

[259] The expression "conscience beyond superego" is derived from Heinz Kittsteiner's study of the origins of modern conscience. H. Kittsteiner, *Die Entstehung des modernen Gewissens*, Suhrkamp Verlag, Frankfurt, 1995, p.400.

[260] K. Winkler, "Ich- Und Über-Ich-Problematik im Umgang mit Normen", pp.70-72. Hartmann had argued that the child's moral development is first dominated by superego structures that are enforced upon the child and then later by the moral capacities of a matured ego. This gradual development is described as a "revaluation of moral values", a process of integration through which "moral law" becomes more and more an ego function. This process of integration is not isolated in the subject, but in constant rela-tion with cultural norms and values that – though the ego-functions are decisive – can either support or manipulate the process. This implies that moral development is de-tached from unconscious elements and mechanisms. Psychoanalytic therapy should strongly support the integration of moral values. H. Hartmann, *Psychoanalyse und mo-ralische Werte*, Fischer Verlag, Frankfurt, 1992, pp.23ff, pp.65ff.

[261] Idem, p.75; M. Klessmann, *Identität und Glaube*, p.45.

In later writings Winkler adds another connection between narcissism, conscience formation and societal norms. Scholars such as Scharfenberg had suggested that a culture of guilt dominated by superego structures seemed outdated. Christopher Lasch had pointed out in *The Culture of Narcissism* (1978) that narcissism had become a general characteristic of (American) civilization arguing that modern man was no longer primarily motivated by guilt, but by anxiety and, as a response to that, narcissism. Anxiety and feelings of insecurity emerge in a society that seems no longer capable of educating and supporting people as responsible human beings through paternal and superego authority structures. In this cultural situation narcissistic traits are taken up as self-protection.[262]

According to Winkler, such a culture of narcissism has important theological implications, because sin and guilt can no longer be defined as a disturbance in the relation between man and fellow man or man and God, but must instead be seen as a failure of one's own ego ideal. This means that theological anthropology must be reconsidered and that a "voice of conscience" should be defined according to the new era. Traditionally Christian conscience was related to the superego structures of guilt and feelings of guilt, but in a culture of narcissism conscience should be related to the ego ideal and associated feelings such as weakness, shame, self doubt and failure. That doesn't mean that guilt and the sense of guilt are to be denied, on the contrary, but they should be integrated in a personality that is primarily to be regarded as the product of a narcissistic maturation process.[263] Scharfenberg's turn to Kohut can be situated in this context.[264]

We have seen that in the early 1970s Scharfenberg had argued for a replacement of a "severe unquestioned superego" by an individually formulated "norm". It was Stollberg who was among the first to propose a differentiation between superego conscience and ego conscience.[265] In the 1970s such a differentiation can also be found in the writings of other scholars such as Riess or Hartung.[266] Ac-

---

[262] Chr. Lasch, *The Culture of Narcissism. American Life in an Age of Diminishing Expectations*, Norton, New York, 1978.

[263] K. Winkler, ""Heile mich, denn ich habe gesündigt". Theologische Überlegungen", in E. Hölscher, M. Klessmann (eds.), *Grundmuster der Seele*, pp.28-38 (33-34); K. Winkler, "Schuld und Schuldgefühl. Die Möglichkeit von Daseinsverfehlung, in idem, pp.80-94 (89-90).

[264] H. Wahl, ""Zwischen" Theologie und Psychoanalyse", p.454.

[265] D. Stollberg, "Das Gewissen in pastoralpsychologischer Sicht". Compare also D. Stollberg, "Tiefenpsychologie oder historisch-kritische Exegese? Identität und Tod des Ich (Gal. 2, 19-20)", in Y. Spiegel (ed.), *Doppeldeutich. Tiefendimensionen biblischer Texte*, Kaiser Verlag, Munich, 1978, pp.215-226.

[266] R. Riess, *Seelsorge. Orientierung, Analysen, Alternativen*, Vandenhoeck & Ruprecht, Göttingen, 1973, pp.53ff.; M. Hartung, *Angst und Schuld in Tiefenpsychologie und Theologie*, pp.114-117.

cording to Auchter, there had always been unease with the Freudian association of superego and conscience. Apparently there was a need to at least differentiate between the sense of guilt in relation to trespassing on collective norms, and the sense of guilt as an injury to personal integrity. The distinction between superego guilt and ego guilt thus runs "like a red line" through all psychoanalytic literature on the problem of guilt.[267] Alternatives to Freud's model were formulated in theories on the two origins of conscience that should be clearly separated: "outer and inner sources". Following Donald Winnicott's distinction between true and false self, Auchter himself differentiates between true authentic conscience and a socially-dependant superego conscience.[268]

From the 1970s onwards the distinction between superego conscience and ego conscience seems to have become almost paradigmatic in pastoral psychological literature on the topic.[269] Superego conscience is associated with enforced morality and as a result of that, a pressing sense of guilt. Ego conscience is generally described in terms of moral autonomy and personal responsibility. The turn to ego psychology and self psychology was not only evoked by the need for theories on maturation processes and reflections on personal growth in faith, but also by the need to rethink and re-establish a relation between individual and collective norms, not only societal norms, but also the shared norms, values and convictions in a community of faith. Ego psychology had turned Freudian psychoanalysis into a psychology of adaptation to group norms.

Riess had argued already in the early 1970s that mature conscience could not be seen detached from the social structure of a group, for conscience "mirrored" the standards and norms of group to which one belongs.[270] Maturation processes were not isolated individual processes: "individual development is always also acquiring of socialization".[271] The individual maturation process could thus also be regarded as a "fusion" process with a social group. He makes perfectly clear that the social group (the church) should meet the demands of the individual and should thus be characterized by "fellowship components" and

---

[267] Th. Auchter, "Von der Unschuld zur Verantwortung. Ein Beitrag zum Diskurs zwischen Psychoanalyse und Theologie", in M. Schlagheck (ed.), *Theologie und Psychologie im Dialog über Schuld*, Bonifatius Verlag, Paderborn, 1996, pp.41-138 (47).

[268] Idem, p.48.

[269] The writings of Winkler and Auchter have already been mentioned. Other examples: H. Pottmeyer, "Heutige Schulderfahrung und das christliche Sprechen von Schuld und Sünde. Verstehensvermittlung als Beitrag zur Schuldbewältigung", in *Schulderfahrung und Schuldbewältigung. Christen im Umgang mit der Schuld*, G. Kaufmann (ed.), Schöningh Verlag, Paderborn/Munich/Vienna/Zurich, 1982, pp.93-114 (106); U. Rauchfleisch, *Psychoanalyse und theologische Ethik. Neue Impulse zum Dialog*, Herder Verlag, Freiburg, Vienna, 1986, pp.21ff., pp.138ff.; R. Riess, "Zeit der Schuldlosen?", p.88; M. Klessmann, *Pastoralpsychologie*, pp.491-493, pp.610ff.

[270] R. Riess, *Seelsorge*, p.192.

[271] Idem, p.208.

"process orientation".[272] In other words, the group mirrors the individual and vice versa.

Hartmann's theory of the adaptation of values and norms as brought forward by Winkler, or Riess' and Klessmann's turn to Erikson's ideas on the positive function religion and social structures have for reaching possibilities for the development of identity (ego-synthesis) and the formation of moral consciousness as result of individual maturation and integration of positive values and norms[273], point in the same direction. Ego psychology and self psychology not only provided theories of individual maturation and faith, but also envisioned a positive view on societal norms and group dynamics, in short, an optimistic view of culture and cultural development. The new psychoanalytic movements thus provided helpful theories for reformulating individual faith in relation to religious community against the background of secularization and a need for new models in pastoral care and community practice. That doesn't mean that the guilt problem is resolved, for as Winkler writes guilt and the sense of guilt are now closely related to individual conscience formation, responsibility and the ability to accept (or adapt to) societal norms.[274] In this context pastoral care has a mediating "conflict stabilizing" role.

This psychological (therapeutic) discourse was thus already a "subtle form of morality" that could easily be allied with more explicit discussions on ethics in pastoral care.[275] Hence in Winkler's writings for example there is also a keen interest in the theories of Lawrence Kohlberg who had described the correspondence between psychological and moral development. From here a step could be made to theories of "man as the ethical subject of his way of life".[276] It has been noticed that this notion of *Lebensführung*, i.e. an autonomous way of life by an autonomous responsible being, developed out of the turn to new psychologies in the 1970s. In the past two decades this has become a dominant is-

---

[272] Idem, p.209. Similar ideas can be find in a 1985 study by Schneider-Flume of Erikson. She writes that "ego-identity and institution strengthen each others vitality" indicating that both individual and group developed along analogous lines and in mutual support. G. Schneider-Flume, *Die Identität des Sünders. Eine Auseinandersetzung theologischer Anthropologie mit dem Konzept der psychosozialen Identität Erik H. Eriksons*, Vandenhoeck & Ruprecht, Göttingen, 1985, pp.86-93 (86).

[273] Idem, pp.83ff.; M. Klessmann, *Identität und Glaube*, pp.33-47. In Erikson's model of developmental stages sense of guilt is closely connected to conscience formation in which ideally the superego does not develop into a strong repressive force intensifying the sense of guilt, but a conscience is constructed through "initiative", that is, being able to integrate positive elements from the cultural ethos and strengthen the ego against superego conscience. Idem, pp.54-55.

[274] K. Winkler, *Seelsorge*, p.356, p.358.

[275] U. Körtner, "Ist die Moral das Ende der Seelsorge, oder ist die Seelsorge am Ende Moral?", in *Wege zum Menschen* 58 (2006), pp.225-245 (225).

[276] K. Winkler, "Zum Umgang mit Normen in der Seelsorge", in *Pastoraltheologie* 80 (1991), pp.26-39.

sue in discussions on pastoral care and ethics.[277] There is thus continuity from psychological models on ego maturation into a discourse on the moral maturation of man.[278]

The context of these discussions in pastoral care is a concern about secularized society. Riess argues that guilt, personal conscience and responsibility have become key issues in a culture that might develop into a "conscience-less" and "guiltless" civilization that yet faces enormous ethical challenges due to the developments in science and in our capacities to control and renew life. The alternative seems to be a return to authoritarian superego structures (in for example fundamentalism). In this situation personal conscience formation and critical responsibility are the key instruments to rethink society and its values in order to create a third option for the future.[279]

In the context of the danger of a "guiltless" culture Winkler strongly stresses the importance of a moral maturation process towards a critical human being, that is to say, critical not only towards identification – the term "enforcement" is no longer applied – with general accepted norms, but also towards oneself in self-observation and self-critique, even in the form of inner feelings of guilt and shame, in order to make possible a self-reconciliation as an element of ego-integration.[280]

The fact that the guilt problem was not broadly debated, but that instead a "silence" occurred, certainly doesn't imply that the problem has gone. The return of religion in the public domain (especially due to the rise of fundamentalism) and the danger of a disintegrated "guiltless" society, means that guilt returns as an issue in rethinking religion in contemporary society, i.e. religion in its function of providing societal coherence (through conscience formation and maturation towards responsibility), and at the same time developing models for moderate religion in-between extremes.

In my opinion, this line of thought ultimately brings us back to issues that Freud discussed and that now seems again the focus of attention: the relation between religion and morality; the relation between the sense of guilt and "advancement in intellectuality"; the inevitability of a sense of guilt in a society

---

[277] U. Körtner, "Ist die Moral das Ende der Seelsorge, oder ist die Seelsorge am Ende Moral?".

[278] An example can be found in a study of ethics by Trutz Rendtorff who clearly relates psychological maturation processes with a capacity to be an autonomous moral being. In this context he refers to Freudian psychoanalysis as a theory of maturation as reality acceptance and hence the acceptance of normal moral behaviour (heterosexuality, marriage). Such an interpretation of Freud can be seen in the light of the influence of ego psychology and self-psychology. T. Rendtorff, *Ethik. Grundelemente, Methodologie und Konkretionen einer ethischen Theologie. Band 2*, Kohlhammer Verlag, Stuttgart/Berlin/Colone, 1991, pp.67-68.

[279] R. Riess, "Zeit der Schuldlosen?", pp.88-89.

[280] K. Winkler, "Zum Umgang mit Normen in der Seelsorge", p.32.

(and religion) that somehow has to find a moderate modus between extreme forces; the question how an individual is socialized and what role tradition, authority and identification play here; the question to what extent traditional theological formulations on guilt (or sin) are, or are not, outdated, still relevant and/or in need of reconfiguration.

4.3.4 Review

From the 1960s onwards Freud and psychoanalysis have had a profound influence on pastoral psychology though it has been rightfully argued that from the 1990s onwards its influence as a dominant paradigm has declined.[281] In my opinion we can fairly say that from a Freudian perspective the climax of the engagement with Freud by pastoral psychology lies in the writings of Scharfenberg from the late 1960s and early 1970s.[282] At that time the Freudian critique of religion functioned as a crowbar to question the dominance of Barthian theology and Thurneysen's model of pastoral care and to open up discussions for further developments. After that early climax Freudian thought remained influential though, in general, in the shadow of new psychoanalytic theories that proved to have a higher constructive potential in pastoral psychology and other disciplines.

Looking back on developments in Scharfenberg's thought – from Freud to self psychology – and on the "debates" concerning guilt, narcissism and conscience formation, the question can be raised as to what motives lie behind the shift from Freudian psychoanalysis towards ego psychology, self psychology and, to a lesser extent, object relations theory.

Scholars such as Scharfenberg and Lauret interpret Freud's writings on religion as analyses of the pathological, immature and illusionary forms of religion. These "caricatures" are clearly associated with superseded institutional and dogmatic superego structures in which the sense of guilt played a key role. The emphasis is now laid on personal faith, on ego-integration and maturation. When Scharfenberg ends is chapter "Beyond the guilt principle" with the remark that in faith a person can truly say "I before God"[283] the road is not only paved for a shift of attention towards narcissism theories, but also the corner stone is laid for reformulating faith beyond Freud's critique of religion. In the writings of Pannenberg and Lauret we see a further step: personal faith and ego-integration are associated with realistic faith and participation in a totality of

---

[281] Chr. Morgenthaler, "Zur Funktion der Psychoanalyse in der gegenwärtigen Pastoral-psychologie. Acht Thesen mit Erläuterungen", in I. Noth. Chr. Morgenthaler (eds.), *Seelsorge und Psychoanalyse*, pp.59-67.

[282] This climax reflects the fact that Freudian psychoanalysis in general was influential in the 1960s, that is to say, in its function as critical theory questioning social structures in society. The writings of Mitscherlich and Herbert Marcuse can serve as examples.

[283] J. Scharfenberg, *Religion zwischen Wahn und Wirklichkeit*, p.208.

meaning. Here we see how the shift towards ego psychology and self psychology goes hand in hand with attempts to reconstruct theology based not on the guilt question, but on the question of meaning in life, as Lauret calls it.[284] In other words, it seems possible to reformulate dogmatic or systematic theology beyond the suspicion that such theology might be motivated by illusionary wishes or enforced guilt-laden religiosity. We are thus back to the issue already addressed in the previous chapters: the true "essence" of religion lies beyond Freud's psychoanalysis.

In my opinion the unease with Freudian thought does not only lie in his view on religion as pathology. There was also the fact that Freud's theories were disturbing in themselves. Here, first, it should be noticed that in the longing for a consistent and integrated subject (ego or self) the "body" is neglected and actually lost from sight. Theories of ego-integration or self-realization aim at unifying the psychical apparatus on the level of consciousness in a process of maturation or even self-transcendence. In Freud's writings – and this is unignorable when one reads his texts – the psychical apparatus is also indeed *apparatus*, closely related to physical impulses and symptoms, organized by drives, and in search of (sexual) satisfaction. Man is characterized by inner conflicts. Yet, these conflicts are situated in the unity of body and mind – the unconscious is the "missing link" relating bodily and psychic processes in a dynamic unity. The body is therefore ever-present in Freudian thought – from his work in the laboratory via the bodily symptoms of the hysteric, infantile sexuality, the drives as "psychical representatives of an endosomatic source of stimulation" and man's own body as a narcissistic love object onto the "psychical consequences of the anatomical distinction between the sexes" or women's penis-envy; from touching and enjoying the body (auto-erotism), eating the body (oral fantasies, totem meal), watching the body (primal scene), beating the body (masochism) onto the bodily surface of the ego. However, when in theological literature Eros is spiritualized, man desires totality of meaning, love for one's fellow man is based on reasonability, or faith is described as a maturation process towards responsibility, the body as *locus* of desire and of the ego is lost from sight. Moreover this means a movement away from Freud's anthropology in which man's bodily urges, instincts and mechanisms rule the unconscious that result in the mental helplessness and inner conflicts the ego is unable to fully control. Apparently, there is an unease about seriously including the body in the concept of integration or faith maturation. A reason for this unease can be found in the fact that the turn to new psychoanalytic theories can be seen as a movement away from theologies that focused on man's sins, guilt and shortcomings. Dialectic theologians such as Thurneysen (and Bach) could associate the "pessimistic" traits of Freudian "anthropology" with their theological views. As a counter reaction maturation, integration, and overcoming of shortcomings

---

[284] B. Lauret, *Schulderfahrung und Gottesfrage bei Nietsche und Freud*, p.21.

(anxiety, guilt) were emphasized. The body, in a sense, would have confronted us again with man's fallibilities and mental maladjustments that theologians were trying to resolve.[285]

Another disturbing element is related to this: Freud did not develop an overall systematic theory, but – as Scharfenberg or Van de Spijker rightfully argue – his thought is in constant development, questioning and re-questioning earlier concepts and structures without reaching a definite end-point, without defining a "message of salvation", an optimum between an inevitable sense of guilt and the advancement in intellectuality, or a picture of a balanced healthy personality adapted to realtity.

Here we find a motive for a turn towards ego psychology and self psychology, because in these theories a steady consistent core in the subject is either presupposed or aimed at, or both.[286] Lauret's study of guilt is a beautiful example of taking Freudian (and Lacanian) thought as a starting point and ending up with steady concepts such as ego strength that can be related to a totality of meaning. Relating Freudian thought to theology (resp. theological anthropol-

---

[285] Dieter Funke has argued that from Descartes and the Enlightenment onwards, the irrational as related to the body and its drives and passions has become subjected to repression and control by rational thought. In Schopenhauer's, Nietzsche's and Freud's thought the irrational reclaims its territory. The concept of the unconscious expresses the unity of body and mind. In theology, Funke argues, the irrational nature of the unconscious and the body is apparently difficult to process: instead the emphasis is laid on rationalization and moralization, instead of seeing religion as an expression of the tragic characteristics of human existence. D. Funke, *Das Schulddilemma. Wege zu einem versöhnten Leben*, Vandenhoeck & Ruprecht, Göttingen, 2000, pp.28-55.

[286] This need to find a core in the subject that can be related to the transcendental or totality of meaning is particularly strong in a 1998 study of the dialogue between theology and psychoanalysis by Anne Steinmeier. Her starting point is Scharfenberg's reading of Freud. She argues that there are tendencies ("dialectic movements") in Freud's psychoanalytic theories – associated with concepts such as truth, love and freedom – that point in the direction of a "self". (According to Steinmeier, religion was subsequently seen by Freud as an "inhibition of the process of becoming a self".) Scharfenberg's ideas on transference and counter-transference as a method in pastoral conversation creating a free conversation that makes healing possible is taken up in a definition of the content of that freedom, namely self-realization in relation to Christ. From there on Steinmeier describes theoretical developments in psychoanalysis as a development in the direction of clearly defined theories of the self. Important for us are her conclusions: the self is a "place"; man is born with a self, but this self needs to be further developed through stages (self-realization); the self is a steady, non-contingent and safe haven in the soul. It is this self in its development that is seen as the "place" where man is in relation to God, because every unique process of self-realization is the process in which God becomes present in the world: *Der Prozeß der Selbstwerdung ist theologisch zu verstehen als Prozeß der Gotteswirklichkeit, wie sie in jedem Leben gegenwärtig ist* (p.200). A. Steinmeier, *Wiedergeboren zur Freiheit. Skizzen eines Dialogs zwischen Theologie und Psychoanalyse*, Vandenhoeck & Ruprecht, Göttingen, 1998.

ogy) seems to go hand in hand with a process of finding steady consistent concepts and principles: Van de Spijker's balance, Meng's realistic utopia, Scharfenberg's Eros and Ananke, and of course the ever present ego that should be
where id and superego were. There is thus a turn to other psychoanalytic theories. Freudian psychoanalysis is after all deconstructive, not only towards outdated religious superego structures, but also towards the (religious) subject, its
maturation processes and its philosophies of life or religious representations.
Consequently, theologians who ultimately seek a positive core in the subject,
whether in terms of ego or self, meaning or balance, love or responsibility, become "un-Freudian", neglecting, ignoring or "neutralizing" the perversities,
weaknesses, regressive, aggressive and destructive forces that are ever present
in Freudian thought. Van de Spijker's "non-discussion" of Freud's thoughts on
the commandment to love one's fellow man might serve as an example. Of
course there are positive elements in Freudian thought: a belief in intellectuality
and sublimation, in great men, in friendship and humour, in love and in the future, but never without the shadow of their counterparts, and never under the
control of consciousness.

   A related aspect can be added: theologians resisted the idea, apparently,
brought forward in the theory of the irrational and immoral unconscious and the
superego as representative of moral enforcement that man can no longer be regarded as personally responsible for his thoughts and acts. The few remarks
Freud made on the issue actually point in a different direction. In a short text on
the issue he points out that the "ego" should assume responsibility for the immoral content of dreams. The reason is a psychological one, not an ethical principle: the ego is "seated" upon and "developed out of" the id. To accept this is
to accept that no-one is "better than he was created", a self-assesment that
guards against "hypocrisy" (illusion) on the one hand and "inhibition" (neurotic
conscientiousness) on the other hand. Freud adds he will leave it to the jurist to
construct social purposes for such responsibility.[287] Responsibility is thus the
affirmation of one's immoral nature. In ego psychology with its focus on the
adaptation to norms and self psychology with its focus on psychic development
in a social context personal responsibility is strongly related to the autonomous
and authentic affirmation of shared norms and values. We thus find two very
different concepts of responsibility that reflect two very different anthropologies.

In my opinion these are main reasons that a broad debate on guilt never took
place. The Freudian sense of guilt as an inevitable characteristic of man's tragic
struggle in life (immoral nature versus morality) was not taken as a starting
point for reflecting on pastoral care or theological anthropology. Instead a turn
to new psychoanalytic theories centered the outlook upon a harmonious

---

[287] S. Freud, *Some Additional Notes on Dream-Interpretation as a Whole, SE XIX*,
pp.131-134.

autonomous responsible religious subject adapting to or affirming shared religious views.

Here, Freud's psychoanalytic views could serve as critical counter-theory again. The constructs of ego conscience and responsibility point in the direction of superego structures that are compelling through the maturation processes and developmental stages in a social and institutional context. Were we to accept Freud's idea that the superego is the larger part of the ego representing the id, the ideals and restrictions, then the so-called autonomous ego-development should be interpreted as a superego commandment that compels the ego towards ongoing maturation and adaptation, towards an ideal that Freud would probably consider illusionary and neuroticizing.

4.4 Debates on exegesis

The development of the dialogue between psychoanalysis and Protestant theology was closely related to the critique of dialectic theology. This is also an important aspect of early attempts from the late 1960s onwards of exploring the possibilities of psychoanalytic interpretations of biblical texts.[288] Helmut Harsch for example argues that such interpretations should be welcomed as an alternative to the anti-psychological attitude in exegesis due to the influence of dialectic theology.[289] Gerhard Wehr asks the question whether there is no alternative in bible interpretation between repetition of outdated traditional thought which is no longer related to contemporary religious experience and a "flight into the modern", a demytholization (Bultmann) which also neglects "the Christian spiritual substance".[290] But which psychoanalysis could be called upon to establish a relation with religious experience or faith?

Not only Harsch and Wehr turn to Jungian depth psychology, but also Kurt Niederwimmer writes that Jesus points towards "the final self-realization of man".[291] His death and resurrection are a "symbol" that despite existential

---

[288] For a survey on psychoanalytic interpretations of biblical texts (until 1999) see M. Leiner, *Psychologie und Exegese. Grundfragen einer textpsychologischen Exegese des Neuen Testaments*, Kaiser Verlag, Gütersloh, 1995, pp.41-76; W. Pratscher, "Tiefenpsychologie und Textauslegung", in S. Kreuzer et al. (eds.), *Proseminar I Altes Testament. Ein Arbeitsbuch*, Kohlhammer Verlag, Stuttgart, 1999, pp.178-188.

[289] H. Harsch, "Psychologische Interpretation biblischer Texte?", in *Wege zum Menschen* 20 (1968), pp.281-289 (281).

[290] G. Wehr, *Wege zu religiöser Erfahrung. Analytische Psychologie im Dienst der Bibelauslegung*, Walter-Verlag, Olten/Freiburg, 1974, pp.14-15.

[291] K. Niederwimmer, *Jesus*, Vandenhoeck & Ruprecht, Göttingen, 1968, pp.86-87. Also K. Niederwimmer, "Tiefenpsychologie und Exegese", in R. Riess (ed.), *Perspektiven der Pastoraltheologie*, Vandenhoeck & Ruprecht, Göttingen, 1974, pp.63-78. Compare V. Metelmann, "Jesus von Nazareth und die christlichen Symbole unter dem Aspekt tiefenpsychologischer Überlegungen", in *Wege zum Menschen* 23 (1971), pp.22-24.

limitations there is a lasting perspective on meaning. Somewhat loosely this idea is inspired by Jungian thought on the collective unconscious, archetypical elements in myth and the function of symbols in resolving inner conflicts.

It was Scharfenberg who took the initiative to formulate a Freudian alternative. In 1971 an edition of *Approaches to Man* was devoted to the subject. Scharfenberg wrote a short introductory text.[292] In Barbara Strehlow's article for this edition a Freudian perspective is further elaborated upon.[293] She focuses on key concepts in Freud's *Moses and Monotheism* such as trauma, defence, repression, latency and the return of the repressed. From there she formulates two central points of attention in a Freudian analysis of texts. First, there are the unconscious presuppositions of the interpreter, that is to say, his libidinal needs, his identifications, his inhibitions, his own repressed wishes and desires. She argues that transference and counter-transference should be the method in psychoanalytic reading and interpretation of texts enabling one to make conscious one's own presuppositions that determine the interpretation. Second, psychoanalytic interpretation could determine whether in a text reality is affirmed or a delusional world is created through, for example, fixation on the father image of God and regression to a father-child relation. In other words, psychoanalytic reading of texts not only evokes recognition of unconscious conflicts and ambivalences of the interpreter, but also those underlying or expressed in the text.

The psychoanalyst and ex-Catholic theologian Eugen Drewermann (1940-) has by far become the most important representative of a "Jungian" line of thought in psychoanalytic bible exegesis. His oeuvre has developed into a landmark in popular theological literature. It all started with his more than 1500 pages long *Strukturen des Bösen* [Structures of Evil] of 1978, a study with a clear aim: "the meaning of our research is not to prove something, but to point at something", namely the "central position of the religious experience of human guilt" and the idea "that man cannot live without God".[294] Thus aimed at is the experience of sin and faith in order to overcome, as he later writes, the split between theology and psychology that characterizes modern exegesis.[295]

Structures of Evil, as Scharfenberg rightfully observed, starts from a single observation: the Jahwist history in the book of Genesis shows structural

---

[292] J. Scharfenberg, "Existentiale und tiefenpsychologische Interpretation biblischer Texte", in *Wege zum Menschen* 23 (1971), pp.1-2.

[293] B. Strehlow, "Ansatzpunkte tiefenpsychologischer Interpretation biblischer Texte bei Sigmund Freud", in idem, pp.16-21.

[294] E. Drewermann, *Strukturen der Bösen. Die jahwistische Urgeschichte in exegetischer Sicht. Band I*, Schöningh Verlag, Paderborn/Munich/Vienna/Zurich, 1988, pp.XII-XIV.

[295] E. Drewermann, *Tiefenpsychologie und Exegese. Band II. Die Wahrheit der Werke und der Worte. Wunder, Vision, Weissagung, Apokalypse, Geschichte, Gleichnis*, Walter-Verlag, Olten, Freiburg, 1985, pp.66ff.; E. Drewermann, *Psychoanalyse und Moraltheologie. Band 1. Angst und Schuld*, Grünewald Verlag, Mainz, 1982, pp.9ff.

resemblances with psychoanalytic theories on the development of the libido.[296] Looking over this study we must draw the conclusion that Drewermann is basically an eclectic thinker who starts off from Freud interpreted through Jung and corrected or supplemented by other psychoanalytic theories.

This Jungian reading of Freud is for example apparent in a passage where Drewermann reflects on the parallel structures between the Jahwist history and psychoanalytic theory, and basically argues that these parallels point in the direction of "similar, innate modes of experiences".[297] He argues that Freud regarded ontogenesis as the repetition of phylogenesis and that therefore the developmental stages of individual psychogenesis could be seen as a recapitulation of prehistoric stages of phylogenesis.[298] This can be synthesized with Jung's theory of the collective unconscious and its archetypes as the instinctual heritage of general human potentials.[299]

Another example of reading Freud through Jung can be found in a paragraph on identification. Without mentioning Jung Freud is said to have argued that identification is a reaction formation against the threat of loosing a love object. Identification is the regressive introjection of a love object. When the love object is God, the image of God will be coloured by the characteristics of the stage of regression. Such an interpretation of identification as basically an inhibition or regression of normal libidinal development can be regarded as Jungian.[300] I will not present other examples. It suffices to say that Drewermann is convinced that Freudian and Jungian theories are not opposed, but "need and supplement each other".[301] Despite the fact that both theories show major differences about the question of subjectivity, Drewermann focuses on those differences that according to him seem promising for supplementation.[302]

Drewermann has a message: man cannot live truthfully and freely when he doesn't "live towards God". In the Jahwist account of prehistory sin is "the endless pathological", a "neurosis before God", a psychological failure in de-

---

[296] J. Scharfenberg, "... und die Bibel hat doch recht – diesmal psychologisch? Zu Eugen Drewermanns Konzept der Sünde als "Neurose vor Gott"", in *Wege zum Menschen* 31 (1979), pp.297-302 (297). E. Drewermann, *Strukturen der Bösen. Die jahwistische Urgeschichte in psychoanalytischer Sicht. Band II*, Schöningh Verlag, Paderborn/Munich/Vienna/Zurich, 1988, pp.2-3.

[297] E. Drewermann, "Zu: J. Scharfenberg, "... und die Bibel hat doch recht – diesmal psychologisch?", in *Wege zum Menschen* 32 (1980), pp.122-123 (122).

[298] E. Drewermann, *Strukturen der Bösen. Band II*, p.3.

[299] Idem, *Band I*, pp.XXXVI-XXXIX.

[300] Already in *The Significance of the Father in the Destiny of the Individual* Jung had brought forward this idea. Freud would later react arguing that identification was a presupposition for object love and that identification should be regarded as a positive mechanism in establishing a self-identity.

[301] E. Drewermann, *Strukturen des Bösen, Band I*, p.XLII.

[302] Idem, pp.XXXV-XL.

velopment.[303] Its symptoms are self hate, existential doubt, anxiety, feelings of guilt, depression, etc. Psychoanalysis however provides a method that can deconstruct neurotic structures and unleash healing powers that lay hidden in the unconscious.[304] Freudian psychoanalysis can help to understand sin and self destruction.[305]

Primarily this is pursued by pointing out parallel structures between the story of the Fall (Gn. 3) and *Totem and Taboo*. The paradise situation (Gn. 2) can be compared with the early oral stage in which infant and mother's breast are in a close unity, but already under the threat of a separation: anxiety clearly precedes the sense of guilt. For his interpretation of the Fall (Gn. 3) he turns to Freud's account of primal history and the origins of the sense of guilt.[306] According to Drewermann the sense of guilt does not originate from the murder of the primal father – in Genesis there is no murder of the father – but from the totem meal which was originally a cannibalistic meal. This issue of the totem meal is symbolically expressed in the story of the forbidden fruit.[307] This means that the sense of guilt should not be related to an Oedipal phase, but actually originates from an oral phase in which "eating" and "fear for loss of love" are important elements.[308] Freud's theory of the origin of the sense of guilt and primal murder are thus corrected with help of the structure of the story of the Fall and Freud's own theory of the various developmental stages. Further elaborating on the cannibalistic meal a third theory is added: Klein's theory of aggression against the mother as source for the sense of guilt.[309] This theory perfectly depicts what the story of the Fall wants to tell: sense of guilt is inevitable; every individual will be driven out of the primal unity with the mother, because of the sadistic impulses against her.

This short depiction of Drewermann's reading of *Totem and Taboo* shows the basic problems in his study. Firstly, there are the parallel structures in

---

[303] Idem, *Band II*, p.XII, p.556. This definition of sin as neurosis is first of all inspired by Jung, but also seems to resemble Thurneysen's ideas on neurosis as symptom of sin. Compare: *Die Psychoneurose ist im letzten Verstande ein Leiden der Seele, die ihren Sinn nicht gefunden hat*". C.G. Jung, "Über die Beziehung der Psychotherapie zur Seelsorge", in *Gesammelte Werke. Band 11*, pp.355-376 (358).

[304] Henning has argued that Drewermann's idea that psychoanalysis is the tool to create healthy faith can be seen as a theory "in the footsteps" of Pfister. In my opinion Pfister is not a major source of inspiration for Drewermann. In *Strukturen des Bösen*, for example, he is not even mentioned. Chr. Henning, "Oskar Pfister – der Beginn einer problematischen Freud-Rezeption innerhalb der Theologie", pp.54ff.

[305] E. Drewermann, *Strukturen des Bösen, Band II*, p.XX.

[306] Idem, pp.178ff.

[307] Idem, pp.197-202.

[308] Basically this early sense of guilt is, according to Drewermann, what Freud had called bad conscience or social anxiety. In Gn. 3 this is reflected in the issue of shame that is closely related to sense of guilt. Idem, pp.203-204.

[309] Idem, pp.188-192.

biblical stories and in psychological development that can be unravelled and interpreted with the help of psychoanalytic theories. Psychoanalysis thus functions as a theological meta-theory based on the idea of universal truths and a promised salvation.[310] Scharfenberg mentions a second problem concerning the parallel structures: psychological models point to progressive development whereas the Jahwist history is an accumulation of disastrous events.[311] Thirdly, there is Drewermann's eclecticism which enables him to freely give a bold psychoanalytic answer to every question raised by exegesis. Whether these theories are consistent with each other is of no concern – after all: they supplement each other. Why and under what conditions one theory can overrule or correct the other, remains an open question.

Concerning his reading of Freud it seems that Drewermann in his depictions of sin as neurosis is not led by the model of obsessional neurosis as developed by Freud[312], but by the model for anxiety neurosis (for it is clear that the sense of guilt is a either a form or an effect of anxiety) and melancholia.[313] There are two main reasons for this choice. Firstly, the obsessional neurosis model, as applied in *Totem and Taboo*, of the primal history could "not be applied for the explanation" of the Jahwist text and was thus "superfluous".[314] The Oedipus complex was not as decisive and dominant in either phylogenesis or ontogenesis as Freud thought. Secondly, there is Drewermann's overall starting point, not only in *Structures of Evil* but also throughout his later writings[315]: faith is opposed to anxiety for the loss of the love object God. "Life without God as the Jahwist understands it has only one structure: anxiety." Anxiety is the "subjective fundamental disposition of human life".[316] It is this anxiety that is both the origin and the core of "neurosis before God".

From the late 1980s onwards the critique of Drewermann's ideas on depth psychology and exegesis grew. In theological literature we can see an emphasis in the critique of his exegetic methods. This is hardly a surprise, for Drewermann had launched a severe attack on the "rationalism of exegesis" in

---

[310] See also D. Funke, "Ewige Urbilder? Einige Anmerkungen zu Drewermanns tiefenpsychologischer Hermeneutik", in B. Benedikt, A. Sobel (eds.), *Der Streit um Drewermann. Was Theolog(inn)en und Psycholog(inn)en kritisieren*, Verlag Sobel, Wiesbaden/Berlin, 1992, pp.52-55; J. Frey, *Eugen Drewermann und die biblische Exegese. Eine methodisch-kritische Analyse*, Mohr Verlag, Tübingen, 1995, pp.80-86.

[311] J. Scharfenberg, "… und die Bibel hat doch recht – diesmal psychologisch?", p.301.

[312] E. Drewermann, *Strukturen des Bösen, Band II*, pp.596-597.

[313] idem, pp.594-595.

[314] Idem, p.596.

[315] See for example E. Drewermann, *Psychoanalyse und Moraltheologie. Band I*, pp.pp.117ff.; E. Drewermann, *Tiefenpsychologie und Exegese. Band I*, pp.1-2, p.12.

[316] *In der Exegese von Gn 2 und Gn 3 haben wir darauf hingewiesen, daß die Angst den Menschen von Gott trenne und die Strukturen seines Daseins grundlegend umqualifiziere; jetzt sehen wir, dass ein Leben ohne Gott im Sinne des J nur eine einzige Struktur besitzt: die Angst.* E. Drewermann, *Strukturen des Bösen, Band II*, p.233.

one of his major studies. The "whole theology" and exegesis as part of it was "nothing but" a long history of the dominance of rationality over subjective experience.[317] Provocative statements such as these evoked critical responses.[318]

In the landscape of psychoanalytic interpretations of biblical texts Jungian depth psychology is clearly dominant. In the 1970s and 1980s occasionally another sound is heard. Interesting, for example, is the 1983 study of the apostle Paul by the biblical scholar Gerd Theissen. He combines various and distinct psychological and psychoanalytic perspectives in his interpretations of passages of text from Paul's letters. When elaborating from a Freudian perspective he focuses on the importance of early childhood experiences in relation to the parents, not only the Oedipal conflicts that are reflected in religion[319], but also the narcissistic feelings of unity and safety.[320] In his study he also presents another, and interestingly enough also Freudian, perspective – although Theissen doesn't recognize it as such: Vergote's structural approach.[321]

In the early 1970s Vergote had written an extensive article on the 7th chapter of Paul's letter to the Romans. His starting point was that psychoanalytic text interpretations should focus on the unconscious motives that underlie and determine both text and reader: interpretation is a quest for meaning in the transferential sphere between text and reader.[322] Psychoanalysis has the task of confronting the anthropological conceptions of the text with those of the reader/interpreter. Applied to Romans 7 it eventually means finding structural anthropological differences and resemblances between the conflicts in Paul's

---

[317] E. Drewermann, *Tiefenpsychologie und Exegese. Band II*, pp.17-18. See also U. Körtner, "Spiritualität ohne Exegese? Pneumatologische Erwägungen zur biblischen Hermeneutik", in *Amt und Gemeinde* 53 (2002), pp.41-54 (44-45).

[318] For example G. Lohfink, R. Pesch (eds.), *Tiefenpsychologie und keine Exegese. Eine Auseinandersetzung mit Eugen Drewermann*, Katholisches Bibelwerk, Stuttgart, 1987; C. Schneider-Harpprecht, "Psychoanalytische Bibelauslegung. Das Beispiel der Hagar-Ismael-Überlieferung", in *Wege zum Menschen* 32 (1991), pp.323-335; J. Blank, "Die Angst vor dem Sturz ins Bodenlose", in B. Benedikt, A. Sobel (eds.), *Der Streit um Drewermann*, pp.21-27; H. Venetz, ""Mit dem Traum, nicht mit dem Wort ist zu beginnen". Tiefenpsychologie als Herausforderung für die Exegese?", in idem, pp.28-38; J. Frey, *Eugen Drewermann und die biblische Exegese.*

[319] G. Theissen, *Psychologische Aspekte paulinischer Theologie*, Vandenhoeck & Ruprecht, Göttingen, 1983, pp.26-30.

[320] Idem, p.30. Here we can clearly detect the influence of the narcissism debate in the 1970s.

[321] Idem, pp.35-36.

[322] A. Vergote, "Der Beitrag der Psychoanalyse zur Exegese. Leben, Gesetz und Ich-Spaltung im 7, Kapitel des Römerbriefs", in X. Léon-Dufour (ed.), *Exegese im Methodenkonflikt. Zwischen Geschichte und Struktur*, Kösel-Verlag, Munich, 1973, pp.73-116 (73-77).

text and those formulated in Freudian/Lacanian psychoanalysis.[323] The aim is to make the historically contingent and unconscious presuppositions of the text visible, enabling a better understanding of the text and thus a better insight into its meaning for the readers.[324] This approach is clearly influenced by Lacan's structural thought and his ideas on the unconscious as language and on the function of elements in the text: how is the "ego" constituted and how does it function in the dynamic relations between Law, flesh and ego; what is the importance of the father for structuring the inner conflicts?

Vergote's article serves as an important guideline for Theissen's interpretation of Romans 7.[325] This is clearly reflected in his analysis of the functional roles of Law and flesh in the unconscious conflict in the text – Law, ego and flesh correspond with superego, ego and id[326] – and his elaborations on the split ego and the positive function of the superego in structuring the ego. However, we should notice here that Theissen, being unfamiliar with Lacanian psychoanalysis and – more importantly – integrating Jungian thought into his analysis of the text, is certainly not following Vergote's line of thought.

In the 1990s Drewermann's depth psychology exegesis were (again) opposed by new Freudian psychoanalytic perspectives. The reason being Drewermann's ideas on eschatological and apocalyptical texts and his analyses of the *Book of Revelations* in *Depth Psychology and Exegesis.*[327] The key issue is the mechanism of transference and counter-transference.

In Drewermann's view the *Book of Revelations* must be seen as "images of self experiences, projections of the self's own psyche into history" and "symbolic stories on eternal truths about man's essence".[328] Gerhard Lohfink and Rudolf Pesch had voiced severe exegetical criticisms of the text, and Drewermann had responded furiously.[329] It was one controversy amidst many, but combined – Drewermann's analysis and defence – they are the starting point for a critical reflection by the psychoanalyst and theologian Hartmut Raguse.

Raguse's study focuses on the reader response evoked by the *Book of Revelations*. According to Raguse, primitive mechanisms are reactivated by the text, namely that of "splitting" and "projective identification". There is an absolute split between good and bad that enables a subject to stay pure and righteous loving a good object (lamb) and yet at the same time enables the same subject to

---

[323] Idem, p.77-78.

[324] Idem, p.81.

[325] G. Theissen, *Psychologische Aspekte paulinischer Theologie*, pp.230-252.

[326] Idem, pp.245-246.

[327] E. Drewermann, *Tiefenpsychologie und Exegese. Band II*, pp.436-591.

[328] Idem, pp.446-447.

[329] G. Lohfink, R. Pesch (eds.), *Tiefenpsychologie und keine Exegese*; E. Drewermann, *"An ihren Fruchten soll ihr sie erkennen". Antwort auf Rudolph Peschs und Gerhard Lohfinks "Tiefenpsychologie und keine Exegese"*, Walter-Verlag, Olten, 1988.

hate an object (or objects) without any limitation in the cruelty of fantasies.[330] Because of this split which precedes an integrated view on objects the sense of guilt is not in issue in the text. The story enables a reader to enjoy his feelings of hate without a sense of guilt and without loosing his purity.

According to Raguse, "Drewermann refuses to take the reader role the text wants him to take"[331], and this is reflected in his interpretation of the text. He argues that Drewermann excludes the hate fantasies from the position of the reader in his desire to read the text positively as a text on healing and integration.[332] And yet, the hate is evoked also in Drewermann as reader: it returns in his furious attack on Lohfink and Pesch. From all this Raguse concludes that Drewermann's analysis of the book of Revelations should not be seen as an interpretation, but rather as a weapon against the text's intentions. Drewermann thus confronts us with a fundamental problem that psychoanalysis raises. He claims an objective position from which he can describe eternal truths, and yet this is exactly what psychoanalysis questions when it argues that every reader (including biblical scholars) is a human being with an unconscious that influences our response to a text that not only transmits cognitive information but also evokes an emotional reaction.

In his 1994 *Der Raum des Textes* [The Sphere of the Text] Raguse's starting point is the "sphere" between text and reader analogous to the sphere between patient and analyst.[333] It is therefore here that Raguse in his reading of Romans 7 seeks alliance with Vergote who, as one of the few psychoanalytic interpreters, did not regard it as his task to analyse the "patient" Paul.[334] Theissen, who did regard the text as an entrance to author Paul[335], is also further elaborated upon.

---

[330] H. Raguse, *Psychoanalyse und biblische Interpretation. Eine Auseinandersetzung mit Eugen Drewermanns Auslegung der Johannes-Apokalypse*, Kohlhammer Verlag, Stuttgart, 1993, pp.155ff., p.162, pp.166-167. Compare also H. Raguse, "Der Jubel der Erlösten über die Vernichtung der Ungläubigen", in *Wege zum Menschen* 42 (1990), pp.449-457 (454-455).

[331] H. Raguse, *Psychoanalyse und biblische Interpretation*, p.161. See also: J. Frey, *Eugen Drewermann und die biblische Exegese*, pp.224-225.

[332] H. Raguse, *Psychoanalyse und biblische Interpretation*, pp.158ff.

[333] H. Raguse, *Der Raum des Textes. Elemente einer transdisziplinären theologischen Hermeneutik*, Kohlhammer Verlag, Stuttgart, 1994.

[334] In Vergote's view the "hidden" meaning of the text cannot be found through a reconstruction of the figure of Paul, nor is the text an expression of Paul's individuality or personal world view. The text instead should be seen as a "fragment" of an "embracing system of meaning". The text is a "fragment", not only in a chain of biblical texts, but beyond that in a "world of thought", a religious tradition. A. Vergote, "Der Beitrag der Psychoanalyse zur Exegese", pp.78-79. In the next chapter we will see that Vergote is referring here to the Lacanian concept of symbolic order which indicates an autonomous chain of signifiers and meaning.

[335] G. Theissen, *Psychologische Aspekte paulinischer Theologie*, p.252.

Raguse's interpretation of Romans 7 is mainly a critical further elaboration on Vergote's and Theissen's interpretations. He questions for example Theissen's association of Law, ego and flesh with superego, ego and id. But most importantly Raguse analyses the concept of sin. Vergote had rightfully argued that in Romans an Oedipal matrix is presented: the Law (of the father) which forbids the desire for the mother and "forces" towards individualization. But Vergote had declined to define sin – he only stated that the flesh should not be associated with evil – and therefore his analysis was unfinished.[336]

Theissen had associated sin with aggression and in fact this idea seemed in concordance with Freud's theory of the primal murder as a result of the interaction of love and hate. The problem with this idea is, however, that aggression is taken up by the superego as a counterforce against "sin".[337] Raguse's alternative is to define sin as perversion, that is, not as the desire to kill the father, but as a will to destroy the father principle and to erect a fatherless-godless world. The Law is then not directed against the flesh and its vitalizing impulses (sexual and aggressive drives), but against "an undifferentiating perversion".[338]

This interpretation of sin is important for Raguse's understanding of guilt and the sense of guilt. When, like Theissen, sin is regarded as a drive or impulse the sense of guilt is a direct consequence of sin, for the sense of guilt emerges out of the conflict between drive and Law. But in Raguse's view – based on his understanding of psychoanalysis as a theory that doesn't liberate people from their inner conflicts, but only makes them aware of them in order to "bear the conflict and to experience one's guilt" (without projecting it)[339] – guilt is necessary and inevitable, not only as a defence against drives, but more importantly as the opposite of the perversion of a total rejection of the father principle.

According to Raguse Romans 7 allows the reader to interpret and experience in fantasy the elements of text in their mutual relations. Given the relations (the Oedipal matrix), the reader can view "the abyss of sin" (rejection of the matrix) without falling in.[340] And when we understand Raguse well, his critique of Drewermann is exactly this: he did reject Oedipal structures regressing

---

[336] H. Raguse, *Der Raum des Textes*, pp.247-248.

[337] Idem, p.255, p.257

[338] Idem, p.260. Compare: *die Sünde ist, gerade auch im Kontext theologischer Interpretationen, weniger als sexuelles, inzestuöses Begehren oder als mörderischer Impuls, sondern als antiödipale Schöpfung einer vaterlosen und die Unterschiede aufhebenden neuen Welt, damit also in Analogie zu perversen Kreationen zu verstehen.* Idem, p.262. In my opinion Vergote's depiction of sin actually points in a similar direction. As we will see in the next chapter, the Oedipal desires of the child are in themselves not evil – they belong to human nature – however, the non-acceptance or rejection of the Name-of-the-Father could be considered sinful.

[339] Idem, p.124. According to Raguse, sense of guilt is thus normal unless it is abnormally high in neurosis. Worse are people incapable of feeling guilty.

[340] Idem, p.274.

to the perversity of a solely motherly world in which he is not guided through texts, but is himself the all-powerful guide in his own mythico-psychological world.

4.5 Rediscovery and reinterpretation of the Freudian "myth"

In the reception of Freud in theology *Totem and Taboo* and *Moses and Monotheism* were not the major studies elaborated upon. In general we can say that *Moses and Monotheism* was a somewhat forgotten work. Scharfenberg had shown an interest in this study in the late 1960s, but afterwards the focus of attention shifted towards those issues that seemed promising in pastoral care. Biblical scholars hardly paid attention to the Moses book.[341]

The main critique of *Totem and Taboo* and *Moses and Monotheism* had always been the application of psychoanalytic theory to cultural phenomena as such and the Freudian "myth" of a single historic act as the origin of religion, cultural institutions, morality and art. The idea that the evolution of culture and religion could be solely explained by the primitive conflictuous constitution of man and that culture and religion primarily had the function of restraining the anti-social drives evoked justified criticism. This theory seemed too simplistic and could find no substantial evidencial support.

As to our topic of the sense of guilt the criticism of Freud's studies had an important effect. Due to the rejection of the Freudian "myth" the main ideas in these studies were also put aside. Firstly, the idea that religion does not originate from innate conceptions or "blue prints" as Jung thought, but should be understood in its historic development. Secondly, there is the idea that the conflicted constitution of man and, as a result, the sense of guilt, plays a dominant role throughout religious traditions. Thirdly, the idea that the Oedipus complex could serve as a structure to relate phenomena to one and another.[342] Fourthly, there is the leading idea that man can only understand himself when he interprets history, i.e. there is an analogous relation between psychoanalytic practice, "autobiographical study" and the analysis of culture and religion.

4.5.1   Rediscovering Moses

In the 1980s the "forgotten" study *Moses and Monotheism* is rediscovered. This rediscovery has in my opinion two stages that both reflect important new readings of Freud. The first is the discovery of the importance of Freud's self-analysis. Ilse Grubrich-Simitis' analysis of the Moses study is important here.[343]

---

[341] R. Rendtorff, "Ägypten und die Mosaische Unterscheidung", in J. Assmann, *Die Mosaische Unterscheidung oder der Preis des Monotheismus*, M. Krüger (ed.), Carl Hanser Verlag, Munich/Vienna, 2003, pp.193-207 (194).

[342] P. Vandermeersch, H. Westerink, *Godsdienstpsychologie*, pp.167-168.

[343] I. Grubrich-Simitis, *Freuds Moses-Studie als Tagtraum*.

She saw the text as a piece of self-analysis and the outcome of a long fascination for Moses, a "day-dream", a reflection on his youth, his father, his Jewish identity and the threat of anti-Semitism. This line of thought has been further developed.[344]

These studies resulted in an important correction in the view of Freud. Firstly, the discovery of the autobiographical element in Freud's writings implies a reconsideration of Freud as a positivist and systematic scientist.[345] Secondly, the rediscovery of Moses has evoked the question of to what extent Freud should be considered – or considered him-self – a Jew, and whether psychoanalysis could be regarded a Jewish science.[346]

This second stage of the rediscovery of *Moses and Monotheism* is closely entangled with the first, especially concerning the "Jewishness" of Freudian psychoanalysis. Yosef Yerushalmi's landmark study on the Moses book is primarily concerned with the question whether psychoanalysis is a Jewish science.[347] In this study a problem was addressed that Grubrich-Simitis had also already reflected upon[348]: Freud's psycho-Lamarckism, i.e. the theory that

---

[344] The psychoanalyst Maciejewski has recently argued that the Moses study can be read in the light of Freud's veiled death wishes against his brother Julius and his sense of guilt that resulted from these. F. Maciejewski, *Der Moses des Sigmund Freud*. In theology Heine has elaborated on the Moses study as an autobiographical study. S. Heine, *Grundlagen der Religionspsychologie*, pp.173ff. In 1999 an issue of *Approaches to Man* was devoted to Freud's *Moses and Monotheism* in which the autobiographical elements in the study were elaborated upon, especially in H. Wahl, "Der Mann Freud und sein monotheistischer Moses", in *Wege zum Menschen* 51 (1999), pp.221-240.
In the Netherlands scholars like Arnold Uleyn, Harry Stroeken and Fred Mampuys reflected on the Moses study as auto-analytical exercise. A. Uleyn, *Psychoanalytisch lezen in de bijbel*, Gooi & Sticht, Hilversum, 1985; A.F.M. Mampuys, *De ik-splijting van de man Mozes en de inscheuring in zijn ik*; H. Stroeken, "Freuds 'De man Mozes en de monotheïstische religie' als autoanalytische exercitie", in *Tijdschrift voor Psychoanalyse* 7 (2001/1), pp.24-34.
[345] In view of developments in the past decades the shift of attention to *Moses and Monotheism* is also a movement away from the "positivist" study *The Future of an Illusion*.
[346] Important publications on this issue are P. Gay, *A Godless Jew*; E. Rice, *Freud and Moses. The Long Journey Home*, State University of New York Press, Albany, 1990.
[347] Y.H. Yerushalmi, *Freud's Moses*.
[348] Grubrich-Simitis had published an unknown Freud text in 1985 called *Overview of the Transference Neuroses* written ca. 1915. In this text Freud argues that the disposition for neuroses originated in the ice age and was ever since passed on from generation to generation. I. Grubrich-Simitis (ed.), *A Phylogenetic Fantasy. Overview of the Transference Neuroses*, The Belknap Press of Harvard University Press, Cambridge (Mass.)/London, 1987, pp.44ff. In this period (around 1915) Lamarck is frequently referred in the correspondence between Freud and Ferenczi. Freud even confesses that his theories are in line with "psycho-Lamarckism". I. Grubrich-Simitis, "Metapsychology

phylogenetic material is passed on from generation to generation.[349] Phylogenetic material not only enclosed psychic dispositions – this had been argued in, for example, the Wolf Man case – but also contents in the form of memory-traces of past generations. In his reconstruction of what Yerushalmi called "tradition" Freud had applied psycho-Lamarckism in his theoretical construct of repression and return of the repressed in Jewish history and the emergence of monotheism. The problem of tradition, its origins and dynamics could be regarded as the central axis of Freud's text and therefore his psycho-Lamarckism posed a problem.

Jacques Derrida and Richard Bernstein opposed Yerushalmi's analysis and proposed solutions to the problem. Derrida spoke of "archive" as transgenerational memory[350] and Bernstein of "tradition" thus reformulating a Freudian position in which the possibility of unconscious transferences of collective memories was stressed. Bernstein argues that Freud's thinking on tradition is revolutionary, because of the idea that "what is most vital in a tradition is genuinely unconscious".[351]

In this context an important scholar in reflecting upon *Moses and Monotheism* is the German Egyptologist Jan Assmann (1938-). Next to numerous publications on Egyptian religion, art and culture, Assmann, together with Aleida Assmann[352] formulated a cultural theory focusing on the concept of cultural memory (*kulturelles Gedächtnis*). In his first major study on this subject Assmann explored the "connective structure" of culture, i.e. the connection between memory, identity and the formation of tradition that constitutes a "collective knowledge and self-image" bound to mutual laws and values and founded on a mutual past.[353] The study focuses on how various societies "imagine" their

and Metabiology. On Sigmund Freud's Draft Overview of the Transference Neuroses", in idem, pp.93ff.

[349] Y.H. Yerushalmi, *Freud's Moses*, pp.54-55.

[350] Derrida argues that Freud merely sees an analogy between the memory of an ancestral experience and a biologically acquired character. The memory of an ancestral experience thus need not be thought of as inherited, but transmitted in the "archive" of language and culture. J. Derrida, *Archive Fever*, p.35.

[351] R.J. Bernstein, *Freud and the Legacy of Moses*, p.63. Bernstein argues that Freud's understanding of religious tradition can be of great value for understanding "the gaps and ruptures in the transmission of tradition". In studying history and religious tradition one should not only focus on the conscious developments, but also on "traces of unconscious memories", periods of "latency" and the dynamics of "the return of the repressed", in short, "the complex interplay of collective forgetting and remembering". Idem, p.64.

[352] For example in A. Assmann, *Erinnerungsräume. Formen und Wandlungen des kulturellen Gedächtnisses*, Beck Verlag, Munich, 1999; A. Assmann, *Zeit und Tradition. Kulturelle Strategien der Dauer*, Böhlau Verlag, Colone/Weimar/Vienna, 1999.

[353] J. Assmann, *Das kulturelle Gedächtnis. Schrift, Erinnerung und politische Identität in frühen Hochkulturen*, Beck Verlag, Munich, 1992, pp.16-17.

identity in their unique constructions of cultural memory. Collective identity is not so much the result of real historic developments, but rather based on how (with what means, motives, and under what circumstances) a society remembers its past in communicative processes. Cultural memory is the complex in which a society, a "we", constructs an identity.[354] In short, "we are what we remember".[355] Therefore, individual memory and identity is always embedded in the participation in collective processes.

The theory of cultural memory is strongly influenced by the writings of the French sociologist Maurice Halbwachs, who, opposed to Freud's focus on individual memory, had introduced the concept of social memory (or collective memory) indicating that individual memory is primarily based on participation in the collective language and communication of a specific group in time and space.[356] Assmann's cultural memory is formulated as a rethinking of Halbwach's social memory, that is to say, it is not a memory embodied in the "horizontal" communication of a specific group of people; it is embodied in texts, symbols, images, rituals, etc. that throughout long periods of time form a tradition in which a subject participates unconsciously. Culture itself "has" a memory embodied in cultural artefacts, texts, "bodies".[357]

This theory of cultural memory is regarded by Assmann as an important correction of Freud's ideas of ontogenetic memory and phylogenetic "archaic heritage" both localized in the individual unconscious. Cultural memory is not innate, but must be seen as an unconscious process of both remembering and forgetting (and not a conscious product of learning) in which one participates, because one is born and socialized in it.[358]

---

[354] An example Assmann mentions is the collective memory of the Jesus movement in the first century. *Nachträglich* – after a period in which the Kingdom was expected to come soon – the Christian community had to construct an identity based not on facts but on oral material. Hence the identity of the group was based on and situated in the collective memory. In a next step "remembered words" were then placed back in a reconstructed geography (Galilea, Jerusalem) and biography (Jesus). Idem, p.41.

[355] J. Assmann, *Thomas Mann und Ägypten. Mythos und Monotheismus in den Josephromanen*, Beck Verlag, Munich, 2006, pp.67-68.

[356] In *Les cadres sociaux de la mémoire* from 1925 Halbwachs had presented an analysis of the Irma dream (*The Interpretation of Dreams*). He argued that the dream should not be interpreted as a hidden wish or as a memory of something that happened in the past, but as a conscious act in which the subject's contact with a social environment is expressed in a constructed memory. M. Halbwachs, *Les cadres sociaux de la mémoire*, G. Namer (ed.), Éditions Albin Michel, Paris, 1994, pp.40ff.

[357] J. Assmann, *Das kulturelle Gedächtnis*, p.19.

[358] J. Assmann, "Sigmund Freud und das kulturelle Gedächtnis", in *Psyche. Zeitschrift für Psychoanalyse und ihre Anwendungen* 2004, 1, pp.1-25. *Wir müssen aber diese Dimension* [kollektive Übertragung, H.W.] *nicht in der individuellen Psyche, sondern im kulturellen Gedächtnis lokalisieren, in das jeder einzelne auf seine weise hineingeboren und hineinsozialisiert wird. (…) Das kulturelle Gedächtnis wird nicht phylogenetisch*

Recently, Maciejewski and Assmann debated the theory of cultural memory focusing on the interaction between individual psyche and culture.[359] Whereas Assmann holds the view that the individual psychic dispositions are the effect of culture and socialization (which in the case of Judaism means: specific historic catastrophes traumatized the Jewish soul creating a fertile soil for monotheism), Maciejewski returns to a classic Freudian position arguing that a psychic trauma (circumcision) predisposed the Jewish soul from which monotheism emanated. There is thus a real primal "deed" that functions as "motor of a specific socialization modus", i.e. the trauma and its psychic effects are used for (later) cultural means/goals.[360]

In my opinion this debate focuses too much on the question of "origin" and "cause" in the history of Judaism, whereas the question of how the interaction between individual and cultural memory is mediated – which is ultimately related to the Oedipus complex – remains largely unreflected. Whether monotheism emanates from a psychic (traumatic) predisposition, or not (when monotheism is inscribed through socialization in the psyche): the question remains how an individual can relate to tradition (identification, sublimation) and how culture can be inscribed.[361] I will return to this topic in the next chapter.

In his 1992 study on cultural memory Freud is mentioned, but not elaborated upon. However, when Assmann reflects on the character of the book of Deuteronomy he argues that this text shows the foundations of a "cultural mnemotechnique" that is still dominating Jewish identity, namely "not to forget" the Promised Land. This memory was originally constructed in the most difficult of circumstances – in exile in Babylon – and is characterized by formulations on the "shocking" return of the repressed, a "memory drama": the Josianic reform and the triumph of monotheism as a return into memory of the original pure monotheism ("Moses") after a long period of decline and "forgetting" throughout the rule of the kings.

---

vererbt, sondern ontogenetisch erworben. J. Assmann, "Archäologie und Psychoanalyse. Zum Einfluß Freuds auf die Kultur- und Religionswissenschaft", in *Psyche. Zeitschrift für Psychoanalyse und ihre Anwendungen* 60 (2006/9-10), pp.1040-1053 (1049).
[359] F. Maciejewski, "Das Unbewußte in der Kultur. Von der Schwierigkeit, die psychoanalytische Kulturtheorie (Freud) in eine kulturwissenschaftliche Gedächtnistheorie (Assmann) zu überführen", in *Psyche. Zeitschrift für Psychoanalyse und ihre Anwendungen* 62 (2008/3), pp.235-252; J. Assmann, "Das Unbewußte in der Kultur: eine Antwort auf Franz Maciejewski", in idem, pp.253-256; "Eine Briefwechsel zwischen Jan Assmann und Franz Maciejewski", in idem, pp.257-265.
[360] Idem, p.258.
[361] Assmann's view of this issue is basically sociological (Durkheim, Halbwachs): groups and individuals socialize in cultural memory through participation in the collective happenings such as feasts and rituals. J. Assmann, *Das kulturelle Gedächtnis*, p.57.

In this scheme Assmann recognizes a Freudian structure: trauma – re-pression – latency – return of the repressed.[362] Already Moses is here a figure in an "afterwards", in a constructed memory. It is exactly at this point where Freud's Moses study proves its importance. It is a study of memory and there-fore not only a text that touches upon the core of psychoanalysis (the recon-struction of the chain of often unconscious memory traces), but also on the question of how cultural memory functions and can be understood. Concerning cultural memory the unconscious not only refers to the repressed memories in individual or collective "psyche", but also to the forgotten texts in archives or the rituals that are no longer performed, and beyond that to traces and roots of collective identity in the "depth of time".[363] This cultural memory is presented as Assmann's solution to the problem of Freud's psycho-Lamarckism.[364] He also points out that he "cannot make much" of Freud's theories on patricide and the generalization of the Oedipus complex from individual to collective mem-ory.[365] His own theory of cultural memory is a correction on these ideas.

Moses as a figure of memory is the topic of Assmann's 1997 study *Moses the Egyptian*. In this study the central concept is that of "Mosaic distinc-tion", i.e. the radical distinction in monotheistic religions between true and false religion, such religions being called "Mosaic" because in cultural memory Moses is regarded as the founding father of monotheism.[366] This distinction in-dicates an intolerance that is not present in polytheism or, as Assmann prefers, "cosmotheism".[367] Monotheism is seen as a counter-religion rejecting every-thing that went previously[368] which finds a biblical expression in the belief in the one true God sharply opposed to false idolatry ("Egypt"). This distinction "between Israel and Egypt" is the subject of the study.[369]

Assmann attempts "to investigate the history of Europe's remembering of Egypt" focusing on a re-examination of the Mosaic distinction.[370] This means a deconstruction of the distinction, necessarily because of the "fact" that the true founder of monotheism was Akhenaton, that Moses might be an Egyptian (as Freud thought), and that a sharp distinction between Israel and Egypt can thus not be made, which ultimately calls for a change of paradigm. The Mosaic dis-

---

[362] Idem, pp.222-228. Compare J. Assmann, *Religion als kulturelles Gedächtnis. Zehn Studien*, Beck Verlag, Munich, 2000, pp.28-34.
[363] Idem, p.37.
[364] *Der Begriff des kulturellen Gedächtnisses entspricht dem, was Derrida "Archiv" und Bernstein "Tradition" nennen.* Idem, p.41.
[365] J. Assmann, *Moses the Egyptian*, p.215.
[366] Idem, pp.1-2.
[367] In polytheism there is no distinction between true and false, only between pure and impure, or holy and profane. J. Assmann, *Religion und kulturelles Gedächtnis*, p.73.
[368] J. Assmann, *Moses the Egyptian*, p.3.
[369] Idem, p.6.
[370] Idem, p.8

tinction should be "abolished" through "deconstructing the Biblical image of Egypt".[371] Such a deconstruction would in fact be a return of the repressed. For according to Assmann, Freud's most important discovery for mnemohistory and theorizing on tradition is the idea of latency and the return of the repressed. There is in fact something like "cultural forgetting" and even "cultural repression". The "repression" of Akhenaton and "Egypt" show this. Deconstructing the biblical image of Egypt, making conscious the Egyptian roots of monotheism as counter-religion should serve to overcome the image of the enemy and intolerance and make a "return" to cosmotheism possible.[372]

In this project Freud is key figure. Analysing Jewish monotheism, the idea of the chosen people, and the origins of anti-Semitism, Freud is part of an enlightened tradition searching to overcome the Mosaic distinction and find possibilities for religious tolerance. What previous scholars could not do, Freud could: relating monotheism to Akhenaton, and associating Moses with Egyptian monotheism. In doing so "Freud is the one who restored the suppressed evidence, who was able to retrieve lost memories and to fully complete and rectify the picture of Egypt".[373]

What are the consequences of this for the Freudian topic of the sense of guilt? Assmann fully acknowledges that guilt is a key issue in *Moses and Monotheism* and that Freud's discovery of the "guilt complex" underlying Mosaic monotheism was part of the search for tolerance (in the sense that guilt might be resolved through reconciliation).[374] Elsewhere this is formulated even more strongly. Guilt is a key element of monotheism. After all, guilt results from the sin of forgetting the worship of the one true God and of participating in idolatry of the "others".[375] In other words, the Mosaic distinction evokes a new kind of guilt, namely guilt as the irreconcilable. Freud had thus made a good point when he argued that sense of guilt was a nuclear element of Judaism, but alas through an invalid argument.

According to Assmann, Freud's ideas on sense of guilt (evoked by the murder of Moses) in the unconscious mental life of the group, its inheritance and spreading over a long period, was based on a limited view on cultural memory. Assmann's alternative theory enables us to regard guilt as equally as central to monotheism as did Freud. Instead of Freud's arguments Assmann refers to biblical texts as a, "superficial", part of cultural memory. And the bible is full of guilt.[376] As a consequence of the deconstruction of the biblical image of

---

[371] Idem, p.210.

[372] Idem, pp.215-218.

[373] Idem, p.148.

[374] Idem, p.166.

[375] J. Assmann, *Religion und kulturelles Gedächtnis*, p.72.

[376] Idem, pp.117ff. Assmann writes that Freud's ignorance of cultural memory is a "blind spot": Freud could have found "hundreds" of biblical passages on themes such as "remembering and forgetting, repression and return, death wish and guilt trauma".

Egypt he argues that biblical guilt has its origins in Egyptian religion and thought on community.[377]

In later publications Assmann has partly revised his ideas on Freud and Mosaic distinction. Rereading *Moses and Monotheism* lead him to conclude that Freud was not trying to deconstruct the Mosaic distinction, but on the contrary viewed Jewish monotheism as an achievement of the chosen people, and regarded his own psychoanalysis as a further "advance in intellectuality".[378]

We should notice that Assmann speaks of guilt whereas Freud analyses the sense of guilt. His theory of cultural memory as a correction of Freud's psycho-Lamarckism implies a turning away from feelings to memory-traces. The cultural memory does not consist of feelings, but of structures, traces and archives. Assmann argues that a blind spot prevented Freud from seeing biblical guilt as more than superficial. Instead he formulated a "superfluous" theoretical construct.[379] We should however not forget that Freud was interested in the origins of the sense of guilt and turned to culture and religion from a clinical perspective. Inner psychic life was his starting point. Assmann's starting point is a socio-cultural theory. Identity is seen here as the effect of socialization.

In my opinion it is exactly here that Freudian thought on psychic development and Assmann's theory of cultural memory can supplement each other. The individual psychic structures should not too easily be put aside in a theory of cultural memory that still has to explain how individuals are embedded in culture, how man is socialized and how exactly individual identity is shaped in the interactions between early psychic formations and culture. Or, as to our topic, how the step can be made from cultural guilt to an individual sense of

---

However, Freud was preoccupied with demonstrating that tradition was unconscious of its underlying motivations. J. Assmann, "Sigmund Freud und das kulturelle Gedächtnis", p.12.

[377] J. Assmann, "Das Herz auf der Waage. Schuld und Sünde im Alten Ägypten", in T. Schabert, D. Clemens (eds.), *Schuld*, Wilhelm Fink Verlag, Munich, 1999, pp.99-147. In this article Assmann reflects on the concept of *Ma'at*, an Egyptian concept indicating "the art of living together", the normative memory of individual identity embedded in membership of a community. Destroying *Ma'at* is regarded as the worst sin effecting guilt. In this respect ancient Egypt can be seen as a guilt culture. Here, guilt is no longer related to Freudian theory, but to a socio-political theory that states that every complex society defining norms of community life – social contract – is inevitably a guilt culture. Idem, pp.118-119. To make possible a distinction between cosmotheistic Egyptian guilt culture and Israelite monotheistic guilt culture, Assmann proposes to make a distinction in the concept of guilt culture between cultures of purification and cultures of sin. In other words, the Mosaic distinction evokes a different meaning of the concept of guilt (idolatry) as opposed to the previous form.

[378] J. Assmann, "Der Fortschritt der Geistigkeit. Sigmund Freuds Konstruktion des Judentums", in *Psyche. Zeitschrift für Psychoanalyse und ihre Anwendungen*, 56 (2002/2), pp.154-171. Also: J. Assmann, *Die Mosaische Unterscheidung*, pp.120-121.

[379] J. Assmann, *Religion und kulturelles Gedächtnis*, p.68.

guilt, and *vice versa*. We will return to the subject of cultural memory in the next chapter.

Assmann's writings seem provocative for theologians, and indeed there have been critical responses, mainly by biblical scholars.[380] The distinction between tolerant cosmotheism and intolerant monotheistic counter-religion especially has been questioned. Nevertheless, the association of monotheism and truth stands out as a daring issue for theologians, philosophers and religious scientists (certainly in an era of growing fundamentalism in world religions). In this respect it is worth noticing that Paul Moyaert, a Belgian philosopher and student of Vergote, has recently published a study on the worship of icons, idolatry and monotheism in which elements of Assmann's work are elaborated upon.[381]

---

[380] Critical articles by biblical scholars (Rolf Rendtorff, Erich Zenger, Klaus Koch, Gerhard Kaiser and Karl-Josef Kuschel) are added in *Die Mosaische Unterscheidung*. Idem, pp.193-286. Also: H. Wahl, "Der Mann Freud und seine monotheistischer Moses"; B. Müller, "Zur Ambivalenz monotheistischer Religionen. Die "Mosaische Unterscheidung", das Problem mit der Macht Gottes und die "leise Stimme" der Vernunft", in *Wege zum Menschen* 57 (2006), pp.119-130.

[381] Moyaert has raised the question whether the prohibition against making an image of God can be solely seen as a counter-idea against the worship of false gods, or whether the prohibition could also be regarded as a claim of God to be worshiped in a unique manner, that is to say, in an optimal manner between nearness and distance. The problem with worshipping an image might be that the image brings God too near. P. Moyaert, *Iconen en beeldverering. Godsdienst als symbolische praktijk*, Uitgeverij SUN, Amsterdam, 2007, pp.55-72.

5   The Flemish connection

5.1 Introduction

In our discussion of the projection debate and its after effects we have seen a
clear critical distance adopted towards Freudian psychoanalysis in the Netherlands. In this chapter we will focus on those theologians (psychologists of religion) – all Catholics – who did positively value Freudian psychoanalysis and
who focused on psychoanalytic theory and methods in the study of the interaction between personality and religion, and on making psychoanalysis fruitful for
various theological disciplines. We will see that guilt and the sense of guilt will
be a dominant issue here. Concretely this means elaborating upon the writings
of Arnold Uleyn, Harry Stroeken and, most importantly, Antoine Vergote and
his followers.

In this chapter I will confess myself as a "Vergotian", but nevertheless
provide a critical reading of his work including his ideas on rethinking Freudian
psychoanalysis. The reason to do so lies in the fact that, although I consider his
work (and that of his students) in psychology of religion and psychoanalysis
most fruitful for further thinking about the relationship between personality and
religion (with consequences for other theological disciplines), some of his concepts need reconfiguration when applied to modern religious phenomena in a
secularized society. This review of Vergote's work will thus provide a theoretical framework for eventually summarizing and discussing the importance of the
Freudian sense of guilt in the final chapter.

In our discussion of the projection debate in the Netherlands and its after-effects
we have seen that Fortmann discussed Freud's theories on the sense of guilt in
the context of mental health. Ever since the issue of the sense of guilt has
croped up, time and again, in the literature on pastoral and mental care. It seems
though to remain confined to incidental publications and certainly not as part of
a broader debate on "the guilt problem" either from a Protestant or a Catholic
perspective.

Kerssemaker has mentioned several reasons for this apparent lack of interest in the issue.[1] Firstly, the fact that the issue of a sense of guilt does not
seem to be important in a culture dominated by individualism, autonomy and
self-realization. Only when this culture is questioned again – and there is a
growing tendency to do so – can new interest in the issue be detected.[2] (As we

---

[1] J. Kerssemaker, "Ten geleide", in A. Hegger et al. (eds.), *Over schuld en schaamte*,
KSGV, Tilburg, 2005, pp.7-9.
[2] For example R. Ganzevoort et al. (eds.), *Vergeving als opgave. Psychologische realiteit of onmogelijk ideaal?*, KSGV, Tilburg, 2003; A. Hegger et al. (eds.), *Over schuld en
schaamte*.

have seen this argument is also valid for developments in German pastoral psychology.) Secondly, there is the fact that the issue of the sense of guilt is a broad, complex existential-anthropological issue which makes it relatively unattractive to deal with in scientific studies. Thirdly, there is the association with a Reformed tradition in which guilt and sin were and are predominant issues. To avoid a revival of this discourse a debate on guilt and sin seems to be avoided. Lootsma even speaks of a "guilt taboo" in the church, because of this tradition: guilt and sin are carefully avoided in pastoral care out of consideration and embarrassment.[3]

Occasionally this "taboo" was broken. In the 1970s the psychiatrist Van Scheyen discovered that amongst his depressive and psychotic patients a significantly large number of them were raised in an orthodox Reformed environment. In several articles he discussed the relationship between these pathologies and a religious background characterized by a strong conscience function, compulsive avoidance of conflicts and an unstable sense of self-esteem. Sense of guilt (or sense of sin) were dominant and could – under certain circumstances – easily lead to a pathology developing.[4]

In the 1980s the psychologist Aleid Schilder, who came from a family background of orthodox theologians[5], published a study of the relation between depression and Reformed (*gereformeerd*) belief.[6] The study caused quite a stir especially among church members. Schilder argued that a Reformed depression could be distinguished from a "normal" depression, and in fact claimed that Reformed religion was a sick-making religion. Following Fortmann's line of reasoning on mental health Schilder defined health as "integration", as a certain balance between psychic forces, and as "positive participation", indicating that healthy faith should be embedded in a belief system that stimulates psychic in-

---

[3] P. Lootsma, "Schuld, een eigentijds taboe", in idem, pp.28-42. A similar position is formulated by Schreurs who has argued that the issue of guilt especially is associated with "the burden of tradition", that is to say, the "terror of fear" related to a Reformed consciousness of sin and the caricatural neurotic forms of traditional Catholic confession practice. These are the two components of an embarrassment with guilt and good reason – apparently – not to touch upon the issue. N. Schreurs, "De traditie van vergeven. De omslag van schuld naar schaamte en de herontdekking van de vergeving", in A. Berlis, S. van Erp, A. Lascaris (eds.), *Overgeleverd aan de toekomst. Christelijke traditie in een na-traditionele tijd*, Uitgeverij Meinema, Zoetermeer, 2001, pp.81-98 (87).
[4] For example J. van Scheyen, "Bezwaard gemoed in een regio: over relaties tussen endogene (vitale) depressies, religie en suïcide", in *Tijdschrift voor Psychiatrie* 1975/17, pp.775-788. See R. Nauta, *Ik geloof het wel*, pp.169-170.
[5] Her father H.J. Schilder was professor in Old Testament studies at the *Vrijgemaakt Theologische Hogeschool Kampen*. The *vrijgemaakt gereformeerden* were a denomination since 1945 when they split of from the *gereformeerde* churches under leadership of her great-uncle, the dogmatician K. Schilder.
[6] A. Schilder, *Hulpeloos maar schuldig. Het verband tussen een gereformeerde paradox en depressie*, Kok, Kampen, 1987. See also R. Nauta, *Ik geloof het wel*, p.171.

tegration.[7] The opposite was disintegration marked by a sense of guilt. This is why in a religious context where guilt is overemphasized a depression could not only be "twice as strong" as a "normal" depression, but the belief system itself could cause depression. This risk was particularly high in a Reformed belief system that emphasized the "paradox" that man is both "helpless" (predestined and incapable of any good) and "responsible" (free to act either for good or evil).[8] Given such a paradox man is always "guilty".

In Schilder's study Freud is not discussed. In fact, monographs by Dutch Protestant theologians extensively elaborating on Freud and the sense of guilt do not exist – which despite "embarrassments" is still remarkable when we consider the dominance of the issue of guilt in Reformed tradition. The main interest from psychologists of religion in this issue stems from Flemish Catholic theologians.

5.2 Arnold Uleyn

We have argued that the "Fortmann agenda" is characterized by a critical distance towards Freudian psychoanalysis. Arnold Uleyn (1926-), a Belgian catholic theologian and psychoanalyst, is the exception here. In the 1960s he was asked by Fortmann to work with him in Nijmegen. Until 1986 he was indeed assistant professor focusing in his work on the "integration of religion and psychoanalysis", a field that made him exceptional in Nijmegen.[9] In my opinion the reason Fortmann asked Uleyn to come to Nijmegen lies not in this project of integrating religion and psychoanalysis. The reason can be found in Uleyn's first major 1964 study *Pastorale psychologie en schuldervaring* [Pastoral Psychology and Guilt Experience].[10]

Uleyn's study of guilt experience can first of all be situated in the context of catholic discussions on healthy and unhealthy guilt and sense of guilt in the 1950s.[11] Pius XII's distinction between pathological forms of the sense of guilt that needed psychoanalytic treatment and existential forms of guilt that needed acceptance underlies Uleyn's starting point: "man has numerous ways to escape from his conscience and recognition of guilt". The aim in pastoral care is

---

[7] A. Schilder, *Hulpeloos maar schuldig*, p.15, p.87. Compare H.M.M. Fortmann, *Als ziende de Onzienlijke, deel II*, pp.310-311.

[8] A. Schilder, *Hulpeloos maar schuldig*, pp.25ff.

[9] J.A. van Belzen, J. van der Lans (eds.), *Rond godsdienst en psychoanalyse*, p.9.

[10] A. Uleyn, *Pastorale psychologie en schuldervaring. Schuldbelijdenis. Parabels. Verdedigingsmechanismen*, Desclée de Brouwer, Brugge/Utrecht, 1964.

[11] A. Uleyn, *Pastorale psychologie en schuldervaring*, pp.46-47. Uleyn refers to Hesnard's ideas on the recognition of sin as increasing the sense of guilt, and to Pius XII who regards the lack of sin experience a danger in modern times.

"to reawaken recognition of guilt and to proclaim God's grace"[12], i.e. the healthy sense of guilt that presupposes self knowledge of limitations and short-comings in moral acts, and the self knowledge of being a sinner, the acknowl-edgement of the breach between man and his God.[13] In more general terms it is knowledge of the *conditio humana*, the acceptance that man is *homo patiens* limited and therefore suffering. The sense of guilt is a signal functioning "as a motor that helps towards salvation".[14] Such self knowledge is not easily awoken. The central theme in the study is thus research into the ego-structure and its defence mechanisms, a theme that calls for a discussion of psychoana-lytic theory.[15]

The first part of the study is concerned with the relation between recog-nition of guilt, confession and faith in the Bible and in tradition. Biblical stories or for example Saint Augustine's *Confessions* can serve as "mirrors" that make (modern) man recognize his guilt before God.[16] But not everyone will be able to do so. There are "huge inner resistances that hinder self knowledge".[17] The Bi-ble speaks of a "hardened heart"; psychoanalysis speaks of "psychic skotomiza-tion" as an incapability to recognize repressed affects.[18] Hence, in psychoana-lytic theory and in pastoral care something similar is at stake: the "unveiling" of the repressed and the overcoming of defence mechanisms.[19] Uleyn distin-guishes repression/denial, rationalization, projection, compensation, and mini-malization.[20] These mechanisms defend the ego (or "heart", partly conscious and unconscious) not only against unconscious drives and needs, but also against the demands of the outside world and against superego demands, recog-nition of norms, conscience and God.[21]

---

[12] *In zijn hoedanigheid van profeet heeft de zielzorger als opdracht de mensen tot schuldinzicht te brengen. Want zonder de ervaring en belijdenis van onze zondigheid is er geen heil mogelijk.* Idem, p.11.

[13] Idem, p.44

[14] A. Uleyn, "Het eeuwige probleem van de schuldgevoelens", in: *Religiositeit en fanta-sie*, Uitgeverij Ambo, Baarn, 1978, pp.85-97 (89-90).

[15] A. Uleyn, *Pastorale psychologie en schuldervaring*, pp.15-16.

[16] *In de parabels herkent de zondige mens zichzelf als in een spiegel" "dat ben ik!", en wordt hij geholpen om zijn zonde te erkennen en te bekennen.* Idem, p.186. Uleyn's many references to church fathers throughout his study serve to indicate that the basic mechanism depicted in psychoanalysis, such as repression, projection or compensation, are not new discoveries, but in fact reformulations of principles and mechanisms that have always been part of the Christian legacy.

[17] Idem, p.106.

[18] Idem, p.108, p.115.

[19] Idem, pp.138ff.

[20] Idem, pp.150-151.

[21] Idem, p.158, p.169. To my knowledge Uleyn was trained as a psychoanalyst in Vi-enna by Igor Caruso. In Caruso's psychoanalytic ideas had expressed the idea that neu-rosis was an "existential heresy", a replacement of true values (conscience) by false

Freud is discussed first of all in the context of repression. Uleyn's depiction of repression is broad: repressed will be those perceptions that are not in conformity with the dominant appreciations of a personality.[22] This means that not only sexual and aggressive drives can be repressed, as Freud thought, but also conscience, sense of norms, recognition of guilt, or the relation with God.[23] In the chapters on rationalization and projection Freud is hardly discussed. Uleyn's starting point concerning projection is quite similar to that of Vestdijk or Sierksma: projection is part of perception, of actively structuring and creating what is perceived. It is an "attempt to make the unknown familiar".[24] In this context the so called projection or transference of the father image onto God can be understood. After all, everything we know is based on perception, and the image of God is thus based on perceivable familiar images and experiences. Pastoral care should therefore only aim at purifying the God image of possible malformations or one-sidedness.[25] This is indeed a point strongly stressed by Uleyn: the distinction between normal healthy projection and unhealthy projection. Only in the context of the latter Freud is mentioned: projection as a defence mechanism. Freud is further discussed in the context of pathological forms of compensation, for example when Uleyn discusses identification in the context of masochistic conscience formation and crime committed out of a sense of guilt.[26] Again the context is one of a pathological excess.

Throughout the study the sense of guilt is treated functionally. Either it serves as a signal of the recognition that man is limited, sinful and in need of salvation and participation, and in need of unity and meaning in life. Or it hinders such a process of "healing" when it makes man passive, masochistic, neurotic, or disturbs relations with fellow men. The healthy sense of guilt is part of conditio humana, a recognition that had already been expressed throughout Christian tradition. Given the fact that Uleyn treats psychoanalytic theory as a reformulation of mechanisms and principles already acknowledged and expressed in Christian tradition we might have expected elaborations on Freud's ideas on the sense of guilt in religion. But these are not found. Freud is strictly treated in the context of pathological malformations.

We can understand why Fortmann wanted Uleyn as an assistant. A common interest is shared: the references to tradition that might be revitalized;

---

ones. J. Fages, *Geschichte der Psychoanalyse nach Freud*, pp.190-191. In Uleyn's study there are references to Caruso's (and W. Daim's) ideas in the chapter on repression.

[22] Idem, p.187.

[23] Idem, p.200, p.213.

[24] Idem, p.259. *Projecteren staat dan gelijk met orde brengen in een onoverzichtelijke veelheid; pogen zich het onbekende vertrouwd te maken en de ongrijpbare werkelijkheid te bekleden met zichzelf, om ermee te kunnen leven en ergens een houvast te vinden.*

[25] Idem, pp.178-179.

[26] Idem, pp.301ff.

the critique of modern mentality; the elaborations on psychoanalysis limited to the realm of pathological defence formations; pastoral care as restoration of an integrated personality capable of participation with his fellow man and with God.

Uleyn's study of guilt recognition already concerned the issues he focused on in later writings. He pioneered the psychoanalytic interpretation of biblical texts. In the 1970s several articles on this subject were published, later edited in *Psychoanalytisch lezen in de bijbel* [Psychoanalytic reading in the Bible]. Here he presents a depiction of developments in psychoanalysis that shows a shift in views on religion and analogously a shift of attention in the reading of texts.[27] In the first period Freud and his followers study religion "scientifically", that is to say, Freud's philosophy of life is basically positivistic and in general his followers share this view. Religion should be analyzed as an archaeological site where all the human drives, conflicts and mechanisms can be found. However, this "objective" approach is combined with a hostile and normative attitude towards religion. Another period starts with Freud's second topic model and is continued in mainstream psychoanalysis (ego psychology). The focus is on individual personality organization and religion becomes a neglected issue. In a third period, under the influence of self psychology and object relations theory[28] religion is rediscovered and positively valued.[29] Religion is rediscovered in its constructive function of life orientation, in other words, in its function of "giving ultimate meaning".[30]

---

[27] A. Uleyn, *Psychoanalytisch lezen in de bijbel*, pp.10-11. See also A. Uleyn, "Over de moeilijke relatie van psychoanalytici met religieuze zingeving en geloof", in *Ego's en echo's. Opstellen over psychotherapie en religie*, KSGV, Nijmegen, 1999, pp.55-82.

[28] Uleyn adds rightfully that there is a structural resemblance between object relations theory and Lacanian psychoanalysis: both theories focus on subjectivity as developed through interpersonal relationships; both argue that identity does not originate from an innate psychic core. Idem, pp.67-68. Compare P. Vandermeersch, H. Westerink, *Godsdienstpsychologie*, part II, chapter 5.

[29] Uleyn mentions the writings of Scharfenberg and Müller-Pozzi as examples of an influence by Kohut. The influence of object relations theory is seen in American literature (Rizzuto). Interestingly, Uleyn does not want to mention Vergote in this context, because, according to Uleyn, Vergote worked from a theological philosophical point of view and not from a psychoanalytic theory. Therefore he is not representative of developments. This remark is remarkable given the fact that Scharfenberg for example also represents a theological position. We should notice here that Uleyn and Vergote for some reason though both working in the field of psychoanalysis and religion never worked together, were not in close personal contact and hardly refer to each others work. A. Uleyn, "Over de moeilijke relatie van psychoanalytici met religieuze zingeving en geloof", p.72.

[30] Idem, p.80. Here we notice that Uleyn's interest in psychoanalysis must be situated within the framework of the "Fortmann agenda".

Uleyn distinguishes between four perspectives in psychoanalytic reading in the Bible: character analysis of biblical figures; author analysis; text analysis; reader-response analysis.[31] Before presenting corresponding analyses to each of the four perspectives Uleyn presents a "genealogy of Freud's spirituality"[32], that is, a reflection on the values Freud held and the ideals that he envisioned: discipline, self-control, humour, friendship. Independent of Grubrich-Simitis elaborations on this topic, Uleyn unravels Freud's fascination for Moses. It is the history of Freud and his father, the family Bible, his Jewishness, the solidarity with the Jewish people under the threat of anti-Semitism, the growing awareness that his own character, ideals and psychoanalysis are entangled with a Jewish mentality as part of Western civilization and culture.[33] Hence, the image of Freud as materialist or positivist is corrected. The central issue of the sense of guilt in Freud's writings on religion is interpreted by Uleyn as a reflection on his personal history and Jewishness: the sense of guilt as the result of the relation with the father who is hated and admired can be situated in the context of the biblical command to honour one's parents.[34] It all culminates in Freud's "Moses complex", in the recognition of being a son of Moses and wanting to be like Moses.[35]

A second issue that Uleyn focuses on in his writings concerns the problem of healthy versus unhealthy religiosity, especially in the context of psychotherapy. In the late 1970s he argues that it is part of *conditio humana* to want to give meaning to life. There is a deep need for meaning, identity, and life perspective. It is a process of longing and suffering, a process that can be described in the Freudian concepts of repetition, remembrance, and working through.[36] It is a process of growth, but also a process that confronts us with the limitations of life and with guilt.

In later writings there is a shift of attention from the recognition of guilt towards the problem of narcissism. He writes for example on the egoistic narcissistic needs of pastors and therapists, but also on the opposite of this phenomenon, the echo-ism (or good-samaritism), the inclination towards self-sacrifice and overzealous complaisance, and the need to find a position between

---

[31] A. Uleyn, *Psychoanalytisch lezen in de bijbel*, pp.12-13.

[32] Idem, p.52.

[33] Idem, pp.20-21.

[34] Idem, p.32.

[35] Idem, p.37.

[36] A. Uleyn, "Vertroosting, geestelijke gezondheid en religiositeit", in *Religiositeit en fantasie*, pp.9-17.

these extremes.[37] Also the issue of life orientation and *zingeving* is further elaborated upon as an issue of importance in psychotherapy.[38]

5.3 Antoine Vergote

Antoine – or Antoon – Vergote was born in Kortrijk in 1921. Like any Flemish citizen of his generation he is bilingual, this being expressed in his writings (and his name). His key publications are mostly written in French, but partly also in Dutch. His academic career is also situated in this bilingual culture: he was appointed professor in psychology (focusing on psychoanalysis and psychology of religion in which he also lectured in the faculties of philosophy and theology) at both the universities of Leuven and – from 1968 onwards – Louvain-la-Neuve. His influence on the psychology of religion in the Netherlands has been profound due to publications and translations into Dutch and due to the fact that some of his students pursued academic careers in Leuven (Dirk Hutsebaut, Jozef Corveleyn) or the Netherlands (Patrick Vandermeersch). Also in philosophy he had a profound influence on scholars (such as Paul Moyaert) who in their work reflect on religion or concepts related to religion. In this respect it seems fair to say that next to Fortmann, Vergote is the godfather of the second major "school" in the Dutch psychology of religion.

5.3.1 The French connection

This engagement with Freud in German and Dutch-speaking theology cannot be isolated from outside influences. We have already noticed this. The influence of ego psychology, self psychology or object relations theory on pastoral psychology and the psychology of religion is, by and large, Anglo-American in origin. Furthermore we have seen the influence of French scholars. This is a constant throughout our study of Freud, the sense of guilt and its reception. After all, Freud's own psychoanalytic career starts in Paris under the influence of Charcot. A large part of the secondary literature used in *The Interpretation of Dreams* is French. Émile Durkheim is treated in *Totem and Taboo*, Gustave le Bon in *Mass psychology and Ego Analysis*. In the writings of Beth, Van der Leeuw and Fortmann we have noticed the influence of Lévy-Bruhl and his concept of participation. In Assmann's studies of cultural memory we noticed the inspiration of Halbwachs. Important references to Ricoeur can be noticed in the writings of Scharfenberg, Lauret, and also in those of Fortmann.[39] Uleyn occa-

---

[37] A. Uleyn, "Helpen als identiteit. Het Echo-syndroom in de hulpverlening", in *Ego's en echo's*, pp.11-36.

[38] For example A. Uleyn, *Zelfbeeld en godsbeeld. Opstellen over psychotherapie en godsdienstpsychologie*, Ambo, Baarn, 1988. A. Uleyn, "Integratie van levensbeschouwelijke aspecten in de psychiatrische hulpverlening", in *Ego's en echo's*, pp.37-54.

[39] H.M.M. Fortmann, *Als ziende de Onzienlijke, deel I*, pp.515-516, pp.546-547.

sionally refers to Ricoeur as early as 1964 in his study on the recognition of guilt.[40] Now that we want to discuss the work of Antoine Vergote the French connection is particularly important. He studied theology and philosophy in Leuven with a main interest in Husserl's phenomenology and from thereon in Freudian and Lacanian psychoanalysis.

From the 1950s onwards especially Lacan had called for a *retour à Freud* in French psychoanalysis, mainly as a protest against American ego psychology which had become mainstream psychoanalytic theory since the 1930s. This theory had basically turned psychoanalysis into a psychology of adaptation to societal norms. Against this idea Lacan calls upon Freud as a critic of societal norms and as having developed a theory in which the individual desire is to be liberated from burdens. Psychoanalysis is not about adaptation but about its opposite, alienation and "otherness".

Originally Lacan had followed Melanie Klein's line of thought in focusing on ego formation in the pre-Oedipal phase and on primitive aggression in the cannibalistic fantasies of eating, and being devoured, by the mother. From here his attention focused on what he would call the imaginary order, an order first of all characterized by the dual relationship between the child and the all-providing (and all desiring "devouring") mother.[41] It is also the order in which the ego (*moi*) originates from the moment a child (*je*) recognizes itself in an image (*stade de mirroir*). This construct was in fact an elaboration of Freud's narcissism theory. The central meachanism in this stage was that the child can only develop a sense of ego by recognizing itself in someone else, an object – *je est un autre*. This identification which is also an estrangement will necessarily lead to disappointment: the image as ego ideal does not exist, and *je* will never become *moi*. This model for all later identifications was (and is) of course a critique of those psychoanalytic theories insisting on ego-integration (or self-realization).

In the dual structure of the imaginary a "third" is already present, the mother for example lifting up the child in front of the mirror saying "that is you", or in the image which is already corresponding with the father as ideal, that is, as having the "phallus".[42] A next stage starts with symbolic castration.

---

[40] A. Uleyn, *Pastorale psychologie en schuldervaring*, pp.130-131, p.287.

[41] On the imaginary see A. Mooij, *Taal en verlangen. Lacans theorie van de psychoanalyse*, Uitgeverij Boom, Meppel, 1997, pp.77-87; D. Evans, *An Introductory Dictionary of Lacanian Psychoanalysis*, Routledge, London/New York, 1996, pp.82-84; P. Vandermeersch, H. Westerink, *Godsdienstpsychologie*, pp.251-252.

[42] The concept of phallus should be clearly distinct from the penis. The phallus refers to a function in a structure, that is, it signifies the object of the mother's desire beyond the child – Lacan will call this object of desire *objet a*; it signifies what the father is supposed to have; and it thus also signifies the object with which the child identifies. D.

The child is confronted with the father's prohibition to exclusively possess the mother and be possessed by the mother (*Non-du-Père*). The child is in other words confronted with the fact that it cannot be the phallus, that it thus cannot possess everything it (and the mother) wants. The child needs to specify its desires in its own unique identity that is primarily bound to its own name that has been given (*Nom-du-Père*). Thus, the child enters the symbolic order, that is to say, the child is introduced into the cultural world in which it has to seek the fulfilment of specified desires in a symbolic way.[43] This entrance is not just a loss because of the prohibition to desire something unobtainable, but also liberation, for it means the beginning of its own desire originating from a limitation, a lack (*manque*).[44]

Introducing the concept of the symbolic[45] first of all means that Lacan finds a connection with structuralism in linguistics (Ferdinand de Saussure) and cultural anthropology (Claude Lévy-Strauss).[46] From De Saussure Lacan adopts

---

Evans, *An Introductory of Lacanian Psychoanalysis*, pp.140-142; P. Vandermeersch, H. Westerink, *Godsdienstpsychologie*, p.253.
Concerning mother and father we should notice that these not necessarily indicate the biological parents or even human beings. Mother and father are functions in a structure, functions that can be ascribed to for example the "mother" church or the spiritual "father". Such functions have, for example, been described by Saroglou in his study of early monastic tradition among the desert fathers: V. Saroglou, *Paternity as Function. Structuring the Religious Experience*, Rodopi, Amsterdam/Atlanta, 2001.
[43] Lacan's version of the Oedipus complex and the entrance into the symbolic order is first described in J. Lacan, *Le Séminaire. Livre V. Les formations de l'inconscient, 1957-1958*, J.-A. Miller (ed.), Éditions de Seuil, Paris, 1998, pp.143-248.
[44] In Lacanian thought anxiety is related to desire. Anxiety originates from the fantasy that child might be the object of the mother's "devouring" desire. Hence, anxiety should be seen in relation to helplessness against being engulfed by the mother's desire for the uncanny *objet a*. Hence it is an anxiety for an object appearing due to a lack of separation. In this sense, castration is necessary to overcome anxiety. It is for this reason that Lacan's seminar on anxiety starts with the concept of desire. J. Lacan, *L'Angoisse. Séminaire 1962-1963*, Éditions de l'Association Freudienne Internationale, Publication hors commerce, Paris, 2000, pp.10ff.
[45] On this issue see A. Mooij, *Taal en verlangen*, pp.106-147; B. Fink, *The Lacanian Subject. Between Language and Jouissance*, Princeton University Press, Princeton, 1995; D. Evans, *An Introductory Dictionary*, pp.201-203; Ph. van Haute, *Against Adaptation*.
[46] De Saussure had argued that language is the totality of signs as a cultural institution. These signs unite a phoneme (*signifiant*) with a concept (*signifié*), but not an object and a word. In De Saussure's linguistic theory this ultimately means that meaning is not related to a pregiven reservoir of meaningful objects, but that meaning originates from the articulation in language. A. Mooij, *Taal en verlangen*, pp.38-59, pp.106ff.
Lévy-Strauss had argued that symbols do not in themselves refer to a deeper pregiven meaning or primal experience, but only have meaning in relation to other symbols in a specific cultural context: in a culture arbitrary distinctions will be made to create an or-

the idea that meaning is the effect of an autonomous chain of signifiers (language). He adds that there is no meaning without a subject of the speech act, that is to say, the *je* as grammatical subject in a sentence – I am..., I am a.... The subject is split, because *je* is distinct from *moi* that can be expressed in endless ways (subject of the statement). A lasting definition of *moi* is impossible.[47] The subject of the speech act is also called the subject of the unconscious, for the unconscious can be seen as the reservoir of signifiers from which *je* can draw signifiers to express *moi*. The subject does not control or possess this reservoir. This is why in Lacan's vocabulary the unconscious is also *le discours de l'Autre*, the discourse of the Other.[48] Entering the symbolic order means the possibility to express oneself in/with a language that is conceived as already there. As in the imaginary order identity is thus derived from the other/Other.

At this point we will not further discuss Lacan's later writings on the order of the Real, an order that is primarily and negatively defined as not imaginary (expressed in images) and not symbolic (expressed in language).[49] It is important that Lacan's thought on desire and the symbolic order will be taken up by Vergote and applied to religious language and religious phenomena – the third order will not play that dominant role in Vergote's work.

Vergote's interest in psychoanalysis evolved from his philosophical background. In 1958 Vergote had already published an article on the question of why philosophers should be interested in Freudian psychoanalysis, especially those interested in Husserl's phenomenology and in rethinking consciousness and human motivations.[50] This phenomenology would be a returning point of reference throughout his writings. In articles published in 1995 and 1997 Vergote discusses the analogies between and supplementary ideas of Husserl and Freud.[51] Most importantly, in both theories he finds a theory of the unity of ego

---

der. Meaning is given accordingly: some things are holy, sacred, others impure and profane, without a necessary reference to an underlying experience. P. Vandermeersch, H. Westerink, *Godsdienstpsychologie*, p.254.

[47] This is Lacan's starting point for a returning critique on Descartes' *Cogito*. According to Lacan Descartes did try to lastingly define the subject as *res cogitans*.

[48] See Lacan's famous dictum: *L'inconscient, c'est le discours de l'Autre*. J. Lacan, *Écrits I*, Éditions de Seuil, Paris, 1999, p.377.

[49] Central concepts here are *objet a*, *jouissance* and *la chose*, all indicating the inconceivable aim of desire, though the superego (*surmoi*) based on identification with a special trait of the father will always insist on satisfaction of desire within the boundaries of the symbolic law of the father (*le non du père*).

[50] A. Vergote, "L'intérêt philosophique de la psychanalyse freudienne", in *Archives de philosophie* 21 (1958), pp.26-59.

[51] A. Vergote, "The Constitution of the Subject and the Trinitarian Articulation of the Christian Faith", in *Psychoanalysis, Phenomenological Anthropology and Religion*, pp.225-239 (226-227); A. Vergote, "Husserl et Freud sur le corps psychique de

and body, opposed to a traditional body-spirit dichotomy in philosophy.[52] In Freudian thought the concepts of psychical apparatus and pulsional desire (*Triebwunsch*) – Vergote prefers his own concepts of "psychic body" or "libidinal body"[53] – indicate the unifying functioning of the unconscious between body and consciousness. (Therefore the physical register as the "order of cause" that needs explanation and the psychic register as the "order of meaning" that needs interpretation cannot be disentangled.) He proposes that Freud's more elaborate theories of the psychic body could be applied to further develop phenomenology. On the other hand, phenomenology should supplement Freudian thought because it offers a better understanding of human beings as capable of creating civilization. After all, Freud had insufficiently "explained" religion by reducing it to psychic needs and motivations, whereas religious belief is actually embedded and expressed within a cultural-religious framework that is external to individual motivations. Or in Lacanian terms: Freud explained (in his own pseudoscientific fantasies and myths) religion as an imaginary product without noticing the symbolic order. The full complexity of civilization and religion cannot be deduced from the simple scheme of natural needs and motivations.[54] Here we find already some key elements in Vergote's work: religion as a symbolic order; man as a psychic body; sublimation as the creation of culture.

5.3.2   Religion as symbolic order

Our starting point when discussing Vergote's work should be Lacan, for it is through him that Vergote will present his version of a *retour à Freud*. From a theological perspective this turn to psychoanalysis is inevitable. Secularization, the decomposition of church structure or folk Catholicism, the critique of mythology and metaphysics are all indications that there is a "turn to subjectivity" and the subject's supposed ability to construct itself and its relation to reality.[55]

---

l'action", in J. Petit (ed.), *Problemes et Controverses. Les Neurosciences et la philosophie de l'action*, J. Vrin, Paris, 1997, pp.387-396.

[52] According to Vergote, Husserl's concepts of "animal nature", "lived body" (*Leib*) and "egoity" (*Ichlichkeit*) indicate the organizing factors between material nature and mental world.

[53] Compare for example A. Vergote, *De sublimatie*, pp.103ff. (originally published as *La psychanalyse à l'épreuve de la sublimation* in 1997).

[54] See for example A. Vergote, *Religion, Belief and Unbelief*, pp.60-61; A. Vergote, "Psychoanalyse in contact met religie", in A. Vergote, P. Moyaert et al. (eds.), *Psychoanalyse. De mens en zijn lotgevallen*, DNB/Uitgeverij Pelckmans, Kapellen, 1996, pp.281-298 (originally published as *Psychoanalyse. L"homme et ses destines* in 1993); A. Vergote, "Religion after the Critique of Psychoanalysis".

[55] A. Vergote, *Het huis is nooit af. Gedachten over mens en religie*, DNB, Antwerpen/Utrecht, 1974, p.24, pp.247ff.; A. Vergote, *De Heer je God liefhebben. Het eigene van het Christendom*, Uitgeverij Lannoo, Tielt, 1999, pp.34-41 (originally published as *"Tu aimeras le Seigneur ton Dieu..."*. *L'identité chrétienne*, 1997).

In this situation of cultural change faith or beliefs[56] have to be redefined, and because of this turn to subjectivity psychology and especially psychoanalysis are called upon for interpretations and evaluations of the religious subject. In this context we can fairly say that Vergote attempts to make psychoanalytic theory fruitful for theology.[57] We will see that he will use psychoanalysis to criticize this turn to subjectivity as far as it focuses on self-realization and ego-integration, and as far as it views the relation with the divine as an extension of man's natural desires to have, to be, or to know "all".

Making psychoanalytic theory fruitful for theology first of all implies a clear distinction of realms. Psychoanalysis studies the human psychical apparatus and in doing so "one might expect that it has something sensible to say about religion", that it has the value of illuminating religious belief. Religion, on the other hand, involves man in his totality and thus psychoanalysis can learn from religion about themes such as "desire, the meaning of the father figure, the Law and guilt". In other words, "the psychic depth dimension is the ground where psychoanalysis and religion meet". At this meeting point psychoanalysis will analyse these themes in relation to "the primal experiences of man", whereas religion will situate these themes in the relationship with God, a relationship "that is conditioned by the psychic depth dimension, but not determined".[58]

The latter remark is typical of Vergote. It draws the line between the scientific study of human motivations in religious belief and a reductionism one finds in the major psychoanalytic theories as well as in much literature in the psychology or sociology of religion. Psychology of religion and psychoanalysis are not concerned with the question whether religion is true or false. This is outside its competence. In his 1966 *Psychologie religieuse* [Psychology of Religion] this is already expressed when he writes that the psychology of religion studies "religious experiences, acts and expressions"[59] and not "the truth of re-

---

[56] Vergote rejects the idea of a differentiation between belief and faith. "To oppose – as some do – faith to belief, is hermeneutical nonsense with respect to Christian religion." A. Vergote, "Cause and Meaning, Explanation and Interpretation in the Psychology of Religion", in J.A. van Belzen (ed.), *Hermeneutical Approaches in Psychology of Religion*, pp.11-34 (29).

[57] B. Pattyn, "Verlangen, ervaring en openbaring. Het werkelijkheidsbegrip in het denken van A. Vergote", in *Tijdschrift voor Theologie* 31 (1991), pp.381-401 (396). Lecuit has recently shown the significance of Vergote's writings in psychoanalysis and psychology of religion for theological anthropology. J.-B. Lecuit, *L'anthropologie théologique à la lumière de la psychanalyse. La contribution majeure d'Antoine Vergote*, Éditions du Cerf, Paris, 2007.

[58] A. Vergote, "Psychoanalyse in contact met religie", p.281, p.286.

[59] Compare: *Die Psychologie aber, als positive Wissenschaft, befasst sich nur mit den Erscheinungen: sie erforscht die Religion, so wie sie sich im Menschen manifestiert und strukturiert.* A. Vergote, *Religionspsychologie*, p.16. Heine has rightfully argued that it is one Vergote's strong points to define psychology of religion in such away that relig-

ligion", that is to say, "its reality character and the existence of God".[60] This is repeated throughout his writings. Thus, when the limitations of the competence of psychoanalysis are discussed he can refer to Freud's *dictum* that psycho-analysis "is neutral with respect to every *Weltanschauung*".[61] But how is this neutrality that Freud claimed (but didn't apply when he reduced religious per-ceptions to psychic motivations) guarded?

Here the Lacanian differentiation between the imaginary order and the symbolic order comes in. Vergote defines religion as "the entirety of the lin-guistic expressions, emotions, actions and signs that refer to a supernatural be-ing or supernatural beings". This entirety is regarded as "a recognizable entity in the cultural tradition". It is a symbolic system: "the symbolic system of relig-ion" is like a language system "external to the human being" and "localized in the world of cultural signs".[62] It is therefore a "cultural phenomenon", a "net-work of enunciations about supernatural and/or divine beings, of ethics, of prayers and of symbolic signs and acts, through which man enters into a life re-lationship with the divine".[63] Explicitly Vergote refers to Lacan and his intro-duction of the symbolic order as a "realm of signifiers", meaning that the hu-man subject will be involved in a "system of signs" that – external to the subject – give meaning.[64] That is to say, like in Lacan's theory, it precedes the individ-ual and dominates him as soon as he enters the order, (re-)structuring the indi-vidual's identity. It is only within a "religious order of language" that the word God has meaning and content.[65]

Religion is a cultural phenomenon developed throughout history from primitive forms to monotheistic religion. Is it therefore, as Freud thought, a hu-man creation? Vergote strongly emphasizes that religion should not be reduced to human motivations, representations or ideas. The "soul and source" of relig-

---

ion is not psychologized, and vice versa that psychology does not evolve into religion. Instead the human psyche is the location where natural motivations and religion inter-act. Hence, this is the focus of attention in the psychology of religion. S. Heine, *Grund-lagen der Religionspsychologie*, pp.251-255.

[60] A. Vergote, *Religionspsychologie*, pp.12-13.

[61] A. Vergote, "Passion for the Origin and Quest for the Original: Ideology and Reli-gious Truth", in *Psychoanalysis, Phenomenological Anthropology and Religion*, pp.103-132 (124). Also in A. Vergote, *Interprétation du language religieux*, Éditions du Seuil, Paris, 1974, p.49; A. Vergote, "Religion after the Critique of Psychoanalysis", p.18; A. Vergote, *Religion, Belief and Unbelief*, pp.23-31.

[62] Idem, pp.16-22.

[63] A. Vergote, "Psychoanalyse in contact met religie", p.283.

[64] Idem, pp.283-285. Compare: *De term symbolisch neem ik in de zin die bepaalde structuralistisch geïnspireerde strekkingen in de huidige antropologie eraan geven, wanneer zij spreken van een symbolische orde. Daarmede bedoelen zij de betekeniswe-reld die door de taal tot stand gebracht wordt en waarin de betekenis bestaat uit de structurele verhoudingen tussen de termen.* A. Vergote, *Het huis is nooit af*, pp.50-51.

[65] Idem, p.45

ion is found in God's auto-revelation.[66] This is what distinguishes religion from a philosophy of life or from mere ceremonial acts. Hence in *Psychology of Religion* religion is first of all defined as a lived relationship with the divine followed by the formulation that religion is a system of belief representations that emanates from this relation.[67] This soul and source of religion gives it its own reality that somehow can be distinguished from other cultural phenomena.

So how does the individual enter this religious symbolic order? We have seen that in Lacan's theory the father function as *Non-du-Père* and *Nom-du-Père* is crucial. His, the father's, interference in the imaginary dual relationship between child and mother marks the end of the imaginary order and the entrance into the symbolic order. Hence, the symbolic order is "given" by the father (not invented or discovered by the child), in Vergote's view "revealed".[68] The relation with God can only originate when God is revealed to man. As in Lacanian thought the only way to enter the symbolic order is to accept the Name-of-the-Father as "Law".[69] The acceptance (*aanvaarding, instemming*) of the Word of God or the word "God" – Vergote uses both options – is the *conditio sine qua non* for entering in a symbolic relationship with God in (Christian) religion.[70] Such an acceptance is not a strictly private affair. The proclamation of the Word takes place in a community that is seen as the cultural bearer of the symbolic order.[71] Christian religion calls for a personal relationship with God

---

[66] See J.-B. Lecuit, *L'anthropologie théologique à la lumière de la psychanalyse*, p.489.

[67] A. Vergote, *Religionspsychologie*, p.22.

[68] We will not deal here with the (mainly American) feminist critique on Lacan's key concept of Name-of-the-Father: in Vergote's theories this critique is not accounted for.

[69] In my opinion the law character of the Word shows that Vergote accepts Freud's association of religion with morality.

[70] A. Vergote, *Het huis is nooit af*, pp.61-67. See also for example A Vergote, *Interprétation du language religieux*, pp.16-17; A. Vergote, *Religion, Belief and Unbelief*, pp.226-227. In a study of the specific identity of Christianity Vergote's starting point is the Law character of biblical proclamation: the Old Testament *Sjema* and Christ's commandment "Thou shallt love thy God". According to Vergote, it is a key issue in the bible that the self revelation of God on the mountain Horeb forms a unity with the commandment to love him. A. Vergote, *De Heer je God liefhebben*. This is repeated in Vergote's recent interpretation of biblical monotheism which starts off with a paragraph on the auto-revelation of God followed by a paragraph on the Law and the Covenant. A. Vergote, *Humanité de l'homme, divinité de Dieu*, Éditions du Cerf, Paris, 2006, p.127ff. Vergote's discussion of biblical monotheism is, though without direct references to Freud, clearly Freudian in the sense that the key elements of *Moses and Monotheism* are guidelines: revelation of monotheism by Moses, the advancement of intellectuality through high moral standards (Law), and the development of an own identity as chosen people (Covenant).

[71] A. Vergote, *Guilt and Desire. Religious Attitudes and their Pathological Derivatives*, Yale University Press, New Haven/London, 1988, pp.14-15 (originally published as *Dette et désir* in 1978).

(in faith), but religion is not just a personal relationship with God: it is "a practice of a community and is bound up in the life of the community".[72]

From all this we can understand how the psychology of religion and
psychoanalysis can be "neutral". Religion is regarded as being an external and
autonomous symbolic order that has to be revealed. It cannot be reduced to psychic motivations nor regarded as an extension of human desires, experiences or
speculative thought. Psychoanalysis is neutral with respect to every philosophy
of life "precisely because it refuses a teleology that would be a natural force inscribed in archaeology".[73] Religion as symbolic order can be clearly distinguished from so called religiosity situated on an imaginary level, i.e. the level of
creating a God after one's own image.

From this general outline of religion as symbolic order we can continue discussing Vergote's position in the theological and psychological landscape, and in
doing so we will get a clearer picture of Vergote's work and his reading of
Freud.

First of all, Bart Pattyn en Jean-Baptiste Lecuit have shown that Vergote can be situated in a debate in Catholic theology about religious experience.
In the 1930s and 1940s theologians such as Joseph Maréchal (Leuven) and
Henri de Lubac (Lyon) had argued that there is a natural inclination in thought
towards the Absolute or a natural innate desire towards God. These ideas
opened up the possibility of overcoming the traditional distinction between the
"natural" and "supernatural". The writings of the Dutch theologian Edward
Schillebeeckx on religious experience can also be situated in this line of
thought.[74] Contrary to these Vergote pleas for an absolute and radical distinction
between the natural and supernatural along the lines of a distinction between the
imaginary order and the symbolic order. Like the Name-of-the-Father differentiates between nature and culture[75], the Word of the Father differentiates be-

---

[72] A. Vergote, *Religion, Belief and Unbelief*, p.207. Compare: *Ik meen dat alleen de religieuze traditie, door haar getuigenis voor de naam God, Hem kan bekendmaken.* A.
Vergote, *Het huis is nooit af*, p.62.

[73] A. Vergote, "Passion for the Origin and Quest for the Original: Ideology and Religious Truth", p.124. The concepts of archaeology and teleology refer to Ricoeur's
Freud and Philosophy in which he in the final chapter had argued that Freud's archaeological hermeneutics should be combined with a teleological hermeneutics as presented
in the phenomenology of religion (Van der Leeuw) and kerygmatic theology (Barth,
Bultmann).

[74] B. Pattyn, "Verlangen, ervaring en openbaring", pp.381-384; J.-B. Lecuit,
L'anthropologie théologique à la lumière de la psychanalyse, pp.542-548. Compare
also P. Vandermeersch, H. Westerink, *Godsdienstpsychologie*, pp.258-260.

[75] According to Vergote, the Law or Name-of-the-Father makes an incision (*coupure*) in
the "mystical" unity from child and mother. *Cette Loi est celle de l'humanité, celle qui
différencie la culture de la nature.* Lacan's use of the word mystical in relation to the
imaginaire dual relationship is derived from Lévy-Bruhl. A. Vergote, "Le sujet incons-

tween nature and the supernatural. The neutrality of psychology of religion and psychoanalysis is thus also situated in a theological position that doesn't want to reduce Christianity to a form of natural religion.[76]

This becomes especially clear in his 1974 study of the interpretation of religious language. Vergote discusses there the work of Tillich and Bultmann as two examples of defining the relationship between subject and revealed religion. According to Vergote, Tillich's theology is essentially imaginary; there is a natural desire towards the ultimate. The "jump" of the subject from existence to essence indicates that there is no actual revelation of a Wholly Other, but that the ultimate ground is nothing but an imaginary construct that satisfies all human desires.[77] This "image of God" whether it is called "origin, endless, eternal, highest being, first beginning, ultimate ground" is "the enlarged mirror reflection of the ego", that is to say, it is "the double ego of thinking man".[78] Vergote proposes his idea of the "revelation" of a symbolic order that structures the subject as an alternative to metaphysics or philosophy based on either "the order of nature" or "existential subjectivity".[79]

This distinction between the natural and supernatural in terms of a sharp division between the imaginary and symbolic order has important repercussions for his position in debates in the psychology of religion. We have seen that Fortmann, Faber and their followers sought for possibilities to save religious experience from psychoanalytic critique. The projection theory was first rejected, but afterwards, with the aid of new psychoanalytic theories, a growing interest emerged in the constructive capacities of fantasy and imagination in the process of giving meaning. We have seen that these psychic mechanisms were supposed to elevate man above everyday reality. In other words, there is a natural possibility or even inclination towards self-transcendence. In this line of thought Faber could argue that man is *homo religiosus*, and Van der Lans could

---

cient selon Lacan", in G. Lofts, P. Moyaert, *La pensée de Jacques Lacan. Questions historiques – Problèmes théoriques*, Éditions Peeters, Leuven/Paris, 1994, pp.1-22 (18).
[76] A. Vergote, *Het meerstemmige leven. Gedachten over mens en religie*, DNB/Uitgeverij Pelckmans, Kapellen, 1987, p.177.
[77] As to Bultmann's existentialism *mutatis mutandis* the same argument applies: the revealed Word is not a pure "interpellation" in reality; its acceptance is based on an existential recognition which means that man is the measure for the revealed. A. Vergote, *Interprétation du language religieux*, pp.15-17.
[78] A. Vergote, *Het huis is nooit af*, p.49.
[79] A. Vergote, *Interprétation du language religieux*, p.17. In "putting all emphasis on the revealed Word to which people can confess themselves emotionally" Vergote's theological position could be called Barthian, not in the sense that religion must go down in order for a purified faith to emerge, but because of the crucial importance of the revelation of the Word through proclamation situated in a community. B. Pattyn, "Wie zal morgen uitmaken wat onzin is? Vragen rond de moderne scepsis tegenover de traditie", in *Tijdschrift voor Theologie* 38 (1998), pp.339-350 (347); P. Vandermeersch, H. Westerink, *Godsdienstpsychologie*, p.265.

write that man is "disposed to ask the ultimate meaning questions that can result in a religious experience".[80] This religious experience is not the experience of God who reveals himself, but must be regarded as a "core experience" in which "the true authentic self is qualified with a transcendental dimension".[81]

Vergote strongly opposes this position: so called religious tendencies towards mystical unities should not be considered religious.[82] He criticizes the attempts made by for example Lévy-Bruhl to trace back religion to a form of participation in totality, or to what Romain Rolland would have called an "oceanic feeling". Instead even the most primitive religion originates from an immediate experience of the symbolic presence of the divine as Wholly Other.[83] Further on Vergote makes clear that a religious attitude is characterized by an openness towards revelation, but should not be regarded as the outcome of the unfolding of natural religious motivations (needs or desires).[84] This line of thought is continued throughout Vergote's writings: when religion is regarded as being the result of a thought process, a wish, desire or need, it is imaginary, and it is therefore illusionary in the sense Freud meant it.[85]

Consequently, the views held by Fortmann or Van der Lans are problematic. Their theories could be regarded as subjectivism with a belief in "a religious finality in human nature"[86] or at least a religiosity that is situated in the imaginary realm of desire for totality (of meaning). Such desire, need or search for ultimate meaning "explains religion psychologically" (psychologism). To equate religion with a worldview is thus a "denial of the identity of religion".[87] It is therefore obvious that Vergote in a debate with Van der Lans on the object of psychology of religion strongly opposed Van der Lans' plea for a focus of attention on giving ultimate meaning and development of a personal worldview. "Psychology of religion deals with religion" and not with worldviews that

---

[80] J. van der Lans, "Zingeving en zingevingsfuncties van religie bij stress", p.87.

[81] J. van der Lans, "Kernervaring, esthetische emotie en religieuze betekenisgeving", in *Religie ervaren*, pp.128-163 (140).

[82] A. Vergote, *Religionspsychologie*, p.27, p.32.

[83] Idem, pp.55-67.

[84] Idem, chapter 3.

[85] See for example in A. Vergote, *Het huis is nooit af*, pp.66-67; A. Vergote, *Religion, Belief and Unbelief*, pp.237-238; A. Vergote, *Het meerstemmige leven*, p.27, p.110, p.185

[86] A. Vergote, "Experience of the Divine, Experience of God", in *Psychoanalysis, Phenomenological Anthropology and Religion*, pp.133-145 (144).

[87] A. Vergote, "De toekomstige godsdienstpsychologie. Een vooruitzicht", in J.A. van Belzen (ed.), *Op weg naar morgen*, pp.178-193 (183). Vergote argues that religion should not be taken up in a more broadly defined giving meaning system, and that meaning in life should not be regarded as the outcome of a subjective search, but as the acceptance of values and truths.

originate "in the speculative mind which asks questions about the world as totality", that is to say, "the need for an all-embracing knowledge of the world".[88]

Vergote's ideas on an unmotivated religion as a symbolic system that is
revealed through the word (of) God also have consequences for his position in
psychoanalysis. In his writings one will find a critique of ego psychology and
self psychology and their key concepts of ego-integration or self-realization.
These psychologies are considered self-centred focusing solely on subjective
needs and desires that leave no room for an openness towards the Wholly
Other.[89] From this a critique of Jung is obvious: when God and religion are unconscious, that is to say, emanating from archetypical potentials and not distin-
guishable from fantasies or delusions, it is clear that Jung completely reduces
religion to psychic functions and his depth psychology should thus be regarded
as atheistic[90], despite the fact that his psychology is a "gnostic star nebula" that
appears to have a positive attitude towards religion.[91]

But what about Lacan, for didn't he also view the unconscious as the
reservoir of language? Was this not a reduction of the symbolic order to the
psyche, or of "the rationality of theology" to the "unconscious language structures"? Vergote agrees that Lacan's position here is atheistic also, even more
explicitly than in Jung's work.[92] At this point he criticizes Lacan's reading of
Freud. Vergote argues that Lacan wrongfully ignored Freud's distinction between "word-representations" and "thing-representations".[93] Primal unconscious representations should be regarded as "thing-representations", whereas
"word-representations" should be situated on the level of the preconscious and
conscious. The unconscious is thus not primarily structured as language, but

---

[88] A. Vergote, J. van der Lans, "Two opposed viewpoints concerning the object of the
psychology of religion", in J.A. van Belzen, J. van der Lans (eds.), *Current Issues in the
Psychology of Religion. Proceedings of the third Symposium on the Psychology of Religion in Europe*, Rodopi, Amsterdam, 1986, pp.67-81 (67-68). On this debate see J.A.
van Belzen, "Religie, zingeving, spiritualiteit: waar gaat godsdienstpsychologie eigenlijk over?", pp.215-217.
[89] For example in A. Vergote, *Religion, Belief and Unbelief*, pp.46-47.
[90] A. Vergote, "Psychoanalyse in contact met religie", p.286. Compare also Vergote's
critique on "monistic psychology" (for example Rogers and Maslow): A. Vergote, *Religionspsychologie*, pp.124-127.
[91] A. Vergote, "De toekomstige godsdienstpsychologie", p.181.
[92] A. Vergote, "Psychoanalyse in contact met religie", p.286. Lacan writes: "The true
formula of atheism is not God is dead (...) the true formula of atheism is that God is unconscious". Cited in A. Leupin, *Lacan Today. Psychoanalysis, Science, Religion*, Other
Press, New York, 2004, p.116.
[93] S. Freud, *The Unconscious, SE XIV*, pp.201-204. On this issue see J. Corveleyn, "Het
onbewuste", pp.144ff.; J.-B. Lecuit, *L'anthropologie théologique à la lumière de la
psychanalyse*, pp.41-47. Lecuit writes the following: *Vergote appelle inconscient origi-
naire l'inconscient constitué par ces representations-chose, intériorisation
d'expériences archaïques positives.*

originally consists of representations of "things" that are not yet structured through language.[94] In Freud's theory of the unconscious these thing-representations indicate that the drive (as representative of the body) is directed towards concrete objects for its satisfaction (for example the mother's breast). The primary processes are thus concerned with things (the own and the other's body parts), and do not yet have a verbal connotation.[95] The original nature of the unconscious is therefore imaginary and not symbolic. Vergote stresses the importance of the libidinal body in Freudian thought as opposed to the fact "that the body is a real problem for Lacan".[96] In other words, Freud's ideas of the psychical apparatus (or "libidinal body") indicating the unity of body and mind are taken up to indicate the bodily character of the drives, its goals and representations on a strictly imaginary level. The transition towards symbolic relationships articulated in language is a further development that we will discuss in a following paragraph on sublimation. To conclude, Vergote's own *retour à Freud* implies an important correction of Lacanian thought.

The question whether this correction is a strategy adopted in order to safeguard the position of religion as an external symbolic order can be raised, but cannot easily be answered.[97]

---

[94] A. Vergote, *De sublimatie*, p.89.

[95] Freud's unconscious is an *ensemble de representations pulsionelles* impressed in the psyche through *contacts perceptifs-libidinaux avec le monde, les autres et le corps propre. Contrairement à Lacan, Freud affirme le plus nettement que l'inconscient n'est pas structure comme un language.* A. Vergote, "Imaginaire et vérité en psychanalyse. La triade lacanienne", in *Figures de la psychanalyse* 8 (2003), pp.127-136 (134-135).

[96] Ph. van Haute, "About Sublimation. Interview with Antoine Vergote", in *Ethical Perspectives* 5 (1998), pp.218-224 (220)

[97] Wagner and Utsch have argued that Vergote's eagerness to avoid psychologism results in the extreme opposite: a radical distinction between "empirics" and "ontology". Consequently Vergote's view on religiosity is characterized by the "occupation" of the psyche by traditional Christian contents. The natural psychic determinants disappear to the background. In short, either man is dominated by natural psychic motivations or by unconditional religious contents. Therefore Vergote's theories on religiosity seem to be theologically motivated "without psychology". F. Wagner, *Was ist Religion?. Studien zu ihrem Begriff und Thema in Geschichte und Gegenwart*, Verlag Mohr, Gütersloh, 1986, pp.256-261; M. Utsch, *Religionspsychologie. Voraussetzungen, Grundlagen, Forschungsüberblick*, Verlag Kohlhammer, Stuttgart/Berlin/Colone, 1998, pp.170-171. The problem with this argument is that it is derived from a reading of Vergote's 1966 study in the psychology of religion that was translated into German. In that study psychoanalysis does not play a major role which might give the impression that Vergote's perspective is basically theological. However, this distinction between nature and the supernatural is based on the Lacanian division between the imaginary and symbolic. In Vergote's writings one cannot discern whether theology precedes and dominates psychoanalysis or vice versa. He focuses on the interaction from a double perspective. Thus, one should read his texts with suspicion, but not draw conclusions too eagerly.

Before we proceed in discussing Vergote's reading of Freud, it should
be mentioned that his interest in the psychology of religion was not completely
dominated by a psychoanalytic approach. In Leuven and in Louvain-la-Neuve
Vergote was able to set up empirical research in the 1960s that continues until
the present day. In his 1966 study in the psychology of religion the first results
of empirical research concerning father and mother symbols (or structural functions) in God representations can already be found.[98] Over the years this research focused on this issue. It showed that representations of God, traditionally
represented as the Father, were in fact an amalgam of paternal (authority, law-
giver) and maternal (care, availability) components, in which in many cases the
maternal qualities dominated.[99]

A key publication in this research program was *The Parental Figures
and the Representations of God* from 1981. This study is a beautiful example of
empirical research in combination with psychoanalytic interpretation. The contributions of Vergote mainly concern the latter aspect. The starting point is
again a Lacanian perspective on the symbolic order of which maternal and paternal symbols are a part. Here also Vergote points out that God's existence
cannot be reduced to psychic motivations. Instead one should focus on the "interaction between religion and personality: the concrete content of the representation of God is an expression of the psychic personality, but the representation
of God has also a psychologically formative influence on the personality".[100]
This reflects our general outline.

5.3.3   Pulsional desire and sublimation

There is in general a shift of attention in Vergote's major writings from the issue of religious experience, belief and unbelief as a field of interaction between
psyche and religion analyzed with the aid of psychoanalytic theory in the 1960s,

---

[98] A. Vergote, *Religionspsychologie*, pp.232ff.

[99] In Vergote this amalgam of maternal and paternal symbols might be called an optimum, that is to say, it resists two extremes: on the one hand a complete maternal image
of God as the caring and comforting mother which would indicate a religion as deconstructed by Freud in *The Future of an Illusion*, or on the other hand a complete paternal
God image that would paralyze and disintegrate religion – more or less in the way Vestdijk had described Calvinism. A. Vergote, *Religion, Belief and Unbelief*, p.231.

[100] A. Vergote, A. Tamayo, *The Parental Figures and the Representation of God. A
Psychological and Cross-Cultural Study*, Mouton Publishers, The Hague/Paris/New
York, 1981, p.19. This study is the only study of Vergote mentioned by Wulff in his
major handbook on the psychology of religion. Undeniably this is due to the fact that it
is the outcome of empirical research – after all, this is the dominant approach in Anglo-
American psychology of religion. Wulff presents the study as a critique of Freud's thesis that God is an elevated father. The fact that Vergote's major reference is psychoanalytic theory is unjustly ignored. D. Wulff, *Psychology of Religion. Classic and Contemporary Views*, John Wiley & Sons, New York et al., 1991, p.305.

1970s and 1980s towards a more fundamental discussion of psychoanalytic concepts and the further development of reformulations of psychoanalytic theory. In his 1997 study of sublimation the libidinal body is elaborated upon, not because it is a Freudian concept, but because it can be introduced into psychoanalysis to indicate "the more or less unified functioning of the primal unconsciousness".[101] Constitutive here is the body, not taken by Vergote as Lacan's *corps morcelé*, the fragmented body that is unified in narcissism, but instead seen as primarily a lived body in and on which the primal pleasure ego moves freely to those parts from which it expects satisfaction.[102] This is what Freud had called auto-eroticism. Narcissism marks the climax of this stage in which this pleasure ego elevates itself as libidinal object. In this sense, narcissism is an act carried out by the libidinal body itself.[103]

These primary processes, or what Lacan indicated as the imaginary order, can also be indicated with the term "natural man". It is man before he enters culture through language (symbolic order). This concept of libidinal body expresses, as we have seen, the unity of body and psyche in Freudian thought, as do concepts such as psychical apparatus or drive wish. In this context Vergote also speaks of pulsional desire as the active pursuit of objects (thing-representations) that give pleasure.[104] The body thus acts; acts that "can be conceived as a psychological tendency possessing a teleology that is inherent to it".[105] There is desire that "originates from the mind embedded in flesh and blood".[106]

This pulsional desire is situated on the level of the imaginary, which means that it is limitless and boundless in its pursuit of pleasure in objects that promise a reunion with "the great All", the source of life and unconditioned

---

[101] A. Vergote, *De sublimatie*, p.103.

[102] According to Vergote, Lacan's ideas on the fragmented body result from his reading of Freud from the perspective of psychosis. Vergote argues that in psychosis the original more or less unified libidinal body is fragmented.

[103] Idem, pp.108-109; J.-B. Lecuit, *L'anthropologie théologique à la lumière de la psychanalyse*, p.58.

[104] A. Vergote, *De sublimatie*, p.99. We should notice here that in Vergote's view desire aims at *plaisir* and not at *jouissance*. This prevents Vergote from slipping into a Lacanian discourse on the nature of *jouissance* as a violent bodily enjoyment. Instead the desire for *plaisir* in the religious symbolic order takes the form of a desire for *bonheur* or *geluk*, happiness. On Vergote's thought on pulsional desire see further: J.-B. Lecuit, *L'anthropologie théologique à la lumière de la psychanalyse*, pp.47ff.

[105] A. Vergote, "Husserl and Freud on the Psychic Body in Action", p.3.

[106] In the preface of the English translation of *Dette et désir* a passage is missing in comparison to the Dutch translation. As in German the Dutch language has two possible translations for desire, namely *begeerte* (*Begierde*) and *verlangen* (*Sehnsucht*). Vergote opts for *begeerte* which is more easily associated with drives and pleasure. A. Vergote, *Bekentenis en begeerte in de religie. Psychoanalytische verkenning*, DNB/Uitgeverij Pelckmans, Kapellen, 1989, pp.5-6. Compare A. Vergote, *Guilt and Desire*, p.viii.

love. To be everything, to be capable of everything, to be autonomous without limitations, immediate satisfaction, in short "the narcissistic dream" or narcissistic fantasy is desired.[107] This natural omnipotence of desire (for omnipotence) should be taken for what it is: "natural". From this does not emerge a natural desire for the divine. The natural desire is a restless desire seeking objects for satisfaction in this world.[108] Yet, this desire will never be satisfied as no object can provide in this. This unsatisfied desire then opens a "rupture" in which a desire for God can be "planted". After all, there is always some lack (*manque*) and "the dominance of the desire for omnipotence is perhaps never so clearly seen as when it encounters the signifier "God" as the characteristic of human powerlessness".[109]

At this point we see how the libidinal body and religion interact. The signifier "God" bends natural desire in the direction of the divine and at the same time it unveils imaginary desire as illusionary. In this context we can understand Vergote's critique of self-realization or ego-integration as basically concepts that sustain narcissistic desires in what he calls "narcissistic fascination"[110]. Essentially these concepts cannot be harmonized with religion or belief. The fact that a subject is not integrated and not "whole" entails that there is an opening towards the other/Other. Such a relationship also means integration albeit on a symbolic level between individual and other/Other through love: "love is the desire for and enjoyment of the other out of one's own incompleteness".[111] Love is thus a specific desire evoked by the presence of the other as other, or the Other as Other.[112] This "or" should not be read as alternative or compensation when the love between persons fails. On the symbolic level both appear, also next to each other.

Given the fact that desire originates in and from the libidinal body, one should not be surprised at finding erotic metaphors in religious language. It is not a necessary sign of pathology or a failed religious maturation process. This is made clear in Vergote's earlier discussion of the mystic desires and enjoy-

---

[107] A. Vergote, *Religion, Belief and Unbelief*, p.231, p.237.

[108] *Want hoe rusteloos verlangend het menselijk hart ook is, hoezeer hem ook "alle dingen te eng zijn", God is zelden de eerst gegeven pool van het verlangen, integendeel. Het verlangen tast eerst de wereld af, zoals een krab haar sprieten uitzendt.* A. Vergote, *Het meerstemmige leven*, p.79.

[109] A. Vergote, *Religion, Belief and Unbelief*, p.238.

[110] A. Vergote, *Het meerstemmige leven*, p.185. This narcissistic fascination found in a spirituality that aims at self-realization or ego-integration, is focused on an ego ideal that can only evoke a neurotic suffering and a wrath against oneself. Being a Freudian Vergote holds the idea that ego and ego ideal will never be one and same. Hence, these spiritualities can only confront one with imaginary lacks, whereas religion confronts one with a symbolic lack that constitutes a subject as individual personality.

[111] Idem.

[112] Compare also A. Vergote, *De Heer je God liefhebben*, pp.187ff.

ments of Teresa of Avila that had also intrigued Lacan.[113] According to Vergote, she should not be considered a hysteric – as had been suggested in literature – but instead a case of "successful hysteria", that is to say, the sublimation of imperious desires that reach towards symbolic union with the Other and decentre from her own self.[114] This eccentricity creates a *locus* for God in the soul.[115]

We have already seen in previous chapters that Freud's *The Future of an Illusion* is situated in debates with Rank and Pfister. I have argued that this text shows a different perspective on religion and on the father figure in comparison to *Totem and Taboo* and *Moses and Monotheism*. I referred to Vergote,

---

[113] A. Vergote, *Guilt and Desire*, pp.153-202; A. Vergote, *Het meerstemmige leven*, pp.219-232. J. Lacan, *The Seminar of Jacques Lacan, Book XX. On Feminine Sexuality, The Limits of Love and Knowledge, 1972-1973 (Encore)*, J.-A. Miller (ed.), Norton & Company, New York/London, 1999, p.71.

[114] A. Vergote, *Guilt and Desire*, p.157. Vergote argues that "hysteric" enjoyments of Teresa are not necessarily caused by the neurotic dynamics of her mental life, but should be considered "normal" within her cultural context (the religious community). On this issue see J. Corveleyn, "Folk Religiosity or Psychopathology? The Case of the Apparitions of the Virgin in Beauraing, Belgium, 1932-1933", in J.A. van Belzen (ed.), *Psychohistory in Psychology of Religion: Interdisciplinary Studies*, Rodopi, Amsterdam/Atlanta, 2001, pp.239-259.

[115] A. Vergote, *Het meerstemmige leven*, p.225. Vergote's discussion of Teresa of Avila's mystique, especially in *Het meerstemmige leven* (pp.224-225) strongly resembles the ideas of the Lacanian psychoanalyst and theologian Michel de Certeau on modern mystic speech. Although Vergote does not make direct references the resemblances are so strong that a direct influence probably took place. In De Certeau's view the core issue in modern mysticism as expressed in for example the writings of John of the Cross and Teresa of Avila is "inner experience". That is to say, mysticism is no longer related to a hidden aspect in reality, but completely situated in the body and soul of the mystic who has to create a space in him- or herself as a place for God or the Holy Spirit to speak. Mysticism is thus the constitution of an inner dialogue, and the experience of God is situated in a speech act of the mystic in and through whom the Other speaks. Here mystic discourse first establishes a differentiation between the subject of the speech act and the subject of the statement that is later repeated in (Lacanian) psychoanalysis. In other words the *el que habla* of John of the Cross is the historic origin and structurally resembles psychoanalytic *ça parle*, the unconscious Other that speaks in the subject. This mysticism is based on an act of the will of the mystic to create a space in him or herself, and a discourse appearing in that space. De Certeau thus situated psychoanalysis in a historico-religious context. Vergote does not take up this line of historic development, but argues, as does De Certeau, that Teresa of Avila's mysticism centres around a emptied space, a *locus*, in which the Other can appear and speak in an inner *colloquium*. M. de Certeau, *The Mystique Fable. Volume 1. The Sixteenth and Seventeenth Centuries*, University of Chicago Press, Chicago/London, 1992, pp.188ff. (originally published as *La fable mystique* in 1982); M. de Certeau, *Heterologies. Discourse on the Other*, University of Minnesota Press, Minneapolis/London, 1995, pp.36-37.

for it was he who has made this difference explicit. In the context of Vergote's discussions of imaginary pulsional desires Freudian psychoanalysis is the main point of reference, but Freud is also strongly criticized, especially when he took the imaginary desires and needs as the starting point for his explanation of religion in *The Future of an Illusion*. Here, Freud saw religion as originating from the imaginary order in which the child is helpless and desires a caring and ever-present maternal father-God to satisfy all needs. This explanation[116] is an example of psychologism in which the elevated father can hardly be called a father, because he is merely considered a person meeting the child's imaginary demands. A discussion of the "meaning of the Name-of-the-Father" is completely lacking, and a thorough understanding of the complexity of religion is thus lost from sight.

The other texts on religion dealing with guilt, identification and authority are situated in the context of the symbolic (*Totem and Taboo, Moses and Monotheism*). Here, the father is reduced to a "male animal" without "name" or Law. Again, Freud failed to recognize the true meaning of the father.[117] Hence, Freud had brilliant insights – for example on the importance of the father figure in religion or the often obscure motives as "the fertile soil" for religiosity[118] – however he was unable to overcome the two main obstacles that underlie his ideas on culture in general and religion in particular: "the combination of a positivistic philosophy and a pathological point of view".[119] Therefore, he could not see in religion anything else but an illusion to be unmasked by science, or a collective guilt neurosis (when he by analogy applied the model of obsessional neurosis on religion).[120]

This general critique of Freud's studies of culture and religion also applies to his clinical writings. Vergote rejects the Freudian concept of the death drive arguing that it is based on a positivistic biological theory in combination

---

[116] Vergote is not the first and only psychologist of religion criticizing Freud's reductionism or psychologism. Erikson already spoke of Freud's "originological fallacy" ("explaining current behaviour by appealing to its origins in the past"). Meissner quoted Erikson on this in his study on Ignatius of Loyola arguing that psychobiography is not about explanation, but about understanding the motivational life of the individual in a specific cultural context. W.W. Meissner, *Ignatius of Loyola: The Psychology of a Saint*, Yale University Press, New Haven, 1992, p.xix.

[117] A. Vergote, "Religion after the Critique of Psychoanalysis", pp.24-37; A. Vergote, "Psychoanalyse in contact met religie", p.289; A. Vergote, A. Tamayo, *The Parental Figures and the Representation of God*, pp.223-224.

[118] A. Vergote, "Religion after the Critique of Psychoanalysis", p.22.

[119] A. Vergote, *De sublimatie*, p.253.

[120] A similar critique can be found in the work of the psychologist of religion James Jones. He argues that Freud's view of religion from the perspective of psychodynamics flows from Freud's positivism. Instead, he proposes to study the relation between individual and religion as a "reciprocal interaction". J.W. Jones, *Comtemporary Psychoanalysis and Religion*, pp.111-113.

with a pathological view that a negative moment or reaction should originate from a specific negative drive, whereas one could also argue that every further development in psychic life includes a negative moment (against for example a previous situation or an object).[121] This view is based on Vergote's interpretation of the fort-da play presented by Freud in *Beyond the Pleasure Principle* as an argument for the death drive. According to Freud, the child's play with the disappearing and returning bobbin on a string was the painful repetition of the disappearance of the mother. It was a painful repetition beyond the pleasure principle and hence a repetition steming from the death drive.[122] Vergote argues that Freud doesn't need the death drive in order to point out the significance of the play, namely the child's "cultural achievement" to say "no" through play against an imaginary attachment to the mother.[123] In fact this "no" was the outcome of the progression, teleology, of the drives. The child is capable on its own of accepting the absence of the mother through the symbolic act of playing with the bobbin.

The teleology of the pulsional desires brings us to the subject of sublimation.[124] The issue had already been discussed in his 1978 *Dette et désir* [Guilt and Desire] in the context of Teresa of Avila's successful hysteria. There Vergote had already indicated that Freud's theories of sublimation were merely "sketchy".[125] The concept apparently remained problematic for Freud because of his pathological view.[126] In 1997 this issue is taken up in a major study of sublimation, a crucial concept uniting the libidinal body and the drives with cultural creations and cultural life. Freud's ideas are the starting point, though a revision of his

---

[121] A. Vergote, *De sublimatie*, pp.277ff.; Ph. van Haute, "About Sublimation", p.222. A similar argument has been presented by Lear who states that the weakness or failure of the pleasure principle should not necessarily lead to the conclusion that there is another principle at work beyond the pleasure principle. The pleasure principle is not a perfect machinery but a psychic mechanism that is sometimes dysfunctional. J. Lear, *Happiness, Death, and the Remainder of Life*, Harvard University Press, Cambridge (Mass.), 2000, pp.80ff.

[122] S. Freud, *Beyond the Pleasure Principle*, chapter 2.

[123] A. Vergote, *De sublimatie*, pp.124ff.

[124] On the issue of sublimation see also J.-B. Lecuit, *L'anthropologie théologique à la lumière de la psychanalyse*, pp.155-224.

[125] A. Vergote, *Guilt and Desire*, p.157. See also J. Laplanche, J.-B. Pontalis, *Vocabulaire de la psychanalyse*, p.466.

[126] As an example of this pathological view the case of the Wolf Man is illustrative: Freud argues that his patient's sadistic and masochistic tendencies were almost overcome through sublimation in religion. Unfortunately the entrance into the religious doctrine implicated the evocation of an obsessional neurosis. Given the fact that religion is already regarded to be a collective neurosis, this is hardly surprising. Here it becomes clear that sublimation is caught inbetween pathological formations.

theories is unavoidable first of all because of the already mentioned obstacles viz. Freud's positivism and pathological viewpoint.

The starting point is Freud's depiction of sublimation as the channelling of the sexual drives into the pursuit of socially acceptable "higher" aims. The sublimation process is thus at the heart of the normal development of the individual into a civilized being.[127] A major problem here is first of all the idea of the sublimation of the sexual drives, which Freud had put forward in *Three Essays* and had repeated thereafter. The starting point is, according to Vergote, a too broad concept of infantile sexuality equating every desire for an object with sexual desire. Linked to this is the problem that the sexual drive is innate, hence that sexuality is innate. However, when sexuality is innate and every desire for an object is sexual, how can sublimation ever be desexualization?[128] – In the Wolf Man case this already proved to be a difficulty. – It is for this reason Vergote prefers the term libidinal drive or pulsional desire.[129]

Another problem with Freudian thought is that sublimation is on the one hand only an alternative for repression and symptom formation, and on the other hand a movement into the culture that can be defined as collective neurosis. Sublimation can actually be regarded as a defence mechanism aiming at the taming of sexual drives. That means that cultural productions are a kind of symptom formation.[130] Hence, sublimation is caught inbetween pathology, between repression and collective neurosis.

A major problem is also Freud's theory of pleasure as the avoidance of unpleasure and as the minimalization of tension. If the drives are motivated by avoidance of unpleasure, so is sublimation. But when the drives aim at an immediate minimalization of tension it is hard to imagine how sublimation can ever lead to a creative activity. It is thus again hard to see how and in what way sublimation can take place when it is motivated by Freud's pleasure principle. Freud's theory is thus in need of revision by thinking through sublimation.[131]

The drives as pulsional desires do not just aim at the avoidance of unpleasure or at merely the satisfaction of basic needs, but positively aim at en-

---

[127] Vergote refers to Freud's concept of "advancement in intellectuality". J.-B. Lecuit, *L'anthropologie théologique à la lumière de la psychanalyse*, pp.164-169.

[128] See also P. Moyaert, *Begeren en vereren*, p.53.

[129] Here we should notice that in Vergote's ideas of the pulsional desires the distinction between sexual drives and ego drives is no longer predominantly important. Instead the main distinction is that between desires and needs. Only in a later development the body is sexualized under the primacy of the genitals (narcissism). In other words, the libido or pulsional desires precede the sexual desires. J.-B. Lecuit, *L'anthropologique à la lumière de la psychanalyse*, pp.61-64. To avoid a Jungian position in which the drives could be seen as a spontaneous autonomous life force with a "teleology", he argues that the drives should be considered physical, submitted to the pleasure principle, and dependant on culture for new objects.

[130] P. Moyaert, *Begeren en vereren*, p.54.

[131] A. Vergote, *De sublimatie*, pp.30-31.

joyment in activity. Eating is for example not just an act that satisfies a need and the enjoyment is not just the hunger that is stilled; there is also enjoyment in the very act of eating. Intellectual enjoyment is not just found in solving a problem or proving a hypothesis, but more importantly in the creative activity of intellectual thought itself. This is one of Vergote's main revisions of Freudian thought, albeit that Freud, in for example a footnote in *Three Essays*, had himself acknowledged that there was also an enjoyment in sexual activity itself and not only in its completion.[132] However, his strict definition of the pleasure principle prevented him from further reflection on enjoyment in activity. According to Vergote, the little child already pursues this enjoyment in activity in the pleasure it finds in and on its own body and that of others, and in the narcissistic ego-formation that originates out of this libidinal body. In the fort-da play Freud analyzed in *Beyond the Pleasure Principle* there is thus not just a repetition of a painful memory, but more importantly a creative moment when the child in a play stages – "symbolizes" – its own "no" towards the imaginary relation with the mother, its own renouncement of imaginary desires. It is a symbolization[133]

---

[132] S. Freud, *Three Essays*, p.212.

[133] It is tempting to compare Vergote's child play as creative symbolization with Winnicott's theories on symbolization in play (in what he calls the transitional sphere or potential space) in for example *Playing and Reality* (1971), for in both theories play is a crucial moment in the child's development, its separation from the mother, its first cultural experience, and its capacity to symbolize and sublimate. In Winnicott's object relations theory symbolization is the capacity to replace the absence of the mother by a transitional object symbolizing "the union of two separate things, baby and mother, at the point in time and space of the initiation of their very state of separateness". The symbol is thus the replacement of the presence of a real object by a symbolic object. In Vergote's view symbolization is actually quite the contrary, the "no" against the presence of the mother. Symbolization is first of all an active distancing from the mother. Nevertheless, there are some similarities on play and sublimation between Vergote and Winnicott. In my opinion Vergote actually positions himself – though by no means explicit – between Freud and Lacan on the one side and (Klein and) object relation theory (e.g. Winnicott) on the other side. This is not surprising when one considers that Lacan is also an object relation theorist, though of a different kind. Vergote holds onto the Lacanian idea that the child actively separates from the mother, that this separation is definite (the *objet a* indicates the lost object) and that the child then enters the world of language through the Name-of-the-Father. But Vergote also stresses the creativity of the child itself in play, its capacity to create a situation or space in which it can stage a cultural experience. Lacan is de-dramatized and this fact alone brings Vergote closer to Winnicott. D. Winnicott, *Playing and Reality*, Routledge, London/New York, 2005, p.130. On Winnicott see for example S.A. Mitchell, M.J. Black, *Freud and Beyond*, pp.124-134; H. Wahl, "symbolic Experience: Transforming the Selfobject Relation. A new Symbol Theory based on Modern Psychoanalysis", in J.A. van Belzen (ed.), *Hermeneutical Approaches in Psychology of Religion*, pp.241-261; S. Heine, *Grundlagen der Religionspsychologie*, pp.194-208.

carried out by the body itself, and a sublimation as it is articulated in the first syllables the child can express, *o-o-o* and *da*.

Hence, this play is on the border of the imaginary and the symbolic. The pulsional desires and the body activities incline towards transgressing the imaginary order. In the moment they do so, they meet the Law of the father ("no") and language. The fort-da play is thus the moment of interaction between libidinal body and culture. The question here is no longer how culture originates from nature, but how sublimation shows the entanglement of nature and culture.

The lack the child experiences in the absence of the mother is staged in the disappearing bobbin and exactly this "rupture" indicates already an acceptance of the "Law". Does this mean that the drives by themselves can be creative through symbolization? Certainly not in the Jungian sense of the word, for according to Vergote the drives are already situated in the interplay with a cultural environment, that is, the contact with parents and the first explorations of objects. Symbolization is thus anticipation of something happening in this cultural environment (absence of the mother) with the aid of a cultural artefact (bobbin). At this point it is clear that Vergote cannot agree with Freud's equation of symbol and symptom, and does agree with Ricoeur and others that the symbol has a creative quality.[134]

According to Vergote, a theory of religious sublimation should and can be reconstructed when separated from Freud's genetic explanation of religion and his pathological view of religion.[135] Freud's studies of religion however give little clue on how to rethink religious sublimation, despite the fact that he regarded religious sublimation as one of the most important forms of sublimation. Removing Freud's "vaguenesses and blunders" this means that a religion can be seen as an "apparatus" in which the pulsional desires are diverted and brought in congruence with "divine reality". Religious sublimation should thus be seen as the process of diverting desires by mediation of religious signs. Sublimation is the affective movement from the imaginary into the symbolic order, whereas religion itself is a symbolic order that presents a desirable object.[136] The best examples of religious sublimation can thus be found in mysticism, in the personal response ("I believe") to the performative speech act of God ("I am").[137]

---

[134] This is already apparent in the 1966 study in psychology of religion where Vergote refers to Ricoeur in his discussion of the symbol. A. Vergote, *Religionspsychologie*, p.223.

[135] A. Vergote, *De sublimatie*, pp.202-224

[136] Idem, pp.222-224.

[137] In an exegesis of Lacan's ideas on sublimation Van Coillie has argued that sublimation has an impossible aim, namely to combine (imaginary) fantasies of an ultimate desirable object (mother) and the acknowledgement of lack (*manque*) and acceptance of symbolic order. In mysticism this is reflected in the "painful tragic enjoyment" that characterizes the mystic's desires and despair. F. van Coillie, *De ongenode gast. Zes*

As Freud suggests in *Moses and Monotheism* the "normal" sense of guilt in Judaism incites advancement in intellectuality and encourages sublimation.[138] Vergote puts this combination in the foreground when he argues that sublimation marks a transformation of the drives towards a culture/religion that, through the father's "no", not only presents a desirable non-imaginary object, but also incites the normal sense of guilt – as we will see in the next paragraphs. "A normal sense of guilt appears to act as a call not for the suppression but rather for the transformation and sublimation of impulses."[139] There is thus a direct relation between the Name-of-the-Father that incites both desire and guilt, and the sublimation of drives.

5.3.4   Guilt

In the writings of Lacan one finds the notion of "symbolic debt" (*dette symbolique*).[140] The Name-of-the-Father, his "no", his Law, introduces a definitive lack. The imaginary desire for the All-mother has to be given up; the subject is now the subject-who-lacks. This is called symbolic castration: the ultimate object of desire is out of reach; desire will never be completely satisfied. The Name-of-the-Father introducing a distinction between the child and the other/Other forbids (Law) the desire for the All-mother. But these imaginary desires – which Lacan associates with sin – unconsciously remain and hence the introduction in the symbolic order always evokes guilt because of these desires.

Every desire towards the other/Other is accompanied by guilt. On the other hand guilt will also be evoked when one gives ground relative to one's desire. Man is guilty whenever there is a renunciation of his own desires. (As example we can think of Elisabeth von R. in *Studies on Hysteria* who felt guilty for not performing her duty towards her father.) In this way Lacan reformulates Freud's inevitable sense of guilt situated in the tension between drive and conscience and as expressive of both love and hate. In Lacan's version it is not a

---

analytische essays over het verlangen en de dood, Uitgeverij Boom, Amsterdam, 2004, pp.169-190. In Vergote's view one does not find this dramatized Lacanian version of sublimation. The "no" against the mother as affirmation of a sense of autonomy and the "no" of the father are supplementary and not primarily in conflict. At this point Vergote's ideas on sublimation differ from those of Lacan.

[138] S. Freud, *Moses and Monotheism*, p.86.

[139] J. Delumeau, *Sin and Fear. The Emergence of a Western Guilt Culture. 13th-18th Centuries*, St. Martin's Press, New York, 1990, p.297.

[140] J. Lacan, *Le Séminaire. Livre IV. La relation d'objet, 1956-1957*, J.-A. Miller (ed.), Éditions de Seuil, Paris, 1994, chapter 2; J. Lacan, *The Seminar of Jacques Lacan, Book VII. The Ethics of Psychoanalysis 1959-1960*, J.-A. Miller (ed.), Routledge, London, 1992, pp.319-321.

sense of guilt, but guilt as a psychic structure situated in the dynamics of desire and Law.[141]

In this context we can understand why Vergote could write that religion involves man in his totality and thus can illuminate the themes "desire, the meaning of the father figure, the Law and guilt". The sequence of words is an indication of a Lacanian perspective on guilt as it is closely associated with Law, father and desire. Guilt is related to the "normal conflicts between pulsional desires and the Law"; it belongs to a general human disposition towards neurosis; it is situated in the realm of "contingency of existence" and the consciousness of being indebted to an other/Other for existing.[142]

Also Vergote agrees with Lacan's motto *maintenir son désir*. Man should not give up his desire (in the symbolic order!), that is, the dynamic energetic core of his contingent existence.[143] One may add: this desire as energetic core of contingent existence is always accompanied by guilt, for there are always and inevitably moments and circumstances that a subject has to "betray" his desire or is betrayed by others, or is unable to pursue his desires in a civilization that demands restraint. This is what Lacan formulated as ordinary man's "destiny".

Guilt is thus seen as a structural element in man's fundamental psychic constitution (from the moment he has entered the symbolic order), but which can also in some cases and under certain circumstances evolve in the obsessional neurotic sense of guilt as described by Freud. The "cure" is to set free again the dynamics of desire. This train of thought can clearly be traced back to Freud for example when he suggests in *Thoughts for the Times on War and Death* that disillusionment in the goodness and progression of man/civilization is necessary precondition for the duty "to tolerate life"[144], and in *Formulations on the two Principles of Mental Functioning* that the reality principle safeguards the possibility of pleasure within a conflictuous structure including the sense of guilt.

---

[141] This symbolic debt is according to Lacan expressed in the Christian doctrine of original sin, and reformulated by Freud in a secular theory on the primal events (incest prohibition, taboo). Not only Lacan stated in the 1950s that Christianity and psychoanalysis hold similar views on sin and guilt. Delumeau has shown that Reik also observed this analogy in *Myth and Guilt*. J. Delumeau, *Sin and Fear*, p.251.

[142] A. Vergote, "Psychoanalyse in contact met religie", p.289, p.291.

[143] A. Vergote, "Ethiek van de psychoanalyse", in A. Vergote, P. Moyaert, et al. (eds.), *Psychoanalyse. De mens en zijn lotgevallen*, pp.299-323 (312-313, 322-323). *Maintenir son désir* implies again a critique of psychologies that focus on self-realization, ego-integration and autonomy: these aims are essentially non-dynamic and non-interactive. A. Vergote, *Guilt and Desire*, p.16.

[144] S. Freud, *Thoughts for the Times on War and Death*, p.299.

One of Vergote's best known studies, *Guilt and Desire*, is concerned with the two main neuroses, hysteria and obsessional neurosis – Vergote prefers to call the latter a guilt neurosis – in relation to religion, and analyzed from a Freudian-Lacanian perspective. We have already mentioned that Vergote rejects Freud's view of religion as collective neurosis, as well as his genetic explanation of religion.[145] However, "what cannot be denied is that Freud posed the central problem of the humanity of man and of the specifically human capacity to suffer neurosis. In this quest, he encountered religion and he recognized that, in its representations, it is the symbolic guardian of the human drama", and that in the centre of this drama was the figure of the father.[146] Though hindered by his positivism and pathological view Freud did recognize that man's psychic life and key complexes structure religion and are structured by religion. This is the starting point in *Guilt and Desire*.

Vergote's presupposition is that neuroses can be seen as exaggerations of "normal" psychic traits. "The conflictual elements that bring about a neurosis can be found in anyone, but what is certain is that neurosis arises from an aggravated conflict between love and hate."[147] In the context of a religious system this means that normal religiosity cannot easily be opposed to pathological formations. Instead one should focus on the tensions and conflicts of the believer who has to find his way on a religious path that remains "a risky one" with the ever present possibility of straying into pathology.[148] The study of religious neuroses must thus be seen against the background of the analysis of normal psychic traits that structure the relation with God.[149] After all, the psychic life has already been structured up to a certain point, and from hereon a person will approach religion given as a (pre-existing) symbolic order. The exaggeration in hysteria or guilt neurosis can thus also be interpreted as an exaggeration of

---

[145] The core of his critique of Freud's *Totem and Taboo* is the problem of how the obedience to the Law and guilt can emerge in a primitive brute society without Law or faith. In Vergote's view the obedience and guilt can only be established by a Law, that is, through the Name-of-the-Father. In other words, culture cannot originate from guilt, because, vice versa, guilt presupposes culture. A. Vergote, "Religion after the Critique of Psychoanalysis", pp.30-32.

[146] Idem, p.31.

[147] A. Vergote, *Guilt and Desire*, p.57. This idea of the pathological as an exaggeration of normal traits can be traced back to the writings of Freud. See for example S. Freud, *Leonardo da Vinci*, p.131.

[148] A. Vergote, *Guilt and Desire*, p.ix. When such religious pathology occurs, the believer will no longer be able to accept the religious system (for he will focus on specific traits) and will no longer be able to participate in a community.

[149] Compare: "By examining these mentally obstructing conflicts [i.e. neuroses, H.W.] we can better understand the import of impulses that appear arbitrary and confused but in fact concern the most profound depths of our being". Idem.

normal types of personalities with an inclination towards a specific pathology: hysterics, obsessional neurotics, or paranoiacs and perverts.[150]

The relation between psychic life and religion is an interaction. Psychic life colours the representations of God. Vergote's empirical research program focused on this aspect. In *Guilt and Desire* this means that the affective ambivalences and psychic conflicts – desires that can only be constrained when the Law is interiorized – are "transferred onto God and the institution of religion".[151] Vice versa (various forms of) religion can also appeal to certain types of personalities.

The aspect of sin in Christian religion is for example a "fertile soil for guilt" and for overcoming guilt.[152] In Christian tradition sin is "guilt before God"[153], and here, we find the point where guilt can transfer into an aggravated sense of guilt: Christianity does not only present sin as guilt in a symbolic structure, but also demands a personal confession of sin. In this personal appropriation of the symbolic order there is the danger of an exaggeration of guilt into the sense of guilt. A deep felt sense of sin in relation to an All-powerful Father already latently corresponds with a neurotic structure in which feelings of worthlessness and even self-hate are combined with feelings of love.

Further concerning sin, Christian religion is in a particular danger of overemphasizing the aspect of "fault" or "judgement" and thus can make "sick".[154] One might conclude from this that Christian religion does well not to overemphasize specific doctrinal aspects.[155] Like Lacan Vergote indicates that

---

[150] On this see P. Vandermeersch, H. Westerink, *Godsdienstpsychologie*, pp.262-266.

[151] A. Vergote, *Guilt and Desire*, p.58.

[152] Idem, p.43.

[153] A. Vergote, *Religion, Belief and Unbelief*, p.99.

[154] This does not mean that a doctrine focusing on sin is by definition a sick-making religion as Schilder argued. However such a doctrine will appeal to certain personality types in a stronger way, which could lead to pathology. Although from a different psychoanalytic perspective than Vergote, Hirsch has also argued that in Christianity the concept of sin indicates the fact that guilt is part of human existence. Instead of offering a framework for understanding the inevitability of this existential guilt and at the same minimizing the personal sense of guilt, the church often overemphasized the sense of guilt as part of a strategy to implement moral ideas. M. Hirsch, *Schuld und Schuldgefühl*, pp.48-49.

[155] It should be noticed here that Vergote is not a Protestant who is inclined to formulate a core message or doctrine, but a Catholic who is rooted in Flemish folk Catholicism. In *Het meerstemmige leven* Vergote describes folk Catholicism as the traditional religious symbolic order that provides "a house of the Father with many rooms" which is good because it reflects the varieties between people. Here we also find a main reason for not making the "Protestant" distinction between religion and faith. Folk Catholicism is a space for various forms of belief/faith that are in a sense always "impure" and in need of further development. Nevertheless, maturation processes and techniques to improve these should never be too strictly enforced. A. Vergote, *Het meerstemmige leven*,

guilt is situated between desires that are repressed and on the verge of return on the one hand and a Law (interiorized in the superego) that represses with the force of the drives. The Law that is meant to liberate from the desire for the All-mother and set a subject free to become an individual with its own identity can thus as easily develop into the harsh superego of guilt neurosis.[156]

The religious path is a "risky one". The dangers of neuroticization, increase of the sense of guilt and decrease of the dynamics of desire are, as Freud had already recognized, ever present. Vergote mentions the example of the obsessional desire to truly confess one's faith, whereas man is a "pulsional being" that can learn from his spontaneity of bodily desires, but that is incapable of taking his life under control in a single moment of formulating "truly". Such an obsession for true confession however is part of the Christian legacy and can thus easily lead to neurotic effects.

Another major problem in Christian tradition is sexuality which has become an obsession in itself: sexual morality closely related to a sense of guilt has had a neuroticizing effect on many. In fact, the increase in the sense of guilt leads to a decrease in affective life, creativity and freedom of thought causing a certain disintegration of personal, social and religious life.[157] In religion this sometimes seems to be advocated because of the distrust of human drives in general. Such distrust can be found in both Catholicism and Protestantism.

According to Vergote, the two traditions reflect two ways of dealing with drives and the sense of guilt.[158] In Catholic tradition (erotic) desires are more positively valued, but at the same time casuistically ordered and controlled. Protestantism shows the tendency to spiritualize the drives in the service of a higher goal, for example a religious perfectionism where narcissistic desire is combined with a sense of guilt as motivations in a longing to be religiously perfect. According to Vergote, the desires for such a goal are not only to be considered self-centred (hence imaginary), but also related to the sense of guilt, especially because the desire for perfectionism is always also a desire to meet the wishes/desires of someone else (be it another person or God). Being perfect is thus a debt towards the other/Other.

---

pp.233-250. A similar plea can be found in *Religion, Belief and Unbelief* where Vergote criticizes those forms of psychology that strive with "inquisitorial authority" towards "religious purism" denying the existence of "psychic man". After all, all forms of belief are in one way or another embedded in the psychic libidinal life of man. A. Vergote, *Religion, Belief and Unbelief*, pp.263-264.

[156] Compare: *La loi du père est libératrice: elle ne détruit pas le désir, mais elle ouvre à l'enfant l'espace et le temps d'un projet personnel.* J.-B. Lecuit, *L'anthropologie théologique à la lumière de la psychanalyse*, p.133.

[157] In other words Vergote repeats what Vestdijk had already pointed at: sense of sin leads to disintegration of social life.

[158] A. Vergote, *Religion, Belief and Unbelief*, pp.105-106; A. Vergote, *Bekentenis en begeerte in de religie*, pp.117-118. (The passage on different valuations of desire in Protestantism and Catholicism is lacking in the English translation.)

Sin as guilt before God indicates that in Christian religion sin is related to the acceptance of the Word of the God. We recall Raguse's critique of Vergote (4.4): he declined to clearly define sin in his exegesis of Paul's letter to the Romans. According to Vergote, sin first of all indicates a structural relation between natural man (with his pulsional desires) and God. It is therefore not to be associated with "fault" or "evil". Man cannot blame himself for being "natural", that is to say, man's existence is indefinite, unfinished, not because of the inscription of an original existential (or ontological) fault, but because of a lack (*manque*).

So what about fault and evil? Overlooking Vergote's writings one should say that a rejection of the Name-of-the-Father creates the situation in which the imaginary desires are maintained and aggressively pursued. "There must exist a negative correlation between real aggression and the awareness of guilt." In other words, "the question as to what occurs when guilt feelings are rejected is inevitable".[159] This question is completely in line with Freud's elaborations in *Civilization and its Discontents* or *Moses and Monotheism* on the necessity of a certain amount of a sense of guilt in order to keep civilization intact and make an "advancement in intellectuality" possible.

Does this mean that aggression is thus "evil"? We should be careful here in drawing this conclusion, for as in Raguse's thought, the superego can only resist the urges of the drives with the energy drawn from them. The fact that Vergote associates the rise of aggression in society with secularization seems to indicate that the decisive "evil" is "guilt rejection"[160], i.e. the rejection of the Name-of-the-Father.[161] From this perspective Vergote can consequently state that sin is the unconscious fantasy of narcissistic omnipotence, i.e. auto-divinization.[162] In this way (imaginary) sin is the opposite of (symbolic) guilt, as sin is a rejection of the Name-of-the-Father and guilt accompanies the acceptance of this Name.

Man needs a certain amount of guilt; guilt is normal and to be distinguished from its exaggerated unhealthy forms in the neurotic sense of guilt. In the previous chapter we have seen that in German theology Catholic scholars

---

[159] A. Vergote, *Religion, Belief and Unbelief*, p.106.

[160] Idem.

[161] From a Lacanian perspective this raises a question that Vergote, to my knowledge, has not been able to answer. Lacan interprets psychosis in his 1955-6 seminar entitled *The Psychoses* as a rejection of the name of the father and a continuance of the imaginary order in delusion. In short, the symbolic order doesn't function. Strictly speaking Vergote would have to assume that because of the rejection of the Name-of-the-Father a psychotic cannot be religious. Clinical experience however indicates – Jung and Freud already noticed this – that psychotic delusions are often "religious". This weak spot in Vergote's thought is related of course to the sharp distinction between imaginary and symbolic order, and the key function of the father in between.

[162] J.-B. Lecuit, *L'anthropologie théologique à la lumière de la psychanalyse*, pp.581-585.

emphasized the difference between a healthy and an unhealthy sense of guilt, and plead for the acceptance of a normal sense of guilt in combination with a critical attitude towards narcissism. This scheme can also be detected in Vergote's writings. *Guilt and Desire* with its analyses of healthy and unhealthy forms of religiosity can be situated in the same Catholic tradition of thought on the matter. Despite the fact that normality can hardly be separated from the risk of pathological exaggerations, and that normality is never a lasting blissful state of health and harmony, this study is still about analyzing unhealthy religion in order to establish what is healthy. But like Freud was avoiding generalizations and messages of salvation concerning an optimum of sense of guilt or a balance between Eros and Ananke, Vergote does not present a clear definition of what should be called moderate traditional religion that is able to deal with guilt in an optimal way.

Religious guilt, positively formulated, is part of belief in which the Word of the Father is accepted and the past imaginary "sins of the flesh"[163] can be acknowledged (as belonging to the past) and confessed.[164] However this religious guilt can easily take the neurotic form of exaggerated feelings of guilt as analyzed by "Freud, Hesnard and others".[165] In that case the imaginary sinful desires are seen as a fault for which one is still responsible. One forgets that man by nature is sinful, that man is not by nature a moral or religious being. The acceptance of the Law marks the moment after which such a being can be developed in the cultural domain. Man should thus not be held responsible[166] for being born a "natural" being.[167] Nor is there a primal "fault" as Freud thought in *Totem and Taboo* that could still legitimize a severe superego.[168] In other words, religious guilt is evoked by a religious Law that installs a specific relation between man as subject-who-lacks and his God. This religious guilt cannot be explained solely by a "general human sense of guilt", but psychoanalysis can

---

[163] A. Vergote, "Der Beitrag der Psychoanalyse zur Exegese", p.107.

[164] A. Vergote, *Religion, Belief and Unbelief*, p.101. Confession of sin should not be mistaken for a confession of "shortcomings and mistakes".

[165] A. Vergote, *Religionspsychologie*, p.253.

[166] As to responsibility, in Lacan's view the Law makes us responsible as far as this responsibility is related to our contingent existence. In fact the Law marks the end of a limitless responsibility that is situated in the realm of the imaginary, namely as the "responsibility" to pursue one's desire for the All-mother, or in more concrete terms, as a responsibility for "everything" – which is sometimes found among pastors in what Uleyn called echo-ism or good-samaritism. On this issue see P. Moyaert, *Ethiek en sublimatie. Over "De ethiek van de psychoanalyse" van Jacques Lacan*, SUN, Nijmegen, 1994, pp.139-143.

[167] In a recent study Vergote calls human nature simply *l"humanité de l"homme* as humanity with the spontaneous potential to give birth to "culture", or also refers to this human nature with Heidegger's concept of *Dasein*. A. Vergote, *Humanité de l"homme*, pp.15-16, p.54.

[168] Compare A. Vergote, "Psychoanalyse in contact met religie", p.291.

make apparent why the proclamation of the Word of God can appeal to people as a message that interacts with the experiences that are constitutive for humanity: "the relation between Law, father and desire" and thus also guilt.[169]

In this context belief (or faith) is seen as dynamic, that is, interactive with and in the symbolic order, in the search for integrity, not as ego-integration, but as an eccentric desire for a personal relation with God characterized by love, and a relationship with others in a community (love, responsibility). Belief is dynamic: it is a desire. It is therefore always uncertain and unfinished; modulated by man's psychic life it is conflictual and full of tension.[170] "Faith can only remain alive by constantly renewing itself."[171] The Law that liberates desire from imaginary preoccupations institutes this activity. An important quality of faith is therefore a lack of inhibition, open-mindedness. In an era of severe criticism of religion, also from a psychoanalytic perspective, such faith can best be described as "second naivety".[172] As in the writings of Ricoeur this does not mean a new naivety after the critique of religion is processed, but instead it means an inner critical attitude integrated in personal belief – critical towards imaginary desires to have, to be and to know All. Hence faith implies a consciousness of guilt. In comparison to Lacan who treats symbolic debt and desire as structures without content, Vergote is able to relate these structures with contents in religion: the experience or consciousness of being "guilty", being indebted to God not only because of imaginary sinful desires, but also because of the fact that existence is "given"; the desire in faith towards a love relation with God.

5.3.5   Review

From the above it is clear that Vergote read Freud first of all through Lacan. The basic structures of Lacanian thought are omnipresent in his work and provide the main framework for his interpretation of Freud. But we have also seen another tendency: a critique of Lacan through Freud. Indeed, Vergote made his own *retour à Freud* which enabled him to criticize Lacan especially concerning the unconscious, the body and the psychic structures without content.

We can fairly say that Vergote remains faithful to the central ideas of Freudian thought: the role of the father; the psychical apparatus and pulsional desires (drives); the unconscious (and the thing-representations); the ambivalences of love and hate; narcissism, identification and sense of guilt; sublimation. Reformulations of key issues are made in the light of a critique of Freud's positivism and his pathological views, and – most clearly in the study on sublimation – in the context of articulating the interaction between individual and

---

[169] Idem.

[170] A. Vergote, *Religion, Belief and Unbelief*, chapter 4.

[171] Idem, p.278.

[172] A. Vergote, *Het huis is nooit af*, pp.76-84.

religious symbolic order. Expressed even more strongly, Vergote's theory of sublimation is formulated in such a way that it perfectly precedes the acceptance of the Law of the Father, the "no" of the father. In other words, reconfigurations of Freudian thought are made in the light of a specific notion of faith as acceptance of the Word and conformation to a symbolic order. At this point, we should notice that Vergote focuses on Freud's concept of sublimation as capacity to commit to social values. He thus distances from Lacan who had criticized Freud arguing that he actually presented a theory of adaptation (like in later ego psychology).[173]

The pleasure principle is – in my opinion with good arguments – reformulated. Concerning the symbol and symbolization Vergote follows the revisions already made by others (such as Ricoeur) that criticized Freud's equation of symbol and symptom and formulated alternatives in which the symbol generates new meaning.[174] Vergote's ideas on sublimation are especially noteworthy, because he shows a way out of Freud's deadlocks concerning the issue as caught inbetween a pathological view of culture and a theory of the pleasure principle that cannot account for creativity. The interaction with culture is stressed: culture provides the goals that the sublimated drives can be aimed at in pursuit of satisfaction, or better, happiness. In this line of thought the successful hysteria of Teresa of Avila is more than illustrative. It points towards the possibility for further studies on the interaction in documented mysticism between individual and cultural environment in different eras and denominations.[175]

Another important area of investigation is the role of sublimation in meaning giving (*zingeving*). Vergote himself strongly opposed the leading theories on this issue, but his ideas concerning sublimation can be important for further theoretical thinking on *zingeving*, on the way an individual can structure his or her world. We will return to this matter in the next chapter. Vergote's ideas about sublimation also opens up the possibility of analyzing theological thought as a specific activity of the human mind, as "advancements in intellectuality" that is only possible as the result of sublimations of drives in a religious symbolic order. In other words, Vergote's ideas on sublimation and the interaction of individual psychic motives and religious tradition suggest that in theological thought and in dogmatic formulations one will also find the sublimated drives and psychic motivations expressed in the language of a collective history. One may expect that theological thought not only aims at clarifying issues and concepts by means of pure cognition, but that also other more emotional, primitive

---

[173] J. Lacan, *The Seminar of Jacques Lacan, Book VII*, pp.87-88, pp.94-95.

[174] Idem, p.97, p.505. In *Freud and Philosophy* Ricoeur elaborates on the symbol in Freudian thought from the perspective of his earlier writings on sin, guilt and the symbolism of evil in his double publication *Fallible Man* and *The Symbolism of Evil* from 1960 (originally published as *Philosophie de la volonté. Finitude et culpabilité*).

[175] De Certeau and Saroglou have already provided such analyses, albeit confined to Catholic mysticism.

or even bodily psychic motives are involved.[176] (The same goes *mutatis mutandis* for the influence of various personality types and the specific psychic structuring in the various "pathologies" that will also colour theological thought.)

Vergote's critique of the death drive is justified. As we have already seen, Freud's thoughts on this subject were highly speculative and his call upon biology was questionable – which was already acknowledged by Freud himself. We recall that a specific motivation for formulating this theory was presented by Jungian thought and Freud's preoccupation to formulate a strong fundamental drive dichotomy. From this perspective the concepts of Eros and Thanatos were also the result of a rivalry that incited him to formulate his theories beyond the limits of clinical evidence in answer to Jung's speculative thought. After its introduction in *Beyond the Pleasure Principle* the concept of death drive hardly played a substantial role in Freudian psychoanalysis, because it always remained a speculative psychoanalytic dogma expressing the moral conviction that man is by nature 'evil'.[177] In the debate with Melanie Klein *inter alia* for example it was not an issue. In Freud's clinical writings the death drive remained dumb and could only be presupposed underlying the amalgam of feelings clinical analysis was confronted with.[178] All in al, it seemed to find its clearest expression in the negative therapeutic reaction. Yet here, the question arises whether the death drive is really needed to explain this negative therapeutic reaction, or whether this reaction can also be understood as part of the therapeutic process itself.

Vergote is right when he argues that a counterpoint in a progressive movement does not necessarily presuppose a death drive: the existence of ambivalences of love and hate, the inner conflictual forces related to objects, serve as better alternatives here. From the perspective of the sense of guilt one might even go one step further and argue that the death drive was also introduced as source for a sense of guilt beyond analyzable individual psychic life next to the sense of guilt that was hereditary and could be traced back to a primal historic crime. Especially in his analyses of primary and moral masochism Freud had

---

[176] The often unconscious psychic motives that influence or are expressed in theological thought are the subject in a tradition of psychobiographies in the psychology religion, starting with Pfister's article on the apostle Paul, via, for example, Erikson's study of Luther, until more recent psychobiographies such as William Meissner's study of Ignatius of Loyola.

[177] Geyskens and Van Haute have rightfully argued that the death drive is hardly elaborated upon by Freud in his clinical writings after *Beyond the Pleasure Principle* and that "from a theoretical perspective the death drive is a redundant hypothesis". They argue that the hypothesis of the death drive as a biological hypothesis only distracts from what is a central idea in Freudian thought: the traumatic origin (helplessness) of subjectivity. T. Geyskens, Ph. van Haute, *Van doodsdrift tot hechtingstheorie*, pp.11-15.

[178] For example S. Freud, *The Economic Problem of Masochism*, p.164.

argued that the need for punishment could be interpreted as the outcome of the death drive.[179] Hence, in two directions Freud's search for the origins of the sense of guilt led into speculative thought: the death drive beyond the pleasure principle and the myth of the primal murder.[180] Criticizing Freud's pathological view, his positivism and the genetic explanation of religion implies, in my opinion, focusing on the analysis of the sense of guilt as an element in both the nuclear inner psychic complexes and the interaction of the individual with others, culture and religion. In fact, and in line with Vergote, this would mean focusing on the sense of guilt in its differentiated types, forms and strengths. Of course, this is again also a Freudian train of thought.

Vergote's ideas concerning the libidinal body as a translation of the psychical apparatus unifying body and soul, does credit to Freud's theory of the psychical apparatus and the unconscious as "missing link" between body and consciousness. The Freudian drive-dichotomy is however somewhat eagerly put aside in favour of the concept of pulsional desires. The reason for this specific Freud interpretation is the otherwise needed broad definition of (innate biological/biochemical) infantile sexuality Freud presents in *Three Essays*.

Sublimation is therefore no longer sublimation of the sexual drives but of the pulsional desires. It is no longer a desexualization and therefore no longer an element in the conflict between sexual drives (infantile sexuality) and the demands of culture (adult life). As Moyaert observed Vergote does not want to needlessly dramatize human existence – the individual is not as mentally maladapted to life as Lacan had reasoned. Instead, the pulsional desires evoke positive affirmative experiences of autonomy (absence of the mother) and creativity.[181] In this train of thought, the primacy of infantile sexuality is replaced by the idea of sexuality as a secondary development in the service of procreation. Though this idea seems to be Jungian, Vergote based it on an interpretation of Freud's texts: Freud had argued that sexuality in the service of procreation is only established after the genital organization in narcissism. Vergote argues that there is thus no reason to call (parts of) pre-genital organization "sexual".

I agree with Moyaert that calling drives sexual, libidinal or erotic is partly a nominalistic and thus unimportant issue[182], but Vergote's critique of

---

[179] Idem, pp.163-165.

[180] This movement into speculative thought is clearly linked with the problem of the role of biology in psychoanalysis. Formulating his ideas on the death drive Freud turns to biological theory, and his quest for the origin of the sense of guilt in history is related to the problem of the "biological" inheritance of phylogenetic material. It is hence not surprising that scholars such as Quinodoz who defend Freud's thought on the death drive and on the inheritance of phylogenetic material call upon modern biological theory to plead their case. J.-M. Quinodoz, *Reading Freud*, p.127, p.193.

[181] P. Moyaert, *Begeren en vereren*, pp.84-85.

[182] Idem, p.70.

Freudian infantile sexuality does raise problems. The question that arises is whether Vergote can now still speak meaningfully of sublimation when it is regarded as a transformation of one aim of the drive to another "higher" and yet familiar aim of the same drive. It is not clear what specific aims and which specific drives we are then talking about. In other words, sublimation seems to indicate every transformation to a higher goal. It thus becomes a "vague" concept that not only reminds of Freud's vaguenesses on the issue, but also reminds of Jung's ideas on the innate teleology of the drives.

Another effect of Vergote's idea of sexuality as a secondary development is that the relation between narcissism and further object relations and identifications is also "desexualized". We have seen that in Freudian thought there is continuity in this respect, but in Vergotian thought the distinction between the imaginary, including narcissism, and the symbolic is sharply drawn.

Lastly, there are Vergote's ideas about sublimation and sexuality: how should we now understand the connection between sexuality and religiosity found in for example the exaltations of the successful hysteric Teresa of Avila or the orgiastic piety of Zinzendorf? Not only in cases such as these can the question about the relation between sexuality and religion be raised, but also in a broader perspective the relation between sexuality and the religious symbolic order needs further clarification when it can no longer be related to (failing) sublimation of sexual drives.

As to Freud's view of religion Vergote's critique is severe although the starting point for psychoanalytic interest in religion remains Freudian: "The interest of the Freudian psychoanalysis of religion consists in its forcing us to examine the hidden and obscure motives that may be the fertile soil from which it springs."[183] Besides, Freud is right not to detect the source or essence of religion in oceanic feelings or in speculative thought that is only allegedly detached from human motivations and representations.[184] As a cultural phenomenon however religion can never be separated from such motivations and representations. In spite of this Freud's reduction of religion to imaginary needs in *The Future of an Illusion* is a severe misunderstanding of religion as symbolic order. And his attempts to reconstruct a primal history from which religion could originate, was an unjust attempt to reconstruct culture on the basis of man's nature described in analogy with obsessional neurosis.[185] Again Freud neglected religion as a symbolic order and was unable to explain how culture (including language!) could arise out of a lawless herd and identification with a male ape that had never proclaimed any Law.

---

[183] A. Vergote, "Religion after the Critique of Psychoanalysis", p.22.

[184] A. Vergote, "Psychoanalyse in contact met religie", p.283; A. Vergote, "Het imaginaire en het symbolische in het godsbeeld", in *Tijdschrift voor Theologie* 9 (1973/3), pp.310-327 (314).

[185] A. Vergote, "Religion after the Critique of Psychoanalysis", p.33.

The critique of Freud's pathological view cannot be overlooked here. We have seen that this also plays a role in *Guilt and Desire*. The starting point is not pathology in religion, but normality and its exaggerations. Here also the symbolic order is important: the ultimate difference between healthy and unhealthy religion lies in the fact of whether a certain religiosity is considered normal in a community, or whether it is privatized.

The distinction between the imaginary and symbolic orders enables Vergote to argue that concepts such as self-realization and ego-integration should be considered imaginary situated on the axis of a desire for "All". Religion implies "castration", the acknowledgement of Law and guilt, the decentring of the ego in favour of the Other, a de-auto-divinization. The consequences for such a point of view of pastoral psychology and pastoral care should not be overlooked. Vergote himself made little contribution to this field leaving it for practical theologians.

In my opinion Vergote's thought can be of great interest here, certainly when one considers the fact that his ideas on creativity and his de-dramatizing of Lacan opens up the possibility of a more fruitful dialogue with for example Winnicot's object relations theory. We have seen that in German pastoral psychology, but also in Dutch psychology of religion and mental health, the dominant psychoanalytic theories are still ego psychology and self psychology. Vergote's ideas on the dynamics of desire, guilt and acceptance of the Law that never reaches a continuous harmonious state, and his critique of religious perfectionism, stand in critical contrast to those psychologies and anthropologies that suggest an autonomous individual, capable of ego-integration, having an autonomous conscience and a strong sense of responsibility (as part of a matured personality). The maturation and purification processes are held to be realistic and healthy aims.

From a Freudian perspective – as Vergote would argue – such an autonomous individuality means denying the fundamental nature of man as fallible, "guilty" and desiring, and hence dynamic and creative. It elevates a narcissistic fantasy to the level of a realistic ego ideal. It therefore exaggerates and overrates the possibilities and moral duties of man when it aims at ego-integration and the formation of an autonomous responsible conscience. It also negates the positive functions of aggression, guilt and anxiety, when emphasizing psychic balance. After all, in some pastoral psychologies one finds the idea that such "negative" feelings should be minimalized or even be overcome.

From Vergote's point of view such demands on the religious persons can only increase a neuroticizing effect of religion (as Freud had already argued). In fact, the ideal of ego-integration and self-realization only seems to obstruct true religiosity that is characterized by desire, doubt, guilt and sublimation. In short, healthy religiosity and the formation of a religious personality are dependent upon the acceptance of a Law that says "no" to (moral) perfection or (psychic) totality. The dynamics of faith is not safeguarded by constant growth and maturation, but instead by constant renewal. I will return to this issue in the final chapter.

In Vergote's criticism of Freud's view on religion and in his own ideas on religion in general the symbolic order is the key concept. The differentiation between the imaginary and the symbolic order enables Vergote to define psychology of religion as the study of the interaction between personality and religion avoiding reductionism or psychologism. The imaginary is the realm of motivations, needs, desire for totality, giving meaning and philosophy of life, and the search for the self. Religion is of another, symbolic order. This is Vergote's stronghold, and yet finally, probably also the most problematic issue in his theories. Two elements are inseparable here: the revelation of the Word of God and the symbolic order as an autonomous chain of signifiers or system of signs that gives meaning.

As to the revelation of the Word of God or the word "God" we have already seen that this is an application of Lacan's Name-of-the-Father onto religion. The fact that Vergote equates Word of God with word "God" is a clear indication that – as in Lacanian thought – the Word is above all a function, namely that of "castration": the response to the word "God" should be "Yes, you are and I am not".

Pattyn has rightfully argued that it is hard to see what content this Word has. It only appears in its function of opening up a symbolic order in which signs and meaning are inseparable. An immediate interpersonal relation with this "God" seems to be impossible and a structural dialogical relation between ego and Thou is without content.[186]

In addition to Pattyn's critique I would add that the word "God" as function without content does signify an authority that has to be accepted. But how is this authority transmitted? Vergote's emphasis on God's auto-revelation veils an issue that has always been important in Christian religion and that also seems to be of importance in modern religiosity: the authority of religious leaders. Vergote has hardly elaborated upon religious leadership whereas in different religious and spiritual movements the interaction between individual and "religious symbolic order" is mediated by authority figures and spiritual guides. In other words, Vergote treats the Name-of-the-Father as if it has a constant unchangeable meaning whereas the study of interaction between individual and religion should also try to get a grip on changing social-cultural contexts including various types of religious leadership mediating the divine.[187]

---

[186] B. Pattyn, "Wie zal morgen uitmaken wat onzin is?", pp.347-348.

[187] Saroglou presents the example of the abba in early Christian monasticism who is regarded a spiritual guide presenting "the image of Christ" with whom the monks should identify. V. Saroglou, *Paternity as Function*, p.123. In a totally different context I have described the minister in early 17th century orthodox Calvinism who is regarded an au-

The symbolic order as an autonomous chain is an "objective cultural phenomenon", a "network of enunciations about supernatural and/or divine beings, of ethics, of prayers and of symbolic signs and acts, through which man enters into a life relationship with the divine". Religious meaning is safeguarded here by defining religion as a structural language system. But can we still speak of religion as such a system in an age of secularization? It is striking that Vergote's religious material is either derived from Catholic folk religion or mystic tradition, i.e. examples of what Paul Heelas calls "the traditional self that is still embedded in the established order of things", that is, "the tradition-informed ways of life".[188] But what about modern "bricolaged" religiosity or spirituality that can hardly be called a structural language system or an established order of things? Poblems arise not only here but also when thinking about acceptance of the Word and about tradition. What about the early Christians such as the apostle Paul, or Luther and early Protestant believers: did they also accept a pre-given autonomous religious system? What about for example the 16th-century iconoclastic fury: was it a religious fury or actually an act of unbelief? What if parts of religious symbolic order are rejected? Strictly speaking in Vergote's line of thought we would have to say that in such cases one can no longer speak of religion. In his debate with Van der Lans on giving meaning this is actually stated, and in his statements about imaginary "belief" also. One "accepts" religion as symbolic order, or not. There seems to be no in-between.

So how should we assess this concept of religion as symbolic order? First of all, there is the problem of entering this symbolic order through the Word of God. Vergote's attempts to set religion free from the dangers of any psychologism and reductionism, is the main motive for strongly emphasizing the role of revelation.[189] The construct is thus that through divine revelation religion as a cultural order is established. It is the "soul and source" of religion repeated again and again in a performative speech act ("I am") and in response an individual's confession ("I believe"). In his elaborations on the history of religions this is confirmed: at the root of religion is man's encounter with a divinity that reveals himself. In emphasizing the non-human origin of religion Vergote goes thus beyond the limit of the neutrality of psychology of religion and

---

thority, because in his sermons he is not proclaiming the Word himself, but actually only mediating it: the minister is an "angel", "God's mouth to the people", not speaking with his own daily voice, but channelling a godly voice. H. Westerink, *Met het oog van de ziel. Een godsdienstpsychologische en mentaliteitshistorische studie naar mensvisie, zelfonderzoek en geloofsbeleving in het werk van Willem Teelinck (1579-1629)*, Uitgeverij Boekencentrum, Zoetermeer, 2002, chapter 3.

[188] P. Heelas, *New Age Movement. The Celebration of the Self and the Sacralization of Modernity*, Blackwell, Oxford, 1996, p.155.

[189] Compare A. Vergote, *Religion, Belief and Unbelief*, pp.16ff. Vergote indicates that religion as reference to the supernatural first of all indicates that religion does not belong to the realm of nature or human agency.

psychoanalysis in actually presenting an apologetics of revelation. After all, this neutrality implied not making claims on the essence or source of religion and this could only be safeguarded by examining religion strictly as an "observable phenomenon".[190]

But this is not the only problem. Religion is regarded by Vergote as an "entity in the cultural tradition"[191], a cultural phenomenon. Yet he does propose that we enter this cultural phenomenon in a specific way, not through the general function of the Name-of-the-Father introducing the child in the symbolic order, but, by analogy, through the acceptance of the Word of God. Pattyn has rightfully argued that Vergote thus suggests that a religious meaning system can be distinguished from other cultural meaning systems, whereas from a Lacanian point of view the distinction between religious and non-religious symbols and signs cannot be made.[192] In Vergote's view the supernatural source and soul of religion make it a "cultural" phenomenon that as entity should actually be distinguished from other cultural phenomena. And yet, from his definition of religion as a cultural phenomenon such a distinction cannot be made.

When we take Vergote's own starting point and definitions as our starting point these problems might actually be overcome. Religion is a network of enunciations about supernatural and/or divine beings, of ethics, of prayers and of symbolic signs and acts, through which man enters into a life relationship with the divine. It is a cultural phenomenon. As to the essence or source of this cultural phenomenon psychoanalysis and psychology of religion remain neutral. We need not reduce religion to human motivations, needs or ideas, and we need not point out that the source and soul of religion is supernatural. The psychology of religion studies the interaction of personality with religion; psychoanalysis has much to reveal about personality. Concerning the nature of religion the psychology of religion depends on religious sciences. Regarding religion a cultural phenomenon that cannot be considered as of a different nature than other cultural phenomena or distinguished from non-religious symbols and signs, we should reconsider Vergote's view of religion as revealed symbolic order.

In Lacanian psychoanalysis the symbolic order is an autonomous cultural meaning system of signifiers. It functions independently of human nature or physicality. It precedes the individual and the child has to be "introduced" into it. The symbolic order is not something from which one can freely distance oneself or from which one can pick elements. (Distance or choice would only indicate a

[190] Idem, p.27
[191] Idem, p.21. Vergote adopts the anthropologist Clifford Geertz' famous definition of religion: "religion is a system of symbols which acts to establish powerful, pervasive and long-lasting moods and motivations in man by formulating conceptions of a general order of existence, and clothing these conceptions with such an aura of factuality that the moods and motivations seem uniquely realistic".
[192] B. Pattyn, "Verlangen, ervaring en openbaring", p.397.

specific position in the symbolic order.) When it is not rejected (like in psycho-sis) the symbolic order will constitute the subject's relation with reality, namely through language instead of through "real" and imaginary objects. Vergote as-sumes that religious reality is constituted analogously. In other words, the Word of God and religion as symbolic order constitute a supernatural reality, i.e. an-other reality also constituted by language.

Thus we seem to have two realities – cultural and supernatural – both constituted by language. When we proceed from the argument presented above, that religion is a cultural phenomenon in a cultural meaning system and that within the order of language (in Lacanian thought) a distinction between reli-gious and non-religious signs and symbols cannot be made, we will also have to conclude that two language systems constituting different realities cannot exist next to each other. To put it simply: there is only one symbolic order. Religion as cultural phenomenon is part of this. This is important for now we don't have to deal with religion as an autonomous system anymore, but can also study its interaction with other cultural phenomena and deal with the fact that some peo-ple creatively construct their own world views including religious elements.

Lacan's view about the symbolic order primarily indicates that there is no other way for an individual to express its identity than in a symbolic way. One might say that this calls for an acceptance, but such an acceptance should not be interpreted in terms of confirmation or obedience. It is not an affirmation of or submission to a tradition – Vergote would certainly agree to that. It is only the "acceptance" to express identity in a symbolic language that – so to speak – has a history.

So how is identity constituted? Not through acceptance itself, but through identification with what Lacan called *traits unaires*, i.e. a subject iden-tifies with single traits from the person who is object (after the example of Freud's hysterics in *Group Psychology* who contaminate each other with the same symptom).[193] The child first of all identifies with a specific name (the family Name-of-the-Father) and through that with the history and future expec-tations related to that name, but also with specific physical traits. As in Freudian thought this provides the model for future identifications. (I will not repeat my earlier elaborations on this issue.)

As we have already seen, the symbolic order is not something a subject can either take a distance or freely pick elements from; it cannot be possessed or controlled – neurotics try, but fail. Identity in Lacanian thought is always re-lated to an "otherness" from which one is alienated, and the desire that ema-nates from this is never one's own, but always also the desire of someone else. Identity is thus not the formulation of a true self preferably grounded in a real past experience ("This is who I am, because of that") or seen as the final sta-dium of a personal maturation process ("I have fully realized myself"), but by

---

[193] J. Lacan, *L'identification. Séminaire 1961-1962*, Éditions de l'Association Freu-dienne Internationale, Publication hors commerce, Paris, 2000, pp.61ff.

adopting a specific position among the possibilities provided by a certain culture.[194] It is only in a cultural context and in relation to others that people can develop an identity that is their own. This is only partly a matter of conscious choice.

Culture thus appears as providing possibilities in which one positions oneself. This calls for a religion (as part of culture) that doesn't enforce itself in an authoritarian way – the outdated superego obedience character of religion as criticized by Scharfenberg *inter alia*. It calls for a religion that is instead authoritative, by which I mean to indicate a religion that incites a process of critical thinking, of personal involvement as well as critical distance, that presents a symbolic field in which an individual can position himself and through which he can enter into a personal relationship with the divine. This is possible because religion is a cultural phenomenon consisting of authoritative elements that are interrelated but also distinct. The authoritative character of religion is based on its history, on its tradition which should not primarily be associated with (paternal) authority and obedience, but with knowledge.[195] Positioning oneself in a tradition means acknowledging that tradition is consciously and unconsciously "constitutive of our very being-in-the-world" and that in a critical dialogue with tradition self-knowledge can be achieved.

In this way tradition is what I would call (paraphrasing Lacan) *tradition supposé savoir*: it is supposed to know who we are. This is the dominant issue in *Moses and Monotheism*, not only in Freud's view of the apostle Paul and his self-knowledge derived from a critical dialogue with Jewish tradition, but also when we consider this study to be a critical dialogue of Freud with Judaism and Christianity as the two religious traditions in his cultural environment. It is in religious tradition that one finds the "historic truth" about oneself. We can only understand ourselves when we interpret our history. Here we find the Freudian analogy between psychoanalytic practice, autobiographical study, and the analysis of culture and religion. And it is exactly because of this analogy that we can understand Freud's fascination with the sense of guilt in religious tradition as the dark trace towards truth, as in psychoanalytic practice.

In view of this, symbolization should not only be defined as the capacity to say "no" against the imaginary and the first "acceptance" of the father and culture, but also associated with the capacity – though in a limited way – to creatively combine elements of religion in order to position oneself. Religious tradition is not only something in which one is "planted", but also something against someone can develop their own identity. Socialization is not only a process of acceptance, but also of critical evaluation. It is saying "yes" and "no" as far as one can (consciously) say "yes" and "no" in a specific cultural context.

---

[194] P. Vandermeersch, *Unresolved Questions in the Freud/Jung Debate*, p.261.

[195] Here I follow Bernstein and his interpretation of the concept of tradition. R.J. Bernstein, *Freud and the Legacy of Moses*, pp.58-64.

From that position a personal relation (from a subject-who-lacks) with the divine can be developed.

In my view, this is exactly what Freud admired in the apostle Paul: his capacity to creatively give new meaning to religion in a specific cultural context with limited possibilities in the interplay of remembering, repeating and working through. The rediscovery of the repressed was his "advancement in intellectuality", being part of a collective identity and yet also capable of making a personal creative difference. It was a "yes" towards religion and Jewish identity and yet also a "no" against nuclear characteristics of that tradition.

Free critical thinking is limited. Assmann's theory of cultural memory shows convincingly that cultural memory is embodied in a cultural system that consists of texts, symbols, images, rituals, and that shows that identity is embedded in participation in and interaction with cultural collective processes. The idea of cultural memory does not express that being embedded in a cultural system implies acceptance of the full system or even obedience to authority. Cultural memory does not correspond with "visible" tradition, for it functions unconsciously. In cultural memory elements can be repressed and forgotten, or exaggerated and stressed, creating ruptures, conflicts, revolutions and restorations in tradition/society. In the collective archive some material is obliterated, other material rediscovered. In this sense a society is what it remembers. The individual raised in society will become a participant when he identifies with a role or place in this cultural context. At this point there is no need to reject the function of the father and the meaning of the Oedipus complex as elaborated upon by Freud, Lacan and Vergote. Identification introduces the individual into the realm of cultural memory, its dynamics of remembering and forgetting, and the ongoing process of constructing collective identity from past material. On an individual level this socialization means that there will be an interaction between already formed psychic structures and unconscious cultural memory-traces.

This process of socialization and identification with elements of cultural memory raises the question of how the interaction between individual and cultural memory is mediated. What happens to the interaction of personality and religion when traditional "rational" dogmatics is no longer acceptable? Does it also imply that underlying unconscious cultural memory-traces stop functioning? Does a critique of specific paternal structures in religion imply that guilt is no longer a factor of importance?

At this point I agree with Freud, Lacan and Vergote that one needs to consider the role of the father and the Oedipus complex in its function of structuring identity. One is initiated into culture via the dynamics of the first identifications and object choices, i.e. the parental figures. These provide the basic model for later identifications and object choices. Hence when we study bricolaged modern religiosity, religious meaning giving or also fundamentalism – a religious phenomenon that seems strongly characterized by both an overemphasis and rejection of elements of traditional religion – we should focus on the way individuals construct their relation with cultural reality and tradition, and vice versa on the way culture/religion establishes moods, motivations, representations and behaviour in individuals and groups. The psychology of religion focuses not only on the way people give ultimate meaning or construct a philosophy of life in the sphere of the private existential self-transcendence Van der Lans speaks of, it also focuses on the role of "parental" figures that still seem important the initiation into religion in a post-modern era, and the interaction with authoritative cultural and religious phenomena. Herein lies the advantage of the theory of cultural memory, that it can do justice to unconscious memory-traces that work through over long periods of time.

As to guilt and the sense of guilt: we have seen that guilt in religion has often been associated with outdated traditional forms of religion or superseded superego structures. When we take Vergote's starting point as ours that guilt is a part of human psychic structure, as a counter point of desire and related to a specific identity in the symbolic order, and Assmann's theory of cultural memory, we should be careful to simply situate a guilt problem in a past guilt culture or formulate models in which guilt is to be resolved. In German theology there is a tendency to start from the idea that a culture of guilt belongs to the past, that our society is "fatherless" and that we live in a culture of narcissistic self-realization. This is often substantiated referring to the critique of the God-father image and more importantly to the decline of the classic authority figures that enforced obedience (family father, minister, priest). But does this decline mean that the father function[196] is less important, or should we also assume that authority can take different shapes and is differently transmitted. In an era in which the dominant discourse is about self-realization, and in which man is supposed to be autonomous and responsible, the question is: Who tells us and how are we told that we should realize ourselves?; Who provides the models and ideals, and how? And even if individuals could autonomously direct their own self-realization, every ego ideal sets a norm, and every norm incites guilt. From the perspective of Assmann we should also take into account cultural memory. The conscious rejection of superego obedience from the 1960s on does not imply a necessary break with the unconscious cultural memory-traces and structures that work through over long periods of time, certainly not when the danger of a guiltless disintegrated society evokes a new interest in religion in its function of guaranteeing social coherence.

In Vergote's thought (imaginary) sin and (symbolic) guilt can certainly not be equated, but are in a sense opposed. This is important for in current discussions

---

[196] With the concept of father function I refer to Lacan's thought on the Name-of-the-Father. With it I mean to indicate that the father is not primarily the physical biological father or father figure, but a function in the structuring of psychic life, here more concretely, in the structuring of religiosity and in pointing towards the divine.

on the necessity of guilt or sense of guilt in civilization (and religion), one of the major problems is the immediate association of the concept with discourse on sin (and related dogmatic issues such as reconciliation or atonement), i.e. an association with supposedly outdated theology. This fact alone makes it difficult to discuss guilt. There is an apparent unease with the subject, not only in the Netherlands, but also in German pastoral psychology. In for example Lauret's study on guilt experience this unease can be seen: his Lacanian view on imaginary conflicts and symbolic identity does not imply an acknowledgement of symbolic debt. At that point he turns to ego psychology in order to argue that guilt can be resolved. Scharfenberg's ambivalence towards a debate on the guilt problem could also be interpreted as unease with the subject. But this unease with a burdened issue – an unease that often takes the form of silence – does not mean that the subject is of no importance.

It would instead be interesting to ask where and how the human guilt mechanism is activated in contemporary religious belief and practice to evoke or/and canalize the sense of guilt: in the concentration on personal responsibility and conscience formation in faith[197]; in the idealization of a religious leader (guru, charismatic leader); in the debt to oneself to strive for religious perfection or ego-integration or ultimate meaning; in the debt to a pastor who with his empathetic attitude or good-samaritanism desperately desires his congregation to be religious and to engage in activities; in political discourse on the foundations of Western culture or in the deprivatization of religion and the attempts to regain moral influence in the public domain[198]; in still not superseded discussions on sexuality and family politics in religious discourse[199]; in the personal ritual commemorations (shrines, monuments) surrounding deceased loved ones – after all, they only live in memory which constrains us to remember them; in the crisis of identity of immigrants torn between cultures; in the "bad conscience" of ex-believers who broke with the superseded superego structures of the religion of their childhood...

---

[197] This issue cannot be limited to the realm of literature in pastoral psychology as we have discussed this so far. In Protestant evangelical literature there is a clear tendency to revive the aspect of guilt and sense of guilt in the context of reviving the "core message" of Christianity/the bible on sin and salvation. A recent example is T. Schirrmacher, *Scham- oder Schuldgefühl. Die christliche Botschaft angesichts von schuld- und schamorientierten Gewissen und Kulturen*, Verlag für Kultur und Wissenschaft, Bonn, 2005.

[198] See J. Casanova, *Public Religions in the Modern World*, University of Chicago Press, Chicago/London, 1994.

[199] This is not only an issue concerning traditional Catholic and Protestant positions with regards to sexuality (for example homosexuality), but it should also be noticed that in the evangelical movement (Christian fundamentalism) sexual guilt feelings are played upon. M. Argyle, *Psychology and Religion. An Introduction*, Routledge, London/New York, 2000, p.183.

5.3.6   Influence

As to the influence of Vergote on Belgian and Dutch psychology of religion, there are several students and sympathizers working in the psychology of religion and philosophy. Given the fact that in Leuven psychoanalytic approaches were combined with empirical research it is almost obvious that not all of Vergote's students continued in the field of psychoanalysis. Those who did however have some common traits: a *retour à Freud* influenced by Lacan; further elaboration in fields of attention present in Vergote's work.

One of the issues in which a *retour à Freud* can be noticed are discussions on psychotherapy in relation to pastoral care. Jozef Corveleyn (1948-) has argued that concerning religion and philosophy of life a psychologist should be neutral.[200] This neutrality, which Corveleyn calls his *retour à Freud*, implies a critique of those therapies (especially in America) that eagerly integrate spirituality. "A psychologist maybe explores the psyche, but he does not look into the soul." He may help a client to liberate his religious desires. He doesn't have to hinder a spiritual quest, but he should not show the way.[201] The pastor does not have this neutrality nor should he. He is a religious guide who works in the field of the religious.[202] His task is to strengthen the relation between the believer and the divine, a symbolic relation characterized by affectivity (desire).[203] Also, the pastor connects the believer to a community and thus prevents "egocentric self-relatedness".[204] (In these qualifications one clearly sees a Vergotian line of thought reflected.)

Harry Stroeken's[205] main subject throughout his career was the issue of psychotherapy.[206] Concerning Freudian psychotherapy Stroeken has observed that psychoanalysis has much in common with tragedy: both only unveil what has happened, one's role and position in the chain of events. Not without reason the first adjective of therapy was "cathartic", a term derived from tragedy indi-

---

[200] J. Corveleyn, *De psycholoog kijkt niet in de ziel. Thema's uit de klinische godsdienstpsychologie*, KSGV, Tilburg, 2003, p.13, p.22.
[201] Idem, p.28.
[202] Idem, p.65.
[203] Idem, p.68.
[204] Idem, p.71.
[205] Stroeken (1940-) cannot be called a student of Vergote *strictu sensu*, although he took his doctoral degree in Leuven (1978), but can be considered a sympathizer. Given the two large traditions in psychology of religion in the Netherlands (Fortmann and Vergote), Stroeken should at first sight be labelled independent. His writings in psychoanalysis and theology though show clear familiarities with Vergote, albeit that in his style Stroeken is less straightlined and "philosophical".
[206] For example in H. Stroeken, *Kleine psychologie van het gesprek*, Uitgeverij Boom, Amsterdam/Meppel, 1988.

cating that one has to learn to live with one's identity.[207] When the patient is able to do so, one can speak of "cure". From this assessment Stroeken is able to elaborate on the differences between therapist and pastor. He stresses the fact that a pastor is situated in a community of believers and not in the neutral setting of therapy. The therapist offers "cure"; the pastor offers "care". Ultimate questions about the meaning of life (and their expression in religious discourse and rituals) can be discussed in therapy, but they cannot be answered. They are principally related to a world view or religion. Here, we see a differentiation of realms that resembles Corveleyn's.[208]

In the writings of Patrick Vandermeersch (1946-) there is a clear focus on issues such as the integration of Freudian psychoanalysis into the psychology of religion and the denominational aspects and theological perspectives that colour the reception of specific psychoanalytic theories. According to Vandermeersch, psychoanalysis and the psychology of religion are both rooted in a cultural history that is, for an important part, shaped and coloured by the Reformation and Counter-Reformation. Hence, psychoanalysts and psychologists of religion should always be aware of the hermeneutical circle they are involved in: their specific perspectives originate from a specific cultural history; their theories are historically entangled with the religious subjects they want to study. (This implies an awareness of often hidden normative aspects in seemingly neutral theories – this questioning of normativity is another major aspect in his work.[209]) An example is Lacan's fascination for mystique and De Certeau's observation of the historic kinship of Lacanian thought with modern mystique.[210] At this point

---

[207] H. Stroeken, *Zoeken naar zin: psychotherapie en existentiële vragen*, Uitgeverij Boom, Amsterdam, 1999, pp.86ff.

[208] A clear and sharp distinction between the role of the psychologist and the pastor is important in practical theology or pastoral psychology. In the Rogerian tradition however and also in some other contemporary literature on pastoral care a clear distinction between therapist and pastor is neglected, and a therapeutic discourse is preferred to describe pastoral relations. For example Chr. Morgenthaler, *Systemische Seelsorge. Impulse der Familien- und Systemtherapie für die kirchliche Praxis*, Verlag Kohlhammer, Stuttgart, 1999, p.161, pp.167-168. One speaks of "client" or "patient" to indicate that both in therapy and religion the same ideals are at stake, such as autonomy, freedom, responsibility and a capacity to be involved in social relations. In those cases therapeutic neutrality is suggested and at the same time undermined by the simple fact that as pastor one cannot be neutral to religion – one is part of the religious community representing religious tradition. In such a situation clarity is both an advantage – as well as an ethical obligation, I would add – for the pastor and his "client".

[209] For example P. Vandermeersch, *Het gekke verlangen. Psychotherapie en ethiek*, De Nederlandsche Boekhandel, Antwerpen/ Dekker & Van de Vegt, Nijmegen, 1978.

[210] M. de Certeau, *Heterologies*, pp.36-37. Another example is Erikson's ideas on basic trust that seem to originate from a Protestant cultural background in which faith is defined in terms of trust, the application of the ideas on basic trust in a study of the young man Luther, and the positive reception of Erikson's work among Protestant theologians.

Vandermeersch explores an area that had already been recognized by Vergote: the denominational differences that are expressed in for example different views on guilt or human desire, and different practices surrounding these issues.[211]

Another major line of interest in Vandermeersch' writings is the problem with the human body and sexuality in religion, philosophy and psychoanalysis. Here we recall Vergote's emphasis on the libidinal body undoing the Cartesian dualistic view of body and soul, and his statement that Lacan has a problem with the body. Vandermeersch' studies of Christian views on (sexual) desire, its disciplination but also its acceptability in certain types of religious behaviour (for example in mystic exaltation), and his major study of religious flagellation show that the body was repressed in modern philosophy but also maintained its fundamental role in specific religious practices that are likely to be regarded as pathological, because they don't fit the profile of enlightened modern thought.[212] The question that arises here is whether in an age of secularization and post-modernism characterized by the decomposition of theological and philosophical thought systems, the body will return as an important *locus* for religious experience. In fact, in much of modern spirituality this seems to be the case. Although from a seemingly different perspective this is in line with Vergote's ideas on the symbolization by the libidinal body.

Paul Moyaert (1952-), a philosopher in the field of philosophical anthropology and phenomenology, has over the years shown a clear interest in (Lacanian) psychoanalysis and religion. In his 1998 study on the excessiveness of Christianity an issue is taken up that was also discussed by Vergote: the mystic exaltations of Teresa of Avila. [213] Moyaert is particularly interested in this mystique because it provides a good perspective on discussing psychoanalytically distinctive mechanisms and concepts such as idealization, sublimation, identification, being in love, love and desire. The distinctions and relationships between idealization and sublimation are then elaborated upon in yet another monograph. In that study Moyaert discusses at length Vergote's study of sublimation.[214] In general he is inspired Vergote's line of thought, but he criticizes the equation of symbolization and sublimation. The issue of symbolization, finally, is further elaborated upon in a 2007 study on icons and idolatry. Moyaert situates himself in the tradition of Van der Leeuw and his view on the symbol as

---

P. Vandermeersch, "Psychologische lagen in het geloven. Opgraafwerk van een analyticus", in *Tijdschrift voor Theologie* 38 (1999/4), pp.381-407.

[211] A. Vergote, *Religion, Belief and Unbelief*, pp.105-106; A. Vergote, *Bekentenis en begeerte in de religie*, pp.117-118.

[212] P. Vandermeersch, *Passie en beschouwing. De christelijke invloed op het westerse mensbeeld*, Uitgeverij Peeters, Leuven, 1988; P. Vandermeersch, *La chair de la passion. Une histoie de foi: la flagellation*, Éditions du Cerf, Paris, 2002.

[213] P. Moyaert, *De mateloosheid van het Christendom. Over naastenliefde, betekenisincarnatie en mystieke liefde*, SUN, Nijmegen, 1998, part III.

[214] P. Moyaert, *Begeren en vereren*, chapter 2.

the coincidence of two realities (image and divine) and idolatry as symbolic practice.[215] Central in this study is Moyaert's discussion of the Old Testament prohibition against making an image of God which is traced back to a fear of intimacy with God – the image lacks distance. Opposed to a strict prohibition on idolatry (such as in Protestantism) he pleas for a revaluation of idolatry in Christianity as an expression of the "mystic truth" that believers desire the physical nearness of God.

Vergote's critique of Van der Lans' approaches and ideas on giving ultimate meaning, resound in the writings of Stroeken. Concerning this issue he argues that meaning in life is not about the dynamics of needs and satisfaction, but centres around limitation and desire, i.e. the dynamics of distance and love. In this scheme the focus is not on the individual pursuing an ego ideal out of a need, but on the subject-who-lacks and its desire for the other/Other. Hence, desires are embedded in an inter-subjective structure of recognition of love.[216] In this context the human body is a "medium for meaning" and a source for pleasure. Here, meaning in life is also defined in terms of participation, albeit not as imaginary participation in a totality, but as involvement in personal relations between subjects. A crucial element here is distance; desire presupposes distance between the subject and the desired. This distance is created in and through the father function; the relation to oneself, others, the world or the divine can only be mediated through language.

Inspired by Vergote and Uleyn psychoanalytic text interpretation has become a field of interest in both the writings of Vandermeersch[217] and Stroeken. In both their contributions a critique of Drewermann can be noticed and a certain *retour à Freud* is advocated. In a study on psychoanalytic interpretations of biblical texts Stroeken[218], for example, takes up Uleyn's differentia-

---

[215] P. Moyaert, *Iconen en beeldverering*, 2007, p17. Van der Leeuw had defined the symbol as "the participation of the Holy with its actual [profane, sensible, H.W.] form", as for example in Eucharist where wine "is" blood. G. van der Leeuw, *Phänomenologie der Religion*, p.425. As to Van der Leeuw, Moyaert points out that Vergote should be situated in a tradition of phenomenology of religion given the fact that, like in Van der Leeuw's thought, Vergote's ideas on the interaction between individual and religion basically circle around man's capacity to symbolize and to be sensitive for symbols. P. Moyaert, *De mateloosheid van het Christendom*, p.101.

[216] H. Stroeken, *Zoeken naar zin*, pp.32-36. Compare H. Stroeken, *Het geloof is er voor de mens*, Uitgeverij Ambo, Baarn, 1995, pp.64-75.

[217] See for example P. Vandermeersch, "Where Will the Water Stick? Considerations of a Psychoanalyst about the Stories of the Flood", in F. Garcia Martinez, G. Luttikhuizen (eds.), *Interpretations of the Flood*, Brill, Leiden, 1998, pp.167-193; R. Kessler, P. Vandermeersch (eds.), *God, Biblical Stories and Psychoanalytical Understanding*, Peter Lang, Frankfurt, 2001.

[218] J. Smit, H. Stroeken, *Lotgevallen. De bijbel in psychoanalytisch perspectief*, Boom, Amsterdam, Meppel, 1993.

tion between four perspectives in psychoanalytic reading in the Bible (character analysis of biblical figures; author analysis; text analysis; reader-response analysis) as the methodological starting point. One of the texts analysed by Stroeken is the story of the Fall (Gn. 2-3). He is critical about Drewermann's reading of the text and prefers to regard the story as a reflection on *conditio humana* described in a series of separations that mark the process of individuation.[219]

As to the issue of the sense of guilt Vergote's *Guilt and Desire* had a major influence on further elaborations on this topic. Vandermeersch has shown an interest in the issue especially in the light of the influence of Reformation and Counter-Reformation differentiations in guilt and in the practices surrounding the issue. Related to this is his interest in various types of faith/religiosity attached to various personality structures. Vergote's ideas on obsessional neurotic and hysteric faith serves as an important inspiration for further elaborations especially concerning psychotic and paranoiac personality structures and faith.[220]

In a short text by Stroeken on the sense of guilt the influence of Vergote is evident.[221] Stroeken defines guilt as the conflict between "act/desire and norm/ideal". This guilt is often hidden – unconscious as in Freudian thought – in other psychic formations such as for example narcissistic ideals, or underlying physical complaints. Here, Stroeken prefers to speak of guilt (instead of the sense of guilt) by which he means to indicate healthy guilt. This guilt is inevitable for two reasons. Firstly, it is part of *conditio humana*, i.e. the recognition that human nature is limited and imperfect. Secondly, it indicates a structural conflict between act/desire and norm/ideal that results from a normal psychic development. These two perspectives are a combination of Uleyn's and Vergote's views on the matter. Recognition of this guilt is important, for guilt corresponds with responsibility, that is to say, being responsible for one's acts and desires and thus being able to participate in inter-subjective relations. Such healthy guilt recognition can be distinguished from unhealthy forms of the sense of guilt. At this point Stroeken not only refers to the Catholic tradition with its culpabilization of the human (sexual) drives (calling upon Vergote's ideas on collective neurosis), but also refers to Van Scheyen's and Schilder's elaborations on the unhealthy sense of guilt in Protestantism. In view of the association

---

[219] This line of thought is mainly inspired by the work of Françoise Dolto who worked closely together with Lacan.

[220] P. Vandermeersch, *Het voetstuk van het weten. Over psychologie, psychoanalyse en theologie*, SUN, Nijmegen, 1992, p.18. A recent publication in this line of research is a dissertation on mourning and giving meaning among schizophrenic patients: H. Muthert, *Verlies en verlangen. Verliesverwerking bij schizofrenie*, Uitgeverij Van Gorcum, Assen, 2007.

[221] H. Stroeken, *Het geloof is er voor de mens*, pp.52-63.

of sin and guilt, Stroeken remarks that the positive function of guilt was lost from sight in both Catholicism and Protestantism.

Like Vergote Corveleyn combines psychoanalytic theory and empirical research, for example in a large research project in Leuven focusing on guilt and shame in different cultural contexts. In this project, that is still running, different perspectives including psychoanalytic theory are integrated.[222]

In the bibliographies of the psychologists of religion Vandermeersch, Corveleyn and Stroeken, one finds publications in psychoanalysis. Corveleyn for example wrote on the Lacanian ego ideal and the Freudian unconscious.[223] Vandermeersch wrote a major study on the Freud/Jung debate[224], and articles on, for example, narcissism.[225] Stroeken's major publications for the larger part consist of writings in psychoanalysis.[226]

5.4 Conclusion

Considering the fact that the next chapter provides an assessment of the topics and theories as discussed, I will confine myself here to a few observations. The most obvious one is: all scholars discussed in this chapter are Catholic. In chapter 3 we have seen how Vestdijk (a "Protestant") opened up a field of attention concerning a psychological approach to religion in which psychoanalytic perspectives were integrated: projection, sin and guilt, sexuality, intolerance, religious personality typology. From these topics only the issue of projection was taken up and heavily debated. Sierksma defended Vestdijk *and* his own position against Van der Leeuw, calling upon Freudian notions, but without further developing a psychology of religion in which the other issues of Vestdijk's essay could be taken up.

The issue of the sense of guilt was thus lost sight of among Protestant scholars, only to reappear in the writings of Van Scheyen and especially Schil-

---

[222] See for example P. Luyten, J. Corveleyn, J. Fontaine, "schuld en schaamte en de relatie tussen religiositeit en geestelijke gezondheid", in J. Janssen, M.H.F. van Uden, H. van der Ven (eds.), *Schering en inslag*, pp.32-51; J. Fontaine, J. Corveleyn, P. Luyten, et al., "Untying the Gordian Knot of Guilt and Shame. The Structure of Guilt and Shame Reactions", in *Journal for Cross-Cultural Psychology* 2006, 37, pp.273-292.
[223] J. Corveleyn, "Het onbewuste"; B. Vervliet, P. Luyten, J. Corveleyn, "Ik-ideaal en ideaal-ik. Een lacaniaanse benadering", in *Tijdschrift voor Psychoanalyse* 2002/3, pp.173-186.
[224] P. Vandermeersch, *Unresolved Questions in the Freud/Jung Debate.*
[225] P. Vandermeersch, "Het narcisme. De psychoanalytische theorie en haar lotgevallen"
[226] Examples of publications in the field of psychoanalysis are H. Stroeken, *Freud en zijn patienten*, Nijmegen, Stichting Te Elfder Ure, 1985; H. Stroeken, *Psychoanalytisch woordenboek*, Uitgeverij Boom, Amsterdam/Meppel, 1994 (2000, 2008); H. Stroeken, *Dromen. Brein en betekenis*, Uitgeverij Boom, Amsterdam, 2005.

der. What these scholars have in common is a severely negative view of guilt and sin in religion. Especially Schilder's attack on sick-making guilt structures in Protestantism caused a stir *and* embarrassment about a Reformed tradition in which the concept of sin was traditionally predominant. Lootsma is right in this respect: the issue of the sense of guilt was only associated with negative aspects of the Reformed faith tradition, and thus the issue was preferably avoided. In this respect Dutch history shows up resemblances with developments in German theology, where after all a fundamental debate on the "guilt problem" – apart from individual studies – did not take place.

Catholic scholars, standing in a tradition of differentiating between healthy and unhealthy sense of guilt, had less difficulty elaborating on the issue of guilt and the sense of guilt. With the exception of Fortmann and his followers – we have discussed the reasons – these scholars saw no problem in calling upon Freudian psychoanalysis. In effect, not only the "actual structuralizing processes in religion", as Vergote called it, could be studied from a Freudian perspective, but also a more thorough interpretation of Freud's writings became possible. He was no longer just an atheist critic of religion and nothing but a projection theorist, but an analyst of the human psyche in its interaction with a specific cultural and religious environment. It is from this perspective that Freud's positivism and reductionism could be overcome when more attention was paid to what was to be considered of importance for a psychology of religion: the meaning of the body; the psychic needs, wishes and motives; the inner conflicts and libidinal entanglements with objects; the importance of mechanism such as symbolization or sublimation; the father function; the basic anthropological structures of faith; the experience of reality; the inevitability and positive meaning of guilt structures in its various forms.

6   Assessments

Introduction

In the final chapter two issues are of concern. Firstly, concluding assessments regarding the analysis of Freud's reception by theology and religious studies will be made. Our study has shown clear differences as regards to the reception of psychoanalysis by German and Dutch-speaking theology and religious studies – notably, the relation between the phenomenology of religion and psychoanalysis in the Netherlands *versus* the close bond between pastoral psychology and psychoanalysis in German-speaking theology. But also some cross-border influences and mutual developments could be detected – notably, the turn to new psychoanalytic theories in the 1970s or parallel developments in psychoanalytic text interpretation. We will not summarize and recapitulate these different histories, their specific characteristics or the movement of mutual influence. These have been described at length. In this closing the chapter these differences in engagement serve as the forum for formulating general patterns and structures with regards to the reception of Freud in both Dutch and German theology and religious studies, as well as in Protestant and Catholic theology. We will specifically focus our attention on how scholars dealt with Freud's critique of religion, Freudian anthropology and Freud's views on the sense of guilt.

Secondly, in our assessments we will focus on specific issues such as healing, maturation and therapy, giving ultimate meaning, and symbolization and sublimation. Here we will again critically confront Freudian psychoanalysis and theology with the aim of, on the one hand, indicating the difficulties when engaging with Freud's thought in theology and, on the other hand, the future and present possibilities of engagement with Freudian psychoanalysis in a constructive manner.

Dealing with the Freudian critique of religion

In our analyses of Freud's reception by German and Dutch theology and religious studies we have seen a recurring issue: How can psychoanalysis be integrated into theology and how can Freud's critique of religion be dealt with? Before we explore this question it should be noticed that this "how" is preceded by the more basic "why". Our enquiry has resulted in various reasons for turning to psychoanalysis in different contexts. We have seen an interest in psychoanalysis because of its alleged anti-materialism (Bouman (3.1)). Another motive could be found in the context of phenomenology of religion: psychoanalysis was engaged with because of a supposed shared method and objective, a theory of the human subject (Sierksma (3.3)), or as relevant in providing a theory of magic and religion (Beth (2.5), Tuinstra (3.2)). We have seen that Tillich valued psychoanalysis for having "rediscovered" the full depth and meaning of the concepts of sin and grace (2.7). In the writings of both Pfister (2.2) and Scharfenberg (4.2.1) one finds an element that is latent in all of the previous: psychoanalysis is called upon as a critical theory against another dominant view.

Whether against materialism, Barthian theology (Sierksma), anthropological studies (Beth) or outdated theological language (Tillich), psychoanalysis is in a sense regarded as critical counter-theory. In Pfister's and Scharfenberg's critique of outdated theological structures this is most apparent. In Vergote's work the use of psychoanalysis as critical instrument against certain theological perspectives is also clear (5.3.2). Hence, not only Thurneysen has strategic reasons, as Scharfenberg cynically called it, to turn to psychoanalysis. In fact, the element of "strategy" is always present in such reception. This is important, because strategy already implies interpretation. Despite Scharfenberg's or Van de Spijker's starting point that Freud should be read from his own presuppositions, we have found no exception as to the suspicion that Freud was engaged with by theologians within an already developed theological framework or in the light of a set religious conviction.

Of course a pure "objective" reading of Freud is impossible – certainly when one considers oneself as a Freudian who is aware of unconscious motives in text interpretation. The fact that psychoanalysis has a history of debates, conflicts and schisms is already an indication of the multitude of readings of Freud's writings and the various theoretical filters that have been used to interpret his work. Nevertheless and from a Freudian perspective, to "know" this brings us closer to the "truth" than to keep one's presuppositions hidden and unreflected. This awareness is not only a task for theologians who, as Sierksma remarked, are sometimes more interested in defending Christianity than in studying religion[1], but also for those who study religion from a supposed neutral perspective.

So how is Freud read and his critique of religion processed? I think we have found some pivotal recurring patterns. The first is total ignorance, i.e. a non-reading and a non-processing. Since our study deals with reception, non-engagement is not the actual issue, but in a sense of course it is the background for a study of the reception. I consider a non-engagement with psychoanalysis as normal: one simply doesn't take notice or is simply not interested. It happens every day. Only sometimes it seems to be a more conscious assessment. Barth (2.6) is an example here, but there are more.[2]

---

[1] Compare also J.A. van Belzen, "Verder dan Freud? Na een eeuw psychoanalytische godsdienstkritiek", in *Tijdschrift voor Theologie* 48 (2008/1), pp.66-90 (88).

[2] Another example can be found in the writings of Raymund Schwager and his followers at the theological faculty in Innsbruck. Their work is inspired by René Girard and his reading of Freud. However, in their writings on the scapegoat mechanism and dramatic theology Freud seems to be avoided. Symptomatic is the German translation of Girard's *Des choses cachés depuis la foundation du monde*: R. Girard, *Das Ende der*

A second pattern I have already elaborated upon in the preliminary con-clusions of chapter 2 (2.8). In the writings of Pfister, Beth or Tillich, but also in the writings of others one finds that the psychoanalytic critique of religion does not touch upon the true essence of religion that is either seen as being revealed (Tuinstra, Thurneysen (2.6), Vergote (5.3.2)) or regarded as a "totality" beyond Freudian anthropology and religion critique (Pfister, Beth and Tillich (2.8), Fortmann *cum suis* (3.4) and Lauret (4.3.1)).

An intriguing question is whether this essence was already "there" be-fore psychoanalysis was engaged with or whether the receptions of psycho-analysis lead to defining an essence of religion beyond religion critique. In gen-eral we can say that such an essence – for example from a Schleiermacherian theological position (2.2, 3.1) – was already part of the theological framework in which psychoanalysis was processed. But we have also found that this es-sence could, under the pressure of the psychoanalytic critique of religion, be-come more pronounced. The turn to Lévy-Bruhl by Beth or Fortmann can be seen as a further articulation of the essence of religion (mystic participation) beyond psychoanalysis: the demystifications of psychoanalysis were reacted upon by a turn to a more romantic perspective on religion (2.8). In comparison to Van der Leeuw, Tuinstra's stronger emphasis on revelation can also be seen as a response to the engagement with psychoanalysis. The same goes for Ver-gote's emphasis on revelation as the source and soul of "unmotivated" religion. To conclude, the psychoanalytic critique of religion incited theologians to de-fine the essence of religion more sharply.

From this "essence" it was then possible to criticize "non-essence" – the neurotic forms of religion (Pfister *inter alia*), the mythic elements in religion (Beth, Tuinstra), the outdated forms of religion (Scharfenberg *inter alia*), the unhealthy forms of religion (Fortmann *inter alia*). The discourse on illusionary versus true religion/faith is an important factor here. Freud's positivist reduc-tionism could thus be processed: his insights into religious motivations (wishes, needs) enabled theologians to distinguish more clearly between "caricature" and truth. His claim to have explained this "truth" could then be sharply criticized. We can for example notice this in Fortmann's critique of Freud as a projection theorist and at the same time as an important contributor to the knowledge on mental disorders.

A third pattern is related to the previous. Freudian psychoanalysis was often regarded as being confined to unhealthy malformations of religion/faith. This can be found throughout our reconstruction of theological engagement with Freud. There are arguments in favour of such a view: the fact that Freud

---

Gewalt, G. Lohfink (ed.), Herder Verlag, Basel/Freiburg/Vienna, 1983. The third part of Girard's text on psychoanalysis (desire, sexuality, latency, Oedipus complex, death drive) is not translated and is simply left out. The translation thus gives the impression that the book actually culminates in Girard's elaborations on Christianity in the second part.

based his theories on clinical material; the fact that in the application of psycho-analytic theory to cultural phenomena pathologies served as models. And yet, to confine psychoanalysis to the realm of the pathological is a disregard of its ambition to formulate theories of general psychic structures.

Psychoanalysis is more than merely pathology. Throughout his career Freud developed meta-psychological models of the human psyche, notably in the two topic models. The same goes for the theories of the unconscious, the drives, the pleasure principle, narcissism and the Oedipus complex, and mechanisms such as repression, identification and sublimation. To make this fruitful for, for example, the psychology of religion or theological anthropology is a complex task. It means, as Vergote has rightfully argued, that Freud's pathological view has to be overcome and the relation between pathological malformations and normal phenomena has to be redefined. In my opinion Raguse and Vergote are right when they argue that normality and pathology are not opposed, but that pathology is an exaggeration of a "normal" psychic disposition.[3] That means that psychoanalysis cannot be confined to the realm of pathological malformations. It also means that psychoanalysis should consider religion (and culture) from a non-pathological point of view and that hence Freudian thought has to be further developed. Here Vergote's position serves as the alternative for a view that can be found throughout the history of the reception of Freud in theology and religious studies in which Freud's positivism and pathological view are seen as preventing him from taking normal or healthy religion/faith into account.

A fourth pattern follows from the previous ones: a turn away from Freudian psychoanalysis to constructive new psychologies. Freud's critique of religion is then seen as a useful critique of outdated structures, but less suited for the construction of alternatives. From this point of view the broad turn in the 1970s towards ego psychology and self-psychology can be understood. Here maturation and developmental ideals are formulated that seem in congruence with a Protestant view on pastoral care and theology formulated in opposition to an outdated tradition. In Catholic studies tradition is in general more positively valued and the ideals of the new psychologies are more sceptically received.

The guilt problem

In the first part of our study I have shown that the sense of guilt is a key issue throughout Freud's writings, even *the* issue in his writings on culture and religion. From his "tragic" interpretation of *Carmen* until his "historic novel" on Moses this is a continuum in both the clinical and cultural writings. The sense

---

[3] This line of thought can also be detected in the writings of Vandermeersch and Corveleyn. See for example P. Vandermeersch, *Het gekke verlangen*; J. Corveleyn, "Folk Religiosity or Psychopathology?".

of guilt is at the heart of the Oedipus complex that steadily grows in importance in Freud's work and is stubbornly defended against criticism by his followers. This nuclear complex with its analyses of the sense of guilt in various directions (in differentiated pathological structures; in culture and religion) describes the human psyche as conflicted, unstable and irrational. It focuses on identity as the outcome of psychic struggle and the result of a personal history in relation to others and culture.

When we deconstruct *Totem and Taboo* or *Moses and Monotheism* with their myths on patricide and the origin of the sense of guilt as the nuclear motive underlying the development of culture and religion, the central intuition in these studies still stands firmly and even becomes more clear: Judaism and Christianity are religions that attempt to channel and resolve the guilt problem, i.e. in these religions the sense of guilt is processed and expressed. This intuition was partly based on Freud's personal interaction with his own Jewish background and his knowledge of the Bible. It was also an intuition derived from his contact with patients, and based on what he saw and heard of the Catholic Church in Vienna. And yet, the emphasis on the sense of guilt in culture and religion cannot be confined to Freud's biography or observations in *fin-de-siècle* Vienna. The Christian and Jewish traditions are full of guilt, and it was this cultural tradition that intrigued Freud the most: the question how the sense of guilt shaped culture, was processed in it, and influenced individual mental life.[4] This is the main perspective in Freud's cultural studies.

The leading model of interpretation is tragedy, but without a dominant pessimism.[5] Here, Freud finds and applies a model that serves as an alternative for a message of salvation, because in tragedy the full conflict between drive and morality can be depicted without pointing towards a final solution or rearrangement.[6] In tragedy there is no outside force, no Other, that can liberate from the flow of events or that can be held responsible for it. The same goes for the persons involved in the tragedy. Tragedy is thus limited to the staging of conflict and the limitations of human life without appointing personal guilt or fault.[7] As early as *Psychopathic Characters on the Stage* this was already suggested. Freud distinguishes between various "stages" on which the tragic strug-

---

[4] Compare H. Henseler, *Religion – Illusion?*, pp.98-99.

[5] Since this study focuses on the sense of guilt the tragic model in Freud's view on culture and religion stands in the spotlight. We should notice that there are some fields of attention in Freud's writings in which the sense of guilt plays no role of importance and that could be regarded as the one side of the picture of which tragedy is the other side. This mainly concerns Freud's texts on humour.

[6] Compare: "All psychoanalytic theorists take a tragic view of life and agree that it is a continuing frustration of both instincts and humanity's dreams of immortality." B. Beit-Hallami, M. Argyle, *The Psychology of Religious Behaviour, Belief and Experience*, Routledge, London/New York, 1997, p.28.

[7] See P. Moyaert, *Ethiek en sublimatie*, pp.213-216.

gle between "love and duty" unfolds as "social drama", "psychological drama" or "religious drama". Religion is thus a stage where the same tragedy as the one staged in psychic life is performed – religion is the staging of tragedy.[8] In *Totem and Taboo* and *Moses and Monotheism* he then adds that religion is also an attempt to resolve the sense of guilt, in other words, to resolve the tragedy called human life. In vain, we might add, the moments or opportunities of resolution are scarce and thus exactly these moments – as in the case of St Paul – actually more clearly unfold the full religious drama.

This does not mean that Freud presents an anthropology in which man is destined by whatever fate. The drama, the psychic conflict, is the basis for Freud's own "godless" moral views[9] – the advancement in intellectuality, the duty to accept life and death, the development of "normal" object relations (but without the inflation of Eros expressed in the excessive commandment to love fellow man), the taming of drives in sublimation for the sake of culture, the appraisel of humour and common sense. It is in the light of tragedy that the virtues and greatness of a personality can flourish – as in the case of St Paul.

It is this general character of Freudian thought that is difficult to process in theology. In Thurneysen's (2.6), Tillich's (2.7), Harsch's or Lauret's (4.3.1) association of psychoanalysis with estrangement and sin we notice how the "tragedy" is integrated in a model containing the notions of guilt and fault, and salvation. The effect of such an interpretation is however that Freudian theory is regarded as a secular crypto-Christian theory that points towards a discourse on (original) sin in which the relation to God is introduced.

Psychoanalysis thus becomes secular dogmatism depicting sinful man who is in need of salvation. It must be said that Freud seemingly gave reason for this line of thought in his "mythical" theories on Eros and Thanatos and on patricide (*Totem and Taboo*, *Moses and Monotheism*). Freud, while denying that psychoanalysis should represent a world view, did move beyond clinical experience into the realm of speculative thought. This has given rise to the idea that Freudian thought is in a sense unfinished, because he did not develop what according to some scholars would and should have been a consequence of his ideas; philosophy of life, teleology inscribed in archaeology.[10]

Freud's turn to speculative thought and mythic constructs were in my opinion unjustly interpreted as a crypto-Christian theory that could be integrated into a discourse on sin and salvation (or conflict and integration) in man-God relationship. These Freudian constructs are the result of his attempts to find

---

[8] S. Freud, *Psychopathic Characters on the Stage*, p.308.

[9] Ph. Rieff, *The Mind of the Moralist*, p.xxi.

[10] In the 1950s and 1960s there was a tendency, for example in the writings of Ricoeur, to supplement Freud with Hegel or to read Freud from a Hegelian perspective. We have seen that this had an influence on Scharfenberg. We should add Lauret, who was certainly influenced by Ricoeur. We should also not forget that Pfister wrote his dissertation on Biedermann, i.e. on Hegel and Schleiermacher.

sources for phenomena in order to explain and resolve its "symptoms". Unsuccessfully, we might add: the mythical character of the ultimate sources indicates that these sources are "dumb" and that "beyond" clinical and cultural evidence the explanation of either the sense of guilt, the superego or the categorical imperative cannot be provided.[11] This is eventually the only "truth" hidden in Freud's "myths", and with that we are back to tragedy. There is no "Other" as either cause or saviour.

Considering the sense of guilt an important aspect of Freud's thought on this matter was lost from sight: the sense of guilt is not so much a problem that needs to be resolved – the absence of a sense of guilt would in itself be a pathological phenomenon – but in fact it is a constructive element in culture, religion and individual life. It is mainly because of this structural "function" of the Freudian sense of guilt that in Lacanian psychoanalysis – and hence in the writings of Vergote – the term "guilt" is preferred above "sense of guilt" (5.3.4). The latter is especially discussed as the pathological exaggeration of the first.

In the various projects of trying to re-establish a relationship between lived faith and human nature on the one hand and theology or metaphysics on the other hand, Freudian psychoanalysis could be used as critical theory, but also proved a hard nut to crack because it presents anthropology without a message of salvation. The attempts to integrate the former in the latter mostly resulted in silence on the aspects that were least compatible: the irrational unconscious, the body and sexuality, the sense of guilt.

The neglect of these issues can be found in the writings of Pfister (2.3.2), Scharfenberg (4.2.4) and Lauret (4.3.1) with the consequence that the sense of guilt became a forgotten, non-debated or neutralized issue. In the writings of these scholars the tragic model and the inevitability of a sense of guilt constituted a problem as objectives were formulated in terms of moral elevation, healing or integration. Van der Leeuw once correctly stated that those scholars that focus on *homo natura* are inclined to reduce man to the animal drive mechanism, whereas scholars who study *homo transcendens* tend to ignore the fact that man is a natural being.[12] This is indeed a basic problem throughout our study. Freudian anthropology can neither be harmonized with a discourse overemphasizing human potentials such as maturation, ego-integration, self-realization or self-transcendence, nor with theological constructs that aim at resolving the guilt problem.[13]

In general we can say that German Protestant theologians thus tend to turn to post-Freudian psychoanalytic theories that present a different anthropology. This is of course legitimate, but not without problems concerning the issue

---

[11] Compare Ph. van Haute, "Michel Foucault: de psychoanalyse en de wet", in *Tijdschrift voor Filosofie* 55 (1993/3), pp.449-471 (462).

[12] G. van der Leeuw, *Der Mensch und die Religion*, p.17.

[13] On this issue see also W.W. Meissner, *Psychoanalysis and Religious Experience*, p.240.

of a sense of guilt. We have found an almost paradigmatic conviction that guilt is a dominant issue in an outdated guilt culture, whereas in a culture of narcissism other mechanisms are more prominent. The emphasis has shifted from paternal superego structures to ego consciousness, stressing ego conscience formation and responsibility in the context of a social community (4.3.3). However, the emergence of the Western guilt culture as Jean Delumeau has described it shows that the issue of guilt was strongly correlated with the rise of the modern subject as an autonomous, responsible and guilty individual.[14] A discourse on a new era beyond the guilt culture focusing on the classic issues related to the modern subject does raise the question what has actually happened to the "guilt problem". The Mitscherlich thesis of the fatherless society might well function here as a secular myth that enables us to silence the guilt problem, whereas it in fact resounds in a discourse on ego conscience formation in a "guiltless" society that is in need of social cohesion. In fact, a discourse on personal conscience formation and responsibility can be situated in a long Christian tradition. Maybe we could add – inspired by Michel Foucault – that primarily the techniques to incite to responsibility and conscience formation have changed considerably from brutally aggressive "pastoral" empowerment in early modern times (Delumeau) to more and more subtle forms in pastoral care.[15] This issue needs more studying.

Freud has clearly (in his analyses of the modern "guilty" subject) pointed out that in the relation between the narcissistic formation of an ego ideal, conscience and superego formation the issue of a sense of guilt cannot be split off as a sole effect of paternal enforcement. On the contrary, the sense of guilt describes the tension between psychic topics that are formed through identification, a mechanism that is primarily narcissistic (as it describes the identification with one's own body and an ego ideal). Seen from this point of view, Protestant pastoral psychologists not only stand confronted with the task of reconsidering the "guilt problem" in relation to their tradition, but also of critically examining the "guilt problem" in ego conscience formation. It is in this context that Freud's views on the sense of guilt as a dominant issue in both modern individual life and religion regains its importance. The question is then not how the guilt problem is resolved through ego conscience formation, but how in a discourse on ego conscience formation a (typically Protestant?) mode of processing the sense of guilt is continued.

---

[14] J. Delumeau, *Sin and Fear.*

[15] Notably in his *Histoire de la sexualité 1. La volonté de savoir* Foucault argued, against the general opinion that the 1960s had brought sexual liberation, that modernity showed the development of more subtle and wide-spread techniques to influence the subject's sexual identity. Church confession was followed by scientific psychological and secular therapeutic discourses, but this did not change the fact that "we are still Victorians". M. Foucault, *Histoire de la sexualité 1. La volonté de savoir*, Gallimard, Paris, 1976.

In the sceptical attitude of Faber (3.4.5), the Protestant psychologist of religion, towards Freud we find the same elements as discussed above in the context of German pastoral psychology: the emphasis on the cultural change from a civil society to an industrial society in terms of a change in authority structures and a decline of paternalism; the traditional superego structures are deconstructed and replaced by individual faith maturation. In his work there is also a turn towards self psychology as in the writings of Scharfenberg.

Thus in the Dutch Protestant reception of Freud the extraordinary position of Sierksma should be noticed. His sense for tragedy in his depictions of man's eccentricity (man's helplessness and attempts to gain control over his life; man as an animal thrown out of balance) is combined with a certain turn to Freud whereas in his dissertation he clearly favoured Jung. However, his thought is then developed no further into a theological anthropology. On the contrary, his ideas on de-projection must actually be understood in the context of an emancipation of science of religion from theology. Yet, the notion of eccentricity, the acknowledgement of being estranged from oneself (without equating estrangement with sin) and his ideas on helplessness as motive in religion does seem to deserve some reappraisal. It points in the same direction as Vergote's depictions of faith as eccentricity towards a psychic *locus* for the divine. The dynamic of faith is situated in relational patterns to others and the Other (that are indeed others/Other and not an enlarged ego ideal). Sierksma's association of eccentricity with the "uncanny" and with the disruptive experience of the Other (and the subsequent projection as mastering reality) opens up other perspectives on the psychological meaning of divine revelation and further understanding of, for example, a phenomenon like conversion (which can be seen as both disruptive and liberating).

In Catholic pastoral psychology and psychology of religion the issue of debating the "guilt problem" has had a different history ever since Pius XII affirmed the importance of Freudian psychoanalysis in a decennium in which the healthy or unhealthy nature of the sense of guilt was heavily debated (4.3.1, 5.2). The recurring theme here in regard to Freud is to clarify the distinction between the healthy and unhealthy sense of guilt. Tradition is not regarded as something that has been superseded and in fact the sense of guilt or guilt is seen as a necessary part of that tradition. We find this theme in the writings of Goetschi and Hartung, and also in the writings of Uleyn and Vergote.

The first problem here is that Freud is often regarded as having analysed only the unhealthy sense of guilt (compare also Fortmann (3.4.4)). We have already addressed this problem; Freudian psychoanalysis cannot be confined to the realm of pathology. Another problem concerns the tendency to define a healthy sense of guilt in terms of existential guilt as it describes man's natural fallibility and can thus be associated with sin. The "guilt problem" is thus not silenced, but a connection is made with traditional religious representations and concepts that go beyond clinical analysis to function as anthropological concepts. In short, Freudian thought on the sense of guilt could be absorbed by a theological tradition.

In my opinion Vergote has correctly avoided such amalgams (5.3.4). Firstly, his starting point is normality, that is to say, that which is considered normal in a certain cultural setting. In our culture Freudian typology can be used to depict normal psychic structures. Pathology deals with its exaggerated forms. A general distinction in principle between healthy and unhealthy senses of guilt is impossible; instead another distinction is proposed – as in Raguse's work; guilt against absence of guilt. Secondly, guilt is not an existential phenomenon that precedes the individual, but a sense of guilt will necessarily be part of human psychic life from the moment the child enters the symbolic world of language and culture. Consequently, regarding guilt as part of the structuralizing processes a child engages when entering the symbolic order and not an existential phenomenon that precedes the individual, means that guilt in its various forms can be differentiated and analyzed.

Here, it is also important to notice that Vergote seems to be able to combine a tragic depiction of human nature – without the dramatics of Lacanian thought – with theology. It is the dynamics of guilt and desire that are at the heart of faith recognizing human nature as libidinal body and the other/Other as other/Other (and not as self-transcendence). In this way psychoanalysis can still be a critical theory questioning hidden agendas, neuroticizing ideals and imaginary constructs by consequently asking what man desires in the light of his history and in the libidinal entanglements that shape his reality; I will return to this issue when we discuss *zingeving*.

On therapy, healing and maturation

A recurring issue in our study is the issue of healing. Pfister, Scharfenberg and others stressed that the objective of psychotherapy was to liberate, to "heal", from those traumas that prevented further maturation or sublimation. But is this the heart of Freudian psychotherapy? In my opinion Raguse is right when he states that psychoanalysis doesn't liberate from inner conflicts, but only makes us aware of these conflicts in order to bear them (4.4). Stroeken has observed that psychotherapy has much in common with tragedy.[16]

---

[16] H. Stroeken, *Zoeken naar zin*, p.90. Assoun has shown that concerning "cure" in psychoanalysis there is a Nietzschean trait in Freudian thought: therapy is the tragic "repetition of the same": recollection (repetition of a representation), activation (repetition as action) and working-through (repetition as a riposte of resistances). In other words, there is no salvational element here, no outside influence, but only liberation in terms of repetition. P.-L. Assoun, *Freud and Nietzsche*, Athlone Press, London, 2000, pp.178-181. Compare also H. Politzer, *Freud und das Tragische*, W. Hemecker (ed.), Edition Gutenberg, Wiener Neustadt, 2003, p.52, p.146.

In fact this assessment follows from an interpretation of Freudian psychotherapy as a technique evolving around the mechanism of transference and counter-transference. This mechanism means that unconscious motives and wishes cannot be made conscious by taking some sort of objective position towards one's unconsciousness, but only in the process of transference and counter-transference, and repeating and working through memory-traces. It is a technique that evokes self-observation, but without the possibility of an objective position in which one can take a distance from oneself. On the contrary, the self-observation confronts radically with the fact that one cannot escape oneself, or as matter of fact be liberated from one's past. Freud does call therapy a "liberation" and "healing", but only in the sense that the personal past is remembered and worked through in order to make conscious the "historic truth", i.e. a reconstruction of a personal history that clarifies the relation between past events and present symptoms.[17]

According to Freud a psychoanalyst should be neutral in psychotherapy, just as he should be impartial to any *Weltanschauung*.[18] Throughout his writings on therapeutic technique this is a line not to be crossed. That doesn't mean that he is an indifferent observer: the mechanism of transference and counter-transference indicates that feelings of sympathy or resistance play a role in the therapist's attitude and the success of the therapeutic process. The neutrality concerns the objective of therapy: the therapist does not present a message of salvation that corresponds with the analyst's own world view. The reconstruction of "historic truth" does not evolve into a moral judgement of the patient's religious convictions or philosophy of life.

We can say that psychotherapy is about the reconstruction and articulation of the patient's desires as the "answer" to the primal question "who am I".[19] Freud already recognized that the sense of guilt plays a crucial role here in the negative therapeutic reaction as a "desire" not to be cured: the sense of guilt is apparently a nuclear element of an indissoluble identity. Freud's articulation of neutrality serves this reconstruction and articulation of the patient's desires and sense of guilt without obstructive normative interactions of the analyst's desires.

The issue of neutrality is an issue of ethics. The patient entrusts his desires to an analyst in a therapeutic setting in which the patient – knowing the

---

[17] Lambertino has rightfully argued for a differentiation between liberation and freedom. Although an individual can be "liberated" from compulsive thoughts or symptoms, he/she will not be free, because the psyche is always determined by its instinctual nature and mechanisms. A. Lambertino, *Psychoanalyse und Moral bei Freud*, p.363, p.387.

[18] S. Freud, O. Pfister, *Psychoanalysis and Faith*, pp.15-19; S. Freud, *The Future of an Illusion*, p.36.

[19] A. Vergote, "Ethiek van de psychoanalyse"; W. Krikilion, "De ethiek van het verlangen in de psychotherapie", in E. Maeckelberghe, H. Westerink (eds.), *Gekke verlangens. Opstellen in ethiek en godsdienstpsychologie voor Patrick Vandermeersch*, Uitgeverij Kok, Kampen, 2008, pp.116-131.

methods and objectives of psychoanalytic therapy – may expect that his personal expressions and articulations do not encounter the normative interventions of analyst. He may count on "sympathetic understanding" and stimulation in the reconstruction, not on the presentation of a normative model with which the patient should identify or a world view to which to adapt. This neutrality is part of a "therapeutic contract" that should not be violated.

It is because of this that psychotherapy should be clearly distinguished from pastoral care. I agree with Corveleyn on this matter in that the pastor represents religious tradition and community (5.3.6). He is a religious guide. This distinction of realms between pastor and therapist is important and useful, not only as a critical instrument against the spiritualization of therapy (notably in America) or a Rogerian pastoral care model, but also in the context of our study of the reception of Freud by theology.

We have seen that, for example, in Scharfenberg's pastoral psychology this distinction is struggled with (4.2.2). Both pastoral care and psychotherapy first of all aim at an open dialogue without enforcements of norms and world views. But the correlation doesn't end here, for according to Scharfenberg psychotherapy presents a secular version of a Christian ideal: the liberation of love. This correlation however is problematic for two reasons. Firstly, the fact that the pastor doesn't enforce norms, but empathetically listens to a person's life story, doesn't imply that therapy and pastoral care correlate. The neutrality of a therapist is still principally to be distinguished from the pastor's position in a religious tradition and community. Secondly, without being reflected explicitly, a psychotherapeutic discourse on articulation of desire (and guilt) develops into a pastoral conversation on resolving guilt and maturation in faith. The suggested correlation thus slips into a discourse in which a single ideal model is presented: mature faith, ego-integration. This is the point where neutrality becomes a message of salvation, and where the normativity of the "therapist" will obstruct a pure analytic process. Suggesting a correlation between psychotherapy and pastoral care thus raises an ethical problem, because it means suggesting neutrality whereas pastoral care cannot and will not be neutral. Even more strongly, to suggest that a pastor is also a therapist – a claim not made by Scharfenberg, but sometimes found in literature – means that a pastor considers himself to be capable of making the right assessments between neutrality and normativity depending on the situation. Such control of registers of speech can be compared with Drewermann's perverse position as all-powerful guide (4.4). It is the refusal of taking a specific limited role.

Pastors can learn some important lessons from Freudian psychotherapy. Firstly, they can learn that they themselves are not psychologists, therapists or psychoanalyst, but have a unique role. Secondly, there is the issue of transference and counter-transference in both pastoral care and in text interpretation. In both fields this means taking into account emotional responses towards a person or text that not only evokes conscious cognitive mental processes, but also responses that are motivated by unconscious processes. In other words, there can be no objectivity. The main point here is that the pastor/interpreter is aware of the fact that his position and perspective is always specific and limited (being part of the hermeneutic circle), and that it serves both pastoral care and text interpretation to make this perspective explicit. I agree with Raguse on text interpretation in this respect. As already mentioned, in pastoral psychology the mechanism of transference and counter-transference has been valued by Scharfenberg (4.2.2), Uleyn (5.2) and others. Thirdly, there is the issue that psychotherapy is about the articulation of one's desires, which may obviously include religious desires. Contrary to pastoral psychology (as far we discussed it) that tends to offer general models and ideals of ego-integration or mature faith, taking the articulation of personal religious desire as a starting point is innovative.

In contemporary literature in practical theology and psychology of religion there is a growing interest in so called "lived religion"[20] and in the narrative hermeneutical approaches to life biographies.[21] In the context of secularization, de-institutionalization and fragmented "bricolaged" religiosity, the religious subject can no longer be regarded as someone who has adopted a tradition, a thought system or the authority of institutions. Instead, the religious subject produces religion and "bricolaged" religiosity thus becomes the primal object of reflection. The starting points are the individually articulated religious desires often in critical dialogue with tradition and institution. Individual life stories become the source for not only understanding post-modern religiosity, but also prompt further theological reflection. It is in this context that Freud's ideas on the sense of guilt and his elaborations of the different types of sense of

---

[20] See for example W. Failing, H.-G. Heimbrock, *Gelebte Religion wahrnehmen. Lebenswelt – Alltagskultur – Religionspraxis*, Kohlhammer Verlag, Stuttgart/Berlin/Colone, 1998; W. Gräb. *Lebensgeschichten – Lebensentwürfe – Sinndeutungen. Eine Praktische Theologie gelebter Religion*, Kaiser Verlag, Gütersloh, 2000; R. Ganzevoort, *De hand van God en andere verhalen. Over veelkleurige vroomheid en botsende beelden*, Uitgeverij Meinema, Zoetermeer, 2006. Whether practical theology is concerned with "lived Christian religion" (Failing and Heimbrock) or "lived religion" (Gräb, Ganzevoort), these scholars share the view that a practical theology that focuses on lived religion means a change of paradigm: practical theology is no longer about a (pastoral) theology or doctrine of church practice. After all, lived religion is situated in critical dialogue with church practice and often found outside church institutions as a lived religious potential for critically rethinking future church practices. This shift of paradigm towards lived religion includes a turn to social sciences and religious studies.

[21] See for example U. Popp-Baier, *Das Heilige im Profanen. Religiöse Orientierungen im Alltag. Eine qualitative Studie zu religiösen Orientierungen von Frauen aus der charismatisch-evangelikalen Bewegung*, Rodopi, Amsterdam/Atlanta, 1998; A. van Heeswijk, N. ter Linden, M.H.F. van Uden, T.H. Zock (eds.), *Op verhaal komen. Religieuze biografie en geestelijke gezondheid*, KSGV, Tilburg, 2006; R. Ganzevoort, J. Visser, *Zorg voor het verhaal. Achtergrond, methode en inhoud van pastorale begeleiding*, Uitgeverij Meinema, Zoetermeer, 2007.

guilt in various pathologies, and Vergote's ideas on religious desire and guilt become important again.[22]

Leaving behind generalizations about a culture of guilt and a culture of narcissism, and instead focusing on individual religiosity means concentrating on how individuals articulate their faith in relation to themselves, God, others and tradition. Since such a starting point implies insight into the interaction between religious representations and psychic processes, a Freudian typology including various forms of a sense of guilt could be helpful here to interpret and understand life stories, i.e. Freudian psychoanalysis could help to gain insight into the personal psychic dynamics in interaction with religion. Maybe this means that in many stories individual religiosity is characterized by narcissistic structures in which a powerful ego ideal in the form of a Self is identified with. But it also enables us to detect other more hidden aspects of religious life: masochistic and neurotic tendencies in, for example, ritualization or an over-zealous sense of responsibility.

Vergote has given an impulse to such differentiations in religiosity in *Guilt and Desire* with its elaborations on obsessional neurotic and hysteric religiosity (5.3.4). Although pastors (and other spiritual care-takers) certainly need not to be experts in psychoanalysis, they do require basic knowledge of the dynamics of the interaction of psychic life and religion. This will not only be for the benefit of the conversation partner, but also for a critical self reflection by the pastor. Here the psychology of religion as an interdisciplinary study of man's psychic structures in interaction with religion can be of importance for practical theology.

This starting point (lived religiosity, narrative approaches) excludes generalizations on healthy religion or mature faith. We have seen throughout our study that guilt (or anxiety) is a "problem" that should be resolved and that somehow psychoanalysis was regarded as helpful in a process of maturation and/or healing. The dominance of a discourse on maturation, healing, and also autonomy and ego-integration has been questioned from various perspectives.

Henning Luther's unfinished oeuvre in practical theology has been an important inspiration here.[23] His ideas on the subject's religiosity as a starting

---

[22] We should add here that after Freud other types of differentiations between various forms of the sense of guilt have been developed. In his study on guilt and the sense of guilt Hirsch mentions "basic sense of guilt", "sense of guilt out of vitality", "sense of guilt out of a tendency towards autonomy" and "traumatic sense of guilt". M. Hirsch, *Schuld und Schuldgefühl*, pp.69-76, pp.128-289. In addition we can mention the two types of sense of guilt as distinguished by Melanie Klein – persecutory sense of guilt and depressive sense of guilt. On this see R. Speziale-Bagliacca, *Guilt. Revenge, Remorse and Responsibility after Freud*, Brunner-Routledge, Hove/New York, 2004, pp.24-32.

[23] H. Luther, *Religion und Alltag. Bausteine zu einer Praktische Theologie des Subjekts*, Radius Verlag, Stuttgart, 1992.

point for practical theology are a key reference in the turn to "lived religion". His critique of ego-integration and faith maturation – not motivated by Freudian psychoanalysis, but by Emanuel Levinas" philosophy – and his ideas on the fragmentary constitution of the subject have been taken up by others in their critical discussion of this dominant discourse.[24]

What is as yet "lacking" in this turn to the subject's biography and its fragmented psychic constitution is a return to Freudian psychoanalytic theory that can account for this in opposition to a discourse built on ego-psychology and self-psychology. Recent publications on guilt and the sense of guilt by German psychoanalysts seem to provide this. From the perspective of existential psychoanalysis Mathias Hirsch (compare Goetschi[25]) has argued that guilt is a "basic phenomenon in human existence".[26] This is expressed in, for example, the biblical story of creation and Fall, which Hirsch interprets as a story on *conditio humana*, i.e. the *So-und-nicht-anders-Sein* of human existence; the fallible and limited human nature between animal and God.[27] This train of thought can also be found in a study of the guilt problem by the psychoanalyst Dieter Funke. From a variety of psychoanalytic perspectives (including Freudian) he too elaborates on the story of creation and Fall as a story of human existence, man's unfinished, eccentric and conflicted nature.[28] This implies that guilt is an inevitable factor in human existence. These are certainly important studies on guilt in a dialogue between psychoanalysis and religion. There are also similarities with Vergote's point of view, certainly concerning a critique of psychological optimism in pastoral psychology and of Christian theology that tends to evoke and/or increase the sense of guilt in a discourse on original sin (as fault) and salvation (by God).

The major difference here, however, is the use of the term guilt to indicate man's nature. It is taken out of a clinical context as well as a cultural-historic context and functions as an existential concept that describes *conditio humana* and that serves as the enigmatic ground for the emergence of various forms of the sense of guilt.[29] We are thus born guilty, and this is exactly the po-

---

[24] See for example G. Schneider-Flume, *Leben ist kostbar. Wider die Tyrannei des gelingenden Lebens*, Vandenhoeck & Ruprecht, Göttingen, 2002.

[25] When Hirsch speaks about *Daseinsanalyse* he refers to scholars such as Condreau, Heidegger and Binswanger, i.e. the same scholars Goetschi calls upon when he discusses *anthropologische Psychotherapie*. M. Hirsch, *Schuld und Schuldgefühl*, pp.40ff.

[26] Idem, p.9.

[27] Idem, pp.25ff, p.41, pp.45ff.

[28] Funke explicitly calls upon Henning Luther's ideas on the fragmented unfinished identity and, interestingly, refers to Plessner's thought on eccentricity. D. Funke, *Das Schulddilemma*, pp.50-53, p.71.

[29] Funke writes for example: *Schuld ist also eine Dimension, die dem Da-Sein des Kleinkindes von Anfang an innewohnt.* In comparison to Vergote (or Lacan) guilt does not arise when the imaginary symbiotic relation with the mother is interfered with by

sition that Vergote wants to avoid by associating guilt with the psychodynamics of the symbolic order and not with something "behind" this order. Seen from this perspective, Hirsch and Funke repeat Freud's mistake of searching beyond the analyzable for a speculative monocausal source of the sense of guilt (the death drive). Nevertheless, Funke's study especially presents a challenge to theologians to rethink traditional theological concepts such as sin and salvation and to further elaborate along the lines of Henning Luther on the unfinished subject in search of meaning.

Vergote's *retour à Freud* (and those of his students) is a systematic outline of psychoanalysis and religion that does credit to individual religiosity without developing into generalizations on healthy religion, mature faith and ego-integration including resolving guilt or anxiety, and at the same time avoids the immediate association of guilt with fault – on the contrary, sin is characterized by lack of guilt structures. In this way he can account for normal guilt that is a nuclear part of the psychic structures that characterize (normal neurotic) identity, but without making guilt into an existential feature of man's nature. A strong religious sense of guilt indicates a pathological exaggeration of a basically normal psychic structure. Nevertheless, normal and hence healthy is the unfinished identity of man, the dynamics of desire and guilt that are always at risk of becoming "unhealthy" and that never provide a stable psychic core, but also enable us to express identity and to vitalize faith. Guilt is thus seen as a normal element in man's libidinal entanglements with himself, others and the Other in a specific cultural and historic context, and even constitutive for the relation with others/Other as others/Other. Moreover, guilt doesn't precede these entanglements.

That guilt is not necessarily to be equated with "fault", but can be regarded as a normal psychic structure that is part of one's identity, is important, not only as a critical alternative to – as Freud would call it – the neuroticizing discourse on healing, but also as a psychoanalytic perspective in discussions on the relation between pastoral care and ethics. We have seen, especially in the chapter on German pastoral psychology, that the reception of ego psychology and self psychology – in themselves already forms of subtle moralizing – could be allied with discussions on ethics in pastoral care, notably concerning the issue of *Lebensführung*. Here, the moral imperative is less subtle, even when it is wrapped in a reasonable discourse on responsibility and a general critical attitude (including self-critique) in the context of the danger of a "guiltless" society (5.3.3).

Here we find an issue that Freud once formulated as the paradox that the most responsible persons are often the ones that have the strongest feelings of guilt, and that Vergote in other terms described as the Christian paradox in which salvation from sin is always offered in a discourse that first inscribes sin.

---

the father's "no", but precedes this imaginary bond as an innate dimension that already colours the relation between mother and child. Idem, pp.80-81.

It is precisely here that normal guilt could easily cross over into exaggerated feelings of guilt or an overemphasized responsibility. In this sense the "guilt problem" is an element in moralizing discourse on maturation, moral development, ego-integration and critical faith.

According to Vergote, there is always a danger of evoking an exaggeration of feelings of guilt in Christian discourse, whereas in fact Christianity provides – or should provide – a moderate way in between extremes, structuring the psychic elements that characterize the relation between man and God in a complex unity. This moderation is endangered when faith is associated with an imaginary ego ideal in the form of ego-integration that tends to evoke a sense of guilt and anxiety at the moment a "fault" is made. In other words, recognition of guilt as structural part of human psychic life avoids the overemphasized importance of privatized *Lebensführung* characterized by self-critique (feeling guilty about one's faults) and faith maturation. According to Vergote, being part of a tradition counters privatization in which an individual is made responsible (in a dominant discourse) for his maturation towards an unreachable personal ideal.[30] Religion thus opposes "narcissistic fascination" and instead inscribes a person in a tradition of expressions of the relation between God and man.

Although I disagree with Vergote with regards to his sheer negative view on narcissism (due to the distinction between imaginary vs. symbolic order) and instead would like to stress the continuity between narcissism and Oedipus complex, I hold Vergote's ideas on symbolic guilt as valuable. Guilt can be seen as an "inevitable" part of the dynamics of desire and faith. Here it is important that Vergote follows Freud in his depictions of various types of psychic structuring that should be accounted for in the interaction with religion. Psychic life colours the representations of God. That means, as Freud was already inclined to differentiate between various forms of guilt according to the "pathology" in which it functioned, that there is a tension between personal recognition of guilt and a traditional Christian "answer" to this recognition in a discourse on sin (as fault) and salvation (by God).

The believer who has to find his way on the religious path can easily be hindered when confronted with general theological schemes that may not always be a stimulant to his specific dynamics of faith. The art of pastoral care is to use the variety of traditional and contemporary expressions of the relation between man and God in order to stimulate the dynamics of faith in individual "lived religion", without concentrating too much on a single normative doctrine

---

[30] Popp-Baier has argued something similar, namely that the psychology of religion stands before the task of describing modern religious pluralism in order to find ways for establishing moderate religion in between two extremes that appear to be currently dominant, i.e. religious fanaticism (Christian fundamentalism) that wants to revive and strengthen faith systems on the one hand and privatized religious meaning systems on the other hand. U. Popp-Baier, *Das Heilige im Profanen*, pp.1-6.

or scheme, or on the interests and needs of a religious institution.[31] In this context the expression and confession of guilt as an element in the relation between man and God can be important as it expresses the inevitability and necessity of being both an individual and "unfinished". In line with Vergote *cum suis*, but also Henning Luther and Funke, the function of religion is to articulate and integrate psychic elements without restoring or constructing an imaginary identity. Articulating guilt can be part of this disturbing, as well as constructive, function of religion, albeit with moderation and caution; there is no need for an articulation or confession of guilt when someone is actually wrestling with feelings of worthlessness because of failing a narcissistic ideal.

Giving ultimate meaning

We have discussed the Dutch projection debate and we have seen how fundamental issues in this debate remain influential especially in *the* current dominant topic in Dutch psychology of religion and spiritual care, the issue of giving ultimate meaning (3.4). The focus in the projection debate was on one general mechanism organizing the subject's perceptions. After Fortmann this did not change fundamentally, albeit that projection could now be more positively valued through new psychoanalytic theories. When in current literature giving meaning is regarded as a general human function of which a religious search for meaning is a specific mode, the theological background as we have analysed it becomes somewhat obscured. Nevertheless, it is clear that in Fortmann's and Van der Lans' writings – in a sense reviving Van der Leeuw's phenomenology against Sierksma's critique – religious experience and mystic participation are "saved" in a secularized society that through the subject-object dichotomy has become estranged from a religious attitude. Religiosity is a personal participation in a meaningful coherence despite a secularized cultural environment.[32]

---

[31] I agree with Nauta and Ganzevoort that the starting point in pastoral care is the lived religion of the pastorant; pastoral care is not the application of theological doctrine in conversation. It is within lived religion that the dynamics of faith should be stimulated, not through an empathic attitude of merely listening, but through a dialogical attitude in which the pastor brings in his own theological (hermeneutical) expertise (of Scripture and tradition) as "counter opinion" or "counter voice", thus inviting further explicit religious desire. Ganzevoort speaks of dialogue between first order theology (pastorant) and second order theology (pastor). R. Ganzevoort, "De pastor(ant) als theoloog. De theologische kwaliteit van het pastorale gesprek", in *Gereformeerd Theologisch Tijdschrift* 100 (2000/3), pp.114-123; R. Nauta, *Paradoxaal leiderschap. Schetsen voor een psychologie van de pastor*, Valkhof Pers, Nijmegen, 2006; R. Ganzevoort, J. Visser, *Zorg voor het verhaal*, pp.213ff.
[32] This "romantic" critique of modern society in which the sense of religiosity and totality of meaning is lost in rationalism can not only be found in the Dutch tradition calling upon Van der Leeuw, but also in German theology. Evidence can be found in Pannenberg's study of anthropology when he elaborates on Johan Huizinga's theory of the

The issue of giving ultimate meaning is a typical issue for Dutch psychology of religion, but also in German practical theology the issue of "meaning" is of growing importance. Here, again, Henning Luther must be mentioned. He saw the function of religion as its "capacity to generate meaning" complementary to the structuring of everyday experiences.[33] This capacity is first of all disturbing; it doesn't contribute to self-realization, ego-integration or the construction of a final coherence of meaning. On the contrary, it confronts these ideals and calls for an unfinished identity and the "practice of the acceptance of contingency".[34] In this line of thought faith, hope and love are seen as opposed to the objective of a totality of meaning associated with self-realization.[35]

Of course, we cannot confine the issue of meaning, meaning giving and meaning systems to the realm of psychology of religion, spiritual care or practical theology. The issue is to be situated in broader cultural perspective as well. Peter Berger has argued in several studies that the issue of the quest for meaning has become dominant in a pluralistic modern society that since Reformation and Enlightenment lacks all-embracing meaning systems that provide a steady framework for structuring experiences.[36] In contemporary times, he argues, the main challenge for religion is to find a moderate religious path of inter-religious dialogue between the two extremes of religious relativism (privatized self-centred religion) and fundamentalism.[37] Human sciences have the task of "pre-

---

"play" (in *Homo Ludens*, 1938) as a principle of (meaningful) unity in culture. From this modern man has become estranged. W. Pannenberg, *Anthropologie in theologischer Perspektive*, pp.316-328. Kuiper has convincingly argued that Huizinga and Van der Leeuw (two scholars who were in direct and close contact) basically share the same views as to the idealization of primitive mentality and the critique of modern culture. Y. Kuiper, "The Primitive and the Past. Van der Leeuw and Huizinga as Critics of Culture", in H. Kippenberg, B. Luchesi, *Religionswissenschaft und Kulturkritik*, pp.113-125.

[33] H. Luther, "schwellen und Passage. Alltägliche Transzendenzen", in *Religion und Alltag*, pp.212-223 (212-213). Luther does not regard religiosity as the effect of the acceptance of dogmas and creeds, but sees religiosity as the critical exegesis of and discussion with institutionalized religion. R. Ganzevoort, *De hand van God*, p.148.

[34] W. Gräb, *Lebensgeschichten – Lebensentwürfe – Sinndeutungen*, p.59.

[35] Compare also G. Schneider-Flume, *Leben ist kostbar*, chapter 4 ("faith without totality of meaning").

[36] As sign of the times we have seen that in the writings of Tillich and Pannenberg the issue of (coherence of) meaning and search for meaning is prominent. In their writings, one might argue, the concept of meaning functions ultimately to (re)construct an all-embracing metaphysical meaning system. W. Stoker, *Is the Quest for Meaning the Quest for God? The Religious Ascription of Meaning in Relation to the Secular Ascription of Meaning. A Theological Study*, Rodopi, Amsterdam/Atlanta, 1996.

[37] See for example P. Berger, *A far Glory. The Quest for Faith in an Age of Credulity*, The Free Press, New York, 1992; P. Berger, T. Luckmann, *Modernität, Pluralismus und Sinnkrise. Orientierung des modernen Menschen*, Verlag Bertelsmann Stiftung, Gütersloh, 1995.

paring the way" for such a moderate "in between".[38] The contribution of psychoanalysis in the psychology of religion (without loosing its neutrality) could
be twofold. Firstly, psychoanalysis can help understand how the subject's relation with the social cultural environment – or even "reality" – is structured.
Secondly, psychoanalysis shows that "giving meaning" implies interpretation of
one's personal and/or collective history.

So, how can Freud fit into this discussion on meaning and "giving ultimate meaning"? In my opinion there are two issues that are particularly relevant: firstly, the issue of perception in the quest for meaning/*zingeving*, and
secondly, the issue of imaginary versus symbolic religious meaning.

We have seen that the projection debate in the Netherlands regarded the
issue of projection as a matter of perception. The background was Van der
Leeuw's phenomenology which was about the subjective understanding of the
object as far as it showed itself. Vestdijk and Sierksma basically explored the
question of how the subject perceives the world, and why and what it is that he
perceives. Already in the title of his study, "Envisioning the Invisible", Fortmann expresses the fact that his book is about perception; it is even about "saving" religious perception since religiosity is regarded as the response to the fact
that "there is something to see". This train of thought is continued in the writings of Van der Lans who regards "giving meaning" as a general human function of structuring perceptions into a coherent world view.[39] It is thus not surprising that key words in the discussion on *zingeving* are associated with
perception; *wereldbeeld* (world view), *verbeelding* (imagination), *levens-
beschouwing* (outlook on life).

The question of course is whether giving (ultimate) meaning is basically
or solely a matter of perception. We recall that Freud had problems with the issue of projection and perception. The mechanism of projection was a displace-
ment from "internal" to "external", a making visible in the outside world of inner affects. In animism it was a primitive mechanism constituting a
Weltanschauung before the development of abstract language made possible
another relation with the external world.[40] As Freud soon found out, projection
could thus not explain religion nor could religion be reduced to it. More generally expressed, projection could not explain the subject's relation with reality. In
Formulations on the Two Principles of Mental Functioning it is clear that Freud
does not regard perception as the cornerstone of the subject's relation with reality. Instead, he focuses on the reality principle as heir of the pleasure principle,
and argues that man's relation with reality is difficult to influence with a call
upon verifiable "real" representations (reality testing). The actual structuring
processes are the libidinal identifications and object relations, i.e. what man

---

[38] U. Popp-Baier, *Das Heilige im Profanen*, p.6.

[39] J. van der Lans, "Zingeving en zingevingsfuncties van religie bij stress". Compare
also T.H. Zock, *Niet van deze wereld?*, 15.

[40] S. Freud, *Totem and Taboo*, p.64.

needs and desires, loves and hates. It is because of this that the paper ended with a short discussion on the sense of guilt. In *Totem and Taboo* this was eventually also the main theme, not projection (perception). Freud's second topic model stresses even more the importance of concepts such as identification and object relations. In *The Ego and the Id* Freud's main interest concern's the superego's relation with the id thus stressing the psychic elements and structures that are not a matter of perception: the sense of guilt, the influence from tradition, the Oedipus complex that moulds the undifferentiated id into a concrete identity.

So Freud's writings shed a very different light on "giving meaning".[41] Vergote had already expressed this as early as 1966 arguing that reading Freud's writings on religion from the perspective of projection meant that the actual structuralizing processes in religion were lost from sight.[42] This critique still stands. In the discussion on *zingeving* the focus of attention is clearly on perception and the cognitive mental functions that organize these perceptions into a coherent world view. In itself the research on this issue is valuable, but needs, in my opinion, supplementation when we want to further understand how people give meaning to their lives and how such a process interacts with religion.[43] We do not need to recapitulate the first part of this book in order to establish a clear train of thought. In Freudian psychoanalysis there are a variety of mechanisms to describe the organization of affective relations between the subject and the world; idealization, introjection, sublimation, transference, identification, object love, projection. In this context the sense of guilt is a principal affect describing the tension between drive and conscience (as interiorized other), love and hate (i.e. the ambivalence of feelings towards the other), etc., which is either a motive for involved in, or an effect of, such mechanisms. A further conceptual analysis is required here, in line with Vergote, Moyaert and others, about the resemblances and differentiations between these mechanisms.

---

[41] From a Freudian point of view we might additionally ask whether *zingeving*-processes defined in terms of ordering perceptions in a coherent world view that provide wellbeing and experiences of authenticity are not an anthropological abstractions or at least luxus. Freud's ideas on the duty to tolerate life or on the avoidance of unhappiness point in a direction that Freud himself not always clearly envisioned, but nevertheless articulated: religion is not the art of being happy or the creation of a coherent world view, but instead the staging of human tragedy and inter-subjectivity with the possibility of comfort and self knowledge.

[42] A. Vergote, *Religionspsychologie*, pp.244-247. Also, A. Vergote, "Projection and Intolerance versus Symbolization".

[43] I use the term supplementation, because the application of psychoanalysis in the psychology of religion (or in any other scientific discipline) can only have the form of an application of a variety of perspectives. The reason is quite simple: there is not a single correct reading of Freud, nor is there an objective application of psychoanalytic theory without a personal or cultural resonance being involved – as the history of the psychology of religion shows. P. Vandermeersch, H. Westerink, *Godsdienstpsychologie*.

Such a supplementation is important, firstly, because it questions the concept of religion that is central in Dutch debates. Secondly, by adding another perspective on religion, Freudian psychoanalysis provides an instrument for understanding key religious, and specifically Christian, concepts. The focus should then not be on Freud's reductionism, on the quest for origins and explanations, but on the central aspect in his work that is far more promising: understanding the interaction between religion and the individual from the perspective of the individual's libidinal structuring processes.

We have seen that from Van der Leeuw onwards we find the idea that man is *homo religiosus*, i.e. predispositioned to ask for ultimate meaning that will restore man's natural religious attitude (mystic participation, second primitivity) (3.1). This is a core experience of self-transcendence, an experience of a totality of meaning in a secularized society. The focus is thus on a specific "authentic" experience as a ground for the development of a religious world view. We have seen that giving meaning is regarded a general human psychic function. This suggests neutrality as to religion, but underlying the issue of *zingeving* is still a specific concept of religiosity, namely as participation in a totality of meaning in a secular cultural environment that evidently does not provide this meaning. The fundamental question is whether this concept of religion is not a typical twentieth century concept formulated as a romantic answer to the gradual decline of Western religious traditions and its social structures and cultural patterns[44], and as alternative for the demystifying critique of culture and religion as presented in, for example, psychoanalysis.[45]

Whatever the answer to this question, Freud has a different perspective on religion arguing that religions are not precipitates of experience or end results of thinking, but – generally speaking – the results and expressions of man's libidinal entanglement with others and the world that can only be understood by working through history (personal and cultural). As Vergote argued, these entanglements can be recognized in key Christian concepts; "covenant, law, promise, father, filiation, death and resurrection".[46] We might add that faith

---

[44] It has been argued that Van der Leeuw's concept of religion – "a search for (revelation of) ultimate meaning" – is basically a nostalgic search for a religious participation that is in danger of being lost in modernity. The focus is thus on (phenomenological) experience and ultimate meaning. J. Waardenburg, "The Problem of Representing Religions and Religion. Phenomenology of Religion in the Netherlands 1918-1939", in H. Kippenberg, B. Luchesi (eds.), *Religionswissenschaft und Kulturkritik*, pp.31-56 (55).

[45] Marcus and Fischer have argued that two ideal-typical forms of critique of culture can be found throughout the twentieth century, firstly, the demystifying critique of culture that unveils hidden motives (social needs, power structures) and, secondly, a romantic style of cultural critique calling to mind the decline of community of mental hygiene in modern society. G.E. Marcus, M.M.J. Fischer, *Anthropology as Cultural Critique. An experimental Moment in the Human Sciences*, University of Chicago Press, Chicago/London, 1986, pp.113ff.

[46] A. Vergote, "Projection and Intolerance versus symbolisation", p.100.

is often defined in theology as a relation with God (and not as a fusing experience with God) and that this relation can be described in terms of love, guilt, awe, obedience, salvation, reconciliation, care, etc. Intersubjectivity provides the material out of which Christian language, symbols, faith and behaviour are made. It is within this framework that an experience of the divine can be processed and has meaning.[47] Seen from this perspective, participation in totality is not a neutral umbrella term for all religiosity, nor is it in congruence with Christian "intersubjective" language that suggests distance between man and God. This brings us to the second issue that we will shortly address.

A distinction between imaginary and symbolic order cannot be found in Freud's writings, and it must be said that Freud hardly paid explicit attention to religious language. In *Totem and Taboo*, for example, the origins of language are not discussed, although Freud does associate religion (as distinct from animism) with the capacity to use language. In *Moses and Monotheism* this is repeated when he writes that through language the realm of intellectuality is opened "in which ideas, memories and inferences became decisive in contrast to lower psychical activity".[48] He describes it as victory of intellectuality (father) over sensuality (mother). These are indications that Freud did consider the development of language as a crucial moment in the origin of culture and religion. In a sense this idea is expressed in *The Future of an Illusion* when we consider that Freud discusses religion as dogmatic religion, i.e. religion expressed in language on "facts and conditions",[49] as also when we consider Freud's interest in religious commandments.

It was Lacan who, combining psychoanalysis with linguistics and cultural anthropology, first used the concepts of imaginary vs. symbolic order in order to make a clear distinction between the child's imaginary relation with the mother (focusing on the child's narcissistic needs and wishes) and a symbolic order that is organized by the Name-of-the-Father and in which desires and identity are mediated through language (5.3.1). Language thus first of all creates distance from an immediate dual imaginary relation with the all-providing mother. Applied to the realm of religion Vergote has stressed this function of religion as symbolic order (5.3.2). His critique of Freud's interpretation of religion in *The Future of an Illusion*, on natural religion, on Tillich's jump towards ultimate ground or on Van der Lans' view of the *homo religiosus* who is disposed to search for ultimate meaning and participation, focuses on a tendency to nostalgically regard religious desire or faith as a substitute for the (need for the)

---

[47] A. Vergote, "Experience of the Divine, Experience of God", p.135.

[48] S. Freud, *Moses and Monotheism*, p.113.

[49] S. Freud, *The Future of an Illusion*, p.25.

other/Other as all-providing.[50] Calling upon Lacan's sharp distinction between the imaginary and symbolic order, Vergote does not so much apply this distinction in order to describe types of religion but uses it as an instrument to normatively assess imaginary "religious" constructs as "unbelief", suggesting that these are enlargements or projections of the individual's need for non-separation and totality.[51]

I have already criticized Vergote's concept of religion as revealed symbolic order and suggested some modifications (5.3.5). Contrary to Vergote's distinction between non-religious imaginary meaning constructs and religion as symbolic order, it is more fruitful – taking lived religion in a post-modern age as a starting point – to use the concepts of imaginary and symbolic order only as an instrument to analyse religion, spirituality and giving ultimate meaning processes.

On a theoretical level, this means the two orders[52] can be used as an instrument to reflect on the concepts of religion and religiosity as applied in psychology of religion itself. At this point I consider Vergote's diagnosis of Freud's view of religion in *The Future of an Illusion* or Van der Lans' ideas on giving ultimate meaning as correct; here, religion is primarily (and explicitly) viewed from the perspective of imaginary needs and wishes. More or less opposed to Van der Lans *cum suis*, Antoine Mooij and Stroeken have elaborated on giving ultimate meaning from a psychoanalytic perspective. They both argue that meaning in life is not about the dynamics of needs and satisfaction, but centres around the dynamics of distance and love. In this scheme the focus is not on the individual pursuing an ego ideal out of a need, but on the subject-who-lacks and its desire for the other/Other.[53] Meaning in life is also defined in terms of participation, albeit not as imaginary participation in a totality, but as involvement in inter-subjectivity. This is the realm in which desire and the sense of guilt appear in their positive function as constitutive for identity and faith. This is important, because in the romantic nostalgic account of religion underlying the discussions on giving ultimate meaning in a modern secularized society, the

---

[50] To be clear here, this is also a point of critique in the direction of, for example, Winnicott's object relation theory in which symbolization is basically a process of substituting for the absent mother.

[51] Though Vergote argues that the "imaginary" experience of participation in totality is a precondition for religious experience, it is not a "true" religious experience, but a pre-religious one. In "mature religion" wish-religion is changed into "true religiosity". A. Vergote, *Religionspsychologie*, pp. 102-116, pp.386-387.

[52] It should be noticed here that Lacan was originally deeply influenced by Melanie Klein; the two Lacanian orders in a sense still reflect the basic Kleinian "orders", paranoid-schizoid position and depressive position, albeit that Lacan much more stresses the importance of the father. Nevertheless, the Kleinian positions offer a comparable tool for analysing forms of religiosity. An example can be found in the writings of Raguse.

[53] A. Mooij, *Psychiatrie, recht en de menselijke maat*, Uitgeverij Boom, Amsterdam/Meppel, 1998, pp.19-23 (23); H. Stroeken, *Zoeken naar zin*, pp.32-36.

fact that religiosity (and *zingeving*) in lived religion needs symbolic structuring in order not to become either privatized religion or fundamentalism is sometimes overlooked. In other words, the meaning of religious language is overlooked in a discussion that focuses on religious core-experiences and merely treats language as far as it concerns the symbolization of the absent other.

As to the issue of the sense of guilt, we have already noticed the fact that the issue is not predominant in discussions on giving ultimate meaning. This is no surprise, not only given the history of the topic, but also given the predominant imaginary account of religion (as participation in totality of meaning and experience of the authentic self). However, in an imaginary account of religiosity the absence of the issue of sense of guilt should not lead us to conclude that the sense of guilt doesn't play a role of importance in lived religion. The very fact that the religious *zingeving*-processes are often seen as starting in times of crisis and depression, and the need for redefining a world view that provides mental and social wellbeing[54], already indicates that the discrepancy between ego and ego ideal is a central problem here. The symptoms of problems in giving meaning do not contradict this idea. Van der Lans mentions "self doubt" and "feelings of worthlessness", symptoms that from a Freudian perspective (on melancholia) can be associated with the sense of guilt. In my opinion, it is not only Van der Lans' focus on cognitive psychic functions and the goal-oriented characteristics of giving meaning processes that prevents him from further elaborating on these symptoms, but also the very fact that his view on giving ultimate meaning is narrowed down to a theme of depression and wellbeing, i.e. a melancholic narcissistic theme that focuses on the individual's self-regard. Other structuralizing processes as Vergote mentioned them – father, Law, desire, guilt – are outside this perspective. The ideas of Mooij and Stroeken on meaning in life are thus important as a critical corrective to the predominant perspectives. This does not imply that *zingeving* as depicted by Van der Lans should be characterized as non-religious or pre-religious (Vergote), but it will provoke a more profound discussion on the meaning of intersubjective structures. Can wellbeing and meaning in life be defined in terms of absence of feelings of guilt, shame or anxiety, or does religious language as a reflection of and on man's libidinal entanglements also present a positive account of these feelings as implicit in these entanglements? But then again, this touches upon different definitions of religion and religiosity.

Symbolization and sublimation

Throughout our study we have seen further elaborations on Freud's "sketchy" ideas on sublimation and symbolization. Freud's vagueness concerning sublimation inspired his early and later followers to define and apply the issue in

---

[54] J. van der Lans, "Zingeving en zingevingsfuncties van religie bij stress", p.77.

various ways, though not without overcoming sketchy thought. We have seen that the issue plays an important role in the writings of Pfister (2.3.1), Scharfenberg (4.2.1) and Heimbrock (4.3.1), but whereas one might have expected further theoretical elaborations on this issue, sublimation remains a rather vague mechanism of desexualization, and religious and moral sublation/maturation.

Scharfenberg speaks of a "broadening of possibilities" through sublimation that overcomes the existential limitations of life. But what exactly does he mean by that? He refers to sublimation as "redirection" of the drives and calls upon Ricoeur's Hegelian interpretation of Freud, arguing that Freud's thought was at least potentially progressive.[55] Later he focuses on symbolization and the sublation (Hegel's *Aufhebung*) of inner conflicts to a higher level of integration.[56] There is thus a relation between sublimation and symbolization suggested, albeit not explicitly. As to the latter issue, Freud's equation of symbol (sign) and symptom proved problematic and, as in the case of sublimation, caught in a web of reductionism and pathological views.[57]

Scharfenberg's call upon Lorenzer and Ricoeur enabled him to formulate a more constructive theory of the symbol. At this point we should notice an element that links Scharfenberg to Vergote: both their views on sublimation and symbolization are influenced by a Hegelian interpretation of Freud. In the writings of Scharfenberg we have already noticed this influence, an influence that is mainly inspired by Ricoeur.[58] In Vergote's thought, in which symbolization and sublimation coincide (as both mechanisms describe the process of drive renunciation and aiming the drives at acceptable goals in culture), a Hegelian perspective is inspired by Lacan.[59] It becomes apparent in Vergote's definition of

---

[55] J. Scharfenberg, *Sigmund Freud und seine Religionskritik*, pp.162-164.

[56] Compare J. Scharfenberg, *Einführung in der Pastoralpsychologie*, pp.54-60, p.182; J. Scharfenberg, H. Kämpfer, *Mit Symbolen leben*, p.173.

[57] Idem, pp.51ff.

[58] Ricoeur's interpretation of Freud is not only influential in the writings of Scharfenberg: this interpretation is also crucial in Lauret's study of guilt experience. He disapproves of Ricoeur's analysis of archaeology in Freudian psychoanalysis. According to Lauret, Freud himself criticized this archaeology and the subject's contingency when he argued that the ego should be were the id was, that is to say, ego-integration in a symbolic order that provides meaning. B. Lauret, *Schulderfahrung und Gottesfrage bei Nietzsche und Freud*, pp.281-289. Also in the writings of others (Fortmann *inter alia*) we find elaborations on Ricoeur, notably on the concept of "second naivety".

[59] P. Moyaert, *Begeren en vereren*, p.74. There is a noteworthy historic connection between Lacan, Vergote and Ricoeur. Ricoeur's interest in psychoanalysis was triggered by an early article of Vergote on psychoanalysis and Husserl's phenomenology. Inspired by this article, Ricoeur followed the seminars of Lacan and started to study Freud. This lead to the publication of his 1965 *L'interprétation* (*Freud and Philosophy*). Lacan, furious that he was hardly referred to by Ricoeur, reacted with the publication of his *Écrits* (1966). F. Dosse, *Paul Ricoeur. Les sens d"une vie*, Éditions la découverte, Paris, 1997, pp.321-326. For an overview of the relations between Lacan, Vergote and

the symbol as a "unity in differentiation", and symbolization as both an affirmation of separation (from the imaginary relation with the mother) and reintegration through language.[60]

Scharfenberg and Vergote, who both had a profound influence on other scholars, turned to a Hegelian interpretation of Freud in order to reformulate sublimation and/or symbolization. From a strict Freudian perspective one might question this Hegelian interpretation in general and Vergote's equation of sublimation and symbolization in particular. After all, in Freud's thought not progression, whether individual or cultural, but psychic conflict and the return of the repressed is central.[61]

Moyaert has argued that Vergote is right in defining symbolization as a mechanism aiming at unity and reintegration. However, sublimation should not be confused with this mechanism as sublimation is the capacity to take into culture what in human life is not aimed at integration. Sublimation presupposes symbolization as it takes up symbols in order to relate them to what is not integratable. Hence, sublimation points to the capacity to accept the fact that life holds irreconcilable and destructive "evil".[62] In my opinion, we have touched upon this idea in for example Freud's remarks on responsibility as acceptance of one's "immoral nature" (4.3.4); also, Freud's critique on illusions (the belief in moral progress) points in this direction – disillusionment brings us closer to the "truth" about human nature and thus leads to a more realistic assessment of oneself and civilization.

With this "evil" Moyaert indicates that the nature of the drives and the most primitive representations have a "core" that cannot be integrated or redirected. He refers to Lacan's concept of "extimacy", which indicates something eccentric in the subject's inner psychic life. To make it more concrete and visible Lacan had referred to a saying of Luther: "You are the waste matter which falls into the world from the devil's anus".[63] Whatever we think of this provoca-

---

Ricoeur see P. Vandermeersch, "The Failure of Second Naiveté. Some Landmarks in the History of French Psychology of Religion".

[60] A. Vergote, *Religion, Belief and Unbelief*, pp.303ff.; A. Vergote, *De sublimatie*, pp.120-131, p.174.

[61] A. Drassinower, *Freud's Theory of Culture. Eros, Loss, and Politics*, Rowman & Littlefield, Lanham et al., 2003, p.57.

[62] P. Moyaert, *Begeren en vereren*, p.76.

[63] Idem, p.79; J. Lacan, *The Ethics of Psychoanalysis*, p.93. We might supplement this with a range of comparable images found in for example pietistic literature. In my dissertation on self analysis and conscience formation in the writings of the orthodox Reformed minister Teellinck I found similar statements – man is nothing but "filth", "excrement","smelly swamp", "rotting bones" – all indicating the fundamental corruption of the human body and hence the impossibility to be sure about salvation, because of the attachment to this body. This "corporal monstrosity" can be compared with Lacan's concept of the Real indicating what cannot be symbolized. As in the case of Teellinck however it can be sublimated, that is to say, it can be taken into culture in a belief sys-

tive quotation, the point is clear: there is an immoral core in human nature that cannot be integrated in whatever ideal; it resists sublation. Seen from the perspective of Moyaert, sublimation adds to symbolization a truth about human nature. It is this element that gives religious language its depths as it is able to express in language the deepest forsakenness, despair or darkness.

Not only from Moyaert's critique of Vergote is a further discussion of sublimation and symbolization possible. There is also another route. In his text on sublimation Vergote points out that the child (in the *fort-da*-play) has creativity of his own as well as a capacity to say "no" to the imaginary order and to work through the absence of the mother in an ambiguous but clearly also a positive way. It is capable of a cultural achievement that can be interpreted as a reaching out towards the symbolic order. In this analysis of symbolization in play, Vergote, in my opinion, positions himself in-between Lacan and object relations theory (Winnicott). Vergote's play is in fact a "transitional sphere" between imaginary order and symbolic order. When we consider Winnicott's definition of the transitional object as the symbolization of "the union of two separate things, baby and mother, at the point in time and space of the initiation of their very state of separateness"[64] the similarities with Vergote's view on symbolization is remarkable. This however, should not tempt us to rush to conclusions. Despite the similarities there are important differences: the child's "no" against the mother versus the regained presence of the mother in the symbol; the importance of the father function in Lacanian thought; the Lacanian model of alienation and conflict versus Winnicott's model of a conflicted harmony. Nevertheless, given the fact that Lacan can be considered an object relations theorist himself and that Vergote moves in the direction of Winnicott, a fruitful dialogue between two different psychoanalytic traditions on sublimation and symbolization could start here.

For the psychology of religion the work of Moyaert and a further dialogue between the Lacanian and Winnicottian views on sublimation and symbolization is of great importance. After all, these issues are still central to psychoanalytic approaches in the psychology of religion. As to the sense of guilt, the relation between sublimation and the sense of guilt needs further elucidation. We have seen that Vergote took up Freud's suggestion in *Moses and Monotheism* that the "normal" sense of guilt in Judaism incites advancement in intellectuality and encourages sublimation, when he argued that the *Non-du-Père* incites desire, guilt and the sublimation of drives. What then would it mean when we follow Moyaert's critique? Maybe here Freud's suggestion that religion is an attempt to resolve the sense of guilt and at the same time provides the structures that cultivate the sense of guilt, points in the direction of an answer: the "fact" that not everything can be resolved, forgiven or reconciled;

---

tem in which, from a human perspective, a full harmonization through symbolization is impossible. H. Westerink, *Met het oog van de ziel*, pp.284-289.
[64] D.W. Winnicott, *Playing and Reality*, p.130.

there is a primitive "real" core that cannot be symbolized and that yet again and again is approached in religious language. Freud tried to grasp this core in his "myths" of the primal murder and the primal scene, but at this point we can better paraphrase Assmann: why create a mythical construction when the bible is full of "waste matter", the impure that cannot be touched and yet accompanies the history of Israel like a stain?[65]

Guilt traditions

We have throughout our analysis of the reception of Freudian psychoanalysis in theology and religious studies seen that Protestant and Catholic approaches to Freud differ. We cannot conclusively speak of a typical Protestant or a typical Catholic reception of psychoanalysis, because there are always exceptions or cross-influences that contradict such a typology. And yet, it is "typical" that ever since Pope Pius XII made a differentiation between the healthy and unhealthy sense of guilt in the 1950s, we find this scheme of healthy vs. unhealthy sense of guilt returning in Catholic literature. Roughly speaking, the same goes for Protestant pastoral psychology that, emancipating itself from Thurneysen's pastoral care model of proclamation of salvation from sin, did in a sense continue the model of sin and salvation when focussing on resolving the guilt problem through ego-integration or self-realization.

The two Christian branches also reflect different perspectives on narcissism and religious tradition. Again roughly speaking, Catholic scholars tend to positively value the meaning of tradition and thus negatively value narcissism, whereas Protestant scholars tend to be more critical towards traditional religious thought and positively assess narcissistic traits that support individual faith development.

Differences such as these have been noticed in literature, but have not been thoroughly analysed. We have seen some examples of short elaborations on differences in religious mentality in Catholicism and Protestantism. At this point, we touch upon an issue that goes beyond a simple typology concerning the differences in the engagement with psychoanalysis in theology and religious studies, namely the issue whether the different approaches to the guilt problem

---

[65] This impurity, though related to sin and guilt, should not be equated with these concepts. Ricoeur can be referred to here as he described the representation of evil in a process starting with the experience of defilement and transgressing into sin and guilt. This tripartite process shows, in my opinion, a certain similarity with Lacan's distinction between Real, Imaginary and Symbolic. The Real coincides with physical defilement. The Imaginary can be related to the level of sin as the latter is seen as "sin before God" (dual relationship, mirror) or sin as destruction of the *Imago Dei*. Guilt is the subjective moment of recognition and internalization of sin and fallibility, and thus situated on the level of the Symbolic. P. Ricoeur, *Philosophie de la volonté. Finitude et culpabilité II. La symbolique du mal*, Éditions Montaigne, Paris, 1960, pp.31-144.

reflect not only different strategies in various religious traditions of how to deal with guilt and the sense of guilt, but also reflect different conceptualizations of guilt in these traditions in the first place. In short: Is there something like a Protestant or Catholic sense of guilt?[66]

There are – surprisingly – few comparative studies on different conceptualizations of faith, sin and guilt in Protestantism and Catholicism.[67] Delumeau's study on the emergence of a Western guilt culture is in fact the most important study here. He concludes from an abundance of material that in 16th and 17th centuries the discourse on sin, guilt and fear becomes "excessive" in both Protestantism and Catholicism. It is exactly here, in the excess, that "typical" differences can be clearly seen. On the one hand, in Catholicism there is the excess of casuistic, of unravelling and classifying sinful desires, thoughts, gestures and acts, with a clear focus (as Foucault had already argued) on sexual sins that need to be confessed in order for the confessor to gain absolution. This practice "deflected attention from questions about the general corruption of human nature".[68] On the other hand, in orthodox forms of Protestantism (Puritanism, Pietism) sin and guilt were closely related to concepts such as original sin and predestination which lead to "a pervasive sense of thorough human sinfulness".[69] Eventually, here also a kind of casuistic was developed, not focussing on sexual thoughts and acts that should be processed in confession, but on the signs of sin and faith according to schemes of progress.[70] Here the believer should certainly not focus on the variety of sins committed, but on the contrary

----

[66] The issue here is not whether there are typical Protestant or Catholic emotions. The question here is whether the interpretation models provided by Catholic and Protestant traditions and that structure and resolve sin, fault and guilt, incite a typical recognition or experience of guilt that is "automatically" associated with other representations, experiences and feelings.

[67] An article on differences between orthodox Protestant and orthodox Catholic concerning guilt experiences is interesting here. The Protestant belief in which being guilty is part of the human condition incites a more non-constructive experience of guilt in comparison to Catholic guilt-experiences. P. Walinga, J. Corveleyn, J. van Saane, "Guilt and Religion: The Influence of Orthodox Protestant and Orthodox Catholic Conceptions of Guilt on Guilt-Experience", in *Archive for the Psychology of Religion* 27 (2005), 113-135.

[68] W.D. Myers, *"Poor Sinning Folk". Confession and Conscience in Counter-Reformation Germany*, Cornell University Press, Ithaca/London, 1996, p.199. On the Reformation's critique of sacramental confession as blueprint for further Contra-Reformation and Reformation belief and practice concerning sin and confession see Th.N. Tentler, *Sin and Confession on the Eve of the Reformation*, Princeton University Press, Princeton, 1977, notably chaper 6.

[69] W.D. Myers, *"Poor Sinning Folk"*, p.199.

[70] Classics in Puritanism are Perkins' "Golden Chain" and of course Bunyan's "Pilgrim's Progress".

he should focus on his spiritual progress.[71] Maybe here we find already a historic source for the differences in the views on sublimation, on making distinctions between healthy and unhealthy forms of guilt, on resolving the guilt problem in ego-integration, on tradition and on narcissism.

When the reception of Freudian psychoanalysis in theology and religious studies is not only dependent on the individual or collective interests and preoccupations of scholars, but also influenced by religious traditions in which models of interpretation, thought and practice are handed down, then we should also raise the question of how psychoanalysis itself relates to these traditions. Foucault, for example, argued that the psychoanalytic talking cure was a secular continuation of the Catholic confession practice.[72] Yet, Freud not only produced a secular variant of Christian practice. Freud himself situates his thought in a religious tradition when he not only identifies himself with Moses or St Paul, but also identifies psychoanalysis with the advancement in intellectuality that tries to capture in words its repressed counterpart, the sense of guilt. Seen from this perspective Freud's interest in the sense of guilt of his patients is more than a reflection on Viennese *fin-de-siècle* mentality, and his reflections on the sense of guilt in culture and religion are more than the applied extension of his practice at the Berggasse.

Also, Freud was aware that understanding the "secular" sense of guilt he found in his patients and cultural environment could only be fully comprehended when this sense of guilt could be situated in a cultural and religious tradition in which this "secular" sense of guilt was already a key element, whether repressed, canalized and/or expressed.[73] The individual cannot escape this past

---

[71] A fundamental difference here is the fact that Catholic believers are called upon to confess their sins before a priest who represents the religious institution and tradition, whereas the Protestant believer is made personally responsible for his own spiritual development.

[72] M. Foucault, *La volonté de savoir*. Osmond, in a study of body and soul dialogues in 17th century religious literature, concludes that Freud's superego and id merely replaced the vocabulary of the inner conflict between body (sin) and soul as the predominant expression of man's self-perception in early modernity. R. Osmond, *Mutual Accusation. Seventeenth-Century Body and Soul Dialogues in Their Literary and Theological Context*, University of Toronto Press, Toronto/Buffalo/London, 1990, pp.185-186. De Certeau has written that certain "Christian phantoms" that characterize modern mysticism return in Lacan's ideas on the separation between the subject of the statement and the subject of the speech-act, in his thought on the "lack", symbolic debt and separation, and in further reflections on the death drive. This relation between Lacan and modern mysticism could be comparable to Freud's relation to Jewish tradition. M. de Certeau, *Heterologies*, pp.36-37.

[73] Freud's preoccupation with the sense of guilt and his continuing search for its sources is often simply labelled with the term "reductionism". Research on the influence of Christian mentality on the emergence of psychoanalysis might also open another perspective: when Freud analysed symptoms in order to find a hidden source for the sense

collective history, this chain of identifications with superegos that together form a tradition.[74] It can only work through this history in order to make this legacy its own.

In Freudian anthropology the subject is regarded an individual and cultural construct. The structuralizing psychic processes are coloured by pathological types and cultural historic contexts. These central aspects of Freudian anthropology thus opened up a scientific perspective on which scholars could elaborate: the emergence of a guilt culture (Delumeau); the practices, techniques and power structures that are involved in the self-perception of individuals (Foucault); the importance of religious language for the constitution of an ever shifting identity in modernity (De Certeau); the meaning and structure of cultural memory (Assmann (4.5.1)) and the interplay of unconscious and conscious memory traces (Bernstein); the importance of the father figure in religion and the often unconscious motives involved in religiosity (Vergote (5.3)); and the various ways in which religious traditions and denomination deal with the sense of guilt.

Here we touch upon the relation between the psychology of religion and the history of mentality. The psychology of religion as the study of the interaction between individual psychic life and religion in a specific cultural context also has a historic branch of which the psycho-biographies are the most prominent components: from Pfister's studies on Zinzendorf and St Paul until contemporary studies in psycho-biography/psychohistory.[75] Already Freud questioned the status of psycho-biographies as sometimes naïve applications of psychoanalytic schemes that were supposed to explain personality.[76] In other words, there is the danger of reductionism and psychologism. However, when psychoanalysis "only" offers interpretive schemes in order to understand certain aspects of a personality, such studies do give us a better understanding of the

---

of guilt, he was in fact following a procedure that can be found throughout the history of Christianity (and starting at least with the early Western monastic traditions and the confessions of St. Augustine), namely the analysis of "symptoms" (thoughts, needs, acts, dreams, longings, vices, virtues) in order to find a hidden deeper source influencing mental life.

[74] Concerning the superego Foucault and Kittsteiner have argued that the Freudian concept of superego does not describe a universal structure of the mind, but is the historic product of developments in Western thought starting with Reformation conscience formation and then crossing over into an enlightened "conscience of virtue". Thus, modernity is characterized by the internalization of good and evil in the inner life causing a bipolar psychic structure of ego versus conscience. This is the foundation on which Freud constructs his ideas of the superego as the seat of internalized morality. H. Kittsteiner, *Die Entstehung des modernen Gewissens*. For an application of this theory see A.E. Goldberg, *Sex, Religion and the Making of Modern Madness. The Eberbach Asylum and German Society 1815-1849*, Oxford University Press, Oxford, 1999, pp.71ff.

[75] For example see W.W. Meissner, *Ignatius of Loyola*.

[76] S. Freud, *Leonardo da Vinci*, p.130; S. Freud, *An Autobiographical Study*, p.65.

historic individual and his or her religiosity in a cultural religious context. This is then also the limitation of these studies: from the individual psycho-biography a collective mentality[77] cannot be reconstructed. Yet when the psycho-biographer takes into account the fact that the historic individual is part of collective mentality then he can also contribute to this field. Personal identity is the result of the interaction between psychic interiority and the outside symbolic cultural world that together determine the individual's self-perception, possibilities and limitations.[78] When psychology of religion studies the interaction between individual and religion as part of a cultural system, and when the individual is socialized into a collective mentality or cultural memory, it is clear that the borders between the psychology of religion and the history of mentality become fluid as both disciplines work with historic lived religion inscribed in texts and artefacts.[79]

---

[77] By collective mentality I mean not only that an individual participates in the totality of mental representations of a certain group at a certain time in history, but also that the individual (and group) participates in a collective mentality that covers a longer period of time and that consists of more unconscious patterns of thought and memories that provide the individual structures for interpretation and mental processing. In the French history of mentality this "unconscious" collective mentality that covers a longer period of time is called *longue durée* (Fernand Braudel) or "the inertia of mental structures" (Michel Vovelle). M. Vovelle, *Ideologies and Mentalities*, Polity Press, Cambridge, 1990, p.8, pp.126ff. This description of collective mentality as formulated in the French history of mentality strongly resemblances Assmann's theories cultural memory. This is not surprising when we notice the fact that Assmann is influenced by Halbwachs, who was a member of the French *Annales* school from which history of mentality emerged. We are thus dealing here with theories that show a family resemblance.

[78] Again, religion is not a symbolic system that appeals to people who actively and intentionally search for a coherent world view (Van der Lans, Zock). On the contrary, the symbolic cultural world confronts us with possibilities and limitations that set the religious desire in motion (Vergote).

[79] At this point we should notice the influence of Freud again. There is no coincidence in Assmann's "rediscovery" of Freud's Moses text: the history of mentality has as much been influenced by Freud as the psychology of religion. Whatever the justified critique of Freud's writings on culture, religion and art, these studies were milestones that profoundly influenced the history of mentality. An example can be found in Norbert Elias" *Über den Prozeß der Zivilisation* (1939). Elias was a founding father of the history of mentality, who in his *magnum opus* developed a theory of the development of civilization (through differentiations in societal functions and pressure of competition) from a culture of shame into a culture of guilt in which an enforced moral culture gradually took the form of self control (modulation of the drives) guarded by conscience and superego. Freud's ideas on the cultural superego and the conflict between ego and conscience were profoundly influential here. N. Elias, *Über den Prozeß der Zivilisation. Soziogenetische und psychogenetische Untersuchungen, 2 Bände*, Suhrkamp, Frankfurt, 1997.

The history of mentality and cultural psychology confront psychology with the fact that subjectivity is culturally constituted.[80] That doesn't just mean that people in different eras and cultures think and desire something different than we, but more radically it means that people think and desire in different ways, that self-perception, sexuality, cognition, mental health, the expressions of the sense of guilt are historically determined. We can follow Clifford Geertz's statement: "There is no such thing as human nature independent of culture".[81] This idea can already be found in Freud's writings: Oedipus and Hamlet show that the inner conflicts are perceived in various ways, and that, even more radically, repression (and even the unconscious), conscience formation and experience of a sense of guilt cannot be detached from history. This is in fact an application of clinical experience: the individual obtains self-knowledge by working through his own history. By extension, this means working through collective history. There is a second idea here that should also be noticed: the individual obtains self-knowledge from being confronted with another person's identity. In Freud's writings, these two are indistinguishable: in individual and collective history one finds the savage in oneself, the other that confronts civilized man with another identity inside himself and that forces him to reassess himself.[82] These ideas on subjectivity – identity as a cultural-historic construct in contrast to another identity that, as Foucault has described at length is often excluded or disciplined (for example, the madman) because of this "otherness"[83] – are important for a psychology of religion that tries to grasp the individual's religious life in a specific cultural context.

The study of the varieties of subjectivity has been somewhat neglected in the psychology of religion. The reason for this, in my opinion, can be found throughout our study: psychologists of religion have strongly affiliated themselves with a "project" that started in the 1950s and 1960s: the contribution of the human sciences in rethinking and re-establishing the relation between church/theology and faith practice. In the Netherlands this is particularly clear in the Fortmann tradition (3.4.5). In German theology this is reflected in the fact that psychology of religion is inappropriately identified with pastoral psychol-

---

[80] For an introduction to this issue see J.A. van Belzen, "Cultural Psychology of Religion Synchronic and Diachronic", in J.A. van Belzen (ed.), *Hermeneutical Approaches in Psychology of Religion*, pp.109-127.

[81] Cited in idem, p.112.

[82] Cultural anthropologists such as Geza Roheim, Bronislaw Malinowski, Margaret Mead, Georges Devereux or Edmond and Cécile Ortigues defended or confronted Freudian psychoanalysis with this other starting from a clear distinction between various cultural systems. Here, we find research in which findings of psychoanalysis are integrated in the study of different mentalities, psychological structures or variations in psychopathologies in other cultural contexts. This is an important field of research (cultural anthropology, cultural psychology, ethno-psychiatry) that has also been somewhat neglected in psychology of religion.

[83] M. Foucault, *Histoire de la folie à l'âge classique*, Gallimard, Paris, 1972.

ogy. In this project, scholars were more interested in what Scharfenberg called the principle of anthropological constancy (4.2.1) underlying the individual and denominational differences or in what Fortmann indicated with the second primitivity he wanted to save in a modern world (3.4.3). On a pastoral level this is reflected in the emphasis on empathy. In other words, the emphasis was not on subjectivity as historic construct or on the other as other, but on the invariable anthropological structures that underlie cultural diversity. In current literature on lived religion however we can notice a call for a certain shift of attention.[84] Lived religion as the starting point in theological disciplines, calls for a phenomenology of lived religion which implies an analysis of subjectivity and self-perception as historic constructs. Here, Freudian anthropology may well provide an alternative theoretical point of departure as it focuses on the subject as contingent and conflictuous construct and already presents a "typology" of personality types (pathological types).

The "return" of religion in the public domain, the rise of New Age spirituality and especially the rise of fundamentalism (both Christian and Muslim) are important for a growing interest in lived religion in a multi-religious intercultural context. Here, psychologists of religion can make important contributions towards providing a better understanding of psychological motives in different forms of religiosity and spirituality. Again, Freudian psychoanalysis is important here. I will mention, though only briefly, some main points of attention here. A main point of interest could be the importance of the body in various religious practices. It is likely – this is a hypothesis – that the decomposition of traditional theological superstructures implies a genuine shift in faith (as mental act) from "word oriented" cognitive functions to more "primitive" mental structures: faith as more situated on the level of intimacy or bodily sensations, or more associated with ritual practices. This is an important field of attention and raises questions when we, for example, consider the strong secularization in European Protestantism. As to the issue of the sense of guilt in a multi-religious context, we need to understand more about conscience formation, superego structures and the sense of guilt in Islamic culture and religion.[85] The differen-

---

[84] Ganzevoort, for example, calls for a more culture and inter-religious oriented practical theology in the context of theology as less guided by "confession" and more by the science of religion.

[85] Here, the same goes *mutatis mutandis* as for the study of differences between various Christian traditions: it is a study into different mentalities reflected and expressed in religion. Not only are the differences in mentality (from a historic perspective) important here. Psychoanalytic perspectives could also be integrated in qualitative (and quantitative) empirical research comparing psychological motives cross-culturally.

tiation between imaginary and symbolic structures might be an instrument to further study spirituality or fundamentalism in relation to religious tradition.[86]

Rediscovering the lost issues

To make Freudian psychoanalysis fruitful in theology and religious studies in general or the psychology of religion in particular, is a challenge. It first of all means, as Vergote has rightly argued, being critical of Freud's positivistic and pathological views, and his "mythico-dogmatic" constructs and explanations. In other words, one should be critical towards Freud's critique of religion. Only then – this implies a thorough knowledge of psychoanalytic theory – it is possible to more clearly envision the constructive elements in Freudian thought that enable us to understand man's religiosity, or, as Vergote said, the "actual structuralizing processes in religion". Here, the focus is on Freudian psychoanalysis as a theory and method to analyse individual psychic life in interaction with a specific cultural and religious environment. As we have seen, Freud focused on the sense of guilt in various cultural and religious contexts: ritualism, totemism, Christianity, and, as he later reformulated it, in the Judaic tradition.

We have seen that it proved difficult, even impossible, to reconcile Freud's tragic conceptions of human psychic life and culture with theological anthropologies that start off from the essentialist premise of man as *homo religiosus*, or formulate clear objectives regarding healthy faith, moral and religious maturation and the resolvement of inner conflicts, or the search for a psychic *locus* as point of reference in a stable religious philosophy of life or as identified with God's reality (self-realization as God-realization). Freudian psychoanalysis will thus always have a critical voice in the direction of certain theological conceptualizations. Yet here also, psychoanalysis has a constructive potential – it provides fundamental theories of human psychic life and its interactions with others, with culture and with reality. A theologian may thus expect important findings that help understand the nature of faith as a mental act[87] and of man's religious behaviour.

Vergote has shown that it might even be possible to construct a theological anthropology based on Freudian/Lacanian psychoanalysis when psychoanalysis is reformulated and further developed and when the psychic structuralizing processes are at the centre of attention. Not the autonomous ego, the wished-for harmonious psychic life or naïve conceptions of religious perfection-

---

[86] When, as Popp-Baier argues, psychology of religion can show the way in between religious extremes is here rethinking moderate religion starts: not in authentic core-experience, but in the interpretation of one's personal (and cultural) history, the reflections on one's religious tradition and in the social interaction with others and their religious traditions, as constitutive for an own religious identity that not only envisions the Other as desirable Other, but also recognizes the other as desiring other.

[87] Traditionally this is indicated with the concept of *fides qua creditur*.

ism, but man as bodily pulsional being, his fallibility in guilt and desire, his libidinal relations with himself, others and reality are taken as the starting point. Some of Freud's most prominent nuclear ideas are thus accounted for: man as a unity of bodily, unconscious and conscious processes; psychic conflict, including the sense of guilt; the libidinal nature of object relations. These are the main characteristics of Freudian anthropology as to be distinguished from anthropologies that start off from innate ontological potencies (such as a natural intuition or desire for the divine).

Our study of the reception of Freud's psychoanalytic theories in German and Dutch-speaking theology and religious studies has shown that these nuclear elements of Freudian thought were in fact "the lost issues". The human body was virtually absent in the writings of theologians that dealt with integrating psychoanalysis in a theological framework. The issue of psychic conflict and the sense of guilt was overshadowed by and "neutralized" in a discourse on maturation and integration. The libidinal entanglement with objects and reality was not a major issue in discussions on giving ultimate meaning and religious perception. It is precisely because of these past "lost issues" that Freudian psychoanalysis still has an important theoretical potential in reflecting upon the nature of faith as a mental act.

Literature

K. Abraham, *Psychoanalytische Studien zur Charakterbildung und andere Studien*, J. Cremerius (ed.), Fischer Verlag, Frankfurt, 1969.

H.A. Alma, *De parabel van de blinden. Psychologie en het verlangen naar zin*, Humanistics University Press, Utrecht, 2005.

O. Andersson, *Studies in the Prehistory of Psychoanalysis. The Aetiology of psychoneuroses and some related themes in Sigmund Freud's scientific writings and letters 1886-1896*, Svenska Bokförlaget, Stockholm, 1962.

H. Anzenberger, *Der Mensch im Horizont von Sein und Sinn. Die Anthropologie Paul Tillichs im Dialog mit Humanwissenschaften (Rupert Riedl, Erich Fromm und Viktor E. Frankl)*, EOS Verlag, St. Ottilien, 1998.

D. Anzieu, *Freud's Self-Analysis*, Hogarth Press, London, 1986.

M. Argyle, *Psychology and Religion. An Introduction*, Routledge, London/New York, 2000.

A. Assmann, *Erinnerungsräume. Formen und Wandlungen des kulturellen Gedächtnisses*, Beck Verlag, Munich, 1999.

A. Assmann, *Zeit und Tradition. Kulturelle Strategien der Dauer*, Böhlau Verlag, Colone/Weimar/Vienna, 1999.

J. Assmann, "Archäologie und Psychoanalyse. Zum Einfluß Freuds auf die Kultur- und Religionswissenschaft", in *Psyche. Zeitschrift für Psychoanalyse und ihre Anwendungen* 60 (2006/9-10), pp.1040-1053.

J. Assmann, F. Maciewski, "Eine Briefwechsel zwischen Jan Assmann und Franz Maciejewski", in *Psyche. Zeitschrift für Psychoanalyse und ihre Anwendungen* 62 (2008/3), pp.257-265.

J. Assmann, "Der Fortschritt der Geistigkeit. Sigmund Freuds Konstruktion des Judentums", in *Psyche. Zeitschrift für Psychoanalyse und ihre Anwendungen* 56 (2002/2), pp.154-171.

J. Assmann, "Das Herz auf der Waage. Schuld und Sünde im Alten Ägypten", in T. Schabert, D. Clemens (eds.), *Schuld*, Wilhelm Fink Verlag, Munich, 1999, pp.99-147.

J. Assmann, *Das kulturelle Gedächtnis. Schrift, Erinnerung und politische Identität in frühen Hochkulturen*, Beck Verlag, Munich, 1992.

J. Assmann, *Die Mosaische Unterscheidung oder der Preis des Monotheismus*, M. Krüger (ed.), Hanser Verlag, Munich/Vienna, 2003.

J. Assmann, *Moses the Egyptian. The Memory of Egypt in Western Monotheism*, Harvard University Press, Cambridge (Mass.)/London, 1997.

J. Assmann, *Religion als kulturelles Gedächtnis. Zehn Studien*, Beck Verlag, Munich, 2000.

J. Assmann, "Sigmund Freud und das kulturelle Gedächtnis", in *Psyche. Zeitschrift für Psychoanalyse und ihre Anwendungen* 2004, 1, pp.1-25.

J. Assmann, *Thomas Mann und Ägypten. Mythos und Monotheismus in den Josephromanen*, Beck Verlag, Munich, 2006.

J. Assmann, "Das Unbewußte in der Kultur: eine Antwort auf Franz Macie-jewski", in *Psyche. Zeitschrift für Psychoanalyse und ihre Anwendungen* 62 (2008/3), pp.253-256.

P.-L. Assoun, *Freud and Nietzsche*, Athlone Press, London, 2000.

Th. Auchter, "Psychoanalytische Überlegungen zum Thema Liebe", in *Wege zum Menschen* 27 (1975), pp.137-150.

Th. Auchter, "Von der Unschuld zur Verantwortung. Ein Beitrag zum Diskurs zwischen Psychoanalyse und Theologie", in M. Schlagheck (ed.), *Theologie und Psychologie im Dialog über Schuld*, Bonifatius Verlag, Paderborn, 1996, pp.41-138.

Th. Auchter, "Zum Schuldverständnis in der Psychoanalyse im Alten und Neu-en Testament", in *Wege zum Menschen* 30 (1978), pp.208-224.

H.-L. Bach, *"Heilung und Heil, Heilung und Erlösung". Eine Untersuchung der theologisch-soteriologische Implikationen der Seelenheilkunde nach S. Freud und C.G. Jung*, Munster, 1980.

K. Barth, *Die kirchliche Dogmatik*, Evangelischer Verlag, Zollikon-Zurich, 1932-1967.

B. Beit-Hallami, M. Argyle, *The Psychology of Religious Behaviour, Belief and Experience*, Routledge, London/New York, 1997.

J.A. van Belzen (ed.), *Aspects in Context. Studies in the History of Psychology of Religion*, Rodopi, Amsterdam/Atlanta, 2000.

J.A. van Belzen, "Between Feast and Famine. A Sketch pf the Psychology of Religion in the Netherlands", in *International Journal for the Psychology of Religion* 4 (1994) pp.181-197.

J.A. van Belzen (ed.), *Hermeneutical Approaches in Psychology of Religion*, Rodopi, Atlanta/Amsterdam, 1997.

J.A. van Belzen, "Leendert Bouman (1869-1936) en de gereformeerde psychia-trie", in *Maandblad voor de geestelijke volksgezondheid* 43 (1988), pp.817-836.

J.A. van Belzen (ed.), *Op weg naar morgen. Godsdienstpsychologie in Neder-land. Teksten II*, Uitgeverij Kok, Kampen, 2000.

J.A. van Belzen, *Psychologie en het raadsel van de religie. Beschouwingen bij een eeuw godsdienstpsychologie in Nederland*, Uitgeverij Boom, Amsterdam, 2007.

J.A. van Belzen, "Reflections on the Passing Away of a Trailblazer: Joachim Scharfenberg, 1927-1996", in *The International Journal for the Psychology of Religion* 7 (1997), pp.53-55.

J.A. van Belzen, *Religie, melancholie en zelf. Een historische en psychologische studie over een psychiatrisch ego-document uit de negentiende eeuw*, Uitgeverij Kok, Kampen, 2004.

J.A. van Belzen, *Rümke, religie en godsdienstpsychologie. Achtergronden en vooronderstellingen*, Uitgeverij Kok, Kampen, 1991.

J.A. van Belzen (ed.), *Van gisteren tot heden. Godsdienstpsychologie in Neder-land. Teksten I*, Uitgeverij Kok, Kampen, 1999.

J.A. van Belzen, "Verder dan Freud? Na een eeuw psychoanalytische gods-dienstkritiek", in *Tijdschrift voor Theologie* 48 (2008/1), pp.66-90.

B. Benedikt, A. Sobel (eds.), *Der Streit um Drewermann. Was Theolog(inn)en und Psycholog(inn)en kritisieren*, Verlag Sobel, Wiesbaden/Berlin, 1992.

P. Berger, *A far Glory. The Quest for Faith in an Age of Credulity*, The Free Press, New York, 1992.

P. Berger, T. Luckmann, *Modernität, Pluralismus und Sinnkrise. Orientierung des modernen Menschen*, Verlag Bertelsmann Stiftung, Gütersloh, 1995.

H. Bernheim, *Hypnosis and Suggestion in Psychotherapy*, University Books, New York, 1964.

R.J. Bernstein, *Freud and the Legacy of Moses*, Cambridge University Press, Cambridge, 1998.

K. Beth, "Brieven van Karl Beth aan Gerardus van der Leeuw. 1921-1938", University Library Groningen, unpublished.

K. Beth, *Einführung in die vergleichende Religionsgeschichte*, Teubner Verlag, Leipzig/Berlin, 1920.

K. Beth, *Religion und Magie. Ein religionsgeschichtlicher Beitrag zur psychologischen Grundlegung der religiösen Prinzipienlehre*, Teubner Verlag, Leipzig/Berlin, 1927.

K. Beth, *Religion und Magie bei den Naturvölkern. Ein religionsgeschichtlicher Beitrag zur Frage nach den Anfängen der Religion*, Teubner Verlag, Leipzig/Berlin, 1914.

K. Beth (ed.), *Religionspsychologie. Veröffentlichungen des Wiener Religionspsychologischen Forschungs-Institutes durch die Internationale Religionspsychologische Gesellschaft, Heft 1-2*, Braumüller Verlag, Wien/Leipzig, 1926.

K. Beth, "Religionspsychologie und Seelsorge", in *Zeitschrift für Religionspsychologie* 1 (1928), pp.5-25.

A. Biedermann, *Christliche Dogmatik*, Reimer Verlag, Berlin, 1884.

J.M.W. Binneveld, "De ontwikkeling van de institutionele zorg voor krankzinnigen in Nederland in de 19de eeuw", in J.M.W. Binneveld et al. (eds.), *Een psychiatrisch verleden. Uit de geschiedenis van de psychiatrie*, Uitgeverij Ambo, Baarn, 1982, pp.94-119.

L. Binswanger, *Einführung in die Probleme der allgemeinen Psychologie*, Springer Verlag, Berlin, 1922.

A. de Block, *Vragen aan Freud. Psychoanalyse en de menselijke natuur*, Uitgeverij Boom, Amsterdam, 2003.

L. Bouman, "De Psycho-Analyse van Freud", in *Psychiatrische en Neurologische Bladen* 16 (1912), pp.346-363.

K. Brath, "Goethe und Freud – eine besondere Seelenverwandtschaft", in *Psychologie Heute* 26 (1999), pp.38-43.

J.O. van de Breevaart, *Authority in Question. Analysis of a Polemical Controversy on Religion in the Netherlands, 1948-1998*, Uitgeverij Eburon, Delft, 2005.

E. Brunner, *Die Mystik und das Wort*, Verlag Mohr, Tübingen, 1924.

M. Buber, *Schuld und Schuldgefühle*, Verlag Lambert Schneider, Heidelberg, 1958.

I. Bulhof, *Freud en Nederland. De interpretatie en invloed van zijn ideeën*, Uitgeverij Ambo, Baarn, 1983.

I. Bulhof, "Psychoanalysis in the Netherlands", in *Comparative Studies in Society and History* 24 (1982), pp.572-588.

J. Casanova, *Public Religions in the Modern World*, University of Chicago Press, Chicago/London, 1994.

E. Cassirer, *Philosophie der symbolischen Formen. Erster Teil. Der Sprache, Gesammelte Werke 11*, C. Rosenkranz (ed.), Meiner Verlag, Hamburg, 2001.

E. Cassirer, *Philosophie der symbolischen Formen. Zweiter Teil. Das mythische Denken, Gesammelte Werke 12*, C. Rosenkranz (ed.), Meiner Verlag, Hamburg, 2002.

M. de Certeau, *Heterologies. Discourse on the Other*, University of Minnesota Press, Minneapolis/London, 1995.

M. de Certeau, *The Mystique Fable. Volume 1. The Sixteenth and Seventeenth Centuries*, University of Chicago Press, Chicago/London, 1992.

J.-M. Charcot, *Leçons sur les maladies du système nerveux faites à la Salpêtrière. Tome III*, Progrès Médical, Paris, 1877.

J.-M. Charcot, *Neue Vorlesungen über die Krankheiten des Nervensystems insbesondere über Hysterie*, Toeplitz und Deuticke, Leipzig/Vienna, 1886.

F. van Coillie, *De ongenode gast. Zes analytische essays over het verlangen en de dood*, Uitgeverij Boom, Amsterdam, 2004.

T.D. Cooper, *Paul Tillich and Psychology. Historic and Contemprary Explorations in Theology, Psychotherapy, and Ethics*, Mercer University Press, Macon, 2006.

J. Corveleyn, "Folk Religiosity or Psychopathology? The Case of the Apparitions of the Virgin in Beauraing, Belgium, 1932-1933", in J.A. van Belzen (ed.), *Psychohistory in Psychology of Religion: Interdisciplinary Studies*, Rodopi, Amsterdam/Atlanta, 2001, pp.239-259.

J. Corveleyn, *De psycholoog kijkt niet in de ziel. Thema's uit de klinische godsdienstpsychologie*, KSGV, Tilburg, 2003.

J. Cremerius (ed.), *Die Rezeption der Psychoanalyse in der Soziologie, Psychologie und Theologie im deutschsprachigen Raum bis 1940*, Suhrkamp Verlag, Frankfurt, 1981.

G.W. Dawes, *The Historical Jesus Question. The Challenge of History to Religious Authority*, Westminster John Knox Press, Louisville/London/Leiden, 2001.

J. Delumeau, *Sin and Fear. The Emergence of a Western Guilt Culture. 13th-18th Centuries*, St. Martin's Press, New York, 1990.

L. Derckx, *Wrok & begeerte: Een pastoraal-psychologisch onderzoek naar de praktijk van hoofdzonden in een cultuur van narcisme*, Uitgeverij Damon, Budel, 2006.

J. Derrida, *Archive Fever. A Freudian Impression*, University of Chicago Press, Chicago, London, 1996.

J.J. DiCenso, *The Other Freud. Religion, Culture and Psychoanalysis*, Routledge, London/New York, 1999.

F. Dosse, *Paul Ricoeur. Les sens d'une vie*, Éditions la découverte, Paris, 1997.

A. Drassinower, *Freud's Theory of Culture. Eros, Loss, and Politics*, Rowman & Littlefield, Lanham et al., 2003.

D.F. Dreisbach, "Essence, Existence, and the Fall: Paul Tillich's Analysis of Existence", in *Harvard Theological Review* 73 (1980/2), pp.521-538.

E. Drewermann, *"An ihren Fruchten soll ihr sie erkennen". Antwort auf Rudolph Peschs und Gerhard Lohfinks "Tiefenpsychologie und keine Exegese"*, Walter-Verlag, Olten, 1988.

E. Drewermann, *Psychoanalyse und Moraltheologie. Band 1. Angst und Schuld*, Grünewald Verlag, Mainz, 1982.

E. Drewermann, *Strukturen der Bösen. Die jahwistische Urgeschichte in exegetischer Sicht. Band I-III*, Schöningh Verlag, Paderborn/Munich/Vienna/Zurich, 1988.

E. Drewermann, *Tiefenpsychologie und Exegese. Band II. Die Wahrheit der Werke und der Worte. Wunder, Vision, Weissagung, Apokalypse, Geschichte, Gleichnis*, Walter-Verlag, Olten, Freiburg, 1985.

E. Drewermann, "Zu: J. Scharfenberg, '... und die Bibel hat doch recht – diesmal psychologisch?'", in *Wege zum Menschen* 32 (1980), pp.122-123.

N. Elias, *Über den Prozeß der Zivilisation. Soziogenetische und psychogenetische Untersuchungen, 2 Bände*, Suhrkamp, Frankfurt, 1997.

D. Evans, *An Introductory Dictionary of Lacanian Psychoanalysis*, Routledge, London/New York, 1996.

H. Faber, *Geloof en ongeloof in een industrieel tijdperk. Een verkenning*, Uitgeverij Van Gorcum, Assen, 1969.

H. Faber, "Een nieuwe kijk op projectie als godsdienstig verschijnsel", in *Nederlands Theologisch Tijdschrift* 39 (1985), pp.110-127.

H. Faber, *Psychology of Religion*, SCM Press, London, 1976.

H. Faber, "Zicht op de structuur van de godsdienstige ervaring: twee boeken", in *Nederlands Theologisch* Tijdschrift 36 (1982), pp.311-331.

J.-B. Fages, *Geschichte der Psychoanalyse nach Freud*, Ullstein Materialien, Frankfurt/Berlin/Vienna, 1981.

W. Failing, H.-G. Heimbrock, *Gelebte Religion wahrnehmen. Lebenswelt – Alltagskultur – Religionspraxis*, Kohlhammer Verlag, Stuttgart/Berlin/Colone, 1998.

L. Feuerbach, *Das Wesen des Christentums*, Reclam, Stuttgart, 1994.

B. Fink, *The Lacanian Subject. Between Language and Jouissance*, Princeton University Press, Princeton, 1995.

J. Fontaine, J. Corveleyn, P. Luyten et al., "Untying the Gordian Knot of Guilt and Shame. The Structure of Guilt and Shame Reactions", in *Journal for Cross-Cultural Psychology* 37 (2006/3), pp.273-292.

H.M.M. Fortmann, *Als ziende de Onzienlijke. Een cultuurpsychologische studie over de religieuze waarneming en de zogenaamde religieuze projectie, delen I-II*, Uitgeverij Gooi en Sticht, Hilversum, 1981.

H.M.M. Fortmann, *Heel de mens. Reflecties over de menselijke mogelijkheden*, W. Berger (ed.), Uitgeverij Ambo, Baarn/Bilthoven, 1972.

M. Foucault, *Histoire de la folie à l'âge classique*, Gallimard, Paris, 1972.

M. Foucault, *Histoire de la sexualité 1. La volonté de savoir*, Gallimard, Paris, 1976.

J. Frazer, *The Golden Bough. A Study in Magic and Religion*, MacMillan, London, 1974.

S. Freud, *Gesammelte Werke, 18 Bände*, A. Freud et al. (eds.), Fischer Verlag, Frankfurt, 1940-1968.

S. Freud, *The Standard Edition of the Complete Psychological Works of Sigmund Freud (SE), Volumes I-XXIV*, J. Strachey (ed.), Hogarth Press and The Institute of Psycho-Analysis, London, 1953-1966.

S. Freud, *Werken. 11 delen*, W. Oranje et al. (eds.), Uitgeverij Boom, Amsterdam, 2006.

S. Freud, K. Abraham, *A Psychoanalytic Dialogue. The Letters of Sigmund Freud and Karl Abraham*, H. Abraham, E. Freud (eds.), Basic Books, New York, 1965.

S. Freud, L. Andreas-Salomé, *Sigmund Freud. Lou Andreas-Salomé. Briefwechsel*, E. Pfeiffer (ed.), Fischer, Frankfurt, 1966.

S. Freud, *The Complete Letters of Sigmund Freud to Wilhelm Fliess 1887-1904*, J.M. Masson (ed.), Harvard University Press, Cambridge (Mass.)/London, 1985.

S. Freud, G. Groddeck, *Georg Groddeck. Sigmund Freud. Briefwechsel*, Limes Verlag, Wiesbaden/Munich, 1985.

S. Freud, *Letters of Sigmund Freud*, E.L. Freud (ed.), Basic Books, New York, 1960.

S. Freud, O. Pfister, *Psychoanalysis und Faith. The Letters of Sigmund Freud and Oskar Pfister*, H. Meng, E. Freud (eds.), Basic Books, New York, 1963.

J. Frey, *Eugen Drewermann und die biblische Exegese. Eine methodisch-kritische Analyse*, Mohr Verlag, Tübingen, 1995.

D. Funke, *Das Schulddilemma. Wege zu einem versöhnten Leben*, Vandenhoeck & Ruprecht, Göttingen, 2000.

R. Ganzevoort, *De hand van God en andere verhalen. Over veelkleurige vroomheid en botsende beelden*, Uitgeverij Meinema, Zoetermeer, 2006.

R. Ganzevoort, "De pastor(ant) als theoloog. De theologische kwaliteit van het pastorale gesprek", in *Gereformeerd Theologisch Tijdschrift* 100 (2000/3), pp.114-123.

R. Ganzevoort et al. (eds.), *Vergeving als opgave. Psychologische realiteit of onmogelijk ideaal?*, KSGV, Tilburg, 2003.

R. Ganzevoort, J. Visser, *Zorg voor het verhaal. Achtergrond, methode en inhoud van pastorale begeleiding*, Uitgeverij Meinema, Zoetermeer, 2007.

P. Gay, *Freud: A Life for Our Time*, Norton & Company, New York/London, 1988.

P. Gay, *A Godless Jew. Freud, Atheism, and the Making of Psychoanalysis*, Yale University Press, New Haven/London, 1987.

T. Geyskens, Ph. van Haute, *Van doodsdrift tot hechtingstheorie. Het primaat van het kind bij Freud, Klein en Hermann*, Uitgeverij Boom, Amsterdam, 2003.

T. Geyskens, "Freuds Letters to Fliess. From Seduction to Sexual Biology, from Psychopathology to a Clinical Anthropology", in *International Journal for Psychoanalysis* 82 (2001), pp.861-876.

T. Geyskens, *Never Remembered. Freud's Construction of Infantile Sexuality*, Nijmegen, 2002.

R. Girard, *Das Ende der Gewalt*, G. Lohfink (ed.), Herder Verlag, Basel/Freiburg/Vienna, 1983.

K. Girgensohn, *Der seelische Aufbau des religiösen Erlebens. Eine religionspsychologische Untersuchung auf experimenteller Grundlage*, Hirzel Verlag, Leipzig, 1921.

G. Gödde, *Traditionslinien des "Unbewußten". Schopenhauer – Nietzsche – Freud*, Edition Discord, Tübingen, 1999.

R. Goetschi, *Der Mensch und seine Schuld. Das Schuldverständnis der Psychotherapie in seiner Bedeutung für Theologie und Seelsorge*, Benziger Verlag, Zurich, Einsiedeln/Colone, 1976.

C.G. Goetz, M. Bonduelle, T. Gelfand, *Charcot. Constructing Neurology*, Oxford University Press, New York/Oxford, 1995.

A.E. Goldberg, *Sex, Religion and the Making of Modern Madness. The Eberbach Asylum and German Society 1815-1849*, Oxford University Press, Oxford, 1999.

A. Görres, K. Rahner, *Das Böse. Wege zu seiner Bewältigung in Psychotherapie und Christentum*, Herder Verlag, Freiburg/Basel/Vienna, 1982.

W. Gräb. *Lebensgeschichten – Lebensentwürfe – Sinndeutungen. Eine Praktische Theologie gelebter Religion*, Kaiser Verlag, Gütersloh, 2000.

K. Grau, *"Healing Power"- Ansätze zu einer Theologie der Heilung im Werk Paul Tillichs*, LIT Verlag, Munster/Hamburg/London, 1999.

I. Grubrich-Simitis, *Freuds Moses-Studie als Tagtraum. Ein biographischer Essay*, Verlag Internationale Psychoanalyse, Weinheim, 1991

I. Grubrich-Simitis (ed.), *A Phylogenetic Fantasy. Overview of the Transference Neuroses*, The Belknap Press of Harvard University Press, Cambridge (Mass.)/London, 1987.

O. Haendler, *Grundriss der Praktischen Theologie*, Alfred Töpelmann Verlag, Berlin, 1957.

O. Haendler, *Tiefenpsychologie, Theologie und Seelsorge. Ausgewählte Aufsätze*, J. Scharfenberg, K. Winkler (eds.), Vandenhoeck & Ruprecht, Göttingen, 1971.

M. Halbwachs, *Les cadres sociaux de la mémoire*, G. Namer (ed.), Éditions Albin Michel, Paris, 1994.

H. Harsch, "Psychologische Interpretation biblischer Texte?", in *Wege zum Menschen* 20 (1968), pp.281-289.

H. Harsch, *Das Schuldproblem in Theologie und Tiefenpsychologie*, Quelle & Meyer, Tübingen, 1965.

E. von Hartmann, *Philosophie des Unbewußten. Versuch einer Weltanschauung*, Varl Duncker's Verlag, Berlin, 1869.

H. Hartmann, *Psychoanalyse und moralische Werte*, Fischer, Frankfurt, 1992.

M. Hartung, *Angst und Schuld in Tiefenpsychologie und Theologie*, Kohlhammer Verlag, Stuttgart, 1979.

Ph. van Haute, "About Sublimation. Interview with Antoine Vergote", in *Ethical Perspectives* 5 (1998), pp.218-224.

Ph. van Haute, *Against Adaptation. Lacan's 'subversion'of the subject*, Other Press, New York, 2002.

Ph. van Haute, "Michel Foucault: de psychoanalyse en de wet", in *Tijdschrift voor Filosofie* 55 (1993/3), pp.449-471.

A. Hegger et al. (eds.), *Over schuld en schaamte*, KSGV, Tilburg, 2005.

P. Heelas, *New Age Movement. The Celebration of the Self and the Sacralization of Modernity*, Blackwell, Oxford, 1996.

A. van Heeswijk, N. ter Linden, M.H.F. van Uden, T.H. Zock (eds.), *Op verhaal komen. Religieuze biografie en geestelijke gezondheid*, KSGV, Tilburg, 2006.

H.-G. Heimbrock, *Phantasie und Christlicher Glaube. Zum Dialog zwischen Theologie und Psychoanalyse*, Kaiser Verlag, Munich, 1977.

S. Heine, "Erkennen und Scham. Sigmund Freuds biblisches Menschenbild", in *Verbum et Ecclesia* 27 (2006/3), pp.869-885.

S. Heine, *Grundlagen der Religionspsychologie. Modelle und Methoden*, Vandenhoeck & Ruprecht, Göttingen, 2005.

Chr. Henning, "Die Funktion der Religionspsychologie in der Protestantischen Theologie um 1900", in Chr. Henning, E. Nestler (eds.), *Religion und Religiosität zwischen Theologie und Psychologie: Bad Boller Beiträge zur Religionspsychologie*, Lang Verlag, Frankfurt, 1998, pp.27-78.

Chr. Henning, "Phönix aus der Asche. Die Wiedergeburt des Christentums aus dem Geist der Psychoanalyse bei Oskar Pfister (1873-1956)", in V. Drehsen, W.

Sparn (eds.), *Vom Weltbildwandel zur Weltanschauungsanalyse. Krisenwahrnehmung und Krisenbewältigung um 1900*, Akademie Verlag, Berlin, 1996, pp.131-165.

Chr. Henning, S. Murken, E. Nestler (eds.), *Einführung in die Religionspsychologie*, Schöningh Verlag, Paderborn/Munich/Vienna/Zurich, 2003.

Chr. Henning, "Gescheiterte Beziehung? Ein Einblick in das Verhältnis von Theologie und Psychologie in der Zeit zwischen 192 und 1960", in *Praktische Theologie. Zeitschrift für Religion, Gesellschaft und Kirche* 35 (2000/2), pp.85-97.

Chr. Henning, "Zankapfel Psychoanalyse. Ein Rückblick auf das gespannte Verhältnis von evangelischer Theologie und Psychologie im 20. Jahrhundert", in Chr. Henning, E. Nestler (eds.), *Religionspsychologie heute*, Lang Verlag, Frankfurt, 2000, pp.67-102.

H. Henseler, *Religion – Illusion? Eine psychoanalytische Deutung*, Steidl Verlag, Göttingen, 1995.

M. Hirsch, *Schuld und Schuldgefühl. Zur Psychoanalyse von Trauma und Introjekt*, Vandenhoeck & Ruprecht, Göttingen, 1997.

D. Hoch, "Vom Umgang mit Schuld. Geschichte einer Tagung", in *Wege zum Menschen* 32 (1980), pp.239-253.

M. Hoffmann, *Selbstliebe. Eine grundlegendes Prinzip von Ethos*, Schöningh Verlag, Paderborn/Munich/Vienna/Zurich, 2002.

W. Hofstee, *Goden en mensen. De godsdienstwetenschap van Gerardus van der Leeuw*, Uitgeverij Kok, Kampen, 1997.

E. Hölscher, M. Klessmann (eds.), *Grundmuster der Seele. Pastoralpsychologische Perspektiven von Klaus Winkler*, Vandenhoeck & Ruprecht, Göttingen, 2003.

P. Homans (ed.), *The Dialogue between Theology and Psychology*, The University of Chicago Press, Chicago/London, 1968.

A. Houtepen, *Uit aarde, naar Gods beeld. Theologische antropologie*, Uitgeverij Meinema, Zoetermeer, 2006.

J. van Iersel, *Wetenschap als eigenbelang. Godsdienstwetenschap en dieptepsychologie in het werk van dr. F. Sierksma (1917-1977)*, Uitgeverij Dora, Rosmalen, 1991.

S. Isaacs, "Privation and Guilt", in *International Journal of Psychoanalysis* 10 (1929), pp.335-347.

G.A. James, *Interpreting Religion. The Phenomenological Approaches of Daniël Chantepie de la Saussaye, W. Brede Kristensen, and Gerardus van der Leeuw*, The Catholic University of America Press, Washington, 1995.

J. Janssen, *Nederland als religieuze proeftuin*, KSGV, Nijmegen, 1998.

J. Janssen, *Religie in Nederland: kiezen of delen?*, KSGV, Tilburg, 2007.

J. Janssen, M.H.F. van Uden, H. van der Ven (eds.), *Schering en inslag. Opstellen over religie in de hedendaagse cultuur*, KSGV, Nijmegen, 1998.

K. Jaspers, *Allgemeine Psychopathologie*, Springer Verlag, Berlin/Göttingen/Heidelberg, 1959.

J. Jeremias, *Die Theorie der Projektion im religionkritischen Denken Sigmund Freuds und Erich Fromms*, Oldenburg, 1978.

E. Jones, *The Life and Work of Sigmund Freud, Volumes 1-3*, Basic Books, New York, 1959

E. Jones, "The Origin and Structure of the Super-Ego", in *International Journal of Psychoanalysis* 7 (1926), pp.303-311.

E. Jones, *Papers on Psycho-Analysis*, Baillière, London, 1950.

J.W. Jones, *Contemporary Psychoanalysis and Religion. Transference and Transcendence*, Yale University Press, New Haven/London, 1991.

N. Jongsma-Tieleman, *Godsdienst als speelruimte van verbeelding. Een godsdienstpsychologische studie*, Uitgeverij Kok, Kampen, 1996.

C.G. Jung, *Gesammelte Werke. Band 11*, Rascher Verlag, Zurich/Stuttgart, 1963.

C.G. Jung, *Psychology of the Unconscious. A Study of the Transformations and Symbolisms of the Libido. A Contribution to the History of Evolution of Thought*, Princeton University Press, Princeton, 1991.

I. Karle, *Seelsorge in der Moderne. Eine Kritik der psychoanalytisch orientierten Seelsorgelehre*, Neukirchener Verlag, Neukirchen, 1996.

R. Kessler, P. Vandermeersch (eds.), *God, Biblical Stories and Psychoanalytical Understanding*, Lang Verlag, Frankfurt, 2001.

H. Kippenberg, *Die Entdeckung der Religionsgeschichte. Religionswissenschaft und Moderne*, Beck Verlag, Munich, 1997.

H. Kippenberg, B. Luchesi (eds.), *Religionswissenschaft und Kulturkritik*, Diagonal Verlag, Marburg, 1991.

H. Kittsteiner, *Die Entstehung des modernen Gewissens*, Suhrkamp Verlag, Frankfurt, 1995.

M. Klein, *Love, Guilt and Reparation and Other Works, 1921-1945*, R.E. Money-Kyrle (ed.), Hogarth Press, London, 1975.

M. Klessmann, *Identität und Glaube. Zum Verhältnis von psychischer Struktur und Glaube*, Kaiser Verlag, Munich, 1980

M. Klessmann, *Pastoralpsychologie. Ein Lehrbuch*, Neukirchener Verlag, Neukirchen, 2004.

U. Körtner, "Ist die Moral das Ende der Seelsorge, oder ist die Seelsorge am Ende Moral?", in *Wege zum Menschen* 58 (2006), pp.225-245.

U. Körtner, "Spiritualität ohne Exegese? Pneumatologische Erwägungen zur biblischen Hermeneutik", in *Amt und Gemeinde* 53 (2002), pp.41-54.

W. Krikilion, "De ethiek van het verlangen in de psychotherapie", in E. Maeckelberghe, H. Westerink (eds.), *Gekke verlangens. Opstellen in ethiek en godsdienstpsychologie voor Patrick Vandermeersch*, Uitgeverij Kok, Kampen, 2008, pp.116-131.

H. Kuitert, *Voor een tijd een plaats van God. Een karakteristiek van de mens*, Uitgeverij Ten Have, Baarn, 2002.

J. Lacan, *L'Angoisse. Séminaire 1962-1963*, Éditions de l'Association Freudienne Internationale, Publication hors commerce, Paris, 2000.

J. Lacan, *Écrits I*, Éditions de Seuil, Paris, 1999.

J. Lacan, *The Seminar of Jacques Lacan, Book VII. The Ethics of Psychoanalysis 1959-1960*, J.-A. Miller (ed.), Routledge, London, 1992.

J. Lacan, *L'identification. Séminaire 1961-1962*, Éditions de l'Association Freudienne Internationale, Publication hors commerce, Paris, 2000.

J. Lacan, *Le Séminaire. Livre IV. La relation d'objet, 1956-1957*, J. Miller (ed.), Éditions de Seuil, Paris, 1994.

J. Lacan, *Le Séminaire. Livre V. Les formations de l'inconscient, 1957-1958*, J. Miller (ed.), Éditions de Seuil, Paris, 1998.

J. Lacan, *The Seminar of Jacques Lacan, Book XX. On Feminine Sexuality, The Limits of Love and Knowledge, 1972-1973 (Encore)*, J. Miller (ed.), Norton & Company, New York/London, 1999.

A. Lambertino, *Psychoanalyse und Moral bei Freud*, Bouvier Verlag, Bonn, 1994.

J. Lampl-De Groot, "Ich-Ideal und Über-Ich", in *Psyche* 17 (1963), pp.321-332.

J. van der Lans, *Religie ervaren. Godsdienstpsychologische opstellen*, KSGV, Tilburg, 2006.

J. van der Lans, *Religieuze ervaring en meditatie*, Uitgeverij Benschop en Thissen, Nijmegen, 1978.

J. van der Lans, L. Vergouwen, "Religiositeit en fantasie. Een beschouwing over onderzoeksgegevens omtrent het omgaan met religieuze beelden", in J.A. van Belzen, J. van der Lans (eds.), *Rond godsdienst en psychoanalyse. Essays voor dr. Arnold Uleyn*, Uitgeverij Kok, Kampen, 1986, pp.88-101.

J. Laplanche, J.-B. Pontalis, *Vocabulaire de la psychanalyse*, Presses Universitaires de France, Paris, 1967.

V. Läpple, J. Scharfenberg (eds.), *Psychotherapie und Seelsorge*, Wissenschaftliche Buchgesellschaft, Darmstadt, 1977.

Chr. Lasch, *The Culture of Narcissism. American Life in an Age of Diminishing Expectations*, Norton, New York, 1978.

B. Lauret, *Schulderfahrung und Gottesfrage bei Nietzsche und Freud*, Kaiser Verlag, Munich, 1977.

J. Lear, *Happiness, Death, and the Remainder of Life*, Harvard University Press, Cambridge (Mass.), 2000.

J.-B. Lecuit, *L'anthropologie théologique à la lumière de la psychanalyse. La contribution majeure d'Antoine Vergote*, Éditions du Cerf, Paris, 2007.

L. Leertouwer, "Primitive Religion in Dutch Religious Studies", in *Numen. International Review for the History of Religion* 38 (1991), pp.198-213.

G. van der Leeuw, *Der Mensch und die Religion. Anthropologischer Versuch*, Verlag Haus zum Falken, Basel, 1941.

G. van der Leeuw, *Phänomenologie der Religion*, Mohr Siebeck Verlag, Tübingen, 1933.

G. van der Leeuw, *Plaats en taak van de godsdienstgeschiedenis in de theologische wetenschap*, Uitgeverij Wolters, Groningen, 1918.

G. van der Leeuw, *De primitieve mensch en de religie. Anthropologische studie*, Uitgeverij Wolters, Groningen/Batavia, 1937.

G. van der Leeuw, *La structure de la mentalité primitive*, Alcan, Paris, 1928.

G. van der Leeuw, "Strukturpsychologie und Theologie", in *Zeitschrift für Theologie und Kirche* 9 (1928), pp.321-349.

G. van der Leeuw, "Über einige neuere Ergebnisse der psychologischen Forschung und ihre Anwendungen auf die Geschichte, insonderheit die Religionsgeschichte", in *Studi e materiali di storia delle religioni* 2 (1926), pp.1-43.

M. Leiner, *Psychologie und Exegese. Grundfragen einer textpsychologischen Exegese des Neuen Testaments*, Kaiser Verlag, Gütersloh, 1995.

A. Leupin, *Lacan Today. Psychoanalysis, Science, Religion*, Other Press, New York, 2004.

L. Lévy-Bruhl, *Les functions mentales dans les sociétés inférieures*, Alcan, Paris, 1922.

L. Lévy-Bruhl, *La mentalité primitive*, Presses Universitaires de France, Paris, 1947.

Chr. Link, *Theologische Perspektiven nach Marx und Freud*, Kohlhammer Verlag, Stuttgart, 1971.

W. Loch, "Heilung als Ich-Integration", in *Zur Theorie, Technik und Therapie der Psychoanalyse*, Fischer, Frankfurt, 1972, pp.135-155.

G. Lohfink, R. Pesch (eds.), *Tiefenpsychologie und keine Exegese. Eine Auseinandersetzung mit Eugen Drewermann*, Katholisches Bibelwerk, Stuttgart, 1987.

A. Lorenzer, *Kritik des psychoanalytischen Symbolbegriffs*, Suhrkamp Verlag, Frankfurt, 1970.

H. Luther, *Religion und Alltag. Bausteine zu einer Praktische Theologie des Subjekts*, Radius Verlag, Stuttgart, 1992.

F. Maciejewski, *Der Moses des Sigmund Freud. Ein unheimlicher Bruder*, Vandenhoeck & Ruprecht, Göttingen, 2006.

F. Maciejewski, "Das Unbewußte in der Kultur. Von der Schwierigkeit, die psychoanalytische Kulturtheorie (Freud) in eine kulturwissenschaftliche Gedächtnistheorie (Assmann) zu überführen", in *Psyche. Zeitschrift für Psychoanalyse und ihre Anwendungen* 62 (2008/3), pp.235-252.

A.F.M. Mampuys, *De ik-splijting van de man Mozes en de inscheuring van zijn ik. Een commentaar bij Freuds Mozeswerk, zijn ik-splijtingstekst en de Wolfmanscasus*, Groningen, 1997.

G.E. Marcus, M.M.J. Fischer, *Anthropology as Cultural Critique. An experimental Moment in the Human Sciences*, University of Chicago Press, Chicago/London, 1986.

W.W. Meissner, *Ignatius of Loyola: The Psychology of a Saint*, Yale University Press, New Haven, 1992.

W.W. Meissner, *Psychoanalysis and Religious Experience*, Yale University Press, New Haven/London, 1984.

W. Meng, *Narziβmus und christliche Religion. Selbstliebe – Nächstenliebe – Gottesliebe*, Theologischer Verlag Zürich, Zurich, 1997.

V. Metelmann, "Jesus von Nazareth und die christlichen Symbole unter dem Aspekt tiefenpsychologischer Überlegungen", in *Wege zum Menschen* 23 (1971), pp.22-24.

S.A. Mitchell, M.J. Black, *Freud and Beyond. A History of Modern Psychoanalytic Thought*, Basic Books, New York, 1995.

A. Mitscherlich, *Auf dem Weg zur Vaterlosen Gesellschaft. Ideen zur Sozialpsychologie*, Piper & Co. Verlag, München, 1969.

A.F. Molendijk, *The Emergence of the Science of Religion in the Netherlands*, Brill, Leiden/Boston, 2005.

J. Moltmann, *Der gekreuzigte Gott. Das Kreuz Christi als Grund und Kritik christlicher Theologie*, Kaiser Verlag, Munich, 1973.

A. Mooij, *Psychiatrie, recht en de menselijke maat*, Uitgeverij Boom, Amsterdam/Meppel, 1998.

A. Mooij, *Taal en verlangen. Lacans theorie van de psychoanalyse*, Uitgeverij Boom, Meppel, 1997.

Chr. Morgenthaler, *Systemische Seelsorge. Impulse der Familien- und Systemtherapie für die kirchliche Praxis*, Verlag Kohlhammer, Stuttgart, 1999.

P. Moyaert, *Begeren en vereren. Idealisering en sublimering*, Uitgeverij SUN, Nijmegen, 2002.

P. Moyaert, *Ethiek en sublimatie. Over 'De ethiek van de psychoanalyse' van Jacques Lacan*, Uitgeverij SUN, Nijmegen, 1994.

P. Moyaert, *Iconen en beeldverering. Godsdienst als symbolische praktijk*, Uitgeverij SUN, Amsterdam, 2007.

P. Moyaert, *De mateloosheid van het Christendom. Over naastenliefde, betekenisincarnatie en mystieke liefde*, Uitgeverij SUN, Nijmegen, 1998.

B. Müller, "Zur Ambivalenz monotheistischer Religionen. Die "Mosaische Unterscheidung", das Problem mit der Macht Gottes und die "leise Stimme" der Vernunft", in *Wege zum Menschen* 57 (2006), pp.119-130.

H. Müller-Pozzi, "Gott- Erbe des verlorenen Paradieses. Ursprung und Wesen der Gottesidee im Lichte psychoanalytischer Konzepte", in *Wege zum Menschen* 33 (1981), pp.191-203.

H. Müller-Pozzi, "Die Tabuisierung der Religion in der Psychoanalyse", in *Wege zum Menschen* 30 (1978), pp. 194-207.

H. Müller-Pozzi, *Psychologie des Glaubens. Versuch einer Verhältnisbestimmung von Theologie und Psychologie*, Kaiser Verlag, Munich, 1975.

H. Muthert, *Verlies en verlangen. Verliesverwerking bij schizofrenie*, Uitgeverij Van Gorcum, Assen, 2007.

W.D. Myers, *"Poor Sinning Folk". Confession and Conscience in Counter-Reformation Germany*, Cornell University Press, Ithaca/London, 1996.

E. Nase, *Oskar Pfisters analytische Seelsorge*, De Gruyter, Berlin/New York, 1993.

E. Nase, J. Scharfenberg (eds.), *Psychoanalyse und Religion*, Wissenschaftliche Buchgesellschaft, Darmstadt, 1977.

R. Nauta, *Ik geloof het wel.Godsdienstpsychologische studies over mens en religie*, Uitgeverij Van Gorcum, Assen, 1995.

R. Nauta, *Paradoxaal leiderschap. Schetsen voor een psychologie van de pastor*, Valkhof Pers, Nijmegen, 2006.

K. Niederwimmer, *Jesus*, Vandenhoeck & Ruprecht, Göttingen, 1968.

K. Niederwimmer, "Tiefenpsychologie und Exegese", in R. Riess (ed.), *Perspektiven der Pastoraltheologie*, Vandenhoeck & Ruprecht, Göttingen, 1974, pp.63-78.

I. Noth, "Karl Beth über Religionspsychologie, Seelsorge und Freud. Zur Auseinandersetzung der Wiener Theologischen Fakultäten mit der Psychoanalyse", in *Wiener Jahrbuch für Theologie* 7 (2008), pp.313-326.

I. Noth, Chr. Morgenthaler (eds.), *Seelsorge und Psychoanalyse*, Verlag Kohlhammer, Stuttgart, 2007.

R. Osmond, *Mutual Accusation. Seventeenth-Century Body and Soul Dialogues in Their Literary and Theological Context*, University of Toronto Press, Toronto/Buffalo/London, 1990.

W. Pannenberg, "Aggression und die theologische Lehre von der Sünde", in *Zeitschrift für Evangelische Ethik* 21 (1977), pp.161-173.

W. Pannenberg, *Anthropologie in theologischer Perspektive*, Vandenhoeck & Ruprecht, Göttingen, 1983.

B. Pattyn, "Verlangen, ervaring en openbaring. Het werkelijkheidsbegrip in het denken van A. Vergote", in *Tijdschrift voor Theologie* 31 (1991), pp.381-401.

B. Pattyn, "Wie zal morgen uitmaken wat onzin is? Vragen rond de moderne scepsis tegenover de traditie", in *Tijdschrift voor Theologie* 38 (1998), pp.339-350.

J.M. Perry, *Tillich's Response to Freud: A Christian Answer to the Freudian Critique of Religion*, University Press of America, Lanham/New York/London, 1988.

O. Pfister, *Die Aufgabe der Wissenschaft vom christlichen Glauben in der Gegenwart*, Vandenhoeck & Ruprecht, Göttingen, 1923.

O. Pfister, *Calvins Eingreifen in die Hexer- & Hexenprozesse von Peney 1545 nach seiner Bedeutung für Geschichte & Gegenwart. Ein kritischer Beitrag zur Charakteristik Calvins & zur gegenwärtigen Calvin-Renaissance*, Artemis Verlag, Zurich, 1947.

O. Pfister, "Das Elend unserer wissenschaftliche Glaubenslehre", in *Schweizerische Theologische Zeitschrift* 4 (1905), pp.209-212.

O. Pfister, "Die Entwicklung des Apostels Paulus. Eine religionsgeschichtliche und psychologische Skizze", in *Imago* 6 (1920), pp.243-290.

O. Pfister, *Die Frömmigkeit des Grafen Ludwig von Zinzendorf. Ein psychoanalytischer Beitrag zur Kenntnis der religiösen Sublimierungsprozesse und zur Erklärung der Pietismus*, Deuticke Verlag, Leipzig/Vienna, 1910.

O. Pfister, *Die Genesis der Religionsphilosophie A.E. Biedermanns, untersucht nach Seiten ihren psychologischen Ausbaus*, Zurich, 1898.

O. Pfister, "Die Illusion einer Zukunft. Eine freundschaftliche Auseinandersetzung mit Prof. Dr. Sigm. Freud", in *Imago* 14 (1928), pp.149-184.

O. Pfister, *Psychoanalyse und Weltanschauung*, Internationaler Psychoanalytischer Verlag, Vienna/Leipzig, 1928.

O. Pfister, *Die psychoanalytische Methode. Eine erfahrungswissenschaftlich-systematische Darstellung*, Klinkhardt Verlag, Leipzig, 1921.

O. Pfister, "Die Religionspsychologie am Scheidewege", in *Imago* 8 (1922), pp.368-400.

O. Pfister, *Religiosität und Hysterie*, Internationaler Psychoanalytischer Verlag, Leipzig/Vienna/Zurich, 1928.

O. Pfister, *Was bietet die Psychoanalyse dem Erzieher?*, Klinkhardt Verlag, Leipzig/Berlin, 1917.

O. Pfister, *Die Willensfreiheit: Eine kritisch-systematische Untersuchung*, Reimer Verlag, Berlin, 1904.

O. Pfister, *Zum Kampf um die Psychoanalyse*, Internationaler Psychoanalytischer Verlag, Leipzig,/Vienna/Zurich, 1920.

H. Plessner, *Die Stufen des Organischen und der Mensch. Einleitung in die philosophische Anthropologie*, De Gruyter, Berlin/New York, 1975.

H. Politzer, *Freud und das Tragische*, W. Hemecker (ed.), Edition Gutenberg, Wiener Neustadt, 2003.

H. Pottmeyer, "Heutige Schulderfahrung und das christliche Sprechen von Schuld und Sünde. Verstehensvermittlung als Beitrag zur Schuldbewältigung", in *Schulderfahrung und Schuldbewältigung. Christen im Umgang mit der Schuld*, G. Kaufmann (ed.), Schöningh Verlag, Paderborn/Munich/Vienna/Zurich, 1982, pp.93-114.

U. Popp-Baier, *Das Heilige im Profanen. Religiöse Orientierungen im Alltag. Eine qualitative Studie zu religiösen Orientierungen von Frauen aus der charismatisch-evangelikalen Bewegung*, Rodopi, Amsterdam/Atlanta, 1998.

M. Pratl, *Von der Schuld zum Neubeginn. Die Beichte als Übergangsritual*, LIT Verlag, Vienna/Munster, 2008.

W. Pratscher, "Tiefenpsychologie und Textauslegung", in S. Kreuzer et al. (eds.), *Proseminar I Altes Testament. Ein Arbeitsbuch*, Kohlhammer Verlag, Stuttgart, 1999, pp.178-188.

H.G. Preuss, *Illusion und Wirklichkeit. An den Grenzen von Religion und Psychoanalyse*, Klett Verlag, Stuttgart, 1971.

P. de Quervain, *Psychoanalyse und dialektische Theologie. Zum Freud-Verständnis bei K. Barth, E. Thurneysen und P. Ricoeur*, Verlag Hans Huber, Bern/Stuttgart/Wien, 1977.

J.-M. Quinodoz, *Reading Freud. A Chronological Exploration of Freud's Writings*, Routledge, London/New York, 2005.

H. Raguse, "Der Jubel der Erlösten über die Vernichtung der Ungläubigen", in *Wege zum Menschen* 42 (1990), pp.449-457.

H. Raguse, *Psychoanalyse und biblische Interpretation. Eine Auseinandersetzung mit Eugen Drewermanns Auslegung der Johannes-Apokalypse*, Kohlhammer Verlag, Stuttgart, 1993.

H. Raguse, *Der Raum des Textes. Elemente einer transdisziplinären theologischen Hermeneutik*, Kohlhammer Verlag, Stuttgart, 1994.

O. Rank, *Die Lohengrinsage. Ein Beitrag zu ihrer Motivgestaltung und Deutung*, Deuticke Verlag, Leipzig/Vienna, 1911.

O. Rank, *The Myth of the Birth of the Hero, and other Writings*, P. Freund (ed.), Vintage Books, New York, 1959.

O. Rank, *The Trauma of Birth*, Robert Brunner, New York, 1952.

O. Rank, H. Sachs, "Entwicklung und Ansprüche der Psychoanalyse", in *Imago* 1 (1912), pp.1-16.

U. Rauchfleisch, *Psychoanalyse und theologische Ethik. Neue Impulse zum Dialog*, Herder Verlag, Freiburg/Vienna, 1986.

Th. Reik, "Bemerkungen zu Freuds "Zukunft einer Illusion"", in *Imago* 14 (1928), pp.185-198.

Th. Reik, *Dogma and Compulsion. Psychoanalytic Studies on Religion and Myths*, International Universities Press, New York, 1951.

Th. Reik, *The Psychological Problems of Religion I. Ritual. Psycho-Analytic Studies*, Farrar, Straus and Company, New York, 1946.

T. Rendtorff, *Ethik. Grundelemente, Methodologie und Konkretionen einer ethischen Theologie. Band 2*, Kohlhammer Verlag, Stuttgart/Berlin/Colone, 1991.

E. Rice, *Freud and Moses. The Long Journey Home*, State University of New York Press, Albany, 1990.

P. Ricoeur, *Freud and Philosophy: An Essay on Interpretation*, Yale University Press, New Haven/London, 1970.

P. Ricoeur, *Philosophie de la volonté. Finitude et culpabilité II. La symbolique du mal*, Éditions Montaigne, Paris, 1960.

Ph. Rieff, *Freud: The mind of the Moralist*, Doubleday, New York, 1961.

R. Riess (ed.), *Abschied von der Schuld? Zur Anthropologie und Theologie von Schuldbewusstsein, Opfer und Versöhnung*, Kohlhammer Verlag, Stuttgart/Colone/Berlin, 1996, pp.74-94.

R. Riess, *Seelsorge. Orientierung, Analysen, Alternativen*, Vandenhoeck & Ruprecht, Göttingen, 1973.

C.R. Rogers, *Client-centered Therapy. Its current Practice, Implications and Theory*, Houghton Mifflin, Boston, 1951.

R.R.N. Ross, "The Non-Existence of God: Tillich, Aquinas, and the Pseudo-Dionysius", in *Harvard Theological Review* 68 (1975/2), pp.141-166.

M. Roth, "Oskar Pfister – der Beginn einer problematischen Freud-Rezeption innerhalb der Theologie. Eine Problemanzeige", in *Praktische Theologie. Zeitschrift für Religion, Gesellschaft und Kirche* 35 (2000), pp.40-57.

H.C. Rümke, *Karakter en aanleg in verband met het ongeloof*, Uitgeverij Ten Have, Amsterdam, 1939.

H. Santer, *Persönlichkeit und Gottesbild. Religionspsychologische Impulse für eine Praktische Theologie*, Vandenhoeck & Ruprecht, Göttingen 2003.

V. Saroglou, *Paternity as Function. Structuring the Religious Experience*, Rodopi, Amsterdam/Atlanta, 2001.

J. Scharfenberg, "Bewußtwerdung und Heilung bei Johann Christoph Blumhardt", in F. Wintzer (ed.), *Seelsorge. Texte zum gewandelten Verständnis und zur Praxis der Seelsorge in der Neuzeit*, Kaiser Verlag, Munich, 1985, pp.175-190.

J. Scharfenberg, *Einführung in die Pastoralpsychologie*, Vandenhoeck & Ruprecht, Göttingen, 1985.

J. Scharfenberg, "Existentiale und tiefenpsychologische Interpretation biblischer Texte", in *Wege zum Menschen* 23 (1971), pp.1-2.

J. Scharfenberg, "Identitätskrise und Identitätsfindung im psychoanalytischen Prozeß", in *Wege zum Menschen* 24 (1972), pp.241-252.

J. Scharfenberg, H. Kämpfer, *Mit Symbolen leben. Soziologische, psychologische und religiöse Konfliktbearbeitung*, Walter-Verlag, Olten/Freiburg, 1980.

J. Scharfenberg, "Narzißmus, Identität und Religion", in *Psyche. Zeitschrift für Psychoanalyse und ihre Anwendungen* 27 (1973), pp.949-966.

J. Scharfenberg, *Religion zwischen Wahn und Wirklichkeit. Gesammelte Beiträge zur Korrelation von Psychoanalyse und Theologie*, Furche-Verlag, Hamburg, 1972.

J. Scharfenberg, "Religionspsychologie nach Freud", in *Wege zum Menschen* 27 (1975), pp.433-448.

J. Scharfenberg, *Seelsorge als Gespräch. Zur Theorie und Praxis der seelsorgerischen Gesprächsführung*, Vandenhoeck & Ruprecht, Göttingen, 1991.

J. Scharfenberg, "Seelsorge und Beichte Heute", in *Wege zum Menschen* 24 (1972), pp.80-90.

J. Scharfenberg, "Sigmund Freud", in W. Schmidt (ed.), *Die Religion der Religionskritik*, Claudius Verlag, Munich, 1972, pp.9-17.

J. Scharfenberg, *Sigmund Freud und seine Religionskritik als Herausforderung für den christlichen Glauben*, Vandenhoeck & Ruprecht, Göttingen, 1971.

J. Scharfenberg, "Übertragung und Gegenübertragung in der Seelsorge", in E.R. Kiesow, J. Scharfenberg (eds.), *Forschung und Erfahrung im Dienst der Seel-*

sorge. Festgabe für Otto Haendler zum 70. Geburtstag, Vandenhoeck & Ruprecht, Göttingen, 1961, pp.80-89.

J. Scharfenberg, '... und die Bibel hat doch recht – diesmal psychologisch? Zu Eugen Drewermanns Konzept der Sünde als „Neurose vor Gott"', in *Wege zum Menschen* 31 (1979), pp.297-302.

J. Scharfenberg, 'Zur Deutschen Ausgabe', in E. Stein, *Schuld im Verständnis der Tiefenpsychologie und Religion*, Walter-Verlag, Olten/Freiburg, 1978, p.9.

A. Schilder, *Hulpeloos maar schuldig. Het verband tussen een gereformeerde paradox en depressie*, Uitgeverij Kok, Kampen, 1987.

F. Schleiermacher, *On Religion. Speeches to its Cultured Despisers*, R. Crouter (ed.), Cambridge University Press, Cambridge, 1988.

F. Schleiermacher, *Über die Religion. Reden an die Gebildeten unter ihren Verächtern*, G. Meckenstock (ed.), De Gruyter, Berlijn/New York, 2001.

G. Schneider-Flume, *Grundkurs Dogmatik. Nachdenken über Gottes Geschichte*, Vandenhoeck & Ruprecht, Göttingen, 2004.

G. Schneider-Flume, *Die Identität des Sünders. Eine Auseinandersetzung theologischer Anthropologie mit dem Konzept der psychosozialen Identität Erik H. Eriksons*, Vandenhoeck & Ruprecht, Göttingen, 1985.

G. Schneider-Flume, *Leben ist kostbar. Wider die Tyrannei des gelingenden Lebens*, Vandenhoeck & Ruprecht, Göttingen, 2002.

G. Schneider-Flume, "Narzißmus als theologisches Problem", in *Zeitschrift für Theologie und Kirche* 82 (1985), pp.88-110.

C. Schneider-Harpprecht, "Psychoanalytische Bibelauslegung. Das Beispiel der Hagar-Ismael-Überlieferung", in *Wege zum Menschen* 32 (1991), pp.323-335.

J. van Scheyen, "Bezwaard gemoed in een regio: over relaties tussen endogene (vitale) depressies, religie en suïcide", in *Tijdschrift voor Psychiatrie* 1975/17, pp.775-788.

T. Schirrmacher, *Scham- oder Schuldgefühl. Die christliche Botschaft angesichts von schuld- und schamorientierten Gewissen und Kulturen*, Verlag für Kultur und Wissenschaft, Bonn, 2005.

N. Schreurs, "De traditie van vergeven. De omslag van schuld naar schaamte en de herontdekking van de vergeving", in A. Berlis, S. van Erp, A. Lascaris (eds.), *Overgeleverd aan de toekomst. Christelijke traditie in een na-traditionele tijd*, Uitgeverij Meinema, Zoetermeer, 2001, pp.81-98.

E. Sellin, *Mose und seine Bedeutung für die israelitisch-jüdische Religionsgeschichte*, Deichertsche Verlag, Leipzig, 1922.

F. Sierksma, *Freud, Jung en de religie*, Uitgeverij Van Gorcum, Assen, 1951.

F. Sierksma, *The Gods as we shape them*, Routledge, London, 1960.

F. Sierksma, *De religieuze projectie. Een antropologische en psychologische studie over de projectie-verschijnselen in de godsdiensten*, Uitgeverij Meulenhoff, Amsterdam, 1977.

F. Siersksma, *Tussen twee vuren. Een pamflet en een essay*, Uitgeverij De Bezige Bij, Amsterdam, 1952.

J. Smit, H. Stroeken, *Lotgevallen. De bijbel in psychoanalytisch perspectief*, Uitgeverij Boom, Amsterdam/Meppel, 1993.

R. Speziale-Bagliacca, *Guilt. Revenge, Remorse and Responsibility after Freud*, Brunner-Routledge, Hove/New York, 2004.

H. van de Spijker, *Narzisstische Kompetenz – Selbstliebe – Nächstenliebe. Sigmund Freuds Herausforderung der Theologie und Pastoral*, Herder Verlag, Freiburg/Basel/Vienna, 1993.

L.E. Stange (ed.), *Die Religionswissenschaft in Selbstdarstellungen*, Meiner Verlag, Leipzig, 1926.

A. Steinmeier, *Wiedergeboren zur Freiheit. Skizzen eines Dialogs zwischen Theologie und Psychoanalyse*, Vandenhoeck & Ruprecht, Göttingen, 1998

W. Stoker, *Is the Quest for Meaning the Quest for God?The Religious Ascription of Meaning in Relation to the Secular Ascription of Meaning. A Theological Study*, Rodopi, Amsterdam/Atlanta, 1996.

D. Stollberg, "Das Gewissen in pastoralpsychologischer Sicht", in *Wort und Dienst. Jahrbuch der Kirchlichen Hochschule Bethel* 11 (1971), pp.141-158.

D. Stollberg, "Tiefenpsychologie oder historisch-kritische Exegese? Identität und Tod des Ich (Gal. 2, 19-20)", in Y. Spiegel (ed.), *Doppeldeutich. Tiefendimensionen biblischer Texte*, Kaiser Verlag, Munich, 1978, pp.215-226.

A. Storfer, *Zur Sonderstellung des Vatermordes. Eine rechtgeschichtliche und völkerpsychologische Studie*, Deuticke Verlag, Leipzig/Vienna, 1911.

B. Strehlow, "Ansatzpunkte tiefenpsychologischer Interpretation biblischer Texte bei Sigmund Freud", in *Wege zum Menschen* 23 (1971), pp.16-21.

H. Stroeken, *Dromen. Brein en betekenis*, Uitgeverij Boom, Amsterdam, 2005.

H. Stroeken, *Freud en zijn patienten*, Stichting Te Elfder Ure, Nijmegen, 1985.

H. Stroeken, "Freuds 'De man Mozes en de monotheïstische religie' als autoanalytische exercitie", in *Tijdschrift voor Psychoanalyse* 7 (2001/1), pp.24-34.

H. Stroeken, *Het geloof is er voor de mens*, Uitgeverij Ambo, Baarn, 1995.

H. Stroeken, *Kleine psychologie van het gesprek*, Uitgeverij Boom, Amsterdam/Meppel, 1988.

H. Stroeken, *Psychoanalytisch woordenboek*, Uitgeverij Boom, Amsterdam/Meppel, 1994.

H. Stroeken, *Zoeken naar zin: psychotherapie en existentiële vragen*, Uitgeverij Boom, Amsterdam, 1999.

F.J. Sulloway, *Freud, Biologist of the Mind. Beyond the Psychoanalytic Legend*, Burnett Books, London, 1979.

Th.N. Tentler, *Sin and Confession on the Eve of the Reformation*, Princeton University Press, Princeton, 1977.

G. Theissen, *Psychologische Aspekte paulinischer Theologie*, Vandenhoeck & Ruprecht, Göttingen, 1983.

E. Thurneysen, *Die Lehre von der Seelsorge*, Theologischer Verlag Zürich, Zurich, 1994.

P. Tillich, *Biblical Religion and the Search for Ultimate Reality*, University of Chicago Press, Chicago, 1955.

P. Tillich, *The Courage to be*, Yale University Press, New Haven/London, 2000.

P. Tillich, *Gesammelte Werke, Band VIII*, Evangelisches Verlag, Stuttgart, 1970.

P. Tillich, *Gesammelte Werke, Band XII*, Evangelisches Verlag, Stuttgart, 1971.

P. Tillich, *Main Works, Vol. 1: Philosophical Writings*, G. Wenz (ed.), De Gruyter, New York/Berlin, 1989.

P. Tillich, *Systematic Theology, Volumes 1-3*, University of Chicago Press, Chicago, 1967.

C.L. Tuinstra, *Het symbool in de psychoanalyse. Beschrijving en theologische critiek*, H.J. Paris, Amsterdam, 1933.

A. Uleyn, *Ego's en echo's. Opstellen over psychotherapie en religie*, KSGV, Nijmegen, 1999.

A. Uleyn, *Pastorale psychologie en schuldervaring. Schuldbelijdenis. Parabels. Verdedigingsmechanismen*, Desclée de Brouwer, Brugge/Utrecht, 1964.

A. Uleyn, *Psychoanalytisch lezen in de bijbel*, Uitgeverij Gooi & Sticht, Hilversum, 1985.

A. Uleyn, *Religiositeit en fantasie*, Uitgeverij Ambo, Baarn, 1978.

A. Uleyn, *Zelfbeeld en godsbeeld. Opstellen over psychotherapie en godsdienstpsychologie*, Uitgeverij Ambo, Baarn, 1988.

M. Utsch, *Religionspsychologie. Voraussetzungen, Grundlagen, Forschungsüberblick*, Kohlhammer Verlag, Stuttgart/Berlin/Colone, 1998.

P. Vandermeersch, *La chair de la passion. Une histoie de foi: la flagellation*, Éditions du Cerf, Paris, 2002.

P. Vandermeersch, *Het gekke verlangen. Psychotherapie en ethiek*, De Nederlandsche Boekhandel, Antwerpen/ Dekker & Van de Vegt, Nijmegen, 1978.

P. Vandermeersch, "Het narcisme. De psychoanalytische theorie en haar lotgevallen", in J. Huijts (ed.), *"Ik zei de gek". Tussen zelf-ontkenning en zelfverheerlijking*, Uitgeverij Ambo, Baarn, 1983, pp.31-56.

P. Vandermeersch, *Passie en beschouwing. De christelijke invloed op het westerse mensbeeld*, Uitgeverij Peeters, Leuven, 1988.

P. Vandermeersch, "Psychologische lagen in het geloven. Opgraafwerk van een analyticus", in *Tijdschrift voor Theologie* 38 (1999/4), pp.381-407.

P. Vandermeersch, *Het voetstuk van het weten. Over psychologie, psychoanalyse en theologie*, Uitgeverij SUN, Nijmegen, 1992.

P. Vandermeersch, *Unresolved Questions in the Freud/Jung Debate. On Psychosis, Sexual Identity and Religion*, Leuven University Press, Leuven, 1991.

P. Vandermeersch, "Where Will the Water Stick? Considerations of a Psychoanalyst about the Stories of the Flood", in F. Garcia Martinez, G. Luttikhuizen (eds.), *Interpretations of the Flood*, Uitgeverij Brill, Leiden, 1998, pp.167-193.

P. Vandermeersch, H. Westerink, *Godsdienstpsychologie in cultuurhistorisch perspectief*, Uitgeverij Boom, Amsterdam, 2007.

A. Vergote, "Der Beitrag der Psychoanalyse zur Exegese. Leben, Gesetz und Ich-Spaltung im 7, Kapitel des Römerbriefs", in X. Léon-Dufour (ed.), *Exegese im Methodenkonflikt. Zwischen Geschichte und Struktur*, Kösel-Verlag, Munich, 1973, pp.73-116.

A. Vergote, *Bekentenis en begeerte in de religie. Psychoanalytische verkenning*, DNB/Uitgeverij Pelckmans, Kapellen, 1989.

A. Vergote, *Guilt and Desire. Religious Attitudes and their Pathological Derivatives*, Yale University Press, New Haven/London, 1988.

A. Vergote, *De Heer je God liefhebben. Het eigene van het Christendom*, Uitgeverij Lannoo, Tielt, 1999.

A. Vergote, *Het huis is nooit af. Gedachten over mens en religie*, DNB, Antwerpen/Utrecht, 1974.

A. Vergote, *Humanité de l'homme, divinité de Dieu*, Éditions du Cerf, Paris, 2006.

A. Vergote, "Husserl et Freud sur le corps psychique de l'action", in J. Petit (ed.), *Problemes et Controverses. Les Neurosciences et la philosophie de l'action*, J. Vrin, Paris, 1997, pp.387-396.

A. Vergote, "Het imaginaire en het symbolische in het godsbeeld", in *Tijdschrift voor Theologie* 9 (1973/3), pp.310-327.

A. Vergote, "Imaginaire et vérité en psychanalyse. La triade lacanienne", in *Figures de la psychanalyse* 8 (2003), pp.127-136.

A. Vergote, "L'intérêt philosophique de la psychanalyse freudienne", in *Archives de philosophie* 21 (1958), pp.26-59.

A Vergote, *Interprétation du language religieux*, Éditions du Seuil, Paris, 1974.

A. Vergote, *Het meerstemmige leven. Gedachten over mens en religie*, DNB/Uitgeverij Pelckmans, Kapellen, 1987.

A. Vergote, A. Tamayo, *The Parental Figures and the Representation of God. A Psychological and Cross-Cultural Study*, Mouton Publishers, The Hague/Paris/New York, 1981.

A. Vergote, P. Moyaert et al. (eds.), *Psychoanalyse. De mens en zijn lotgevallen*, DNB/Uitgeverij Pelckmans, Kapellen, 1996.

A. Vergote, *Psychoanalysis, Phenomenological Anthropology and Religion*, J. Coveleyn, D. Hutsebaut (eds.), Leuven University Press, Amsterdam/Atlanta, 1998.

A. Vergote, *Religion, Belief and Unbelief. A Psychological Study*, Leuven University Press, Amsterdam/Atlanta, 1997.

A. Vergote, *Religionspsychologie*, Walter-Verlag, Olten/Freiburg, 1970.

A. Vergote, *De sublimatie. Een uitweg uit Freuds impasses*, Uitgeverij SUN, Amsterdam, 2002.

A. Vergote, "Le sujet inconscient selon Lacan", in G. Lofts, P. Moyaert, *La pensée de Jacques Lacan. Questions historiques – Problèmes théoriques*, Éditions Peeters, Leuven, Paris, 1994, pp.1-22.

A. Vergote, J. van der Lans, "Two opposed viewpoints concerning the object of the psychology of religion", in J.A. van Belzen, J. van der Lans (eds.), *Current Issues in the Psychology of Religion. Proceedings of the third Symposium on the Psychology of Religion in Europe*, Rodopi, Amsterdam, 1986, pp.67-81.

H. Vermorel, M. Vermorel, *Sigmund Freud et Romain Rolland. Correspondance 1923-1936. De la sensation océanique au Trouble du souvenir sur l'Acropole*, Presses Universitaires de France, Paris, 1993.

B. Vervliet, P. Luyten, J. Corveleyn, "Ik-ideaal en ideaal-ik. Een lacaniaanse benadering", in *Tijdschrift voor Psychoanalyse* 9 (2002/3), pp.173-186.

S. Vestdijk, "Het schuldprobleem bij Dostojewski", in *De Poolse Ruiter. Essays*, Uitgeverij Bert Bakker, Den Haag, 1958, pp.76-88.

S. Vestdijk, *De toekomst der religie*, Uitgeverij Meulenhoff, Amsterdam, 1975.

S. Vestdijk, *De vuuraanbidders. Roman uit de tachtigjarige oorlog, deel 3*, Nijgh & Van Ditmar, Den Haag, 1985.

K. Voigt, *Otto Haendler – Leben und Werk. Eine Untersuchung der Strukturen seines Seelsorgeverständnisses*, Lang Verlag, Frankfurt et al, 1993.

G. Vorbrodt, *Beiträge zur religiösen Psychologie: Psychobiologie und Gefühl*, Deichert'sche Verlag, Leipzig, 1904.

M. Vovelle, *Ideologies and Mentalities*, Polity Press, Cambridge, 1990.

F. Wagner, *Was ist Religion? Studien zu ihrem Begriff und Thema in Geschichte und Gegenwart*, Verlag Mohr, Gütersloh, 1986.

H. Wahl, *Narzißmus? Von Freuds Narzißmustheorie zur Selbstpsychologie*, Kohlhammer Verlag, Stuttgart/Berlin/Colone/Mainz, 1985.

H. Wahl, "'Zwischen' Theologie und Psychoanalyse: Joachim Scharfenbergs Impulse für die Religions- und Pastoralpsychologie", in *Wege zum Menschen* 49 (1997), pp.439-458.

P. Walinga, J. Corveleyn, J. van Saane, "Guilt and Religion: The Influence of Orthodox Protestant and Orthodox Catholic Conceptions of Guilt on Guilt-Experience", in *Archive for the Psychology of Religion* 27 (2005), 113-135.

E.R. Wallace, *Freud and Anthropology. A History and Reappraisal*, International Universities Press, New York, 1983.

G. Wehr, *Wege zu religiöser Erfahrung. Analytische Psychologie im Dienst der Bibelauslegung*, Walter-Verlag, Olten/Freiburg, 1974.

J. Weima, *Reiken naar oneindigheid. Inleiding tot de psychologie van de religieuze ervaring*, Uitgeverij Ambo, Baarn, 1981.

J. Werbick, *Schulderfahrung und Bußsakrament*, Matthias-Grünewald-Verlag, Mainz, 1985.

H. Westerink, *A Dark Trace. Sigmund Freud on the Sense of Guilt*, Leuven University Press (*Het schuldgevoel bij Freud. Een duister spoor*, Uitgeverij Boom, Amsterdam, 2005).

H. Westerink, ""Een geweldige illusie": Over de theologische achtergronden van Freuds *Die Zukunft einer Illusion*", in *Nederlands Theologisch Tijdschrift* 59 (2005/3), pp.177-194.

H. Westerink, "The Great Man from Tarsus: Freud on the Apostle Paul", in *Psychoanalytic Quarterly* 76 (2007), pp.217-235.

H. Westerink, *Met het oog van de ziel. Een godsdienstpsychologische en mentaliteitshistorische studie naar mensvisie, zelfonderzoek en geloofsbeleving in het werk van Willem Teelinck (1579-1629)*, Uitgeverij Boekencentrum, Zoetermeer, 2002.

H. Westerink, "Zum Verhältnis von Psychoanalyse und Mythologie. Die Einfluß Heymann Steinthals Völkerpsychologie auf die angewandte Psychoanalyse", in *Psyche. Zeitschrift für Psychoanalyse und ihre Anwendungen*, 62 (2008/3), pp.290-311.

K. Winkler, *Seelsorge*, De Gruyter, New York/Berlin, 2000.

K. Winkler, "Zum Umgang mit Normen in der Seelsorge", in *Pastoraltheologie* 80 (1991), pp.26-39.

D. Winnicott, *Playing and Reality*, Routledge, London/New York, 2005.

D.M. Wulff, *Psychology of Religion. Classic and Contemporary Views*, John Wiley & Sons, New York et al., 1991.

Y.H. Yerushalmi, *Freud's Moses. Judaism Terminable and Interminable*, Yale University Press, New Haven/London, 1991.

S. Ypma, *Tussen God en gekte. Een studie over zekerheid en symbolisering in psychose en geloven*, Uitgeverij Boekencentrum, Zoetermeer, 2001.

H. Zahrnt (ed.), *Jesus und Freud. Ein Symposion von Psychoanalytikern und Theologen*, Piper & Co Verlag, Munich, 1972.

E. Zaretsky, *Freuds Jahrhundert. Die Geschichte der Psychoanalyse*, Zsolnay Verlag, Vienna, 2006.

T.H. Zock, *Niet van deze wereld? Geestelijke verzorging en zingeving vanuit godsdienstpsychologisch perspectief*, KSGV, Tilburg, 2007.

T.H. Zock, *A Psychology of Ultimate Concern. Erik H. Erikson's Contribution to the Psychology of Religion*, Rodopi, Atlanta/Amsterdam, 1990.

Schriften der Innsbrucker Gesellschaft für Psychoanalyse

hrsg. von Univ.-Prof. Dr. Hans Jörg Walter und Univ.-Prof. DDr. Werner Ernst (Universität Innsbruck)

Forum Religionskritik

Herbert Bickel; Helmwart Hierdeis (Hg.)
„Unbehagen in der Kultur" – Variationen zu Sigmund Freuds Kulturkritik
Die Texte dieses Bandes verstehen sich als Beiträge zur Tiefenhermeneutik einer Kultur, wie sie uns in den Gestalten von Bildung, Religion, Ökonomie, Politik, Therapie, Medien und Sexualität entgegentritt. Die meisten von ihnen entstanden anlässlich einer Vorlesungsreihe zu Sigmund Freuds „Unbehagen in der Kultur", die vom Institut für Erziehungswissenschaften der Universität Innsbruck gemeinsam mit der Innsbrucker Gesellschaft für Psychoanalyse veranstaltet wurde.
Bd. 3, 2009, 312 S., 29,90 €, br., ISBN 978-3-8258-1869-2

Reinhard Zaiser
Verdrängung und Neurose, Wunschdenken und Illusion?
Zu Sigmund Freuds psychoanalytischer Religionskritik und noogener Neurose
Thema ist nicht allein Freuds Abwehr und (Re-) Konstruktion der Religion als Illusion und Neurose, sondern die Dialektik, Kritik und Dekonstruktion der Freudschen Psychoanalyse und der psychoanalytischen Religionskritik, die sich wie ein roter Faden durch sein Gesamtwerk zieht, als Metakritik der Psychoanalyse. Konkret kehrt die von Freud verdrängte Religion als Psychoanalyse wieder und entpuppt sich Freud aufgrund seiner eigenen noogenen Neurose (sic!) als Fall für die Logotherapie.
Bd. 6, 2005, 184 S., 19,90 €, br., ISBN 3-8258-8242-x

LIT Verlag Berlin – Münster – Wien – Zürich – London

Auslieferung Deutschland / Österreich / Schweiz: siehe Impressumsseite

Studien zur Ethnopsychologie und Ethnopsychoanalyse

hrsg. von Werner Egli, Gerhard Kubik, Maya Nadig, Johannes Reichmayr und Vera Saller

Gerhard Kubik
Tabu
Erkundungen transkultureller Psychoanalyse in Afrika, Europa und anderen Kulturgebieten
Sigmund Freud, der Begründer der Psychoanalyse, war auch der erste, der Tabus quer durch die Kulturen psychoanalytisch auflöste. Inzwischen ist von uns viel weiteres Terrain erschlossen worden, u.a. in den Initiationsriten, im Spiel und in relgiösen Bereichen. Die im Prinzip dreiteilige Struktur der Tabu-Formeln wurde erkannt. Durch Verinnerlichung der Tabu-Inhalte hilft eine Kultur dem Individuum, mit sozial nicht akzeptierten unbewußten Tendenzen fertig zu werden. Aus diesem Grunde sind Tabus auch eine Neurose-Prophylaxe.
Der vorliegende Band gibt einen Überblick heutiger Tabu-Forschung zum Verständnis der Tiefenpsychologie des Menschen. Er gründet sich auf jahrzehntenlange Feldforschungen des Verfassers und seiner Mitarbeiter in Afrika, Europa und anderen Kulturgebieten.
Umschlagbild: Tabu-Bereiche. Zeichnung des Verfassers.
Bd. 7, 2007, 104 S., 19,90 €, br., ISBN 978-3-8258-9799-4

Brigitta Hug
Babyjahre anderswo
Theorie und transkultureller Vergleich der frühen Kindheiten bei den Gusii, den !Kung San und den Iatmül
Babys überleben anderswo wie in westlichen Gesellschaften nur dann, wenn sie mit innerer Anteilnahme ins Leben getragen werden. Aber nicht überall übernehmen Mütter und/oder Kleinfamilien diese faszinierende und arbeitsintensive Aufgabe. Die erste Lebenszeit wird – so die These der Ethnologin und Psychoanalytikerin Brigitta Hug – sozial organisiert. Je nach wirtschaftlichen und politischen Bedingungen werden Kleinkinder verschieden gepflegt und werden ihnen besondere Eigenschaften und Bedürfnisse zugeschrieben. Der transkulturelle Vergleich der frühen Kindheiten bei den Gusii, den !Kung San und den Iatmül veranschaulicht dies und analysiert gleichzeitig westliches Denken über Babys.
Bd. 8, 2007, 280 S., 24,90 €, br., ISBN 978-3-8258-0127-4

L I T Verlag Berlin – Münster – Wien – Zürich – London
Auslieferung Deutschland / Österreich / Schweiz: siehe Impressumsseite